Television News,
Radio News

Television News, Radio News

Irving E. Fang

School of Journalism and Mass Communication
University of Minnesota

RADA PRESS   ST. PAUL

Copyright © 1980, 1972, 1968 by Irving E. Fang

Television News first edition, Hastings House, September 1968
  Second printing, July 1970
  Third printing, July 1971
Second edition, revised, Hastings House, August 1972
  Second printing, February 1974
  Third printing, August 1974
  Fourth printing, March 1975
  Fifth printing, May 1976
  Sixth printing, October 1977
  Seventh printing, November 1978
Third edition, revised as **Television News, Radio News,** Rada Press, May 1980

Library of Congress catalog card number: **80-50847**

ISBN **0-9604212-0-3**
Formerly ISBN 0-8038-7117-1 and 0-8038-7125-2 (pbk.)

Rada Press, Inc.
2297 Folwell
St. Paul, Minnesota 55108

299351

Printed in the United States of America

Acknowledgments

Several people generously shared their knowledge and experience in the preparation of *Television News, Radio News*. My thanks to Dr. Donald Gillmor, University of Minnesota; Prof. David Dary, University of Kansas; Prof. T. Joseph Scanlon, Carleton University, Ottawa; news director Ron Handberg and chief photographer Joe Sullivan, WCCO-TV, Minneapolis-St. Paul; news director Curt Beckmann (RTNDA President, 1980) and reporter Robert Thornberg, WCCO Radio; news director Stan Turner, chief photographer John Hoffman, and meteorologist Dennis Feltgen, KSTP-TV, Minneapolis-St. Paul; and news director J.B. Eckert, Gopher State Radio Network.

Rick Atterbury designed the book. Douglas Grainger drew the jacket cover. Averie Cohen, WCCO, KSTP, ABC News and UPI Photos provided the photographs. David Hudson and Carol Egan helped pull the book together. I am grateful for the special skills of Dr. James Brown, Anders Himmelstrup, Prof. Harold Wilson, Adrienne Banks, Scott Ferguson, Niels Jensen, Valery Bloft, Grant Williams, and my wife, Junko Fang.

Irving E. Fang

Minneapolis
May, 1980

IRVING E. FANG has been a journalist since 1951 and a professor of journalism since 1969. He has worked as a newspaper reporter and editor in California, Nebraska, South Carolina and Alabama. He worked for Reuters in London and the *Daily Times* of Nigeria. He was with KABC-TV Los Angeles, and ABC News in Los Angeles and New York, working as a news writer, producer, and assistant manager of the network election unit, where he continues as a consultant. Prof. Fang is in charge of the broadcast journalism sequence at the University of Minnesota. He holds a B.A. in English, an M.A. in journalism, and a Ph.D. in speech from UCLA.

His books are *Television News* (Hastings House, second edition 1972); *Television/Radio News Workbook* (Hastings House, 1971), and *Those Radio Commentators!* (Iowa State University Press, 1977), winner of a 1978 Broadcast Preceptor Award and a selection of the Nostalgia Book Club. *Television News, Radio News* is a revision of his earlier *Television News.*

Dedicated to the memory
of Elmer Davis.
Broadcast journalism
will find no better model.

Contents

Preface   **11**

Section A: **WRITING**

1.   **Writing for the Ear**   **19**

Evolution of Broadcast News Style

Broadcast News Writing

Accuracy

"That's what the wire copy said."

"Hey, Fred, listen to this…"

Clear Writing

The Easy Listening Formula

The Abstraction Ladder

Colorful Writing

2.   **News Copy**   **29**

The Script

"Throwaway" Leads and Transitions

Summary Lead or Item Lead

Question Leads
Narrative Treatment
Jargon
Redundancy
Gobbledygook
Other Confusion
Covering Yourself
Action Verbs
Freight Train Phrases
Attribution
Contractions, Quotes, *Said*, Slang
Metaphor and Simile
Repetition
Simplicity, Informality, Sparkle
Numbers
Personalization
Sex Bias
Emphasis
Examples of Leads

3.   The Lead-In   49

Newscaster Alone
Chromakey
Video Intro
Roll-Thru
Standupper/Wraparound
Going to Commercial
Headlines?

4.   The Picture Story   65

An Absence of Detail
Leaving an Impression
Tying Copy to Pictures
Telling It the Way It Happened
Making Connections
What Interests You?
The Local Angle

"How much time can you give me?"
Editing a Speech

Section B: **RADIO**

5.   The Radio Reporter   87

Getting the Equipment Ready
Taping and Note Taking
Radio Reporting Techniques
Remote Tape Reports
Editing the Tape
Editing Problems
Preparing the Newscast
Errors

6.   Radio News   97

Advantages and Drawbacks
Three Radio News Operations
Costs
Audio News Services
Newscast Schedule
All-News Radio
Mobile Units
Tape Recording

Section C: **TELEVISION**

7.   The Television Reporter   115

Guidelines
The Interviewee's Knowledge
The Reporter's Knowledge
Digging for Facts
Politicians and Reporters
"Don't let him off the hook."
Individuality
Three Case Studies

Covering a News Conference
Editing Problems
Reverse Angle Questions
Lack of Alternatives
Add a Dash of Humility

8.   A Television News Day   135

The Bulletin
Daily Assignments
The Day
The News Director
The Producer
The Writer
Building the Newscast
The Director
Control Room and Studio
Rehearsal

9.   The Newscaster   157

Charles Kuralt and All That Hair
"Eyewitless News"
Doing It Right
A Sense of the News
Rapport
Guide to Pronunciation
Reading the Script
Formats
Television Sets

Section D: NEWSCASTS

10.   Getting It Together   171

Sources of News
Wire Services
Other Media as Sources

Sources for Visuals
The Community
Covering Beats
Processing the News
Processing Film
Videotape
Audio Tape
Graphics
Copy
Script Assembly
News Values

11.   News for Everyone   185

It's Still a Small Town
Broadcast News vs. Newspaper News
The News vs. What Really Happened
Unwrapping the Truth
Local Stations Try Fresh Approaches
Stock Market Reports
Of Tenors, Turnips and Teachers
The Older Audience
The Younger Audience

12.   Weather   199

The Nightly Report
Value of Weather News
Weather Jargon
Sources of Weather News
Professional Meteorologists
"Happy" Weather
Illustrating the Weather
Radar

13.   Sports   207

The Sports Reporter

Sports News Ethics
Sports Jargon
The Wider World of Sports

Section E: CONSTRAINTS AND CONCERNS

14.   Speaking Out in Editorials and Documentaries   217

The Reluctant Broadcaster
Broadcasters Who Speak Out
Documentaries
What's Your Viewpoint?
Consumer Problems
Editorials, Not Editorializing
The Fairness Doctrine
The Fairness Doctrine: Pro and Con
Red Lion
Section 315
Broadcasting and the First Amendment

15.   The Law   235

Libel
The Right of Privacy
Journalists' Privilege
Court Gag Orders
Access to Public Meetings
Obscenity
Lotteries

16.   Mike and Camera in the Courtroom   249

Hauptmann
Canon 35
Sheppard
Estes
In Camera or On Camera
Sirhan
The Alabama Plan

Judges Use Video
Common Sense Conduct

17.   The Profession   261

Is It or Isn't It?
Standards
Ethics
Education
The Profession
The Resumé
Town and Gown
Research
The Library

18.   Show Biz   273

The Other End of the Tube
The ''Show Biz'' Issue
Consultants and Show Biz
The Consultants
Consultants' Research
Advice on News Content?
''Happy Talk'' and ''Tabloid'' News
Finding ''Talent''
News or NEWZAK?
Why Consultants?

19.   The Round Events Peg and the Square News Hole   285

''That story right after this....''
''Why do you want to show that stuff?''
Kidnapings, Hijackings, Riots
''Why can't you be objective?''
Evidence of Bias
Checkbook Journalism
''Why don't you put on some good news for a change?''
''What can *we* do about what *you* show?''
The Pseudo-Event

Section F: PICTURES

20.   Shooting the Story   309

A Fire
A Collision
A Murder
A Riot
A Parade
Lost Child at Police Station
News Staging

21.   Electronic News Gathering   323

How It Developed
All ENG
Tool or Toy
Ethical Questions
You Can Let the Camera Run
Other Advantages
Pooling
Costs
Which Picture Is Better?
The Television Camera
Video Transmission
Film-to-Videotape
The Videotape Machine
Reel-to-Reel Editing
Computer Editing
The Future

22.   TV Photography   345

Some Basic Concepts
The Sound Camera
The Zoom Lens
The Silent Camera
Accessories
Lighting

Film and Processing
Super 8

23.   Sound   355
Equipment
Problems and Solutions

24.   Film Editing   363
The Editing Process
Equipment
Splicing
Where to Splice
Overlap Cuts
Double Chaining
Double System

25.   Stills   375
Outside Sources
Library Stills
Maps
Cartoons
Supers
Slides
Animation

Glossary   381

Reference Notes   393

Index   401

PHOTOGRAPHS

15 Herbert Kaplow, left, and Frank Reynolds, ABC News
16 WCCO-TV, Minneapolis-St.Paul, newsroom
18 Newscast from WCCO-TV newsroom
48 Camera with TelePrompTer
64 Photographer with ENG camera and deck, WCCO-TV
84 WCCO radio interview
86 Interviewing Minnesota Governor Wendell Anderson, WCCO Radio
111 Radio newsroom, KSTP, Minneapolis-St. Paul
112 Technical director at switcher, WCCO-TV
114 KSTP-TV reporter doing an interview
133 Reporter checking a fact, KSTP-TV
134 Satellite weather photos
155 Director, left, and producer in television control room, WCCO-TV
156 Max Robinson, ABC News
168 ABC Radio network news
170 UPI broadcast wire
197 Covering a fire
198 Meteorologist, WCCO-TV
213 Covering participatory sports, KSTP-TV
214 Confrontation, Americus, Georgia, *UPI Photos*
216 Newscast, WCCO-TV
234 Character generator
259 Artist's courtroom sketch
260 Ann Compton, ABC News
284 Shootout, Winston-Salem, N.C., 1971, *UPI Photos*
305 Vietnam war photographer, ABC News
306 Taping a sports event, KSTP-TV
308 ENG photographer, KSTP-TV
321 3/4'' tape editing, WCCO-TV
322 Live feed via microwave, KSTP-TV
344 Using a horizontal film editing bench
362 Reporter and film editor at work, KSTP-TV
373 Double system film editing
374 ABC News artist

Preface

In the second edition of *Television News,* I compared television news to a mirror, saying, "In this capability to hold a mirror up to its community, television news cannot be equalled."

It was a sloppy comparison.

A mirror offers a full view of reality for as long as you choose to look. Television news gives us a moment of reality — or a reasonable facsimile thereof — captured here and there, a collection of snapshots frozen in time and space.

You don't find many mirrors in television newsrooms.

You do find cameras.

A lot of Americans are hungry news consumers. So are a lot of Canadians and thoughtful people in many countries. Newspapers, news magazines, current political biography all find a ready welcome. So do television and radio news, which at their best give the *feel* of what has happened, the actions, the emotions. "We reach people who count, not who are counted," is the boast of some media. People who *count,* the news makers and shakers, also listen to radio and watch television news, and what the broadcast journalist communicates to them may influence a chain of events.

It is a heavy responsibility.

Others get news about the world beyond their neighborhood and their jobs from television alone. They don't buy books. The postman stuffs no news magazines into their mail box. The newspaper boy bicycles past their house. They listen to no radio news except for the headlines that briefly interrupt their music. Only television news talks to them about their city's pollution, their state's taxes, their nation's political campaigns, their world's nasty little wars.

If the television journalist does not communicate clearly, some people

— citizens and voters — will not understand what is happening. If the television journalist does not communicate interestingly, some people will not care what is happening. If the television journalist does not communicate accurately, some Americans will have a distorted notion of what is happening.

It is a heavy responsibility.

The journalist carries this responsibility daily along a rocky path. Snags and thorns pull at him, the rocks give way, sometimes rocks are thrown at him, and he sometimes trips over his own feet as he runs to deliver his messages before the sun sets.

Thinking about those snags, rocks and clumsy feet is not a frivolous task, nor inconsequential. Television news has become too important. Those who prepare it and deliver it ought to look at everything they do with an unflinching gaze. Even if they don't, others do, as we all learned after one speech in Des Moines let loose tens of thousands of angry letters, telegrams and phone calls to the networks and local stations.

If television news were ineffectual, it would be let alone.

It is not.

The anger following Spiro Agnew's speech has subsided. Agnew himself has left the political arena and so have the others in that administration who fueled the fires of television news criticism. Now a national poll shows television news to be more trusted than any other institution.

Television news did not deserve all that criticism.

It does not deserve all that trust. Not yet.

Those who work in television news, and also those who do not, cannot afford to let suspicion grow about the honesty and soundness of what is at times our best means of giving people the news. Charles Evans Hughes said:

> We have in this Country but one security. You may think that the Constitution is your security — it is nothing but a piece of paper. You may think that the statutes are your security — they are nothing but words in a book. You may think that an elaborate mechanism of government is your security — it is nothing at all, unless you have sound and uncorrupted public opinion to give life to your Constitution, to give vitality to your statutes, to make efficient your government machinery.

A 1972 Roper Poll reported that one person in seven thought the government should control television news programs. Among people with a grade school education or less, the percentage was more than one person in five.

Why do people watch television news? The obvious answer is: to become informed about the day's events. Yet we read disturbing studies telling us that most viewers can recall little of the news they just saw. Perhaps for many viewers, television news is a kind of early warning radar telling them the world won't blow up today, their taxes won't go up and neither will the price of a pound of hamburger. Or perhaps television news is a kind of entertainment. Answers can come only from research, but the research that televison stations have been willing to sponsor has been private and unpublished, done by commercial firms solely to increase audience size.

Television news left its childhood a long time ago. Memory now dims of newspapermen who brought clackers to news conferences in order to ruin film sound tracks. We saw television news help to hold this nation together when a president fell in Dallas. Through television we felt a war across 10,000 miles. Through television we watched men walk upon the moon. We traveled with another president from the bold opening to China to the humiliating closing of Watergate. As three world famous leaders clasped their hands over a peace treaty for the Middle East, we were witness. As hundreds of thousands of Iranians chanted hatred of America, our stomachs sank.

Radio news holds its special place in our communications system. Rumor of important news — a tornado, an assassination, a war — sends citizens scurrying not to television sets or the corner newsstand, but to the nearest radio. Its dial is quickly twisted to where the news flows most completely, most clearly, most accurately, most interestingly. Even a normal news day finds the radio journalist setting a hastier pace than his competitors at the other media as his newscast deadlines tumble toward him like the ocean's waves, spaced every so many minutes.

Speaking about all journalism, Howard K. Smith said, "I would guess that, after formal schooling is over for the average citizen, at least four-fifths of what he continues to learn about his community, about his state and city, and about his nation and the world, come filtered through the observations of a journalist." [1]

Former NBC president Robert Kintner said:

> On the day when those of us who have given our lives to the medium are called to account for our time, the heaviest weight on our side of the balance will be this expansion of reality for tens of millions of people. Today many people of relatively little formal education, who read slowly and without pleasure, have met with and probably understood more of the world around them than any but a handful of sophisticated and curious minds understood fifty years ago. [2]

The world day by day moves closer to that peculiar place that Canada's Marshall McLuhan calls the global village. The United States already is a section of that village, with television news watched nightly in more than 50 million homes and radio news heard daily in cars, houses, offices, boats and cabins, on street corners, beaches and mountain trails. Like it or not, electronic information involves everyone with everyone else, North with South, white with black, old with young.

Go to any corner of this nation, walk through any neighborhood, and you will find television aerials poking up. The roof may leak, but those skinny sticks of metal protrude from it. Go to any corner of this nation and you will hear somebody's ragged music. The table may sag, but a transistor radio perches on it. Sometimes, in the midst of all the televised fantasy and the radio racket, the news comes through.

WRITING

Writing for the Ear

News Copy

The Lead-In

The Picture Story

Writing for the Ear

1

One good word is worth a thousand pictures.

— *Eric Sevareid*

Consider your listener. Consider your viewer. Ask yourself, what does he or she look like? The answer should not be, "That's a stupid question. Listeners and viewers look like everyone." Indeed they do, but the writer who imagines an audience of everyone imagines nothing. He writes with no one in mind, which is a mistake.

For the news writer, the reporter and the newscaster, the audience is a single person, not a great faceless mass. One person. For the radio journalist, that one listener may be a commuter driving his car along a freeway, listening at 55 MPH as he changes lanes. For the television journalist, that one viewer may be a housewife trying to catch the news while supper is cooking and she's ironing and the kids are yelling. Or the one viewer is her husband, home from his eight-hour shift, tired and irritated, wondering when the newscaster will finally shut up. That driver, that housewife, that factory worker is the audience. There is no convention of political scientists listening intently to catch every nuance of the information presented. If you, in delivering, reporting or writing the news, confuse that tired workingman or bore him, he can turn you off — CLICK! — just like that. From that moment, all your clever imagery, all your projected sincerity, all your carefully edited film and tape, presented at considerable expense, and all the rest of your news department's hard work is wasted, so far as that viewer is concerned. He may not come back tomorrow. He may never tune in again.

You can, if you wish, pander to him in an effort to enthrall him (or her). Play up the sex stories, the crime stories and the light features, especially what used to be called cheesecake, while you provide a minimum of important news. Some news directors do this, especially during rating periods when the station buys space in the newspapers and along the sides of buses to advertise a "courageous" examination of marijuana in the nearest university sorority houses, or some such. This kind of journalism equates with the diet pill business in medicine and the promotion of whiplash injuries in law.

Or, you can give your tired worker the important news of the day in a manner which *will* interest him, which will have him call out, "Say, Maud, did you hear that?" Although he may still be waiting for the ball scores, he is watching the news to learn what has happened today. He pays taxes, he has children in school, his family breathes the air and drinks the water, he doesn't want food and gas prices to go up, he doesn't want to lose his job and he doesn't want to go to war. Above all, he is nobody's fool. If you can present the news to him clearly, so that he can understand it, and interestingly, so that he pays attention to it, he will stay tuned and you will be acquitting yourself professionally.

Evolution of Broadcast News Style

In the course of two centuries of American journalism, a unique style of newspaper writing evolved. Its most distinctive feature is the "inverted pyramid." The most important facts are told first, followed by lesser facts in descending order of importance. The first sentence usually has the "five W's": Who, What, When, Where, Why; and sometimes How is thrown in for good measure. The headline first tells the story in microcosm. The 5-W lead retells it more clearly and with a little detail. The next three paragraphs or so may provide a further retelling, with still further detail. The remainder of the story may retell it all again, this time in chronological form with additional detail.

This writing style has been developed to a high degree by — and tends to be peculiar to — American newspapers. It is not the style of Fleet Street, whose sub-editors prefer a less stilted style, narrative rather than structured. Nor is it universally liked, or used, by all American newspaper reporters.

It can be a horror, like this lead sentence which appeared in a St. Paul, Minnesota, newspaper: "A young GI, who as editor of war dispatches heard on military broadcasts in Vietnam said the Army censors news to American troops in the war zone, has been reassigned, U.S. officials said Thursday in Saigon."

The inverted pyramid style has one big advantage over a chronological or narrative style of writing. It enables a busy newspaper copy editor to trim a story, either in copy or type, from the bottom as the page is assembled. And so, because stories are written to be trimmed from the bottom if necessary, important elements of each story are retained, despite drastic chopping.

When radio news emerged in the twenties and thirties, it was written by men trained in the newspaper tradition. Radio news was fed through newspaper wire services or stylistic copies of newspaper wires. Gradually, however, it became apparent that radio news must not be just spoken newspaper copy. A listener cannot skim broadcast news items looking for a story in which he is interested. In radio and television, trimming from the bottom means throwing out entire stories.

Another difference between newspapers and broadcast news is that, in broadcasting, a narrative treatment immediately after the lead sounds more natural than the retelling of a story in an ever-expanding lead. Further, some words and word pairs which look perfectly good in print feel awkward on the tongue ("youths," for example). A newscaster plowing through a long sentence must catch his breath in the middle, a physiological fact that the newspaper writer need not consider. The broadcast news listener's continuity of thought is threatened by lengthy noun clauses between subject and verb, or between transitive verb and direct object. (For instance, "Senator Brown, who visited Judge Jones yesterday after a talk with Congressman Smith, cancelled all other appointments.")

Over the years, radio news writers altered newspaper style to suit their own medium. The changes were ad hoc: if an innovation sounded good, it stayed, and was used again another time. No overall style was imposed in radio news writing. Although radio news drew men like Edward R. Murrow, who was trained in public speaking, the fountainhead of radio news writing has been journalism, not rhetoric.

Broadcast News Writing

Television news grew out of radio news, just as radio news grew out of newspaper journalism. Like Topsy — and like radio news — it just grew. It, too, evolved on an ad hoc basis to suit a new medium. Although there are many similarities, the style of radio news writing is not completely the style of television news writing. When videotape or film is shown, words must relate to pictures. Audio and video elements work in concert to tell the story. Silence is sometimes part of the television script. A good radio story is often trimmed or rejected for television because it is not "visual." A good television visual story is often rejected by a radio news editor because it is weak.

The television news or documentary writer who fails to balance audio and video elements, or who thinks the sound will take care of itself, is practically begging to be misunderstood. Experiments by university researchers indicate that words compete poorly with pictures if the words separately clamor for the viewers' attention. As an example, it is foolish policy to grab any piece of war locale film in order to illustrate the latest wire copy from that locale. If the film shows a village with a medium shot of a chicken scampering across a dusty road, the copy can report anything from a political upheaval to a major battle, and a lot of viewers will remember nothing but that chicken.

An effective bit of humor can occasionally be derived from sharply contrasting what the television audience sees with what it hears. For example, a feature story about a flying grandmother began with film of a private plane taxiing toward the camera while the newscaster said something like, "Everyone knows that when a grandmother reaches her sixties, she likes nothing better than to stay at home with her rocking chair, her knitting and her pussy cat." (SOUND UP FULL FOR ENGINE ROAR). "David Brinkley's Journal" showed scenes of automobile graveyards, highways jammed with billboards, and streets jammed with pawn shops, with no audio but a recording of "America the Beautiful." It was effective, powerful rather than humorous, with the kind of impact Simon and Garfunkel delivered with their "Seven O'Clock News," as they sang "Silent Night" against a radio newscast of tragedies. Two elements can also be contrasted by tight intercutting. When Oklahoma ended statewide prohibition, an Oklahoma City television news photographer shot film of "dry" ladies outside a liquor store stubbornly singing "Onward Christian Soldiers." He also shot close-up film of the liquor store cash register ringing up sales. A film editor intercut the two scenes, with each phrase of the song followed by the counterpoint ringing of the cash register.

Accuracy

No preaching, just a little story, a cautionary tale. It happened to a cub reporter on a small daily newspaper in southern Indiana. His story of a trial involving attempted rape mixed up the name of the judge and the name of the defendant. Instead of suing, the judge wrote this letter to the newspaper:

"I enclose a Xerox copy from your paper which has just been handed to me. I appreciate the fact that, because of bad circulation, your paper is understaffed and your writers are poorly trained. The subject matter of this article was highly technical and, therefore, the writer of this article could not be expected to get it right the very first time. I, therefore, am going to point out some of the idiom used in court and identify the cast of characters.

"First, the judge (that's me) sits up front of the courtroom on a raised dais with a robe on and scowls at people. Secondly, the defendant is the fellow sitting at counsel table representing truth and justice. The press are those people sitting over at the side of the courtroom with long hair, whiskers, and barefooted.

"Now in criminal proceedings, the judge is not charged with crime. The defendant is charged with crime. The judge does not claim alibi. The defendant claims alibi. The judge does not have to have an alibi. He is the head honcho.

"I am sure that if your writer carefully reviews the above information he may eventually be able to get his article correct.

"I wish you to know, in passing, that I am a great admirer of the

Fourth Estate, and sometimes get very emotional when I observe their crusade for truth and justice. Therefore you have my permission to pass these instructions on to other newspapers who are in like situations so that they may benefit from these simple instructions."[1]

"That's what the wire copy said."

Never write anything you don't fully understand.

"That's what the wire copy said" is the feeblest excuse around.

If *you* don't understand it, how do you expect anyone else to understand it? If you suspect the information in a wire service item, you can call the wire service and ask them to check it out. You can also call the source of the story or someone near the source. Should time be pressing and the source is too far away or unavailable, then you should "write around" the suspicious information or qualify it.

"Hey, Fred, listen to this..."

Not only is a 5-W lead unnecessary in broadcast copy, it is most undesirable, for it throws a great deal of information at the listener all at once. Equally undesirable is any large and formal assemblage of facts. Veteran broadcast journalists, professors and textbooks exhort the student and the young journalist to write in a conversational style, but worry as the young writer will, a conversational lead still eludes him.

You might try this mental trick. (It may not work for you, but it's worth a try.) Vocally precede a lead with the phrase, "Hey, Fred, listen to this...." Then read your lead. If the words sound cumbersome and stiff, rewrite them. You may find that "Hey, Fred (or "Mom" or "Uncle Charlie," if you prefer), listen to this...." is a useful phrase which keeps you from writing awkward leads full of little facts which hardly anyone could care about or remember.

If you preface a story with such a phrase, say it aloud, then read your copy aloud. In any case, read your copy aloud.

On the left is copy which was read on a television newscast over silent film of a school ceremony held outdoors. On the right is a version rewritten in a conversational style and considerably shortened. Read each version aloud, preceding each reading with "Hey, Fred, listen to this...."

Original	Rewrite
New facilities at Breck School were dedicated this afternoon in the name of the Reverend Canon F. Douglas Henderson. Canon Henderson is recognized for seventeen years of leadership as rector and headmaster of the school. The new additions to existing facilities included a science hall, lib-	Breck School has a new science hall, a new library, a new girls' gym, and a new hockey arena. And today, they dedicated them. Breck is a co-educational college prep school, with 500 students.

rary, girls' gym, and hockey arena.
Breck is a co-educational college prep
school with an enrollment of about
500. The school has often been cited
for new innovations in traditional educational methods.

Note that the rewritten version says "they" without revealing who "they" are. In context, especially with film showing who "they" are, "they" needs no more elaboration than "it" does when we observe that "it's raining." The original version, filled with details viewers will not absorb, reads as if it were written by a publicity man whose broadcast experience is limited to changing stations.

Clear Writing

The most important consideration of a broadcast news style is clarity. Radio and television news share this need. Unlike the newspaper reader, the radio listener or television viewer cannot go back over a sentence to fathom its meaning. Either he understands it the first time through, or he loses it forever. Any listener who stops to think, "What was that he just said?", loses not only that bit of news, but also the news that is being told while he is puzzling over the last bit.

A young Minnesota radio station reporter phoned a house where a man reportedly had fallen into a septic tank.

"Have they extricated him yet?" the reporter asked. (Or, so goes the tale.)

"Extricated him, hell," was the reply. "They have to get him out first."

Clear writing is not a matter of luck. Nor does it automatically develop in a writer. Clarity of writing style has been studied for two generations as a behavioral science called "readability." Its best known advocate is Rudolf Flesch. In its early days, readability was the province of educators who searched for formulas to measure children's schoolbooks. Later, Robert Gunning and a few others applied their skills to dispel the fog in business writing, periodical publications and news wire copy. Today, readability researchers use computers and follow investigative lines similar to those of linguists seeking machine translation of language. Among the products of labored research, which at one time included hand counts of the letters in thousands of words, have been formulas which objectivity test for clarity.

Without a formula, there are only two ways to determine whether a news story is understandable to a broadcast audience. One way is to test the audience. Several research studies have done just that, reading news items to groups of volunteers, then questioning them. This method may provide guidelines to the researcher, but it obviously cannot be used by the news writer to provide guidelines for the story he has just written. Therefore, he turns to the second way to decide whether his copy is clear. He evaluates it based on his experience. Or his editor does. Either way, the judgment is subjective. Sometimes, this judgment is very good. Sometimes it is not.

In deriving formulas, readability researchers have used such yardsticks as lists of difficult words, average sentence length, number of prepositional phrases, average letters-per-word, use of "personal" words and sentences, complexity of sentences, ratio of clauses, percentage of abstract words, number of pronouns, and much, much more.

For the news writer faced with the practical task of checking his copy, most formulas are too complex to be of value. He needs a guide to clear writing he can remember easily and apply easily. He needs a guide he can also mentally put aside. Such a guide will become integrated into his total writing experience, called up involuntarily when a sentence sounds or looks cumbersome.

The Easy Listening Formula

With the need for a simple, practical formula in mind, the author, aided by a computer, did his doctoral dissertation on the subject of clear writing in television news. From an analysis of 36 network and local scripts, plus stories from six major U.S. newspapers, a total of 152,890 words, a writing formula emerged. It is called ELF, for Easy Listening Formula, but it is also useful to test newspaper copy and any other prose written primarily to communicate information.

The East Listening Formula is simply this: *In any sentence, count each syllable above one per word.* Take a second look at any sentence scoring above 20. It may be perfectly clear, but chances are it can be improved by trimming adjectives or adverbs, extracting clauses or dividing into two sentences.

A one-syllable word is not counted: hat, check, girl.

A two-syllable word counts one: bowler, grabbing, hostess.

A three-syllable word counts two: fedora, accepting, senora.

As words are replaced by longer words, we climb the abstraction ladder. We also climb ladders we might call "difficulty" and "infrequency." Put plainly, long words are usually harder to understand than short words — not always, but usually. As Winston Churchill put it, "Short words are best, and old words, when short, are best of all." One-syllable words are often either familiar verbs, pronouns, function words (the "glue" words which hold content words together), or concrete nouns. Polysyllabic words (like the word "polysyllabic" itself) are often abstract nouns or seldom-used verbs or adjectives. Obviously, there are exceptions to these statements, but language as a whole hews closely enough to the "long-hard, short-easy" pattern to make the *length* of a word a rough guide to its difficulty. But there are exceptions, like "hews." One obvious reason for the pattern is our natural tendency to shorten words we use often. Gasoline becomes gas. Telephone becomes phone. Television shrinks to TV.

The Easy Listening Formula is based on the concept that a sentence is a package for information. The ELF permits considerable variety in writing. It does not require short, static sentences to produce a pleasingly low score. Here is a sentence with an ELF score of zero: "This is the cow that kicked the dog that chased the cat that killed the rat that ate the malt that lay in the house that Jack built.'' It is also a clear sentence. Children have delighted in it for ages. Notice that it contains not one abstract noun. What sends the Easy Listening Formula soaring is a long sentence full of long words.

To sum up, long words often communicate abstract ideas: capitalism, totalitarianism, communication, psychotherapy. In writing news, we cannot always escape long words. However, when we must get an abstraction across the air waves, we should do so as simply as possible. The abstract information should be sent in "small packages" — that is, short sentences.

Writing is a way to transmit information, attitudes and emotions from one brain to other brains. We may regard television as a medium for information, attitudes and emotions, using writing-read-aloud and pictures. We employ television as our medium because it carries farther than sticking our heads out the window and shouting. What are important are the information, attitudes and emotions — not television, not the means of communicating. Writing, radio, television and shouting are means to communicate, and nothing more. Let us disagree with Marshall McLuhan as concerns news, and say that the medium is not the message. The message is the message. However, if we fail to communicate the message — which is the content of each day's newscast — if we do not get our information across to the viewers clearly so that they understand the news, then we are wasting paper, ink, breath, vocal chords, film, tape, a great deal of money and everyone's time, including our own.

The Abstraction Ladder

In *Language in Thought and Action*, S.I. Hayakawa uses a cow named Bessie to explain how we abstract words.[2] Near the bottom of the abstraction ladder is the one and only Bessie, the name we give to that particular creature grazing over there, whom we can see and touch and describe from her big brown eyes to the way she switches her tail. If we climb one rung of the abstraction ladder we come to the word "cow." We still have a picture although we have lost some of the characteristics of the cow we call Bessie. Climbing higher, we come to "livestock." That's somewhat blurry. Harder to picture. More characteristics gone. Higher still, we find "farm assets." Next, "asset." Finally, at the top of the abstraction ladder, "wealth." If we try to visualize that, we are forced back down the abstraction ladder, perhaps to a pile of coins.

Sometimes we have to talk about "farm assets" in reporting news, but when we do we should be aware that we are way up on the abstraction ladder. What we are discussing is hard to comprehend, to give form, to put edges around. When we can manage it, we'd do better to write about Bessie.

As examples of how this is done, here are the leads on two front page stories of one issue of *The Wall Street Journal*:

> During the final two nights of last October and the first two of November, four 30-man guerrilla teams led by North Korean Lieutenant Chong

Dong-choon slipped ashore on South Korea's rugged and bleak eastern coast. They quickly faded into the mountains.

This story concerned North Korean subversion of South Korea. Do we want to read on? You bet we do.

Here's the second lead:

DETROIT. Just before dusk on a recent snowy afternoon, a car on the crowded Edsel Ford Expressway near here skidded on a patch of ice. It came to a halt broadside across three lanes of fast-moving traffic. A trailing car plowed into it, followed by another and another.

Again, a narrative treatment and concrete words low on the abstraction ladder carry us into the story. The story begins with just that: *a story*. This story dealt with multiple car collisions and their insurance problems.

If *The Wall Street Journal* chooses to talk to its highly literate readers in short, clear sentences and in terms they can visualize, and if the *Journal* can do so with complex economic and political matters, a broadcast newsman might conclude there is not much information that he cannot offer up just as simply and clearly.

Newspaper reporter Fred Othman advised young reporters:

Tell about the taste of things and, especially, smells. People like to hear about smells. Both good and bad. Take the man smoking a Turkish cigarette; it smells like burnt chicken feathers. Say so.

Don't write about ideas, or even things, but about the people who have the ideas, or who build (or break) the things. Let the ideas and the things be described, but by all means make them incidental. Get as many personal references into the story as possible.

Conflict between two men is better than conflict between two armies. If the battlers are doing it with words, quote them accurately. Really accurately. If they mangle the language or split infinitives, let them do so in your story; makes 'em sound like humans. Entirely too many people, when quoted, sound like English professors. [3]

A word of caution here, and a plea for charity. True, many people speak in ungrammatical, broken sentences. Probably so do you. If you would like to see your own words quoted so that you sound "human," even if you sound foolish or uneducated, then let the bad grammar of others show. Otherwise, be considerate of the person you quote. Do not read his words so that he sounds ignorant. If you must change a word to make a statement grammatical, then change the word, so long as you don't alter the meaning.

Colorful Writing

Clear writing will produce a competent news writer, considering style alone. But by itself, it will not produce a quotable writer. Few things in life give a worker more satisfaction than the praise of his fellows for his workmanship. The journalist is no exception. There is deep satisfaction in having a phrase cited by a co-worker. "Hey, did you hear Charlie's tag on that lost horse story?" Or having the studio crew break into laughter when the newscaster reads a line. Or having them suddenly grow attentive, suddenly grave. For example, one newscaster was so moved by copy reporting the death of a beloved actress that he was unable to finish reading it. He sat there, on camera, biting his lip until the director went to black.

The sources of color are many. They include metaphors, similes, pungent verbs, humor, topical allusion, and the narrative tale. Use them sparingly and build them upon the framework of clear writing.

For the Student

1. Describe a listener or viewer that you would write for.

2. Why should newspaper and broadcast news writing styles differ?

3. Rewrite a newspaper story into broadcast news style. Take an ELF count for each sentence. Which story has a lower ELF average?

4. Now rewrite that story to *raise* the average markedly. Show each version to a friend. Which does he or she prefer? Why?

5. Choose an abstract noun from one of your leads and build an abstraction ladder up and down as far as you can go.

News Copy

2

The high linguistic crimes committed by television's newscasters and advertisers have impoverished the richest language in the world.

— Jean Stafford
New York Times

Journalism has been called a process of elimination, an unfortunate definition that has led to some bad jokes, but it fits.

Some advice: if a word isn't needed, omit it. If a sentence adds nothing to the communication of information, omit it. Padding is just a hindrance to thinking. Don't try to write everything there is to say about a person or an event or an idea. You can't do it. And if you could, who would want to hear it?

Despite its masthead, *The New York Times* does not give us "All the news that's fit to print." *The Atlanta Journal* does not "Cover Dixie like the dew." And the radio newscaster does not give us "a complete summary" of the news, whatever that means. "Complete summary" is a contradiction. If it's complete it's not a summary. If it's a summary, it's not complete.

The summary of headlines comprising what some stations call "all the news" led William Small of NBC to imagine the following lead if Moses were living now: "Today, at Mount Sinai, Moses came down with Ten Commandments, the most important three of which are...."

What should you tell in a news story? Tell what is important or interesting, based on your judgment, which derives from your training, skill and experience. Then stop. Do not use a piece of information just because you happen to have it. A news story is not a dumping place for data. Waste baskets were built for that purpose.

Some guidelines:

1. Always be prepared to revise copy.
2. Edit for brevity.
3. Look for deadwood.
4. Trim adjectives and adverbs.

Here's an example: "Police said (that, according to their information,) the militant students would not agree (with the idea) that the building should be vacated." And if the students themselves were in the building, the last clause could be shortened to "...to leave the building."

The Script

Here are some rules:

1. Type copy. Don't write in longhand. If changes involve more than two or three words, type them in. If only two or three words, print them. If the page looks messy, retype it.
2. Double space or triple space.
3. Put only one story on a page.
4. Slug each story with one or two words in the upper left corner, followed by your last name and the date: FIRE-JONES-7/3. If your newsroom has a different slug-line style, follow it.
5. If your story continues onto a second page, print MORE in big letters and/or draw an arrow pointing down. On the top of the second page, type FIRST ADD, then the slug word: FIRST ADD FIRE.
6. Put script page numbers in the upper right corner when the script is assembled.
7. Never break a sentence on a page. Try not to break a paragraph on a page.
8. Never break a word on a line.
9. Don't change a word gingerly, like this: tomo(r)row; or like this: ~~tomorow.~~ tomorrow Change it boldly: TOMORROW.
10. For television, don't write in the bottom one-fourth of the paper. The newscaster has to look too far away from the camera lens to read it. For radio, it doesn't matter.
11. Be sure your typewriter ribbon is black enough and your typewriter keys are clean.
12. Leave margins.
13. Radio copy goes the full width of the page. Television copy is split down the middle, with an inch of white space between video and audio. If the station's practice is to put video material on the left and audio matter on the right, keep it that way.
14. Figure on 4 seconds to a full line of copy, 2 seconds to a half-line, as a rough guide.
15. Words to be read aloud should be typed upper and lower case. ALL OTHER WORDS, BOTH VIDEO AND AUDIO INFORMATION, SHOULD BE TYPED IN CAPS.
16. Use a series of dots . . . to indicate a pause. Use pairs of dashes -- two dashes on each side -- to set off a phrase. Use parentheses (now and again) for "throwaway" phrases. In broadcast copy, punctuation has no function other than clarity.

17. Use hyphens for clarity, despite dictionary usage: *anti-aircraft, re-establish.*

18. All elements of a number should be written so that they can be read from left to right, and symbols should be spelled out. Some readers prefer to see it this way: $4,687.14. Others like: Four thousand six hundred 87 dollars and 14 cents. Also acceptable: 4 thousand 687 dollars and 14 cents. Better yet, round off the number: 47 hundred dollars *or* nearly 47 hundred dollars. 14.3% should be written: 14 — point — 3 percent. June 16 should be written: June 16th *or* June sixteenth. 1972 can be left as is. The decade can be written as: the 1970's, *or* the nineteen-seventies. Fractions are written out: two-thirds, one-half *or* half (NOT: a half; a million sounds like *eight* million.) Set off telephone numbers with hyphens: Central 6-5-4-3-1. The number 1 looks like the letter l, so write *one* and *eleven* unless the one is part of a larger number.

19. Underline words to be emphasized. Not should usually be underlined or spelled in caps.

20. Use phonetic spelling for unfamiliar names. Capitalize the stressed syllable: *He drove from Cairo (KAY-ro), Illinois, to Paris (PAY-ris), Kentucky.*

21. Spell correctly, even though only one or two staff members will see your copy. Misspelled words can cause confusion and can lead to mispronunciation. Keep a dictionary and a gazeteer or atlas. Besides, why let your co-workers think you are stupid?

22. Read your copy aloud. Whisper if you like. You'll catch awkward phrasing or a succession of silly sounding or sissy sounding sibilants. Veteran broadcast journalists subvocalize as they write.

23. Don't abbreviate, except for Mr., Mrs., Dr. and St. as in St. Paul. Use initials if you want them read aloud: the F.B.I. *or* the F-B-I. Where the initials are not all that familiar, precede or follow them with the full name: *the S.D.S. — Students for a Democratic Society.* Where the initials form an acronym, don't use periods or dashes: *NATO.*

"Throwaway" Leads and Transitions

A short sentence or a sentence fragment at the start of a broadcast news item acts like a headline. It tells the listener what to expect. It is also a one-sentence lead-in to a story, a billboard at the start of a newscast, or a tease preceding a commercial:

> *A wet finish to the State Fair...*
> *Another day in the auto strike...*
> *Three accidents are in the news...*
> *Today's storm was one for the record books...*
> *And school opens tomorrow...maybe...*

Beware of the forced transition phrase. Because one story follows another does not mean the stories must be connected. Even when a connection exists, the news writer should not feel obliged to write a bridge (or "a coupling pin"). Spare us from cute leads like:

> *A war of a different sort happened here at home when the mayor and the city council tangled over the location of the new airport.*

Summary Lead or Item Lead

The reporter who covered last night's city council meeting has a problem deciding what to lead with, because three items on the agenda have about the same news value. He can choose one item to lead with and concentrate on, then touch upon the others, or he can write a summary lead, an "umbrella lead" which tries to cover all the important items. Of necessity, a summary lead will have to be less specific than a lead dealing with just one item, and that is the problem with using summary leads in broadcasting. A lead which is less specific must be more abstract, more vague. Here is an example of a summary lead, plus two sentences:

> *The Los Angeles School Board has approved a complex integration plan for the nation's second largest school system.*
>
> *That plan includes a one-year halt on forced busing and shorter rides for students who are bused. The proposal also gives parents a say in how L.A. schools will be integrated.*

The summary lead with the phrase, "complex integration plan," covers at least three items: a one-year halt on forced busing, shorter rides, and giving parents a say in integration. "Complex integration plan" is an abstract phrase, hard to understand or define.

Here is the same story, using a single item in the lead:

> *In Los Angeles, the School Board decided that for the next year students would not be bused to schools against their will.*
>
> *And many students who do take the bus will have shorter rides.*
>
> *The School Board also decided to give parents a say in how L.A. schools will be integrated.*

Question Leads

Be careful. On the air they tend to sound like introductions to commercials. Used sparingly, the question lead adds to the conversational mood the newscaster tries to create.

Narrative Treatment

Sometimes David Brinkley succeeded in telling us what happened because he told what happened first, what happened next, and what happened after that. The wonder of it is that writers don't copy his writing style the way reporters and newscasters copy his delivery. The narrative writing style is as old as "Once upon a time...." which got buried somewhere in the folds of the 5-W lead.

On the left is a silent film story used on the air by one station (with the names changed). On the right, a narrative rewrite.

Original	Rewrite
LIVE	**LIVE**
A Lincoln High School student has failed in a bid to get back into school.	Howard Green wants to get back to Lincoln High School. So far, he can't.
FILM	**FILM**
At a meeting this afternoon the County Board of Education rejected an appeal by the parents of Howard Green, who was expelled for allegedly violating school regulations regarding the use of dangerous drugs. Although the youth admitted taking barbiturates, an attorney hired by his parents claims medical tests indicated he had not consumed drugs. The attorney says the parents, Mr. and Mrs. John Green, indicate they will go to court if necessary to get their son reinstated.	The school expelled him for taking barbiturates. Howard admitted it. But his parents hired a lawyer. And this afternoon the County Board of Education heard the lawyer say that Howard did not take drugs...and there are medical tests to prove it. The Board thought it over...agreed with the school... and rejected the appeal. Howard can't return because he broke the rule about taking drugs. But his parents, Mr. and Mrs. John Green, say they aren't quitting. They're ready to go to court to get Howard back into Lincoln High.

This example was offered by CBS Radio's Charles Osgood:

Early this morning a Metro construction worker named Edward Herndon was working at the Gallery Place Station on Seventh Street.

Normally Herndon worked below ground as a miner, but he was above ground this morning.

A passing truck set the platform to vibrating, toppling a three-ton hydraulic rig. Herndon, who was 33 years old, was crushed to death under the machine.

Jargon

Exactly what is a *six-alarm fire* anyhow? What is the difference between six alarms and five alarms?

Perhaps you know, or perhaps you don't know but still use it in copy because you assume that everyone else knows, and no matter what it means, everyone will surely know it was a big fire, right?

What is an *ad hoc committee*?

What is a *viable alternative*? What is the difference between an alternative that is *viable* and some other kind of *alternative*?

How many viewers will know what a *debriefing* is? A *zero-based budget*? An *inversion layer*? *Zero precipitation*? Do you know?

The Mary Tyler Moore Show may have gone off the air, but Ted Baxter is alive and well in hundreds of television newsrooms and thousands of radio newsrooms.

Redundancy

News writers sometimes tack words onto other words to no purpose. "In basketball tonight..." becomes "In basketball action tonight...", presumably to distinguish it from passive basketball. "Showers" become "shower activity" in case we might be thinking of rain that doesn't move.

NBC's Edwin Newman, who has collected redundancies, noted that we have "famine conditions" instead of famines, "different kinds" instead of kinds, "an urban crisis situation" instead of an urban crisis. We no longer have rules and prospects and news, but ground rules, future prospects and newsworthy happenings. We no longer worry about our safety. It's our personal safety. Companies don't grow. They have positive growth. A triumph becomes a successful triumph. A slaying is a fatal slaying. [1]

Gobbledygook

Nobody grows old these days. Instead, people become senior citizens or golden agers. Kids are no longer lazy in school; they're underachievers. Military prisoners are not tortured; they undergo deep interrogation (unless they're our soldiers, in which case they are tortured). The poor have vanished from our slums, replaced by the culturally disadvantaged. For that matter, the slums have vanished, replaced by the inner city.

Wherever something unpleasant exists, it seems we can make it disappear by giving it a nice ringing phrase. Bureaucrats create many of these euphemisms, but journalists proliferate them, which is a shame because journalists should know better.

Accuracy and clarity remain the touchstones. If a delicate phrasing more accurately and clearly identifies a condition, the delicate phrasing should be used, but if the old Anglo-Saxon word does the job better, the old word should be used. Learn to suspect new terms which government officials, military briefing officers and professors drop at news conferences. But at this point there is nothing much you can or should do about senior citizens. They're here to stay. The old folks have gone.

Other Confusion

Most stories reported *today* happened *today*, especially if they are reported on an evening newscast. Unless there is something special about the event occurring today, such as a reference to an event yesterday or tomorrow, avoid the temptation. Leave *today* out.

If time is important, if you want to show how fresh the news story is, or if leaving the "when" out bothers you, try *this morning, this afternoon, this evening,* or *tonight.*

Avoid "the former" and "the latter." They are confusing.

Beware of "it." Be sure its referent will be understood by listeners. If in doubt, repeat the original word or phrase or identification.

Again, don't lead with an unfamiliar name. Instead of: *Herman Hicks was fined 15 dollars by a municipal court judge,* make it: *A municipal court judge fined Herman Hicks 15 dollars.*

If you lead with a familiar name, precede it with a title or an identification: *The football hero of the nineteen forties...Tom Harmon...*

The usual broadcasting practice is to give the identification first, the name second, no matter where in the story they appear.

Covering Yourself

Accused and *alleged* are used in copy as magic incantations to ward off libel suits. How effective they are is problematic.

The accused rapist was arraigned this morning tells us that a rapist, who is accused, was arraigned, not that this is a fellow who must be presumed innocent until proven guilty by a court of law. *Police captured the alleged killer* introduces us to a killer, not a presumed innocent. *Accused* and *alleged* mean nothing in a legal sense before a preliminary hearing.

After a preliminary hearing and before the trial verdict, it would be better to say, "Joe Doakes, accused of rape..." than "Accused rapist Joe Doakes..."

A different concern arises when the writer is faced with two casualty figures, say *15 dead* reported by the AP and *18 dead* reported by UPI. In this case, use the lower figure if you use only one, or use them both, like this: *Early reports say at least 15 persons are dead, and perhaps as many as 18.*

Action Verbs

These are usually active, not passive, verbs which *describe* what occurred rather than merely *reporting* it.

Poor: A temperature inversion brought eye-burning smog and then heavy fog into the Los Angeles basin Friday, shutting airports and making driving hazardous.

Better: Another temperature inversion in Los Angeles. Drivers whose eyes smarted from the smog later had to peer through a gray gloom as heavy fog rolled in. The airports turned away incoming planes.

Freight Train Phrases

Professor Edward Bliss, a worthy friend of the English language, frequently advises broadcast journalists to shun freight train expressions: "House Ethics Committee Chairman Democratic Representative John Flynt of Georgia..."

Do not refer to people as objects: "The 45-year-old Johnson..." or "The conservative Johnson..." Better: "Johnson, who is 45,..."

Attribution

Attribute a statement to its source when the statement is controversial ("All the Democrats do is spend and tax, spend and tax."), when the source is needed to establish credibility ("Smoking a pack of cigarettes a day definitely shortens the average life span by four years."), and when the source is part of the story ("The governor will not run for re-election.").

Don't attribute without a reason.

If the source is trustworthy and obvious, don't attribute. For example:

Poor: *The vice president in charge of production at Mammoth Studios, Harvey R. Lurch, says shooting begins next week on "Son of Anchorman."*

Better: *Shooting begins next week on the Mammoth Studios picture, "Son of Anchorman."*

Don't use vague or pointless attribution, such as "unimpeachable source" or "highly placed informants," unless you are a diplomatic correspondent.

Limit attribution: *Police said*, not *Assistant Police Chief Melvin Grover said* (unless there is a reason for using Grover's name).

Start the sentence with the attribution.

Contractions, Quotes, *Said*, Slang

Use contractions, but don't feel that broadcast style requires contractions. Broadcast style requires only a natural, conversational manner of writing and speaking. If you are more comfortable with "should not" you should not feel obligated to write "shouldn't." But eschew "ain't."

Quotation marks by themselves may not sufficiently separate a direct quote from other copy, but they should be used, along with an introductory phrase, as a signal to the news reader to pause and shift vocal tone. With a lengthy quote add a concluding phrase:

The mayor said — and I quote — "Let's work together."

The mayor called it "a misguided, overblown project."

Quoting the mayor: "We have no other choice."

The mayor's exact words were: "Not while I still draw breath."

The mayor said — to use his words — "Councilman Jones is dead wrong."

The mayor praised what he called, "The company's concern for the health of our community."

Break up a long quote by inserting a phrase like: *And still quoting the mayor*, or, *The mayor went on to say*, or, *The mayor continued....*

At the end of a long quote, add, *The words of the mayor*, or sometimes, *end of quotation*. Do not write *unquote* or *end quote*, for they sound stilted.

Use quotation marks because, as stated above, they alert the reader to provide a pause or inflection.

When you quote someone saying "I," be sure the copy is written so that no one thinks the newscaster is referring to himself.

Said and *says* are perfectly good words no matter how many times you use them. *Points out* is tricky. So is *claims*.

Told is better than *said in a speech to....*

Promised is another good word, where it fits.

Using a slang word depends on whether it gets in the way of communication. Some slang is O.K. Other slang words get a lot of folks uptight, and we'd be out of our gourds to do a number on our viewers, dig?

A couple of words about dialects: Don't ever.

Metaphor and Simile

Metaphors embed themselves in a language. Yesterday's metaphor becomes today's household word and, by a metamorphosis, the only word which will do, the only word which expresses exactly what we want to express. Because words are symbols, because words stand for things, actions, qualities and relationships, we can almost regard language itself as a body of former metaphors. By definition, a metaphor is a word of phrase which substitutes for another word or phrase. A comparison is implied rather than stated, as in a simile, which sets out the comparison with "like" or "as."

Of all stylistic devices, metaphors and similes are probably the best known and most abused:

> *Tiger Jones flew out of his corner of the ring like a bulldozer, with that right arm cocked for a haymaker.*

It takes imagination to find a fresh metaphor or simile, one which brings the listener an involvement in a mood. That mood might be as somber as a state funeral, as light as a humorous Harry Reasoner commentary, as tense as a battleground on the day before battle, or as pathetic as a battleground on the day after. The metaphors and similes either add to the mood or, by not adding to it, automatically detract from it. In sum, metaphors and similes are too important to be written thoughtlessly. It isn't necessary to use metaphors. It is necessary to avoid stale metaphors, meaningless metaphors. If you want a slogan to hang above your desk in place of THINK, you might consider:

EXPUNGE

CLICHES

> Poor: *Speculation was rampant in local and Eastern financial circles today as to the possibility of a merger between Douglas Aircraft Co. and giant North American Aviation, Inc., of El Segundo.*

Better: *Some financiers here and in the East are saying that Douglas Aircraft Co. may merge with North Aviation of El Segundo.*

The rule for using metaphors and similes should be: Use a figure of speech only if you can justify using it.

The mixing of metaphors, like the mixing of many colors, produces only a muddy picture. The careless mixing of metaphors is easily found in news writing:

Poor: *A deluge of late selling on the New York stock exchange tumbled prices to their lowest level of the year. The market suffered a similar low blow early this morning and just managed to recover before the second wave of selling hit.*

Better: *A wave of late selling on the New York stock exchange tumbled prices to their lowest level of the year. The market had just managed to recover from an early morning selling wave when the second wave came.*

Repetition

Note that the revised version uses *wave* three times. Repetition is a useful writing device, particularly in writing meant for the ear. The idea contained in a word is reinforced by repeating the word. But repeating should be conscious and with purpose. Repeating a word because you cannot think of another, because it jumped to mind, or because you will not bother to take the time to look in a dictionary or a thesaurus for a better word marks you as careless.

Simplicity, Informality, Sparkle

Mark Twain, who was paid by the word, said, "I never write 'metropolis' for seven cents when I can get the same price for 'city'."

The UPI radio manual advises us to:

send, not transmit or dispatch
call, not summon
buy, not purchase
leave, not depart or evacuate
act, not take action
try, not attempt
arrest, not take into custody
show, not display or exhibit
get, not obtain
need, not require
see, not witness
help, not aid or assist
break, not fracture
build, not erect or construct
meet, not confer, convene, or hold a conference

And don't hold your breath until you hear some kid holler, "Oh, I just sustained a contusion" or "I've suffered an abrasion" or "I've received a laceration." Bruises, scrapes and cuts are *in* these days.

A difference between broadcast writing and writing for print is the conversational style of the former. Within the limits imposed by the need for brevity and clarity in imparting information, the rule for writing for the ear is *write as you talk.*

Incomplete sentences and truncated words mark the conversational style. *...Much cheaper than a 'copter, too — six thousand dollars, as compared with 30 thousand.* (KNXT News).

We have already observed that a sharp contrast between audio and video elements of a story may create an effective bit of humor. There are other ways to make the viewer smile, to brighten his hour, and do so without resorting to "happy talk." Learning them is worthwhile, because the day's news report is so often an unrelieved catalog of death and taxes. No one reports about the bus which safely negotiated the hairpin turn.

Obviously, not every story ought to be brightened with a felicitous phrase. If the news is grim, let it remain grim. Where it is not, a touch of sparkle here and there helps. However, too many light touches are worse than none at all, because then the writing intrudes on the story rather than enhances it, and the news report sounds corny, sophomoric.

Here are some sources of sparkle: 1. famous quotes, including poetry, and proverbs; 2. commercial slogans; 3. twists on popular movie and song titles; 4. allusions to unrelated but well known news events, historical events, or persons; 5. irony; 6. understatement (less often used than hyperbole but often more effective); 7. the pun.

Numbers

A City Council meeting might produce this story:

> The City Council last night tentatively approved a Department of Parks and Recreation budget request of $6,500,000 for the coming fiscal year, an increase of $1,250,000 above the current budget.

What meaning does this story have for the milkman, the machinist, the stenographer, or you? Maybe a vague unease, because somebody wants to spend more on something, and taxes will go up for sure. Had the newscaster reading this item said "sixteen million" or even "sixty million" some viewers, perhaps many viewers, would have sat quietly waiting for some news of interest to them. After all, $6,500,000 doesn't have much physical reality. In dollar bills, could you lift it? In quarters, would it fill your living room to the ceiling? How much of that money affects *me*?

Suppose, instead, the City Council meeting produced this story:

> This year, the cost of running the city's parks is, on the average, two dollars and 63 cents for every man, woman and child living here. Next year, it may go to three and a quarter, up 62 cents. The Department of Parks and Recreation is asking for the increase...and last night the City Council tentatively agreed to it.

Now the milkman, the stenographer, you and I have information in a dosage we can gulp down. Are we getting our $2.63 worth? Are the parks well tended and is it such a big deal to spend another 62¢ to keep them from looking scruffy?

Maybe you can personalize even more by naming an average family. If the federal government announces an income tax hike, and you work on a station in, say, Louisville, it is easy to localize the story by saying, "Kentuckians will pay more when...." There's a better way, but it takes a little trouble:

> "Arthur Simpson, his wife and their two children live in east Louisville on Simpson's weekly take-home pay of two hundred 24 dollars and 47 cents. Starting January first, they'll have to manage on two hundred 18 dollars and eleven cents. What happens to the other six dollars and 36 cents? Uncle Sam is taking a bigger bite out of Simpson's paycheck...and mine...and yours...."

It is easy to get enchanted with numbers. Numbers are obvious, and come easily to hand. "Three men were injured..." "A budget of 6 million 500 thousand dollars."..etc. But life is more than numbers. Instead of learning that the City Council approved a record budget of $6,500,000, the viewer might prefer to learn that the City Health Bureau will have a little more money to do its job next year, but not enough to add a dormitory to the School of Nursing, while the Department of Sanitation will get considerably less than it asked for, and will have to do without new garbage trucks.

Obviously, this kind of writing forces the journalist to pay more attention to the budget statement, make a couple of phone calls and consider what is meaningful to people. A sum like $6,500,000 isn't meaningful to many people. If you heard it on the radio, you'd forget it immediately. You wouldn't care if the budget was $6,500,000 or $7,500,000, and yet the difference is enough to make you a millionaire. Now you're interested! Somebody is now talking about making *you* rich!

The point is, do not use numbers just because you have them at hand. If the City Council passes a six and one-half million dollar budget, you must mention that sum in a story about the new budget. But you do not have to lead with it, and you do not have to limit yourself to it.

The rule here is: *a number which means little to you will mean little to most listeners.*

The same rule applies to "Three men were injured..." This is such a standard lead that an editor may jump down your throat if you fail to use it. But it would be more interesting to say that a dump truck filled with sand took a corner too sharply and tipped over. The three men inside were taken to the hospital. All were cut and bruised, and one of them, John Rogers, may have a skull fracture.

You cannot get away from numbers, but play down the flood of numeric facts which come your way. Approximate numbers where you can and make them meaningful where you can.

Personalization

In broadcast news writing, a degree of personalization is achieved by tying the viewer, the newscaster and the community together by using such pronouns as "we," "us" and "our." For example, it is better to write "The City Council voted to raise *our taxes*" than to write "The City Council voted to raise taxes" or "The City Council voted to raise your taxes." Also: "We are due for some rain tonight"; "The income tax form will not confuse us this year as much as it did last year"; and so forth.

However, newsroom policy decisions guide the use of "our" in the sentence, "Our bombers again hit hard at enemy positions." Some news directors prefer the strictly neutral, "U.S. bombers..." or "American bombers..." Other news directors consider the use of "our" in this context to be acceptable.

Sex Bias

The feminist movement has reached into our language to change job titles, patterns of reference, and other words which belittle or discriminate against women. Activists have encountered both success and failure, both support and opposition in their efforts to free the English language of bias, which, they argue, becomes bias in fact.

And so it is *journalist* or *reporter*, not *newsman*.

Anchor or *newscaster*, not *anchorman*.

Photographer, not *cameraman*. *Sound technician*, not *soundman*. *Desk assistant*, not *copyboy*.

In other fields we have *business executive, mail carrier, fire fighter, police officer, city councillor, supervisor* (not *foreman*), *member of Congress*, or *representative, student* (not *coed*), and *feminist* (not *womens libber*).

Chairperson has not gone down quite so easily. *His* is still with us for lack of a satisfactory neutral reference to the third person singular, *his or her* or *his/her* generally being regarded as awkward and *their* being regarded as grammatically beyond the pale.

Still, much has been accomplished. If "John Rogers" doesn't require his marital status advertised, neither does "Mary Rogers." Many elderly women still prefer *Mrs.* or *Miss*; younger women prefer *Ms.* or nothing at all. If the newsroom does not have a policy, judgment must be substituted, judgment usually being better than policies anyway.

When a boy reaches 18, he is a *man*. When a girl reaches 18, she is a *woman*.

We have not reached the time when we will refer to "John Rogers" as "the father of two" with the aplomb that has us writing about "Mary Rogers" as "the mother of two." And we quail at describing defendant John Rogers as "an attractive blond," while we show less hesitation at describing defendant Mary Rogers as "an attractive blonde." Old habits die hard, but changes have been made and more changes, no doubt, are coming.

Rule: If the gender identification is pertinent, use it. If not, don't.

Emphasis

An advertisement for the American Telephone and Telegraph Company's Bell Telephone Laboratories showed a dour man and a headline which read, THIS MAN IS NOT SMILING. The copy claimed that this headline was informationless. "It tells you nothing you haven't already learned from looking at the picture," alleged the ad writer, who went on, "If someone tells you your own name, he again transmits no information: you already know it. He doesn't resolve any uncertainty for you. This idea — that whatever resolves uncertainty is information — was used by Dr. Claude E. Shannon during his years at the Bell Telephone Laboratories to define and measure information for the first time in a way that was usuable to scientists."

Shannon's mathematical equations serve as the basis for communication theory. Communications engineers must be forever in his debt. However, the ad writer was quite wrong when he said the headline, quoted above, contained no information. The reason: the ad writer is unable to tell whether the reader has already learned, by looking at the picture, that the man is not smiling. To be sure, if someone asked the reader whether the man was smiling or not, the reader would reply in the negative, possibly accompanied by some choice words about the mentality of the questioner. But the headline called attention to the fact. Without the headline, the fact might have been overlooked.

Let us apply this to television news. Let us identify the man as John Jones, a local banker just arrested for embezzlement. We have either this still or some film of Jones with the same expression on this face. The copy might read:

VIDEO	AUDIO
CU: JONES. 15 SECS.	Jones was obviously unhappy as our camera caught him at this troubled moment in his life. His eyes were slightly bloodshot. His lips were pursed. A worried frown creased his brow. His face seemed to reflect a mixture of anger and despair.

Of course, we do not write such copy, but if we did, can it be said that we offer no information? What we have provided is emphasis. We have taken a small bit of information and, by hammering at it, have driven it home to the television viewers. At least, we hope we have done so, but chances are if we were to ask the viewers, five minutes later, how Jones appeared, a few might answer, "He looked fine."

Among the dictionary definitions of information are "the telling of something" and "knowledge acquired." For some people, information will not be acquired by being told only once, in passing, along with the thousand other bits of information they will receive in the course of a newscast. They may have to be told again and again, perhaps in different ways. The television journalist can count himself successful if viewers retain just the core of the information he tries to transmit by word and picture. Very few will recall the details.

Examples of Leads

Original

A cut-back in the shipment of Canadian crude oil to Minnesota refineries may cause a shortage of oil by winter....State energy analysts called the cut-back potentially serious.

Rewrite

State oil experts say Minnesota may run short of oil this winter because of Canadian cut-backs.

Original

Minnegasco and NSP customers who use natural gas will be paying more for it beginning in December. An estimated 4 to 8 percent increase will be effective December 27th.

Rewrite

Most of us will be paying more for natural gas starting right after Christmas. A 50 dollar gas bill will go up two to four dollars.

Original

There is a drop of minority students enrolled at the University of Minnesota Law School. This year's class of 249 first year students has the smallest number of minorities in seven years. There are only ten minority students compared with twice that number last year. The number of women enrolled has also declined. Until this year the number of women applicants had been increasing.

Rewrite

Fewer minority students are enrolled at the University of Minnesota Law School... the smallest number in seven years. There are 10 minority students in a class of 249. Last year there were 20. And, for the first time, fewer women applied than the year before, and fewer were enrolled.

Original

A feud between the U.S. Senate and the House of Representatives has left the Federal government without money to keep operating past tomorrow, at least technically. The Senate killed an emergency money bill designed to keep the government afloat for another month. That would give Congress time to agree on a fiscal budget for next year. The House would not compromise when the Senate asked it to reconsider some language in the bill forbidding the use of Federal money to pay for most abortions.

Rewrite

The Federal government has no money to operate past tomorrow, at least technically. The Senate killed an emergency money bill because the House would not compromise on forbidding Federal funds for abortions.

Original

Five members of the Brainerd City Council are expected to receive contempt of court citations today for deciding not to fluoridate the city's water supply. Ramsey District Judge Harold Schultz said that the council members face fines of 250 dollars a day and even possible imprisonment. Schultz will decide on what action he will take on Monday.

Rewrite

Five members of the Brainerd City Council face jail terms and fines for refusing to fluoridate the city water supply. Ramsey Judge Harold Schultz said council members could be fined up to 250 dollars a day each. He'll announce his decision Monday.

Original

A fuel explosion and fire at a Marine Corps camp in Japan has killed one person and injured at least 46. High winds from a typhoon knocked the fuel tank over causing it to explode and set fire to several buildings.

Rewrite

In Japan, a typhoon knocked over a fuel tank at a U.S. Marine base. It exploded, killing one marine and injuring at least 46 others.

Original

The possible move of the Baltimore Colts to another city may be settled today at the N.F.L.'s mid-season meeting in Dallas.

Rewrite

They're meeting in Dallas today to decide if the Baltimore Colts stay in Baltimore.

Original

Blizzard warnings are in effect today across western Kansas and west-central Nebraska as a windy snow storm moves eastward through the central and southern states. The storm has already killed eight people.

Rewrite

A blizzard which already has killed eight people is moving eastward through the midwest and the south.

Original

A gasoline shortage will soon sweep across the country and Minnesota will be the hardest hit state. So says the executive director of the Minnesota Service Stations Association, Brian Ettesvold.

Rewrite

An expert on gasoline supplies says Minnesota next month may suffer the worst gasoline shortage in the nation.

Original

Have law agencies already lost the war on drugs? The General Accounting Office of Congress says illegal drug use is so popular and so profitable for traffickers that the problem has become too much for the U.S. to handle alone. Even after decades of greatly publicized police action against drug suppliers, G.A.O. says business has never been better. The G.A.O. report recommended the establishment of a consortium of victim countries to develop a global plan of action.

Rewrite

A Congressional study says the drug problem has become too big for the United States to handle alone. It recommended that countries with a lot of addicts work together.

Original

The Federal Trade Commission ruled that American Medical Association members can advertise their services. The A.M.A. was unlawfully placing restrictions on advertising and on the soliciting of patients.

Rewrite

The Federal Trade Commission ruled that doctors can now advertise. The F.T.C. says the American Medical Association cannot prevent doctors from selling their services any way they want to.

Original

A free exhibition of Hubert Humphrey mementos is currently on display on the third floor of Coffman Union. Two hundred objects and 50 photographs on the late Minnesota politician are shown in the exhibit. The display is open to the public from 7 a.m. to 11 p.m. Monday through Thursday, 7 a.m. to 11 a.m. Friday and Saturday, and 1 p.m. to 11 p.m. on Sunday. The exhibit will run from now until October 31.

Rewrite

Hubert Humphrey mementos are on display at Coffman Union. Admission is free. The exhibit can be seen until the end of October.

Original

The governments of Vietnam and the Vietnamese-controlled Heng Samrin government in Cambodia, or Kampuchea, announced jointly that the Mekong River could now be used to ship aid to Phnom Penh.

Rewrite

Vietnam and Cambodia have agreed to allow aid shipments to come up the Mekong River.

Original

Consumer food prices rose point nine percent in September.

Rewrite

Food prices rose again in September. The week's groceries that cost 50 dollars in August went up to 50 dollars and 45 cents in September.

For the Student

1. Monitor each newscast in your reception area for writing style. What conclusions can you reach?

2. Write a news story in inverted pyramid style. Rewrite it in narrative style.

3. Scan the front page of a newspaper. Draw a circle around each word or phrase of jargon or gobbledygook.

4. Now circle every number on the page.

5. Rewrite the story with the most numbers, eliminating as many as you can without losing the essential information of the story. Which version would be easier to remember if heard over the air?

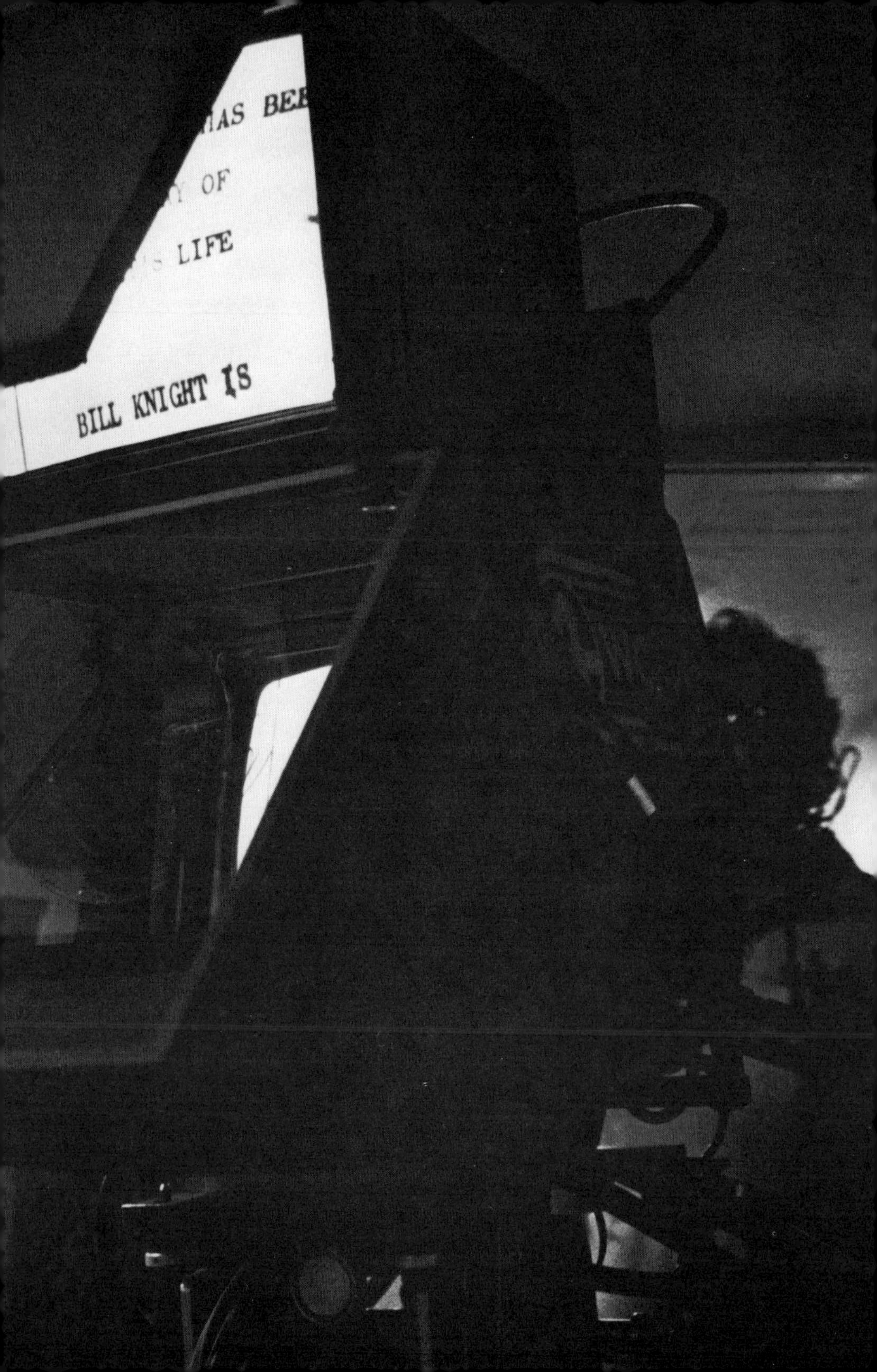
LIFE
BILL KNIGHT IS

The Lead-In   3

A loud voice which reaches from coast to coast is not necessarily uttering truths more profound than those that may be heard in the classroom, bar or country store.

— *Edward R. Murrow*

Almost all the meaningful sound in a sound-on-film (shortened in scripts to SOF), a sound-on-tape piece, or a radio actuality, is talk. Almost every lead-in — or "intro" — is an introduction to someone saying something.

That someone may be a reporter: "Dairy farmers in Starke and Howard counties have been threatening to spill their milk rather than sell it at today's prices. Today they made good their threat. Here's a report from Nancy Patterson."

That someone may also be the person interviewed although a direct switch from the newscaster to the interviewee is more common in radio than in television: "Dairy farmers in Starke and Howard counties have been threatening to spill their milk rather than sell it at today's prices. Alfred Nelson milks 150 cows on his farm northeast of Starke City."

The lead-in itself may be done by:

1. A newscaster or a reporter in the studio, the "Eyewitness News" format.

2. A newscaster with a Chromakey or rear projection still or freeze frame behind him.

3. A still (card or slide) photo, map, cartoon, title card or prop.

4. Silent film.

5. Sound film with the volume lowered in the control room, so that the sound serves as a background to the newscaster's voice.

6. A "standupper" by the reporter who covered the story, which is itself SOF.

While each of these methods has its place, some are more desirable than others. A newscaster is more interesting to watch when he has a still behind him. "Sound under" film is preferable to silent film. And film is usually preferable to a still photo. Nevertheless, a mix of all these methods is probably best of all, based on the adage that variety lends enchantment. But with the exigencies of time, available materials and a limited budget, a television journalist must temper what he would like to do with an awareness of what he can do. Let us consider each method in turn.

Newscaster Alone

Going directly from a newscaster to an interviewee's statement is sometimes unavoidable. A news director anywhere has little option but to accept the abrupt cut to sound film if the sound film arrived late from the lab or on video tape (technically not film, but it will be so regarded in this context), if it contained no intro scenes, and no stills are available for rear projection.

Rule: *The newscaster should introduce the story as if no film were to follow.* Unless he has some special reason for referring to the film (e.g., "We were fortunate to get..." or "The prime minister of China made his first appearance before cameras in..."), the newscaster's lead-in should ostensibly ignore the SOF which is to follow. He should not say, "This is what the mayor said about new taxes" or "Here is the mayor," and he should especially avoid unfinished sentences, such as, "The mayor declared..." The reason is simple: film or tape does not always appear when you want it to appear. Even the best run newscasts occasionally suffer the embarrassment of a three-second pause between the newscaster's last word and the mayor's first word. Three seconds is a long time to leave a newscaster "with egg on his face." Yet without film to cut to, the director has no choice but to stay with the newscaster or, what is worse, go to black. Three seconds delay makes a newscast seem amateurish if the newscaster has introduced the film with something like, "The mayor declared..."

It is far better simply to let the film appear after the newscaster has prepared us with background information in the same way he would report any story. For example, "Mayor Tolliver said that the city may be forced to impose a hotel-motel bed tax. It drew immediate opposition from the Chamber of Commerce. The mayor spoke at this morning's City Council meeting." The viewer is now prepared to hear the mayor, and even a Chamber of Commerce official whose statement is "butt-ended" to the mayor's statement, provided the official is identified by a super. The mayor should also be identified by a super. Should the film be delayed, the newscaster will not look foolish. Even if the film breaks in the projector — which also happens sometimes — the newscaster can sometimes go on to the next story, or fill in with pad copy, without the need to apologize.

Here are some examples of lead-in copy used on the air. In each case the last sentence of copy was immediately followed by someone talking, someone who in most instances was identified in the final intro sentence.

Indianapolis winner Sam Hanks — official starter of today's 3-hour cross country navigational race in Los Angeles. 45 blind teenagers from the Braille Institute guided drivers after interpreting course instructions from the Braille System for the blind. One of the navigators....Jerry Arakawa....

Tomorrow at noon, the 35 foot yawl Viking will sail from Redondo Beach harbor bound for Hawaii. This afternoon we spoke with the pleasure craft's owner, John Brockman, about the trip.

Beauty contestants from Los Angeles gathered at the International Hotel this afternoon to compete for the title of Miss South Los Angeles...part of a run-off for the title, Miss California. We were on hand as the judges announced their decision.

(AFTER ESTABLISHING VIDEO)
This little 3-year-old girl is able to walk again after successful heart surgery at Loma Linda University Hospital. She was given a going away party today by hospital officials and members of the Heart Fund Volunteers. Little Afahan Zafar and her father are from Pakistan and came to this country in a final effort to save her life. The story has a happy ending.

The copy which leads into a taped or filmed statement should not give away what will be said. To use the earlier example, if the mayor says, "It is my reluctant conclusion that a hotel-motel bed tax is the only way to avoid adding to the heavy tax load of the already overburdened home owner," then the lead in should not steal the mayor's thunder. It should not baldly state that "Mayor Tolliver said that the city may be forced to impose a hotel-motel bed tax." Rather, the copy should "set up" the statement. For example: "At the City Council meeting this morning, Mayor Tolliver proposed a new tax...one which immediately drew an angry reply from the Chamber of Commerce and from hotel owners. The mayor's proposal: a tax on travelers, visitors and people who come to the city for conventions." The mayor now appears to use the term "hotel-motel bed tax."

Chromakey

Television news studios are equipped with either slide-actuated rear projection or Chromakey, a color-keyed electronic rear projection system which accommodates not only stills, but can show films, videotape and live transmission in color on the screen behind the newscaster, who must be careful not to wear a blue shirt or suit, for it will appear to have vanished (most systems are keyed to blue).

The studio director must establish his cameras so that the newscaster is close to the RP (or "chroma"), yet does not obscure any significant element of it with his head. If the director has a free camera, he should set it up for a dissolve from a wide shot of the newscaster and the RP to a tight shot of the RP alone. The person in the newsroom who makes the slides ought to know the relationship of newscaster to RP screen. If the newscaster sits to the left of the screen, the slide maker should reverse any profile pictures which face right, away from the newscaster. If the newscaster's head blocks most of the lower left quadrant, the slide maker must be sure no RP map contains an important element in that corner. Of course, no picture containing words may be reversed, because the words would appear backwards.

No slide should be "busy." If the story concerns the death of a literary figure, and the only picture available shows him in the company of four other people, it is advisable to cut him out of the picture and photograph him against a light gray background. A map "moved" (transmitted) on the wirephoto facsimile machine usually needs to be redrawn to remove most of the detail and to add color.

If the SOF to follow is a statement by, say, the British prime minister, the slide maker should not use an old library still of the prime minister as his lead-in. The prime minister probably looks older on film, has removed his/her spectacles and his/her overcoat, and is wearing different clothes. The old still, in short, looks like an old still. Much better: draw a map of the area the prime minister is discussing, such as Zimbabwe-Rhodesia or Britan itself, or use a photo, if the prime minister is discussing a person.

Again, the copy should neither refer directly to the film which follows nor should the newscaster repeat the thoughts or words on film. The newscaster must make reference to the RP and he should do so in the first sentence, but the reference should be oblique, never anything like, "This is the French foreign minister" or "We are looking at a map showing..." unless some special reason exists for calling attention to the RP. That might occur if, for instance, the map were a newly discovered treasure map, or the photograph showed a million dollars worth of Spanish doubloons. Even then, direct reference is not absolutely necessary.

Rules which apply to RPs also apply to pictures and drawings which fill the television screen. A news program which lacks RP projection facilities may show still pictures and drawings either by making slides from the originals or by pasting the original photos and drawings to cards. The cards are placed on a stand, and a studio camera transmits them through the electronic system. If two studio cameras are available, as they would be in a three-camera program, electronic dissolves can create useful and pleasing montages. Slide projectors in two telecine chains can do it too, of course.

The cheapest, simplest and quickest way to put a picture on the air is to slap some paste on its back, stick it to a card and place it in front of a studio camera.

Video Intro

A common way to introduce a person making a statement is with silent or sound-under tape or film. A familiar procedure in covering a static scene story such as a news conference or an interview begins with setting his camera on a tripod and arranging his lights. He must do this before any fixed-time event begins, or he will lose the opening statements while he fumbles with his gear. With his sound camera thus immobilized, the photographer relies on his lighter, handier silent camera to give him the variety of scenes and angles he wants for establishing and cutaway shots. Unless he is under instructions to "edit in the camera," the photographer tries to shoot enough different scenes to cover any approach the writer and the editor might later take to the story.

Minicams and the new film cameras like the CP 16 are light enough on the shoulder so that some photographers never use tripods or backup cameras. The photographer shoots the interview and the cutaways with the same camera.

Over a period of weeks, an imaginative writer or editor will have assembled almost as many different kinds of intros as there are different kinds of stories.

1. The opening scene is often, but not always, an establishing shot: that is, a long shot or medium long shot which encompasses as much of the scene as is practicable. This may be followed by a medium shot of the speaker's table or lectern, followed by a cutaway of spectators, the reporter, one or more cameras, or any of a dozen other shots. Or, instead of a long shot, the opening scene may be the medium shot, followed by a close up of the speaker, followed by a cutaway. Or, the opening scene may be a close up of the speaker, followed by a medium shot or a long shot, in which case the cutaway probably will not be required.

2. Another way to avoid a cutaway, which at best is a necessary artifice, is to use the interview footage immediately preceding the first sound bite used, with or without an establishing shot. In other words, the editor does not begin the first sound bite with the speaker's first words, but backs the film up to include four to six seconds of the speaker before he utters those words. Unless the audio track contains only normal background noise for these four to six seconds, the editor must "bloop" the sound track, i.e., wipe the film with a magnet to erase the sound or dub "audio only" with a tape editor. This film should not be used if the speaker was talking, because his lips would be moving. The film is eminently usable if a reporter was asking a question which the writer chooses not to use. The question is blooped, and the speaker's face in close-up or medium close-up appears as part of the silent intro. A cutaway is not needed. The intro could even be this shot alone, backed up 10 to 15 seconds.

3. In place of a static opening scene, the first film to appear on the air may be the speaker walking into the room. The hubbub accompanying the entrance and the words of greeting to friends and newsmen make an excellent opening if the speaker is famous.

4. If the event occurs in an auditorium or a banquet hall or council meeting, the opening shot may be of the audience. It may also be of an exterior, say a building on campus. It may be a sign on the door or at an entrance gate. Any exterior opening should carry us smoothly, shot by shot, to the speaker. For example, a brass plaque at the entrance to a multi-building factory might be followed by the exterior of the building where our speaker is located, followed by him in a medium long shot — presumably in a room whose equipment is important to the story — followed by a cutaway of the most important piece of equipment, followed by the audio statement.

5. The opening silent film might be a pan of a room full of interesting objects, or several shots of individual objects, followed by audio of the speaker surrounded by the objects. A trade fair, a boat show, or an art exhibit may be treated with such an opening.

6. The intro might be of a plane arriving at an airport, or a car pulling to the curb.

Rule: *Whatever video is used, the writer should be able to defend his choices.* If he begins with an establishing medium long shot, he ought to be able to explain why, although it is unlikely that anyone will ask him to do so. It is a sloppy writer whose instructions to an editor are "Give me 15 seconds of establishing at the head." Any scene which appears on a television newscast — and there may be dozens in each newscast — is there because someone chose that particular shot in preference to everything else. If the selection is careless and arbitrary, the newscast will reflect it.

Just as each scene should be used because there is a reason for using it, the length of each scene should be justified, and usually right down to the last second. The writer ought to make a rational, conscious decision that a shot should last four seconds rather than three. Indeed, a thoughtful writer and a careful editor will occasionally dispute the addition of one second, and in an overlap cut the editor may count frames. All this, of course, assumes that enough time is available to polish a story. Where time permits, pride of craft should emerge in each story. When the writer and film or tape editor race the clock — as all writers and editors must do sometimes — they will instinctively do things right if they are accustomed to thoughtful editing.

Among the reasons for letting a shot run, say, eight seconds instead of five seconds or ten seconds, are these:

1. An audio track which matches the video runs eight seconds.

2. The audio track is needed for just eight seconds.

3. A quote or other copy which for some reason should not be altered runs exactly eight seconds.

4. It takes eight seconds for a pan (a horizontal turning of a stationary camera) to establish, move, and stop. An editor should not cut into or out of a moving pan.

5. Certain actions at either end of the shot must be included, e.g., a man walking into and out of frame.

6. Certain actions at either end of the shot must be omitted, e.g., nasty gestures at the camera by a prisoner, leaving a maximum of 8 seconds of permissible footage of the prisoner.

7. A scene is "worth" eight seconds, or the cutting rhythm calls for a shot here about eight seconds long. These two considerations are highly subjective, but they are often soundly based on years of motion picture cutting experience which develops a feeling for shot value and rhythm.

8. Approximately eight seconds may be needed to permit a smooth dissolve or fade out of a shot which would otherwise be cut for five seconds.

9. A scene may be so "busy" (for example, a lot of words on a sign) that a shorter length will not give the viewer full comprehension.

The total length of an intro to a sound bite usually runs between eight seconds and 20 seconds, with 12 to 15 seconds being common. Little can be said in less than eight seconds which will suitably prepare the viewer for the sound-on-film statement. Anything more than 20 seconds would seem to be pointless or dull, unless the intro film sustains the interest of a silent or sound-under film story.

Rules which govern on-camera, RP, and still introductions to speakers also govern video intros:

1. Copy should match picture.

2. A person seen in medium shot or close up must be identified the first time he appears. The viewer should never wonder who he is looking at.

3. As already mentioned, copy should never begin with phrases like "This is...,""We are looking at..." or "Here we see...." Such words may prove embarrassing for the newscaster if the film is up-cut or rolls late. The viewer then will not be looking at what the newscaster tells him he is looking at.

4. The last words of copy before the sound bite should not refer to the statement by phrases like "The mayor added..." or "Watch this scene," or "He had this to say...." As noted in the last chapter, an exception to this rule occurs when something visually significant is likely to escape the viewer's attention because it happens very quickly or is very small or faint. Even then, the writer can usually refer to the object or action indirectly. For example, if the camera catches the third woman from the left in the back of the room suddenly fainting, the copy need not say, "Watch a woman in the back of the room," although this is permissible digression from the objective reporting of the story. The copy can read, "As the lawyers wrangled, a woman standing in the back of the room fainted from the heat and the excitement." The viewer's attention will be drawn there when

the picture appears just as surely as he would with a "watch her" admonition.

5. The intro copy, in sum, should be a story in microcosm, one that could stand — although weakly — without film.

6. Copy preceding a sound bite should "set up" the statement, but it should neither repeat the words that are coming, nor should it give away their import or surprise, unless a single fact of the story is so overshadowing that nothing else matters. Rather, the writer should indicate the overall tenor of the copy. What follows is "poor" or "better" in certain contexts:

POOR INTRO	BETTER INTRO
Mayor Smith said Councilman Brown was misguided.	Mayor Smith criticized Councilman Brown.
Mayor Smith announced that all playgrounds would be closed.	The mayor had news that is sure to distress the city's children...and their parents.
The mayor surprised newsmen today by declaring, "I will not run for re-election."	The mayor surprised newsmen today by announcing that he will soon retire from public affairs.

The copy, above, which is labelled "poor" is poor only if it is immediately followed by the mayor on film saying, "Councilman Brown is misguided" or "I'm sorry to announce that all playgrounds must be closed" or "Gentlemen, I have decided I will not run for reelection."

The copy is adequate if the mayor does not repeat on tape what the newscaster uses in his introductory copy. Indeed, the copy may be exactly what is called for if the mayor does not make the announcement on tape, but proceeds from that point with an explanation of the announcement; for example, "I say this about Councilman Brown because of his extraordinary opposition to the city beautification program," or, in the case of the playgrounds, "We are acting on advice of the City Health Officer because of two cases of meningitis reported in the county," or, in the case of the re-election, "I have served as mayor and as councilman for 26 years, and now it is time for a rest." With such opening statements on film, the direct or indirect quote becomes a needed part of the informational "set up."

7. The intro copy replaces a reporter's question when that question, as recorded, is inaudible, too long, connected to a prior answer ("In that regard, how can you..."), or asked by the reporter of a competing station, when newsroom policy requires the elimination of competitors' voices. Under any of these conditions, the intro must ask the question, because the tape begins with the person answering it. For example, this lead-in: "On another subject, the governor formally announced that he's not a candidate for the Democratic nomination for vice president. Then he was

asked if he would turn it down." Governor: "I don't see how anyone could turn it down."

Roll-Thru

Two statements are conveniently joined by means of a roll-thru. This is a length of film not meant to be seen on the air, used while a recorder or projector continues rolling at full speed. When one person makes statements at two different times, e.g., a defendant chatting with reporters just before and just after he is sentenced by the judge, a roll-thru joins the statements.

The roll-thru may run five or six seconds, with the newscaster on camera. More commonly, the roll-thru will be video, with the newscaster voicing over it.

The roll-thru is usually a bridge between two sound bites. A story may have several of them (referred to as "roll-thrus," not "rolls-thru"). Statements by different speakers also can be butt-ended: that is, spliced directly without a roll-thru, with supers to identify the speakers.

The tape or film and the copy used in a roll-thru must either time or identify change. For example, between the defendant's two statements, before and after sentencing, the camera may focus on the courtroom door:

VIDEO	AUDIO
:32 VTR	SOUND BITE
	END CUE: "...really innocent."
:05 ROLL-THRU	Jones entered the court to hear his sentence. He was quieter when he returned.
:29 VTR	SOUND BITE
	END CUE: "...serve my time."

As another example, let us assume we have a statement by Mayor Smith saying Councilman Brown is misguided, and a reply by Councilman Brown that Mayor Smith has forgotten his promises to the voters. A five-second roll-thru might consist of three seconds of Councilman Brown's name on his office door, plus a two-second medium long shot of the councilman's office, with Brown seated at his desk.

VIDEO	AUDIO
1:04 MAG	SOF
	END CUE: "...him astray."

:05 ROLL-THRU	But Councilman William Brown was more concerned with budgets than with beauty.
:57 MAG	SOF
	END CUE: "...the taxpayer."

The common practice of intercutting two separate interviews gives viewers the sense that a debate is taking place, because the editing is based on comments about the same topics: for example, each person's statements about pollution abut, followed by their statements on the need for new schools. While this method makes their relative positions clear, the viewer should not be misled into thinking that an actual debate took place, which might lead him to conclude that one of the opponents got the better of it. The newscaster should make it plain that no argument or interchange of views took place, and the viewer is merely hearing isolated comments which have been edited together to help in understanding the positions of the two opponents.

Between two statements by the same person during an interview or news conference, the roll-thru should not show the speaker's face in close up or medium shot (a jump cut unless it is sandwiched between two cutaways). Here, the roll-thru is really a cutaway. An establishing long shot can be used. Better yet: show the back of the speaker's head or a one-quarter profile, with the speaker talking and gesturing, and the reporter, shown in the background head-on, listening. A roll-thru of cutaways which do not include the speaker is less desirable because the roll-thru copy probably sets up the speaker's next statement. In short, if the newscaster is talking about what else Mayor Smith said, let us see Mayor Smith, but let us not see a closeup of his face.

Standupper/Wraparound

The term "standupper" refers to a reporter at the scene describing the event. He "stands up" before the camera, and what he says is his "stand up piece." In radio it is called a "wraparound" or "wrap" because the reporter's words wrap around (precede and follow) the actuality.

The "stand up piece" may be an "intro" and a "close" to a self-contained segment such as a person talking, or it may be an on-camera "intro" and/or "close" to silent film in a double chain story. If the "standupper" is for a double chain, then the reporter delivers an introductory sentence or two and a closing sentence or two while looking directly at the camera, expecting that his portion of his narration will be shown to the audience. He reads the rest of the story from his notes, expecting that the video "B roll" will cover the audio "A roll" of him on camera. He is then reading "voice over." (These terms are by no means universal, but are common enough to be widely recognized.)

In some cases, the "standupper" is simply a short statement delivered by the reporter in the field. This is the weakest kind of field reporting. It is sometimes used when no other meaningful or applicable picture is available, because at least it shows the audience that the television station sent a reporter to the scene of the story. If possible, the reporter should be standing near something significant to the story. Perhaps it is a building in which the action is taking place. Perhaps it is a gate, through which newsmen have been denied access. On one story, network camera crews and reporters flew to Yellowstone Park to film the killing of elk by rangers who were ordered to thin out the herd because of overgrazing. When they arrived, they were denied admittance to where the elk were being slaughtered. At least one network reporter, trying to get an early story out, did a "standupper" beside the bodies of two of the elk. There was nothing else to show.

In an interesting form of double chaining (cutting or dissolving back and forth between two projectors), the A roll carries the interview, and the B roll consists of long shots and medium long shots of the reporter and the interviewee walking along, chatting. The camera never allows us to approach near enough to match mouth movements to the questions and answers we hear. The two people walk into or walk out of frame. The scene of their stroll is germane to the topic they are discussing, e.g., a campus or downtown streets.

The news clip, as it is seen on the air, might begin visually with the A roll, which shows the two men in actual conversation, dissolve into the B roll for the bulk of the clip, and return to the A roll — of the actual conversation — at the conclusion. Or the B roll might carry the entire picture. In either event, an on-camera introduction by the newscaster or the reporter in the studio should precede the film.

In a memo to ABC network correspondents, Gary Franklin commented on some filmed standuppers he had seen, good and bad:

1. A recent demonstration in a European capital. The immigration laws are about to be changed. Protestors marching through the streets. Many skin tones. Turbaned Indians. Robed Africans. Local gendarmes. Shouting. Chanting. Banners. Sidewalk crowds.

ABC correspondent: does standupper against nondescript wall, street sign over his head. No other activity in standup picture. Visually dull. Prognosis: if film is used at all, it will probably be voice-over only, without "picture" of the correspondent.

(Competition standupper, same story: correspondent reports from the middle of the demonstration, the participants pouring past the camera. Very effective.)

2. ABC correspondent in Miami opens piece on $300,000 development homes — with a wide-angle shot, showing correspondent cruising down a canal, past the huge homes, while he is talking.

As a closer, correspondent washes hands in fancy, gold-encrusted sink...shuts off water...turns to camera..."THIS IS -----, ABC, IN A 14-THOUSAND DOLLAR BATHROOM." End. Great.

3. ABC correspondent in Rome, does story on traffic jams which are forcing city to consider tearing down the ancient wall of Rome. "Stand-upper" (in this case, "sitdowner") done inside car. Wide-angle shot reveals other cars outside windows...all stuck in middle of traffic jam. Perfect.

4. Correspondent in Paris...does ABC standupper, with girl in bra and stocking girdle — posing with semi-nude man for advertising photographer...over correspondent's left shoulder. A story on France's advertising revolution, and the media's "use" of sex. Attention-getting — to say the least.

What's the point of all this?

. . . We want to *see* as well as hear our correspondents on the scene... want to *see* them in the proximity of the most important action elements of the stories they're covering.

A reporter standing against a blank wall won't be able to give us much of a substitute for track-only, voice-over.

IMPORTANT POINT: The correspondent-inside-the-scene material need not be extensive. It often requires no more than two or three sentences for the opening...a couple of sentences for the closing...and, if you really want to add an extra touch, a chunk for the middle.

For the sake of covering yourself fully — try to do the *entire* narration — including open and close — later. The duplication won't hurt — and can only help, in case the on-scene material doesn't work out.

At times it may be desirable to show the correspondent at various points within the story — in addition to, or instead of — the open and close. Therefore, *if* you can do the entire on-scene standupper/sitdowner/crouch-downer on camera, while part of the action background...so much the better. Everyone here realizes this isn't always possible...but it should be tried.

Careful, once again: make sure your pace, mood, level, background noise (as well as that certain difference between outdoor and indoor sound) will match throughout the piece. Too often, the opening sentences, recorded on the scene and in the middle of some activity, demonstrate an intensity and pitch not matched by the more relaxed track-only, recorded later, in the hotel room. It makes for some jarring audio-cutting.

In any case, a standupper recorded on an activity-filled street can never match additional narration, recorded after things have died down. Therefore, always try to provide some wild track of the action *noise* (traffic, demonstrators, water lapping against a pier, gunfire, pumps, crowds, a speaker on a podium, aircraft engines, and what have you) which can, if necessary, be *triple*-chained into your story.

To sum up:

Walk with the demonstrators (without getting hurt)...drive through the demolished suburb...sit on the rundown porch with the poverty worker and the indigents...stand amid the crowd of squealing youngsters...walk out from behind the weird statue...smoke the cigarette with the new controversial filter, while you intro the news conference involving the scientists... speak from the seat in the middle of the stadium crowd...let the laboratory worker and his microscope softly dominate the foreground, while you explain from — and are visible in — the background...intro and close from the foreground, while the VIP speaks or shakes hands behind your back...BE A VISUAL PART OF THE STORY!

It can make all the difference between story acceptance and (gulp) story rejection.

The reporter ought to indicate his setting: "Behind me is the courthouse where...," "A biting wind is sweeping down from the mountains as these rescue workers...," "From where we are located we can see...," "The crowbar on this table is the one used..." and so forth, as the camera pans up to the mountain or zooms in on the crowbar.

The close is usually just a wrap-up sentence or two with the reporter's name and location following it: "The people of Sleepy Valley will remember this day for a long time. This is Joe Foss, at the railroad depot in Sleepy Valley."

In addition to the standup open and the standup close, the reporter must provide voice over the accompanying (e.g., B-roll) film. Most standuppers are done against a background of distinctive sounds which will not always match the accompanying film, whose sound is the best natural background to its own picture. Given the option, the editor would choose it instead of the background sound behind the reporter's voice. Rather than provide an unmatched audio background, the reporter should do his voice-over narration in a relatively quiet place, such as a room or a quiet street. The voice-over narration should include the open and close, which will give the editor the option of cutting the entire film voice-over, or cutting either the open or close that way.

Choice of a site for voice-over narration should be made with the standup location in mind. If the standupper was done on a noisy street, the voice-over should be done on a quiet street rather than a hotel room where the difference in acoustics will be evident. If the standupper was done *sotto voce* in the back of an auditorium where a speaker was holding forth, a quiet hallway should serve nicely for the voice-over.

Going to Commercial

Going from a film story directly into a commercial fails to establish the distance which should exist between news and advertising. This direct method also misses an opportunity to confirm the newscast as an entity and the anchor as the person in control of the newscast. Fading from a film to black, then fading into a commercial is bad enough. Cutting from a film to a commercial is unforgivable.

Here are several acceptable methods of going to a commercial:

1. The anchor, the sports editor or weathercaster says simply, "I'll be back in a moment." Or,: "We'll return after this commercial message," "More news after this announcement," etc.

2. The anchor uses a tease: "A new effort to stop plans for the airport. The story...after these words." Less desirable: "...after these words for Sparkle Fish Bath." As a matter of policy, some stations object to any tease copy on ethical grounds; i.e., that the news, including people's misfortunes, is being used as a lure to hold people for a commercial.

3. A tease is voiced over the newscast's logo on a slide.

4. Similar to the tease is the billboard at the start of the newscast, with headlines of the biggest news items and the feature stories. The newscast begins after the opening commercial. A smaller billboard headlines news in the next news segment, between commercials.

5. A freeze frame of the end of a VTR or film clip is kept on the air without sound. The newscast logo and today's date are supered over it, then the director goes to black. He fades in on a commercial. This formatted end of a newscast segment gives the newscast a modern, professional appearance. It tells the viewer that someone took some pains to put this program together.

6. The director cuts to a wide shot of the news set, with several people in view. He holds it for three or four seconds, then fades to black.

Headlines?

Newspapers provide an all-at-once service, what the French call a *coup d'oeil*. One glance at a page and the reader knows from the headlines what stories he will read.

Broadcast journalism offers only a linear service. To get the third story, you must sit through the first two, unless you care only about the weather or the ball scores. In that case you know approximately when the newscaster will relinquish the camera and you tune in then. Some radio newscasts do provide a headline service by giving one-line summaries at the start.

Headlines offer the viewer an advantage that some newsrooms have been aware of. For some years the ABC network news led its newscasts with a "menu board" list of headlines. A few newsrooms continue to offer it, but no newscast, to the author's knowledge, tells the viewer at approximately what time a major story will be reported. Workers in the studio and in the control room know, of course, but the information is not shared with the audience.

In light of the longer newscasts which have been coming to television, a headline service telling what and when ought to be considered.

For the Student

1. Find an interview story in the newspaper. Write a 20 second lead into the first quotation used.

2. Write a 10 second lead into the same quotation.

3. For what kind of story and sound bite might it be better to use a photo as intro, either full screen or Chromakey, instead of VTR or film? A map? A cartoon? Newscaster on camera with no still?

4. Assume that you are a reporter who must do a standupper at each of these locations: outside the wall of a prison in which convicts are holding guards hostage, outside a federal court building in which an important case is being tried, on a military airfield in front of a new fighter plane. Using your imagination (but not too much imagination), write a standupper open and close around a statement by someone at the scene, e.g., the prison warden, the test pilot.

5. Compare the different ways to lead into commercials. Which do you prefer? Why?

The Picture Story 4

I have a peasant's mind. I can only write about what I see.
— Edward R. Murrow

People watch television news, in large measure, because it brings events in action into their homes. We see and hear a fighter plane swooping down, a soldier on patrol stepping carefully. We watch a demonstration, a parade. We follow police searching for a lost child or groping through the wreckage of an airliner. We hear and observe the highlights of a speech, a football game.

We do not watch television only to get the latest news. Radio does a better job. We do not prefer television because we want to get all the news: local, national and international. The newspaper does a better job. We do not prefer television for depth of coverage or penetrating analysis. A news magazine does it better.

We, as television viewers, benefit from our newscasts because they take us to the scenes of the action and show us what is happening and what has recently happened. What we see on the television screen during a newscast can move us more deeply than what we merely hear or read. "A picture is worth a thousand words" applies to a newscast.

An example of the impression that a film (for "film" also read "videotape") story can make occurred when the showing of film from Vietnam of a brief engagement between some attacking G.I.s and three Viet Cong who chose to dig in and fight, rather than melt away in the swampland. The story, sent by war correspondent Don North, was shown on the ABC network at 11 p.m. on a Saturday night. Because those, in San Francisco and New York, responsible for its cutting and presentation knew that what was on film was strong stuff, the editing was done very carefully and with several long distance phone consultations. Viewers' reactions were immediate and vocal, split about 50-50 between those who thought it should not have been presented and those who felt the film brought home the ugliness of the war as it should be brought home. More viewers phoned about this film than about any film ever presented on an ABC weekend newscast until then. One viewer, a Northridge, California housewife, was able to recall scene and word in the two minute 15 second film clip almost exactly, and did so in a moving letter:

I am writing because of something I saw on the ABC Saturday night news.

It was a film report from Vietnam showing fighting between American and North Vietnamese soldiers. Later the film showed American soldiers dragging a wounded North Vietnamese soldier out of his fox-hole. The Vietnamese was wounded so very badly and his face was twisted in pain. As they dragged him out of the hole, an American soldier said, "What's the matter, V.C.? Did I hurt you?" He said this in a whiny, sarcastic voice and he reminded me of a school-yard bully whose victim has finally broken down and cried.

A medic did try to save the soldier's life, but he died. Then he was pulled by the feet, his face dragging in the dirt, and thrown into a hole to be buried.

I couldn't believe what I saw and heard and I couldn't believe that every person watching the newscast wasn't as horrified as I was.

What I want to say is this: There doesn't seem to be any hope for this world when man cannot have sympathy for another man's pain and a man's dead body is treated with disrespect. How can God ever forgive us?

I feel that I must say these things to someone.

Thank you for reading this.

This story from a battle zone in Vietnam used words and pictures to create an indelible impression. Obviously, not every story can do the same. Yet the creation of the indelible impression remains the goal. A film story can inform by reaching the emotions rather than the intellect, by touching rather than telling.

An Absence of Detail

From an understanding of this quality of newsfilm, we can draw an important rule for the editing and writing of a visual story: *Do not cram a story full of details.* Unless a viewer has an exceptionally keen mind and pays full attention to the screen, he is certain to have difficulty absorbing a story containing dozens of minor bits of information in the copy and a succession of varied and "busy" scenes. Certainly, most viewers are not likely to be either moved or informed much by such treatment.

One former Los Angeles newscaster reported the funerals of celebrities without any voice-over whatever. The report of an actor's funeral visually began with a still of the actor, a face familiar to everyone. The still was followed by a dissolve into film of the funeral, including close-ups of celebrities who attended. Finally, a dissolve to a card on which was printed the actor's name and underneath, the years of his birth and death. Then a slow fade to black. And from start to finish, music, not lugubrious, but gentle and light. Nothing more. On the air it all appeared simple and natural. The concealment of art is an art.

An example of a story crammed with facts is printed below, in the left-hand column, from the City News Service of Los Angeles.[1] Admittedly, the story was not written to be read on the air, but it will serve as an example. The AP version, on the right, is a far better treatment of the same news. (A few hours later, CNS rewrote its original story, improving it considerably.):

LOS ANGELES (CNS) — THE FAST THINKING OF A GREYHOUND BUS DRIVER IS CREDITED WITH PREVENTING A MAJOR TRAGEDY WHEN AN 800-FOOT "RIVER OF GASOLINE" IGNITED FOLLOWING A TRAFFIC ACCIDENT ON THE SANTA ANA FREEWAY.

ACCORDING TO BATT. CHIEF CLYDE BRAGDON OF THE COUNTY FIRE DEPT., THE BLAZE ERUPTED FOLLOWING A SERIES OF CRASHES ON THE INBOUND LANES OF THE FREEWAY EAST OF THE WASHINGTON BOULEVARD ON-RAMP SHORTLY AFTER 11 O'CLOCK LAST NIGHT.

THE MASSIVE SCENE OF DESTRUCTION BEGAN WHEN A CAR REPORTEDLY WENT OUT OF CONTROL ON THE RAIN-SLICK FREEWAY, CAUSING SEVERAL OTHER VEHICLES TO SLAM ON THEIR BRAKES TO AVOID THE ERRANT AUTO.

SEVERAL VEHICLES ASSERTEDLY SKIDDED TO A STOP ON THE SLIPPERY FREEWAY, POINTING IN ALL DIRECTIONS. BUT NO DAMAGE OR INJURIES WERE REPORTED.

LOS ANGELES, MARCH 11 (AP) — TWENTY-FIVE PASSENGERS ON A GREYHOUND BUS RAN THROUGH BURNING GASOLINE TO SAFETY LAST NIGHT AS A 15-FOOT WALL OF FLAME RACED TOWARD THEM.

POLICE SAID NOBODY WAS INJURED. WITNESSES GAVE THIS ACCOUNT:

A TANKER TRUCK SLOWED IN HEAVY TRAFFIC ON THE SANTA ANA FREEWAY AND WAS STRUCK BY ANOTHER TRUCK, WRECKING THE TANKER AND SPILLING 1,825 GALLONS OF GASOLINE.

AN UNIDENTIFIED MOTORIST STOPPED AND SET OUT FLARES TO WARN ONCOMING VEHICLES. A FLARE IGNITED THE GASOLINE. THERE WAS AN EXPLOSION AND FLAMES ROSE AS HIGH AS 20 FEET ALONG 200 YARDS OF THE FREEWAY.

AT THIS POINT, A GASOLINE TRUCK AND TRAILER ENTERED THE FREEWAY FROM WASHINGTON BOULEVARD AND IMMEDIATELY BEGAN TO SLOW DOWN TO AVOID THE TANGLE OF STOPPED VEHICLES.

AS THE GASOLINE RIG BRAKED TO A HALT, A HUGE SOUTHERN PACIFIC RAILROAD SEMI-TRUCK AND TRAILER, REPORTEDLY TRAVELING ABOUT 45 MILES PER HOURS, WAS TO JAM ON ITS BRAKES AFTER SUDDENLY COMING UPON THE SCENE.

AS IT SLID TO A STOP, THE SEMI-TRUCK CLIPPED THE END OF THE GASOLINE TRAILER, CAUSING AN 1825-GALLON OF FUEL (SIC) TO SPILL ONTO THE FREEWAY. THE SEMI-TRUCK THEN JACK-KNIFED INTO A FREEWAY GUARD-RAIL.

THE GASOLINE BEGAN FLOWING DOWN THE FREEWAY TO A DRAIN ABOUT 800 FEET AWAY AS OTHER VEHICLES, INCLUDING A GREYHOUND BUS WITH 25 PASSENGERS ABOARD, PULLED TO A STOP.

THE BUS DRIVER, WHO HAS NOT YET BEEN IDENTIFIED, IMMEDIATELY SPOTTED THE DANGER FROM THE ESCAPING GASOLINE AND EVACUATED HIS PASSENGERS. A FEW MOMENTS LATER, A MOTORIST AT THE EAST END OF THE TANGLE PURPORTEDLY PUT OUT FLARES AS A WARNING TO ONCOMING DRIVERS.

ONE OF THE FLARES WAS APPARENTLY TOO CLOSE TO THE DRAIN WHERE THE GASOLINE WAS ESCAPING AND THE FUEL IGNITED, SENDING A RIVER OF FIRE BACK TOWARD THE TANKER AND THE NOW-EMPTY BUS.

THE DRIVER OF THE LOS ANGELES BUS, WILMER TURNER, BRAKED TO A STOP TO AVOID HITTING THE CRASHED TRUCKS. HE REPORTED:

"I SAW GAS SPURTING OUT OF THE TANKER. I GOT OUT OF THE BUS AND WALKED TO THE REAR AND SAW FLAMES. I RAN TO THE FRONT AND YELLED, 'HEY, ALL YOU CATS, GET OFF.' I NEVER SAW A BUS CLEAR SO QUICK."

THE PASSENGERS — MOST OF THEM MARINES ON LIBERTY FROM CAMP PENDLETON 60 MILES TO THE SOUTH AND THEREFORE SCHOOLED IN SNAPPING TO AN ORDER — RACED THROUGH THE FLAMES.

SEVEN UNITS OF COUNTY FIRE-MEN HAS (SIC) RESPONDED AND IMMEDIATELY PUT WATER ON THE FLAMES, PREVENTING AN EXPLO-SION OF THE REMAINING GASOLINE IN THE TANK TRUCK AND ITS TRAIL-ER.

THE BUS, HOWEVER, WAS COMPLETELY DESTROYED BY THE BLAZE, AS WAS THE FIRST TRAILER OF THE SOUTHERN PACIFIC RIG.

OTHER VEHICLES STOPPED AT THE SCENE, INCLUDING THE CARS INVOLVED IN THE INITIAL MISHAP, WERE HURRIEDLY DRIVEN AWAY AND WERE NOT DAMAGED.

A SIGALERT WAS PUT OUT FOR BOTH SIDES OF THE SANTA ANA FREEWAY, AS THE FIRE AND THICK SMOKE PREVENTED TRAVEL ON THE OUTBOUND LANES.

MEANWHILE, A SERIES OF MINOR ACCIDENTS OCCURRED BEHIND THE FLAMING SCENE AS OTHER CARS WERE FORCED TO COME TO A FAST HALT.

BATT. CHIEF BRAGDON ISSUED A PRELIMINARY DAMAGE ESTIMATE OF $31,000, INCLUDING ABOUT 150 FEET OF WOODEN CENTER DIVIDER RAIL WHICH WAS DE-STROYED BY THE FLAMES.
HE ADDED THAT IT SEEMED ALMOST INCREDIBLE THAT NO DEATHS OR INJURIES OCCURRED IN EITHER THE FIRE OR THE CRASH-ES.

FIREMEN REMAINED AT THE SCENE UNTIL THE REMAINING GASOLINE FROM THE RUPTURED TRAILER WAS TRANSFERRED TO ANOTHER TRUCK.

BEFORE THE FIREMEN EXTIN-GUISHED THE BLAZE, THE BUS HAD BEEN BURNED OUT, THE TANKER HAD BEEN DAMAGED AND THE OTHER TRUCK'S TRAILER DESTROYED. FIREMEN SAID IT WAS A MIRACLE THAT 2,700 GALLONS OF GASOLINE IN THE FRONT TANK DID NOT EXPLODE.

A WITNESS SAID ONE MAN'S CLOTHING CAUGHT FIRE AS HE RAN TO SAFETY, BUT HE APPARENTLY ROLLED ON THE FLAMES TO EXTIN-GUISH THEM.

4:40 AM

THE FREEWAY WAS CLOSED
FOR ABOUT TWO HOURS UNTIL
THE FIRE COULD BE EXTINGUISHED
AND ALL THE WRECKAGE RE-
MOVED.
                        3:59 AM

Facts can be jammed into pictures also. A picture by itself consists of facts. A close-up of a face tells us several things about the person: sex, age bracket, race, possibly his emotional state, possibly the state of his health. A medium shot gives us a clue to his financial condition and possibly even his place in society (is he a factory worker? a business leader? a student?). A picture of two women is "busier" than a picture of one woman. A picture showing two women carrying placards we can read is "busier" yet. And so on. A shot held for three seconds followed by a different shot for four seconds demands more of the viewers than one shot held for seven seconds. Two shots of different scenes demand more of viewers than two shots of the same scene, perhaps a long shot and a medium shot. More information is contained in two shots or two different scenes than in a single shot or a single scene, just as more information is captured in a "busy" shot than in a simple one. And so the rule, *Do not cram a story full of details,* applies both to copy and to pictures.

As an example of "busyness," Patrick Trese of NBC News said, "We have absorbed from radio the tremendous fear of dead-air. I know one radio station where two men are on the air at the same time. If one pauses for a moment the other leaps in and starts talking. Sometimes they're talking over each other. There is absolutely no dead-air on *that* station. There is also no sanity. More important, for the audience, there is often no clear idea of what they are trying to convey. What happens orally can happen visually, too. If you talk about something that has no relation to the film, the audience will get no clear view of the picture. You will have talked the film to death." [2]

Leaving an Impression

What television news delivers best is impression. A minute of bombers destroying a bridge and a flyer emerging from an air-sea rescue helicopter, when combined with a few facts about yesterday's raids and losses, will leave the viewer with more than he would retain if the newscaster read a long Associated Press dispatch. Viewers would not absorb the myriad details of the dispatch. The newscaster will not have communicated much. The many minor facts would bounce off minds dulled by other minor facts of no immediate relevance to their lives. In short, the words would be wasted.

The experienced television writer uses just a few key facts. He aims to give viewers an understanding of what has happened. Call it a feeling or an impression. He leaves them with something they can absorb. If he gave them a lot of names and numbers, they would recall nothing.

Yet another aspect of content must be observed. Except for major news, most of the longer television news items are visual. Given a choice between a 30 second report about a budget item being approved and a 30 second ENG tape about a fatal accident, most television stations show the accident footage. Remember, television news is not newspaper news read aloud. Of course, news judgment should always be the deciding factor. If the television news editor decides the budget item has wide significance, it ought to be aired, ENG or no ENG.

Tying Copy to Pictures

The copy and the video will either reinforce each other by carrying related information, or they will compete with each other for the viewer's attention. When this happens, the picture usually wins out. The viewer will recall what he saw, not what he heard. In most cases, this means he will have lost the central fact and the important details of the story. From this, we can draw our second rule of writing and editing a visual story: *Relate words and pictures.*

The relationship should be indirect. An experienced writer does not say, "We are now looking at..." or "This picture shows..." Instead, he reinforces the picture by directing the viewer's attention to whatever is significant in the picture in terms of the story. For example: "On the hillside, a charred and battered helmet was one of the few indications that a battle had been fought here." Or, "The unexpected sunshine drew people to the city's parks."

Television copy must do more than relate to the pictures. Copy must tell the story. Words fill in the factual details pictures omit. But the writer can relate his copy to his pictures while he tells the story. For example, the copy which goes with a seven-second shot of a burned-out store front might read: "The fire then spread northward to the Acme Hardware store. It gutted the store. The estimated loss: 50 thousand dollars."

In rare instances, the writer may want to call attention to something before the audience sees it. If the event is startling and happens very quickly or happens in one corner of the picture, the writer may decide to alert the audience in advance to make sure they do not miss the event and will understand what they are about to see. For example: "As the police searched the alley, the suspect suddenly ran from behind a garage and disappeared over a fence. Watch the garage in the upper right hand corner...(PAUSE)...Officers ran after him. They caught him crouching against the side of a house two blocks away." Dramatic footage can also be shown twice, the second time in slow motion.

In a video story from Vietnam a television photographer included a shot of a soldier being wounded by a mortar shell. The photographer happened to be pointing his camera at a soldier some ten yards distant when the shell exploded. The reporter on the scene later did a double chain narration which contained a sentence alerting the audience to watch the soldier being wounded.

An editor wisely struck out this part of the narration, replacing it with a "slug" — a piece of blank leader. The result was more effective and in much better taste — a pregnant pause in the narration, which in itself focused the viewer's attention to the scene. The mortar blast surprised the audience as much as it did the photographer who happened to shoot it.

In this KNXT, Los Angeles script, observe how a reporter on camera in the studio is assisted in telling the story by a meshing of sound and silent film with a slide and "supers."

TOTAL FILM 3:21 :35 SIL DISSOLVE AT :05 TO SLIDE OF SLAIN POLICEMAN	This is where an Alhambra policeman lost his life today. Sergeant George Davis, thirty-five, married, the father of two small boys.
	His blood was spilled fatally here outside this Alhambra Savings and Loan Company in the six-hundred block of East Main Street. This morning, two armed men walked inside, forced employees to help them gather up about ten-thousand dollars. Upstairs, a bank official heard the noise, and summoned police, while the vault was being robbed.
BACK TO FILM AFTER FIVE SECONDS	
	Officer George Davis was first on the scene, and the robbers decided on a hostage.
1:22 MAG SUPER: DAVIS	SOUND UP..."There was a wee bit of" SOUND OUT..."And then I was shoved right down beside em."
:04 SIL	Meanwhile, another Alhambra officer had arrived on the scene.
:53 MAG SUPER: HOSTAGE	SOUND UP..."Well, as I arrived." SOUND OUT..."And by that time the suspects had driven east on Hidalgo Street."
:24 SIL STUDIO AUDIO	This is the getaway car, found a few blocks away at Grand and Granada, where the suspects crashed into a tree. Found critically wounded inside was a man identified as Edgar Ball Weaver of Los Angeles, on parole from Chino where he served a robbery term.

Police and FBI agents began a house-to-house search which continues for the other suspect who, they believe fled on foot.

DISSOLVE TO STILL OF SUSPECT
AT END OF FILM

He is identified as Jesse James Gilbert, alias James Mansfield and Henry Gatum..an escapee from Folsom Prison where he was serving a burglary term. Police identify him as the man who fired the bullet which killed officer George Davis.

Telling It the Way It Happened

Our third rule of writing and editing video is: *Carry the viewer into the story.*

The family sitting at home in front of the television set tunes into a newscast because they want to learn — and see — what has happened in their community and in the world beyond. They are not tuning into "I Love a Mystery." While artistry belongs in newscasts, artfulness does not. The cunning news item which begins with a big close-up and does not settle down for 30 seconds may be the delight of a movie script writer, but it will bewilder the viewer, who should never have to say after a story, "Now what was that all about?"

Unlike the inverted pyramid structure of newspaper stories, the television news story should be chronological, usually but not always after an opening summary of the main facts, and somewhat conversational. Consider a normal telephone conversation in which an item of news is related:

"Hello, Maud. This is Agnes. Jim just came home and told me the bank was robbed. It was two of them, with stockings over their heads and they got 18 thousand dollars. That's right. I said 18 thousand dollars. It happened just before the bank closed. Jim says these two guys pushed their way into the door just as the guard was about to lock it. They waved guns around and made everyone lie on the floor. Jim says one of them pointed his gun at everyone while the other one went around to the tellers' windows and began shoveling money into a shopping bag, coins and all — and endorsed checks. Jim was scared to death and he said a couple of the girls were crying until the fellow holding the gun went over to them and told them to shut up. They didn't try to get into the vault. I guess they were afraid somebody might have rung the silent alarm. Jim says the whole thing didn't take two minutes. The two guys ran out and jumped in a car and took off. I think the police threw up roadblocks. Anyhow, they got away, so far. Thank God nobody was hurt."

The structure of Agnes' narrative is essentially the structure of a television news story. The lead is contained in the first two sentences, for the essential facts are that the bank was robbed of $18,000 by two gunmen wearing stocking masks. The rest is chronological narrative. Had anyone been injured, you can bet that Agnes would have mentioned it in the beginning, "Jim just came home and told me the bank was robbed and old Mr. Peabody was hit so hard over the head that he's in the hospital."

A newspaper reporter might write the following story about the robbery:

> Two stocking-masked bandits held up the First National Bank, 212 Oak St., at 3 p.m. yesterday, escaping with an estimated $18,000.
>
> Police and state highway patrolmen set up roadblocks on all roads leading from the city, but as of last night the gunmen had eluded the police net.
>
> The loot was in bills, coins and negotiable checks scooped into a shopping bag from the cash drawers of the bank's six tellers' windows.
>
> No attempt was made by the bandits to enter the vault, which was closed but not yet under the time-locking device that prevented its being opened until morning. Police theorized that the bandits ignored the vault, containing an additional $56,000 because of fear that a teller might have set off a silent alarm, bringing officers before the pair had time to get away.
>
> The hold-up began at 3 p.m., as guard Sam Peabody, 62, 3412 Lincoln Ave., was locking the front doors. Two men, wearing nylon stockings over their heads to distort their features, shoved their way through the door...(Etc.)

The newspaper story is chock-a-block with facts. Until we are well into the story, we find no chronological organization. Quite the contrary. Some of the latest news is at the beginning. This is good newspaper and wire service practice, for a fresh lead can be written without having to change the entire story and perhaps reset an entire galley of type.

However, it is not good broadcast news story. The way Agnes tells it is more interesting and more like broadcast news in structure. The radio listener or television viewer finds himself in the role, here, of Maud, who must listen to the story from the beginning to the end rather than in the role of the newspaper reader, who can skip to another news item at any point in this story.

In summary, the broadcast story should be chronological after the lead, interesting, clear, devoid of unrelated details (like the age and address of the guard) and somewhat conversational (not chatty, of course).

The videotape which accompanies the story should be edited to match the copy, but should also make some sense by itself. Opening on a tight shot of a teller's empty drawer is cute and artful but it is not clear, unless the copy says something like: "Two hours ago this drawer held three thousand dollars

in bills, coins, and negotiable checks. There are five other drawers like it.''
(CUT TO MONTAGE OF EMPTY DRAWERS). But even with this explanation,
the viewer remains puzzled. Some viewers may never catch up.

Here is a standard treatment, which tells the story without fuss or fancy
dressing:

VIDEO	AUDIO
LS: BANK EXTERIOR	Two bandits — wearing nylon stockings over their faces — held up the First National Bank, and got away with about 18 thousand dollars.
MS: BANK FRONT DOORS	They forced their way past a guard who was locking the doors at the 3 o'clock closing hour.
LS: BANK INTERIOR	The masked bandits ordered customers and employees to lie face down on the floor.
MS: TELLER WINDOWS	Then, while one bandit held a gun on everyone, the other cleaned out the tellers cages.
CU: EMPTY DRAWERS	He went from drawer to drawer with a shopping bag, filling it with bills, coins and negotiable checks.
MS: TWO WOMEN TELLERS	At one point, his partner walked over to two young women tellers who were lying on the floor weeping, and ordered them to keep quiet. He did not touch them.
MS: VAULT DOOR	The bandits wasted no time on the locked vault, which holds 56 thousand dollars.
MS: POLICE, BANK PERSONNEL	They may have been afraid a teller had rung the silent alarm to summon police.
LS: REAR VIEW, BANK INTERIOR, FRONT DOORS IN BACKGROUND	It took the pair about two minutes to gather up the estimated 18 thousand dollars, and run out of the bank to a waiting car.
MS: POLICE IN BANK	Police have thrown up highway road-blocks.
MS: MARY ANN BEASLEY INTERVIEW WITH MISS BEASLEY	Mary Ann Beasley was one of the tellers who was ordered to stop crying.

Which version does this television story most closely approximate, the one given by Agnes or the one written by the newspaper reporter?

Notice that the choice of shots carries us steadily into the story, starting with an establishing exterior shot. No scene is out of place or likely to confuse the viewer. Notice, too, that each shot matches the copy accompanying it, and that the story is told as it happened, following the summary lead. The story as a whole may be compared to a ladder. The two sides, video and audio, run parallel to each other and are joined at every rung — every scene.

Making Connections

Our fourth general rule for telling the visual story is: *Edit to establish relationships.*

The famous Russian film maker Serge Eisenstein taught that the joining of two pieces of film results in three ideas: the ideas in each piece of film and the idea in their relationship. An example of how this can operate is offered by Marty Smith, of Capital Film Laboratories, Washington:

> Visualize a film of a train coming into a station, requiring about 30 seconds to chug in and stop. It has little intrinsic meaning and is too long. So I must cut it somehow. This I do by cutting in three shots from stock footage of a girl watching the train come in. By doing so, I actually shorten the film and change it by introducing a relationship. The secret of the power of motion pictures is this human need to relate things. Before, you had a train and a girl. They meant only themselves. Cut together, the two are related and a third meaning arises. In reality, they were not together at all. But relating them in the eye of the viewer gives them a brand new meaning unto themselves.[3]

Most picture stories seem to need cutaways. And most cutaways seem to be hackneyed: a camera rolling, a bank of cameras, a reporter's poised pencil, or a sound "pot." These are familiar cutaways for interviews and news conferences. We have seen them a thousand times already, and are likely to see them a thousand more. More imaginative cutaways are available. The subject of the interview has ideas to express. He is talking to people. Why not show people? Perhaps a cluster of them are standing to one side, listening. Perhaps the photographer can get back far enough with his zoom lens pulled back to its widest angle to relate the subject to the entire room, or at least to the reporter.

There have even been instances when an editorial decision was made to throw away the picture story, at least in its conception, in favor of a short, humorous feature consisting of cutaways. Robert Brennan of CBS News once produced a "What's Going On Here?" story out of film submitted of a man in a "Buck Rogers" rocket suit entertaining a crowd. The film showed very little of the take-off, but lots of the crowd. By cutting it to emphasize reactions rather than the event itself, Brennan presented an imaginative little newscast item.

With the rare exception of a scene which is intrinsically shocking, news pictures should not be edited to jar the viewer, or to puzzle him. It may be demanding too much to say that pictures should tell some semblance of a story even without sound, yet this is an ideal which ought to be kept in mind. For example, without words, we make some sense out of the following order of silent scenes:

1. Long shot of an accident scene.
2. Medium shot of one damaged car.
3. Medium shot of another damaged car.
4. An injured man lies on the ground.
5. An ambulance arrives.
6. The injured man, again.
7. Ambulance attendants walk; camera pans, discovers man.
8. Spectators look.
9. Man is put into amblulance.
10. Medium long shot of policeman directing traffic around accident.
11. Medium shot of ambulance pulling away.

Now suppose we eliminate the opening long shot. We do not establish the scene. The result is a slight bewilderment. We see two damaged cars. Are we in a junkyard? We see a man lying on the ground. What is he doing there? A little later we will figure it all out, but we may still be unsatisfied because we have not seen the relationship between the other pieces of film which the opening shot gives us.

Understanding the need for relating scenes is basic to the photographer, the reporter, the writer and the editor, permitting the viewer to see a story that was put together to produce clarity instead of confusion.

The opening shot and the closing shot should run at least five seconds each. Seven seconds might be better. On the air, if the director up-cuts the start of a story with a three-second opening scene, the viewer only sees one or two seconds of the scene, and that is inadequate at the opening and jarring at the close. Both events happen often enough for the editor to take the simple precaution of adding two or three extra seconds to both the first and last scenes. Besides, at the start, many viewers will need those extra seconds to absorb the establishing scene. As for the last shot, Hollywood tradition has accustomed us to the long fadeout.

What Interests You?

Unlike the professional ballplayer, a journalist gets better as he grows older, and his worth increases, provided he takes pride in his work. If he does not, he becomes a hack. The difference between the hack and the competent journalist is imagination. Or, to put it another way, the difference is a willingness on the part of the competent journalist to *think* as he makes the dozens of decisions he routinely faces each working day. The hack tends to react automatically. He bases his decisions, pragmatically, on the easiest way to do something. The competent television writer should be able to defend with logic every scene he chooses, every word he uses.

The British statesman Edmund Burke argued, "If it is not necessary to change, it is necessary not to change." The television journalist, wondering what film sequences to select and what copy to write, might paraphrase Burke's credo: "If it is not necessary to include, it is necessary not to include." Or, less fancifully: if you don't need it, drop it. Each day provides far more news than any newscast has time to present. And if each day doesn't also provide far more pictures or at least opportunities for them than there is time for, the assignment editor should be replaced.

The decisions a writer is called upon to make usually involve winnowing the material available to him. What scenes and facts should he include? The element of information (a scene or a fact) ought to meet either of two tests: is it important to the story? *or,* is it interesting? If the element of information meets neither the standard of interest nor the standard of importance — the standards being those of the writer or editor — the element should be dropped. The day's file of news will contain other important and/or interesting elements to include in the newscast.

The factors of news choice are the factors of attention: what will or ought to make someone pay attention. The most important news to you is news which vitally concerns you: "Mr. Smith, I'm happy to tell you the tumor is benign." "Charles, I've decided to leave you." "Stick 'em up, buddy."

Consider the written news item on a slip of paper passed to the bank teller: "I have a bomb in this paper bag. Give me all your folding money. P.S. Don't make any sudden moves." That news contains these attention-getters:

1. Personal involvement
2. Danger
3. Excitement
4. Economic effect
5. Immediacy (time)
6. Nearness (place)
7. Human interest
8. Novelty

All these elements make an event news. Add two other elements:

9. Magnitude of the event
10. Fame of the person involved

and you have the factors which determine news choice.

Every television news story should have one or more of these factors, but more factors do not necessarily mean more important news. A single factor may lift the news event above every other news event. For example:

"The Pope died today."

The fame of the person involved places this story at the top of virtually everyone's list of news stories on any day, yet other factors of news choice in this story are minimal or non-existent.

The Local Angle

One of the reporting tasks for any news medium is finding "a local angle" in a story with a distant dateline. Usually the local angle will be the name of a local person or the local concerns of a national event; for example, the likely effect on a local shoe factory of a bill to lower tariffs on Italian shoes. Occasionally, a writer produces a local angle where none exists, and in the process makes the distant event more understandable and more personal to his audience. Don Buehler, news director of KSTP radio, St. Paul, delineated an anti-war demonstration in Washington this way for Twin City listeners:

> To visualize Washington today...picture 35W southbound on a Friday afternoon...picture a burning car, or cars...across 35W northbound, cutting off the downtown Minneapolis exits and I-94 eastbound. Picture an overturned truck on Highway 55 and 7th Street...picture a crowd of 500 youths thumping on automobile hoods at Highway 12 and Cedar Lake Road... mentally conceive the 8th Avenue, Broadway, Hennepin and 10th Avenue bridges blocked.
>
> Or note I-94 near St. John's hospital in St. Paul...Snelling closed at County Road C...Shephard Road at a standstill...Lexington choked with demonstrators led by a pediatrician.
>
> You have a mental picture of Washington...gleaming on the banks of the Potomac, in view of the world. If you're familiar with Washington... M Street...through Georgetown...clogged. The 14th Street Bridge...that's where Cal Thomas is stationed.[4]

"How much time can you give me?"

What is news is relative to what else is news. "Man bites dog" is the top story on a lazy July Fourth, when government offices are closed. "Man bites dog" does not get into the newscast on the day war breaks out. In short, there are slow news days and busy ones. The writer must adjust his judgment to the total flow of news. For instance, on a slow news day, he edits an ENG tape running two and a half minutes of a quarrel between two city councilmen over rezoning a residential block to allow construction of a supermarket. The story contains these elements:

VIDEO	AUDIO
1. The street in question, various scenes. 20 secs. silent.	1. Newscaster sets the scene. Where we are, what the quarrel is about.
2. City hall, Councilman Smith's office door, Councilman Smith. 12 secs. silent.	2. Newscaster introduces Smith, who is pushing hard for the rezoning.
3. Smith, 40 secs. sound-on-VTR	3. Smith tells why.
4. Councilman Brown's door, Brown. 8 secs.	4. Newscaster introduces Brown, who is speaking for the folks who live around the corner, and like the neighborhood as is.
5. Brown, 35 secs. sound-on-VTR	5. Brown tells why not.
6. The neighborhood, 5 secs. silent	6. Newscaster says most neighbors agree with Brown.
7. Tightly edited (3 to 8 secs. each) comments by a half-dozen neighbors. Neighbors are filmed outdoors. 30 secs. sound-on-VTR.	7. Four oppose the change, one favors it, one is uncertain.

Half an hour after the tape is edited, an explosion on the other side of town tears open a dry cleaning plant, killing two and injuring seven. Today is no longer a slow news day. The news director automatically re-evaluates the news stories in his line-up, including the quarrel between Smith and Brown. If the quarrel had not erupted on the Council floor that day, the entire story, all two and a half minutes, might have been set aside as a news feature usable tomorrow or the next day. But the quarrel did occur, and this is today's news. The tape will have to be re-cut to about one minute. Out go the comments of the neighbors and the 5-second intro. That shortens the tape to 1:55, with :55 yet to be chopped out. He listens to Smith and Brown on the monitor, and cuts each man to 20 seconds. This leaves 20 seconds to be removed. Out go the silent leads to each man. The writer retypes the opening 20 seconds of copy to include the news of the quarrel and to "intro" Smith and Brown. Supers identifying the men will do the rest. The tape is now one minute long. A minute and a half has been saved for use in the explosion story.

In a radio or television newscast, all stories must fit the inexorable limitations of time. The writer assigned to the story of the governor's arrival or the seizure of a heroin cache will ask, "How much time have I got?" He doesn't want to know how much time he has to write his script but rather to know in advance how much air time will be allowed for the story, so that he can frame his editing decisions within that span of time. The news producer may say, "Keep it under a minute thirty," or he may say, "Take a look at it and see what it's worth." In either case, after screening the tape, the writer may call the news director to say, "This stuff is pretty bad. I'd either keep it to 20 seconds or drop it completely." Or he might say, "We've got some great footage here. Can you let me have two minutes?"

What has happened in this interchange between writer and producer is that the producer was considering the importance of the story based on the day's news-file, and the writer was considering its interest, based on the scenes he has just viewed. Similar conversations occur many times each day in newsrooms across the nation.

Editing a Speech

The television news writer fulfills a unique function when he screens tape of a speech. Willy-nilly, he is a censor.

The photographer, reporter, or producer at the scene are also censors. But unless they are severely limited in the quantity of tape that they may shoot, their censorial functions are limited to "cutting out the dull stuff."

The news writer has many matters to consider as he waits for the VTR to begin:

Time

The amount of time alloted for this story may be allocated in advance by the newscast producer ("Keep it under 1:15"), or it may be the result of haggling, such as:

> *Writer:* "Can we let the senator's speech run two and a half minutes?
> *Producer:* "Impossible. Wrap it up in 45 seconds."
> *Writer:* "I can't do that. Even if I just use the part where he calls the governor a fool, it will be 1:15. Add a 15-second silent intro, you have a minute and a half, and that's without his talking about the highway scandal."
> *Producer:* "Suppose you just use the highway scandal."
> *Writer:* "It's not as strong, and we'll only save 15 seconds."
> *Producer:* I'll give you a minute 10, tops."
> *Writer:* "Make it 1:20."
> *Producer:* "O.K. 1:20, but it better be worth it."

If the producer were assembling a 15 minute newscast, which permits about 11 minutes of actual time for news, a minute and 20 seconds represents a significant slice of the show. The 1:20 must include the silent VTR, or on-camera introduction to the speaker, leaving perhaps 1:05 of a speech that may have gone on for an hour.

Appeal

Most speeches excerpted and presented on a newscast are political. Few politicians, or non-politicians speaking on political matters, sustain general interest very long. A television news audience is far different from a politician's live audience. The live audience has voluntarily surrendered its time and attention to hear the speaker. The television audience is not present to hear the speaker, but to hear the news. News writers tend to assume that the audience has a low threshold of boredom which few speakers can overcome by charisma.

Significance vs. Interest

Frequently the writer finds himself torn between using a significant statement and an interesting one of not much significance. In the above example, the senator's comments on the state's highways quite possible were of greater importance to the citizenry than his waspish criticism of the governor. Yet the writer, who could choose only one, chose the latter. It was more interesting, more likely to hold the attention of the viewers, in his opinion. Another writer, equally capable, might have reached the contrary decision. No doctrinaire rules may be laid down about this. Each writer must choose for himself, again and again. He must base his choices upon his news department's policy and his own predilections. As his experience grows and he himself matures, his choices ought to be wise, popular, and defensible.

Writer's objectivity

It may be generalized that most experienced news writers are objective about most stories. They can cut a speech or a news conference without being affected by their own political opinions. The few who have an ax to grind do not deserve their jobs, for they are propagandists, not journalists. Yet many a decent, objective news writer occasionally finds himself absolutely furious at the mouthings of the man on the screen in front of him. He is sorely tempted to make the speaker look bad. Perhaps the speaker is a Nazi or a Communist, a John Bircher or a New Leftist and the news writer is infuriated, because of his own political bias. If this is the case, the writer ought to turn the editing over to another writer, or ask another person to view the tape with him and share in the decision making. To make such a request is a mark of personal strength.

Self-contained statements

Television-wise politicians use the enthymeme, the aphorism, the pungent phrase, the statement which can be taken alone out of context. They learn to pause between statements, knowing that the medium of videotape or of film transforms the dimension of time into the dimension of length, and that a few inches of ¾-inch tape or of 16-millimeter film length ought to bracket a statement for easy removal from the rest of the speech. What these astute politicians do is not obvious even to the initiated, for the argument wrapped up in a couple of phrases, the short and crisp remark, and the pause are all familiar rhetorical devices. On the other hand, editors shrug their shoulders when the speaker on film declares, "I have seven proposals. One...Two...Three...etc." The editor is not totally without recourse in this situation, but the effective remedy may involve the complexities of double chaining film or insert editing tape, and the editor may feel that the speaker's point number three is not worth the trouble. The editor may decide to choose a less significant part of the speech because it is easier to edit, or because it will look better on the air. This rejection of the better statement also occurs when the speaker entwines it with another statement, perhaps by a reference buried within the statement, such as "My opponent will be rejected by the voters next Tuesday because he is guilty on all these counts, and the voters know it." The wise speaker also avoids involved explanations, pyramided arguments and sentences which begin with conjunctions or transitional words and phrases such as "however," "therefore," "as a result," "because of that," and so on.

For the Student

1. How could VTR of an accident scene detract from the viewer's understanding of what happened?

2. Without telling him why, have a friend watch a newscast while you monitor, noting which stories had film or other visuals. After signoff, ask him to recall as many stories as he can in as much detail as he can. Is there a correlation between visual elements and those news items which left an impression? Is there any other kind of correlation?

3. Read a local front page story in today's newspaper. If you were covering it for television, what scenes would you want to shoot?

4. Based on these scenes, write a television news video version of the story.

5. Monitor one local newscast from each station in your area. Record your impressions of the way voice-over matches video.

RADIO

The Radio Reporter

Radio News

The Radio Reporter   5

Edward R. Murrow: "Are you sure?"
William L. Shirer: "I'm paid to be sure."

Newspaper reporters and network television crews cooled their heels as best they could in the heat outside the iron gates of the Guadalajara residence of the U.S. consul general in Mexico, Terence Leonhardy, who had just been released by the terrorists who had kidnapped him. While they waited in hopes of a story, an enterprising reporter in Minneapolis was getting an interview with him by telephone. WCCO reporter Bob Thornberg, reading on the wires that Leonhardy was a native of North Dakota, quickly found out that he was also a friend of North Dakota's Senator Quentin Burdick. The reporter phoned Burdick to get background on Leonhardy. When Burdick remarked that he had the brand new phone number to the consul general's residence in Mexico, Thornberg suggested a three-way conference call. Burdick agreed and, later, so did Leonhardy, who had given orders that he did not want to talk to reporters, but decided that he did not mind if a Minnesota radio station listened in while he told his old friend that his health was good and what had happened during the kidnapping. After they hung up, the tape of the call was fed to CBS Radio for a network exclusive. The reporters outside the iron gates got nothing at all that day but tired feet.

This story has two morals. First moral: As the AT&T commercial says, "Sometimes long distance is better than being there." The telephone line is often the best path to a radio story. Second moral: Don't underestimate radio news or the resourceful radio reporter. Television has not walked off with all the marbles and never will.

Here's another example of quick thinking:

A robber held up a loan company in a Texas city. The manager pressed the silent burglar alarm. A police dispatcher sent a patrol car. A radio newsman, hearing the dispatcher on his newsroom police monitor, looked up the address in a cross-listed telephone directory and dialed the phone number on his beeper line. At the loan company the phone rang insistently. The robber told the manager to pick it up.

Hello, the manager said.

The reporter said he heard the loan office was being robbed.

The manager allowed how that was now happening.

Now?

Yes.

The reporter paused for a moment's thought. Could he speak to the robber?

He wants you, the manager said.

Another pause, longer.

Hello, the robber said.

The reporter and the robber chatted for a bit, but the conversation was interrupted by the police arriving at the front door. The robber was arrested.

And the radio reporter had it all on tape.

Another moral: It pays to have a cross-listed telephone directory.

Getting the Equipment Ready

Most days in a radio reporter's life are less dramatic, consisting of odd working hours and the routines of beat calls and covering news conferences.

The radio reporter should check the batteries of his cassette recorder and bulk erase some cassettes before starting out. Bulk erasing is important because cassettes may be used in recorders with different alignments for the record head, even among the same brand of recorders. Failure to bulk erase the cassettes can lead to an overlap of sound from the previous recording. The reporter is left with worthless material.

While there are occasions when other more elaborate recorders are used, the radio news work horse is the cassette recorder. Choosing the right cassette is important. A "60" has 60 minutes of total recording time — 30 minutes on each side. A "120" would have 60 minutes on each side, and so forth. If the reporter knows that the recording will be brief, a "45" may be adequate, but shy away from very short cassettes; you may have to flip the tape over at a crucial time. On the other hand, a "120" uses much thinner tape in order to fit the standard cassette size. Thinner tape also has its drawbacks. It should be used in only top quality equipment because thin tape can jam a machine by wrapping around the capstan of a misaligned recorder. A good compromise is a "90," which gives 45 minutes on each side. Few speeches, news conferences or interviews last longer than 45 minutes.

At a news conference, the radio reporter must determine microphone placement. In some cases, a mike is not needed because the location will have an existing sound system with a "mult-box" for recording equipment hook-ups. The "mult-box" has multiple outlets wired to a single microphone. A jack gets the sound to the recorder. "Mult-boxes" may have both the miniature jack outlets needed for radio cassette recorders and the three-pronged jacks used for camera sound. As a precaution, a radio reporter should carry cords or adapters for both types of outlet.

Most "mult-box" outlets are at "mike level," which means the plug goes to the microphone input on the cassette recorder. If a "mult-box" outlet is at "line level," the plug must go to the "auxiliary" or "line input" jack of the cassette recorder. Mismatching impedances results in a sound too faint or too distorted to use.

The reporter should check the sound meter to be sure a recording is being made. There is no need to adjust volume levels on most recorders because they have "automatic gain control" (AGC).

The automatic gain (volume) control can be a problem if a speaker uses forceful gestures. If the microphone is fixed to a podium which is pounded for emphasis during a speech, the automatic gain control picks up strong vibrations that it reads as loud noise. Consequently, the record volume drops automatically. The next several spoken words cannot be heard well until the automatic gain re-adjusts. Radio reporters combat this by using a cushioned mike stand or by taping the mike to a free-standing public address microphone.

Former Minnesota Senator Eugene McCarthy was a threat to automatic gain controlled recordings because he was a microphone fiddler at news conferences. The nearest mike was something for him to toy with while responding to questions. His manner was gentle as he turned the mike from side to side, but some mikes ended up facing the opposite direction. The sliding of the microphones across a solid surface created vibrations that not only recorded as loud scraping sounds, but also screamed to the automatic gain control for relief. Savvy reporters placed their mikes behind others and away from McCarthy's right hand.

Taping and Note Taking

One advantage radio has over television is the ability to keep a recorder going during an entire news conference or speech. Mindful of expensive film, reporters would try to guess when the best statements were coming before signaling the cameraman. Reuseable videotape allows cameras to run for longer periods of time, but photographers have to be up shooting from other angles and they frequently miss good material, leaving their reporters to script those points. Radio, however, will be more likely to have the actual recording.

Letting the radio tape recorder run causes problems, too. The reporter will have more tape to search when scripting the story and selecting actualities. Taking notes, even though the words are being recorded, helps in several ways. First, a reporter is often called upon to ad lib a report from the scene. Second, notes are a protection in case of failure to record properly. The most important reason is that notes offer a chronology to follow when he writes his story. Segments on the cassette tape can be quickly located if the reporter jotted down catch phrases, topic areas and time cues. If the reporter cannot be close enough to his tape recorder to read the footage counter, he should use his wristwatch. Of course, he should know how long it takes his footage counter to go from zero to ten.

Speeches can be harder to cover than news conferences, with no provision made for microphones and recorders. A little planning can help, as it did for a reporter covering a speech at a conference of bishops where elaborate ceremony was planned on a high stage. The podium was accessible only by walking the length of the stage. Since the reporter would have been a glaring intrusion walking that stage to start the recorder for the speech, he made prior arrangements with the speaker, who was most understanding. The recorder was placed on the podium before the dignitaries assembled. When the time came for his speech, the speaker turned on the recorder himself as the reporter gestured in reminder from the front row.

The reporter used a "120" tape, realizing he could not turn off the machine or flip the tape before the speech ended. If the cassette comes to an end, it strains the batteries as the capstan pulls against an immovable tape. When using older tape recorders without automatic shut-offs, reporters must know when the tape runs out, or they face problems with the tape speed before the batteries can be changed. Tape speed slows if batteries run low. The recording will not be true.

Many larger radio stations can remedy important recordings that are off speed by transferring the sound to a variable speed recorder, but it is an elaborate and imperfect process of dubbing.

Radio Reporting Techniques

Aside from equipment considerations, radio reporters need to remember always that the listener is just that — a listener who cannot see the story. The following example will illustrate.

The reporter is interviewing the owner of a specialty gift shop on a guided tour through the store. The reporter should not point to an item and ask "And what about that one there?" The listener, who cannot see the pointing hand, begins to lose the flow of the interview. Better: "Could you tell us something about that tiny glass figurine up on the shelf behind you?"

If the shop keeper uses visual expressions in responding, the reporter should help the listener. Shop owner: "Yes, this little glass Raggedy Ann doll is an exact scale replica of a stuffed doll we have which stands about this tall." Reporter: "Yes, just about to your waist."

A reporter must be quick to identify voices in a multiple guest interview. Complications from an actual post-trial phone interview illustrate the significance of name identifications. A radio engineer recorded a three-way conference call among a man just convicted of kidnapping, the defense attorney, and a reporter.

A million dollar ransom had not been recovered. The reporter asked the convicted kidnapper if he could afford to appeal, but the reply came from the attorney, "Look, money is no object. I'm taking this case all the way to the Supreme Court if I have to." The reporter neglected to remark that the attorney had answered that question. Later an editor at the station aired a report that the "convicted million dollar kidnapper says money is no object. He will appeal."

The post-trial telephone interview is also an example of an advantage radio has. The comments of the defendant and the defense attorney were aired live from the hall outside the courtroom, the first public comment by the principals at a trial of national interest, the Piper kidnapping trial.

Radio reporters should be well versed in proper phone use. Care must be taken to inform the individual that he or she will be recorded. This may be handled casually with public officials who are accustomed to being recorded. They expect it, and are adequately notified with a simple "Tape's rolling!" However, private citizens require a more deliberate approach. As an example, the reporter might say "I'd like to tape record our conversation, if I may, so portions of it can be used on our news. Is that all right with you?"

Nervous about being recorded, some people need reassurances that it is painless. On occasion, reporters have offered to do the recording first, and allow the person to decide afterwards if the recording can be broadcast. Usually this is done when a person is giving an eyewitness account of an accident or some other non-controversial event. It is done to set the individual at ease. Almost always the interviewee will find that being recorded was not difficult, and he or she will have been made comfortable enough to give the reporter a good interview. However, when the interviewee is the subject of controversy and declines recording in an attempt to avoid accountability, then the reporter must not offer such an option, which is an invitation to censorship.

Mark W. Hall, author of *Broadcast Journalism*,[1] has some advice to the reporter doing an interview, including:

1. Identify yourself, your station, and the purpose of your call.

2. Tell the person you are calling that you are recording the interview. If he objects, turn off the tape recorder.

3. If he still objects, explain that you are trying to get a balanced report.

4. If he still objects, ask him why.

5. During an interview, ask open-ended questions, like why.

6. Don't murmur "I see" while he is talking. Keep quiet. Editing will be easier.

7. Don't ask permission to use a comment. Don't agree to let him preview the edited tape.

To which we may add:

8. Be friendly and interested, not pushy.

9. Listen for the natural lead to the story, the "angle."

Remote Tape Reports

The radio news reporter away from his station faces a dilemma if he has an interview of MOS on tape which he is anxious to get on the air quickly. If he is near his car, equipped with a high quality radio transmitting unit capable of taking a tape recorder patch, and he is within transmitting distance of his station, his problem is solved. But what if he is not?

One solution would be to dial his station on a nearby phone, and play the tape, with the tape recorder speaker next to the telephone mouthpiece. Quality: awful.

A common practice among radio newsmen is to establish a hardwire connection using a telephone. This is done by a patch cord from the tape recorder's "Line out" with two alligator clips. The reporter unscrews the mouthpiece of whatever telephone he happens to be near and attaches the alligator clips to the two protruding metal tips. Sometimes microphones with alligator clips are used the same way for live transmission. Many public telephones now have mouthpieces which cannot be unscrewed. Use a private office phone.

Telephone companies frown on this practice, as they do on the attachment of any foreign equipment to their equipment without their own interface gear. The practice flaunts the provisions of their telephone tariff rate structure, which is approved by a state regulatory agency, but — as far as the author has been able to determine — attaching a tape recorder to a telephone is not illegal, provided, of course, the instrument is not damaged. To the best of the author's knowledge, it is not a *crime* and there are no legal penalties. The telephone company may be within its rights to cut the user's service, however. So be warned.

A simple telephone tap, sold in audio equipment stores, consists of a suction cup wired to a plug which goes into the microphone input jack. The suction cup attaches to the outside of the telephone, usually on the base near the transformer or on the receiver behind the earpiece. The tap is used for recording if hard-wired equipment is unavailable. Quality is only fair. Higher quality devices are also on the market.

Besides communications equipment, the reporter's car should carry emergency equipment: a tow line, battery cables, lanterns, flares, etc. In winter when the reporter goes where the blizzard is, he will find foul weather gear useful. More than one journalist has been rewarded with an interview after pulling a driver out of trouble. Also: overshoes in spring for high water, pencils instead of ball point pens in freezing winter, and change for parking meters everywhere. Licensing a remote car as a truck should allow it to park in downtown truck stops, where cars are forbidden.

The urban riots of the 1960's led some stations to paint over the call letters on the sides of their cars. To identify their news vehicles in order to park without getting tickets, reporters acquire or manufacture an I.D. card. Attached to the driver's sun visor with rubber bands, it is flipped into sight when the reporter parks in a yellow or red zone, on a highway shoulder near an accident, or at a fire.

Editing the Tape

In the studio, the actuality must be scripted and readied for broadcast. The "cut," the segment to be used, is then dubbed onto a cartridge, or "cart." A cassette recorder with the "cue-review" feature can be a great advantage in dubbing actualities. It allows the reporter to stop the cassette tape between sentences, even between words. If an edit is needed in the actuality or if the edit cannot be started or stopped cleanly, an intermediate dubbing must be done on a reel-to-reel recorder. This will allow the reporter or an engineer to cut out portions of the tape physically or electronically before the actuality goes on a "cart."

Internal editing is often done when the speaker has included a parenthetical interruption to the thought which a reporter wants. For example: "The explosion left the shop in shambles. There was debris on everything including my sister-in-law's wedding dress way in the back closet. I've been meaning to get that dress back to Harriet, but the car has been on the fritz and we can't get parts for the carburetor. The auto parts store is out of stock. But just look at this place. It's a wreck and our insurance won't cover it." The portion about the car and the auto parts store is an unnecessary detraction. The reporter will cut from "I've been meaning to..." to "...out of stock." Of course, he must not cut anything that affects the meaning of what he retains.

Editing Problems

The reporter must be careful about background noise and speech patterns when making edits. For example, an airplane flying overhead normally would not be a distraction since it is first heard in the distance and then fades out after passing overhead, unless the edit excludes the gradual approach of the airplane. If the background sound suddenly changes, it calls attention to itself. Music in the background of an interview can also be a problem. So can speech patterns. If a person is nearly shouting at the beginning of the selected actuality but is speaking quietly at the end, it will be difficult to lift material out of the middle.

Wind can raise havoc on the tape. Wind strikes microphone membranes like a finger in the eye. It doesn't take much pressure to hurt. Not only will wind record like static, but it will also drive down the automatic gain control. Foam windscreens work best, but even a double wrap with a handkerchief helps in emergencies. Whenever possible, position yourself or the interviewee to block the wind.

A less obvious threat to good recording — but one which can produce the same effect as direct wind — is a faulty microphone cord or a cheap microphone which is not shielded from its cord. When the microphone is moved, even just back and forth during a question-and-answer exchange, cord noise can develop. The reporter with a poor mike should position it between himself and the interviewee, and then not move it other than perhaps a slight tilt to the speaker.

(For addition information about microphones and how to solve audio problems, see CHAPTER 23: SOUND.)

Preparing the Newscast

Allowing time for two 30-second commercials, an intro, a close and a promo, a five-minute newscast may actually contain three and one-half minutes of news. The newscast producer checks the daily operating schedule to learn how much time he must fill. Reading a typewritten line takes about four seconds, with some variation depending upon the reader's rate. At four seconds per line, a three-and-one-half-minute newscast requires 52 full lines of copy. The writer counts his lines down the middle of each page, ignoring those lines which end short of the page center, and counting as a full line any line which reaches the center, but taking into account a line thinned by crossed-out words.

The last item in each newscast should be short, so that it can be dropped if the newscast runs long, and a pad item or two should be attached in case the newscast runs short or a tape jams in the cart machine. Where newscasts end with a "brite" or "kicker," the brite should be read for time, and that time should be subtracted from the total newscast time to determine whether the newscast is running long or short. This process, known as "backtiming" in television as well as radio, gives the newscast a strong finish. For example if a newscast is scheduled to begin at 2:00:00 and end at 2:03:30, with a closing brite which runs fifteen seconds, the announcer backtimes to 2:03:15; that is, he cuts or pads the newscast to a closing time on the clock of 2:03:15, then starts reading the brite.

A five-minute newscast allows little time to present long stories or any but the briefest of actualities, especially if the newscast must cover world and national news plus local news.

A ten-minute newscast, with two and one-half minutes of commercials and other non-news matter to be subtracted, requires 112 lines of copy plus some pad copy, giving the producer much more flexibility than a five-minute newscast. His mix of stories normally can accommodate voicers or wraparounds ("wraps") of up to 1:30 each.

The writer usually types no more than two or three short items to a page. On some stations one story per page is the rule. Actualities, stories with audio carts, should always stand alone on a page.

Some news departments follow a policy of noting the length of the stories on a page, in seconds, at the top of the page. For actuality pages, the length of the intro and close copy is added to the time of the insert. Insert intro and closing words are also noted:

mayor/carson/4-15   total   :39

MAYOR ZIMMERMAN TOLD THE CITY COUNCIL LAST NIGHT THAT
HE COULD NOT SUPPORT A PLAN TO WIRE THE CITY FOR CABLE
TELEVISION. REPORTER JANE CARSON WAS AT THE MEETING.

Opens: "The mayor surprised..."

insert runs   :27

Ends: "...back to committee."

THE COUNCIL HAS CALLED A SPECIAL MEETING FOR NEXT
THURSDAY.

Reading the in-cue not only tells the engineer where to begin the dub, but
also assures the announcer that the right actuality is being aired. The announcer
is also helped by a brief statement in the script of what the actuality contains,
and, immediately after the end cue, the term "DOUBLE OUT" or "ENDS UP"
if either applies. "Double out" means that the words identified as the end cue
were used by the speaker at an earlier moment in the tape, and therefore be
careful not to cut out of the tape when they are heard the first time. "Ends up"
means the end cue words are said by the speaker in a rising tone, so the engineer
and the announcer must be aware that they must cut away from the tape, even
though a rising tone carries the expectation that the speaker has more to say.

A "voice-over," when the sound on the tape is wanted as a background
to the news reader, must also be indicated on the script:

Opens: "There shall never be...."
Runs :18
ENG. NOTE: Ends: "...a strong America." (Pause...voice over
applause)
(ANNCR.) It was the tenth time the President's speech was interrupted
by applause. And each time the subject was national security.
The stronger the statement, the louder the applause by workers
at the munitions plant.
(BRING UP APPLAUSE 3 SECONDS, AND FADE OUT)

When the producer has assembled the script, he takes a carbon copy either
of the entire newscast or of the actuality pages to the control room along with
the recorded cartridges. The carts and script pages are numbered in the order
they are used.

Errors

They happen. If an error gets on the air it should be corrected as soon as possible
because listeners who heard the error may still be tuned in. There is no embarrassment in making a prompt correction.

Sometimes the problem is confusion, not error. Either the writing is unclear or the writer has used a combination of words that read well but sound funny or different than they are intended to be.

For example, "The governor presented the hometown hero with a laurel, and a hearty handshake." That brings to mind the famous comedy team.

Another example: "The governor told the delegates, 'You are all most welcome to our state.' " That sounds like "almost welcome."

Still another, "The governor said he is considering more drastic action." The governor probably meant that he is considering sterner measures than those he has already taken, but some listeners may think the governor has already taken drastic action and now contemplates *additional* drastic action. Proper reading of the phrase "more drastic action" will help, but the writer would be better off by using other words to eliminate the ambiguity.

Working out of a mobile unit is essentially the same for a reporter as working in a studio. The reporter should know its engineering limitations, since the decisions on when to use a mobile unit often hinge on how the mobile unit is equipped. Limitations in range and location also need to be understood.

The radio documentary usually includes a lot of narrative done in the studio, plus on-location sound to add interest. This "background" or "wild" sound can be acquired simply by walking along with a tape recorder collecting the sounds of the neighborhood. A radio reporter working on a prostitution documentary chanced in this way to record an actual offer by a man for sex. As the reporter strolled through an area notorious for prostitution, a man approached from the other direction with a known prostitute. At the moment they passed, the man could be heard to offer $20.

Unlike the usual run of radio news, documentaries afford the flexibility and time to contrast or balance the actualities. If one person declares that "arresting the woman is the best way to keep controls on prostitution," and another person declares that "arresting the man will dry up prostitution quicker than anything," the two actualities may be butted together. Television can juxtapose conflicting answers easily because the viewer sees the individuals talking. In radio, the speakers are not seen, so their voices either must be easily distinguishable or the narrator must briefly identify them.

For the Student

1. Would you like to be a radio reporter? Discuss in class.

2. Accompany a radio reporter in the field.

3. Spend four hours in a radio newsroom.

4. Conduct an interview with an audio tape recorder. Using different cuts from the interview, write two stories.

5. Conduct a five-minute interview as if it were a live report for a radio station, including an opening and a closing.

Radio News   6

News is like salted nuts. The more you inform, the more people want you to inform.

— Richard Wald

Above all, radio is the medium best suited for following a story as it develops. Frequently listeners make decisions based on fresh information. A driver hears that an accident is blocking the road she intends to travel, so she steers an alternate route. Another hears of a school closing, so her child's muffler and cap go back on the hall closet peg and the peanut butter sandwich goes into the refrigerator.

Occasionally these reports can have life-or-death consequences. The report of an accidental release of poisonous gas alerts people to evacuate the area. Reporters take care to describe the routes for the evacuees to follow, and where to go for food and shelter. Blizzards, hurricanes and floods send people to their radios for a voice of guidance.

The better news operations are likely to benefit from listeners' news tips and queries. A man who heard an explosion near his home called a radio station with a good news service to ask, "What was that big explosion I just heard?" A reporter put him on hold while he dialed the police, who received the call just as they learned about an explosion at an asphalt company. The reporter got a lead and the man who phoned got the answer to his question. The reporter developed the news lead by consulting a cross-listed city directory to locate a company next door to the asphalt company. Within minutes he had an eyewitness account of the explosion and fire.

Solid news operations pay off in many ways. The rich get richer.

But be cautious. The citizen who telephones to report an accident she has just witnessed should be thanked, but her information must be checked. A well-intentioned caller may have the wrong information. When the information proves correct about an accident on a main thoroughfare, the station can air an advisory to motorists to detour.

Advantages and Drawbacks

Radio news beats the competitive media in these ways:

1. For bulletin news, it is fast and adaptable compared with the lumbering giant, television, which puts the bulletin on, then ignores the story until the next scheduled newscast unless the story is bad enough to shock the nation. Newspapers are out of the running.

2. When you want the latest news, you can find it on the radio, somewhere on the dial. You may just hear the headlines, but if the story you want is big enough, the headlines will include it.

3. For live coverage of a breaking story, as for bulletins, radio again has the ability to be the lithe, fast runner when compared to the lumbering giant, television. Unless the story warrants a television mobile unit or a helicopter with video transmission gear, radio news will beat it with on-the-scene information now. Again, newspapers are out of the running. A word of caution belongs here. Do not intercept and rebroadcast police or other official broadcasts. It is illegal and may endanger lives. For example, the Federal Aviation Administration criticized several radio broadcasters for transmitting radio conversations between pilots and FBI agents during a hijacking.

4. For economic reasons, radio stations can present a variety of specialized newscasts on a regular basis, which television will not match (a television station *could,* but no station *does*): regular newscasts, sports news, business news, extended weather reports, farm news, science news, political commentary, news for women, feature news. The list goes on. Television is not in the running, but newspapers definitely are. So are magazines.

5. People can hear the news while absorbed in other activities: driving, working, housecleaning, sunbathing, even trying half-heartedly to wake up.

6. For some newsmakers, radio provides a better means than television for getting through to people with complex information. When pictures are either unwanted or unavailable, radio may be the best medium of all for convincing.

7. During blizzards, floods and other emergencies, radio keeps people in touch with what's happening. For some, a lifeline. Of prime importance: school closings, street and highway closings, emergency lane locations, schedules, warnings. Television does not compete. Newspapers cannot.

8. Certain small segments of our society can get news in no other way. Among them: people who live in remote areas and the blind. Automobile commuters fall into this category twice a day.

So much for the advantages. The biggest disadvantage of radio news exists for both the public and the practitioner. Most radio news is sketchy and inadequate. The listener who really wants *news* is merely exasperated unless he can find a station committed to news.

The radio journalist may eventually leave the field in despair, battered by too much rip-'n-read, too many five-minute newscasts written in 15 minutes, too many demands for a fast one-line-in, one-line-out of a taped insert in a newscast which goes on in 30 seconds, not enough time to finish a phone call, no time at all to consider or weigh or think. It is haste, not speed, and the product reflects this in local newscasts across the land. Intelligently crafted newscasts, invariably beamed from intelligently — and profitably — run stations, are oases in a national radio wasteland. Discussion of radio news quality usually terminates in a quarrel over radio broadcasting economics — that is, to permit a journalist to spend more time preparing a newscast means either presenting fewer and/or shorter newscasts, which no responsible journalist wants, or increasing the radio news staff, which costs money.

The difference between a rip-'n-read news operation and a modestly adequate news operation is relatively small. "Modestly adequate" might mean an extra person, hired at a respectable salary, and a budget which will cover a few more stringers and some long distance calls. To satisfy FCC requirements, news is the main "front" which enables stations to renew their licenses. All stations should put up a good front. Some stations do, because their owners care. All stations should care. And if they don't, the news staff must care. Even at a one-person news operation, imagination and energy make a difference.

An angry radio news director told colleagues, "The reason the lousy stations exist is management. Hear their cry, 'we would like to have a better news operation, but you know news is a costly proposition...all stations lose money on news.' Bunk. Our noon news blocks on AM or FM nearly pay the bill for our entire news operation during the year...those ("lousy") operations detract from my news and your news, and still put us in the class of second-rate journalists. We are going to remain in that category until management get their heads together and begin making accusations against each other about sloppy, incompetent newsrooms."

The popular conversation-pit television newscast, with the anchor, editorialist, weathercaster and sportscaster exchanging banter, has not been matched by radio newscasts. KSFO, San Francisco, found warm listener reaction to a variation on the pattern. The newscaster and the disc jockey on duty talked about the news in what was described as "a free-hand, unrehearsed, give-and-take session." The newscaster reported what was happening, the disc jockey asked questions which sprang to his mind, and the listener found himself "drawn into the discussion because the questions being asked by the DJ are the same ones generally that the listener is asking himself."

Three Radio News Operations

A survey by RTNDA, the Radio Television News Directors Association, of more than 800 television and radio stations in the United States and Canada showed these averages:

Radio newsroom employees: 1.08 full time, 1.01 part time.

TV-radio combination newsroom employees: 3.7 full time, 0.9 part time.

Daily radio newscasts that were longer than 5 minutes: average of 3.

95% of the radio newsrooms had tape recorders.

60% - 70% had mobile units of some type.

28% of the radio stations (50% of the television stations) used stringers, but many radio news directors were displeased with what they had.

75% of the news directors, radio and television, reported to management; 25% reported to the program director.

UPI took a survey of radio stations to determine news practices and operating philosophies. Here are three reports from, respectively, a small town, a small city, and a medium-size city.

STATION #1

Market, 6,000; power, 1000 watts; on air, daytimer; owned locally; independent.

Philosophy

Wants to be more than a jukebox, so it has strong local news department with authority to break in with any important news. Features bloc programming, country-pop music (stays away from R-and-R image).

News Operation

Tools: Broadcast wire, two-way mobile, working arrangement with other stations on regional breaks, mutual cooperation with a newspaper.

Staff: News director responsible to manager, one staffer.

General: Uses wire service copy every half hour. 15 minutes at 8:30 a.m. and at noon. Local newscasts at 7:05 a.m. and 5:05 p.m. Ten are under five minutes, 8 are tens and 2 are fifteens. News mixed according to significance. Write two local newscasts and "unashamedly rip-and-read other times. We use nearly all features and in-depthers in our bloc programming, i.e. farm, women's, commentary, sports, record information. Also religious section."

Success Key

"We feature news and information and brag about it and sell it."

News Revenue

News big factor in a "very profitable" P-and-L statement. 18 of 20 newscasts sponsored, and it gets a 30% premium for two local newscasts. Merchants buy time because "they know people listen to us." News sold both spot and package. Listeners say they stay tuned all day because of the variety, the information and the fun provided. One hardware store has been with station steady for 17 years, one drug store for 12 years and three auto dealers 8-10 years.

Editorials

Five days per week, written by general manager. "We've been praised and we've taken our lumps. Above all we've gained stature in the process."

Looking Ahead

Feels there is more and more listener demand for actualities. Now gathers some locally and gets some from Washington headquarters of two major political parties.

STATION #2

Market, 200,000; power, 1000 watts; on air, daytimer; owned, group; independent; TV-affiliated.

Philosophy

"Attention to detail will bring success." Uses two full-time newsmen to produce and broadcast the news. No jockeys. "Newsmen never turn a record or touch a mike switch. They do what they're paid to do. News." Up-tempo music, but no rock 'n' roll, mixed with news.

News Operation

Tools: Broadcast wire, audio service, helicopter, mobile phone, beeper.

Staff: News director responsible to manager, 1½ newsmen, two stringers, arranging working agreement with other stations.

General: 12 newscasts in 12 hours. A fifteen on each hour, except thirties at 7 a.m. and noon and a sixty at 5 p.m. Saturdays and Sundays show tens every hour (but plans to make them fifteens). Non-news personnel NOT permitted to make newscasts. Four times as much news carried today as one year ago. Sports carried 45 past the hour.

Success Key

"We are only five months old in terms of a change in format but have no reservations in saying that news is the only way to go."

News Revenue

"Still struggling to shake the good-minimum news format but can say that news has been our 'saving grace.' We have hired newsmen, produced good news and sold our station on the basis of news concept. Sales have doubled. Listener comments are great and anticipate 50% of our net will come from news in the near future. Six of 12 newscasts sponsored and sold on spot and package basis. We're building community acceptance and long-range solidity this way. And it's paying off. An air-conditioning company moved up its season 45 days on the strength of newscast promotion. A nursery sponsor got one complete landscaping job on basis of a newscast. We can and will corner the market by staying ahead of our competition in news."

Sales aids — promotion

Salesmen carry A.R.B. information, brochures, audition tapes, news oriented sales stories. Advertise in newspapers and on TV.

STATION #3

Market, 495,000; power, 5,000 watts; on air, 24 hours; owned, locally; independent.

Philosophy

Hires only high calibre newsmen, gives them an efficient news center, serves listeners 24 hours per day with whatever is happening.

News Operation

Tools: Broadcast wire, audio service, regional news network covering seven states, 6 mobile units, 1 airplane, 2 leased helicopters, 3 tiny-talkie units, 5 portable recorders, working agreements with stations.

Staff: News director with vice-president's title and responsible only to management, 7 staffers (each working part of day in news center, rest in field and each with a mobile), 10 stringers.

General: Features hard news, editorials, airborne traffic advisories, weather and road conditions, school and industrial closures, features, in depth on big stories. 20 scheduled newscasts: 19 fives and a 55 plus 1 fifteen at 7 a.m., plus 7 headline summaries, all locally produced. Has live sports, voicers, mobile, regional network feeds, audio, special reports from news center. "We interrupt for important news." Volume up 15% in last 12 months by adding four regular news reports; volume up 50% in last five years. Non-news personnel never allowed to air newscasts. Newscasts a mixture of all news according to significance.

Success Key

"Only way an independent can be a real force in a community is through an extremely news-oriented approach. News as it happens from where it is happening. Be vital."

News Revenue

"News, without question, is the reason for our #1 rating." All 20 newscasts sponsored, two with same sponsor for seven years. Sold as spots. Charges 10% premium for all time during AAA drive time periods to defray cost of airborne coverage. 50% of net comes from news: up 25% in five years.

Editorials

Daily, written by news director, general manager and commentator, approved by news director. Has helped commercially and is "credited with the election of a mayor."

Sales aids — promotion

Salesmen have tapes and brochures. Tours of news center.

Costs

Examples abound. A three-person news staff in an Iowa town of 8,000 *turned out* 23 newscasts daily and *turned over* $78,000 a year to the station above newsroom operating costs.

Cost of setting up a small radio news operation will include equipment bought once (presumably), weekly salaries, weekly costs for teletype wires and audio services, and supplies which must be reordered. Naturally, these costs vary. A large radio station in Philidelphia will pay more than a small station in Wet Hat for the same AP wire. It will also pay more for an acceptable journalist for the obvious reason that it can afford to demand a higher degree of skill.

Initial purchases of equipment include standard size typewriters, portable tape recorders, a special telephone installation, a roving police monitor, and perhaps a file cabinet in addition to other office furnishings.

The computer system familiar to newspapers has entered the radio newsroom here and there. Video terminals with keyboards have replaced typewriters. The story typed on a terminal and stored in a computer can be printed as hard copy or can be read by the newscaster directly from the terminal, entirely eliminating paper.

Travel, stringers and tipsters should be budgeted. A radio news stringer is a part-time correspondent, usually in another community within the station's transmission range. Some stringers are paid by the word or by the story. Sometimes their voices are used, sometimes just their information. Stringers may be small town reporters, housewives or students who have the spare time and the flexible schedule needed to cover stories at odd hours, either at their own direction or on assignment from the newsroom (in the latter case they should be paid whether or not the story goes on the air).

Tipsters are found where news is found. The court bailiff, the police sergeant, the fire dispatcher, the probate clerk, the parole officer, the air traffic controller, the highway patrolman, John and Jane Q. Public may all call from time to time with leads which develop into hard news or feature stories. For the tip, the station may pay a few dollars. Word of tipster payments spreads and the news department which establishes a policy of paying for tips soon finds itself getting news tip telephone calls from people who were never solicited. The station will eventually have a substantial network of informants. Many of the tips prove worthless, but lots of wheat lie amid the chaff. All tips should be checked.

A variation of the tipster network is to advertise that the station will pay a specified amount, perhaps $25 or $50, for the tip leading to the best story of the week. Not only is the sum paid but, with his consent, the tipster's name is announced.

Audio News Services

Audio news services enable radio stations to offer their listeners much more than local actualities plus a reading of wire news. APR, the Associated Press Radio network, and UPI Audio each feed hundreds of clients a stream of complete newscasts, sportscasts, stock market updates, agricultural reports, features and actualities over permanently open telephone lines, plus sound signals that switch a tape recorder at each radio station on and off. At this writing, AP, UPI and Mutual are moving to satellite transmission of their audio networks, which improves the quality of sound considerably and eliminates the chance of signal failure from land lines that are subject to going down in storms or being torn up by a farmer's plow. To alert radio news directors, the AP and UPI broadcast wires carry billboards of what is being fed. National Public Radio now uses satellite transmission.

ABC, CBS, NBC, Mutual and some station groups supply their affiliates with a steady flow of national newscasts and actualities. Several smaller organizations and branches of the U.S. government also offer audio feeds. Many are in specialized subject areas, such as finance or religion. Some are free services.

The Wall Street Journal and the Christian Science Monitor installed special news wires at radio stations in exchange for a schedule of commercials. Many agricultural radio stations have a wire from the Commodity News Service in Kansas City.

By 1980, 21 state radio networks were serving stations a mix of state news, sports, weather, plus farm and market reports. Feeds come not only from the network office but from stations up and down the line with something to offer. A typical service, the Missouri network, daily feeds more than 70 stations a news service that includes thirteen state newscasts, three sportscasts, three actualities, two features on Missouri history, and hourly UPI audio newscasts, national sports reports and stock market reports. In addition, the Missouri Network covers college and professional football and basketball games.

Branches of government, politicians, and some private business firms mail audio tape handouts. Some of these spots are quite good and can be edited to make them both better and less commercial.

A number of special radio networks exist in the United States independent of outside business interests. Several stations band together to exchange voice reports, actualities, or live programming. The stations may belong to the same owner, they may be in the same state or region, or they may have a community of interests and be commercially run, like the sizable Black Network, or non-commercial, like a network of college radio stations. For a little extra trouble and expense, the radio station belonging to a regional network extends its reach quite a bit.

Radio newsmen feeding a spot to a network sometimes forget to stop. Radio news consultant Jerry Graham: "There is a tendency to have actualities just for the sake of actualities and to let them run too long. Tight editing is needed. Secondly, reporters in the field have to refine their techniques. They should get to the heart of the story in the first few seconds of their reports, so that the stations that cannot carry a full segment won't lose the important element of a story that may be at the tail end and be cut out."

Voice inserts (called "voicers" or "beepers" even when there is no beep) should be short. Sometimes 30 seconds is too long. Usually it is ample. Not many beepers should be allowed to run as long as 60 seconds. Length, however, depends on substance.

Get live or taped voicers from: a witness to a breaking news event, including those involved, like the bank teller who was just held up and the runner who just won the race and hasn't quite caught his breath; the people who will be affected by a decision, like the homeowner whose taxes are about to rise or the president of the company that won the contract; the important citizen who says surprising things and the important citizen who is miffed at what the other important citizen just said, even if he hadn't heard about it until you called him.

Newscast Schedule

The radio news audience ebbs and flows. It is greatest at three periods of the day: morning, noon, and late afternoon.

Morning (6 a.m. — 10 a.m.): Clock radios wake people with the news. Mothers want to know how to dress children for school. Commuters want to know what freeways are jammed. Car radios keep them company all the way to work. Everyone wants to know what's been happening.

Noon: Radio news accompanies lunch for the housewife, the construction worker, the farmer.

Late afternoon (3 p.m. — 7 p.m.): Commuters again want to know about the traffic. Investors wonder what the Dow did. Everyone wants to know what the day has brought.

Some listeners like to tune in at bedtime. Has the world survived another day? What will tomorrow's weather be? Who won the Detroit game?

Both inside and outside these peak listening periods a pattern of headlines, brief weather reports, 5-minute summaries, and 15-minute newscasts can give form to the daily news schedule. For example, headlines and weather on the half-hour and 5-minute summaries on the hour. Or, 15-minute newscasts on the hour, headlines at the half-hour and 45 minutes past the hour. Or, 5-minute summaries at quarter-past, half-past, and five-to. And so on. Because the audience increases during three periods of the day, the amount of news offered should increase also. That is the time for the daily business digest, the science report, the "news behind the news," news for women, the sports report.

Not all these newscasts are produced locally. Many radio stations affiliate with APR (Associated Press Radio), UPI Audio, CBS, NBC, Mutual, one of the four ABC networks, or a state network. All networks provide newscasts on regular schedules. Affiliate stations sometimes attach local newscasts back-to-back to the network newscasts which include national and international news. There is no "best way" to set up a radio news schedule. Some stations want to duck the competition. Some want to meet the competition head-on. If any rule exists it is this: *Don't change the schedule without a good reason.* Listeners establish radio news habits. A newscast is a constant in the lives of many people, as dependable as the rising of the sun.

All-News Radio

Although a number of radio stations in major cities have gone to an all-news or news-and-information format, "salted nuts" for the listener has not always brought peaches and cream to the station owner. Several stations tried all-news and dropped it. Those who survived are glad they held on for the year or more it took to break old listening habits and build that audience which exists in every major city for all-news radio.

Unlike radio music audiences, all-news audiences pop in and out. For about three years in the mid-Seventies, NBC News provided an all-news feed to subscribing stations, allowing a few minutes every half-hour for local news. It was a noble experiment, but too few stations signed up to make it profitable, so NBC gave it up.

The so-called "20-20" news format — repeated every twenty minutes — has proved popular with audiences. Station managers considering all-news fret over the cost. Staff may double, if it was thin to begin with. Other overhead costs rise. On the other hand, revenue should also rise considerably. Some stations are making more than they ever did spinning platters. Beyond money, the station manager finds himself with influence and prestige in the community beyond anything he had experienced as just a businessman whose business was running a radio station.

All-news format varies with the hour of the day. During morning and evening commuting hours, the pace picks up: shorter stories, more rapid reading rates, more headlines, more frequent time and temperature checks, more sports reports, fewer features. Between 10 a.m. and 3 p.m., many listeners are housewives. A lot of traveling salesmen are out there, too. News tends to get softer: longer stories, more features, slower pacing. Here is a WBBM, Chicago, noon to 1 p.m. format:

> Network news
> Local news
> Weather
> Stock market report
> Editorial
> Local feature
> Headlines
> News summary
> *Direct Line* (an ombudsman service)
> Book reviews
> Hollywood report

Says John Callaway of CBS Radio, "We view news as reporting on the reality of what's happening. War is a reality, sure — but so is a book, so is a play, so is a restaurant. When you give immediacy to them, you're in soft news — and this is a significant part of our approach to housewives' time."

A charge levelled at all-news radio is that most of it is shallow. Said media critic Robert Lewis Shayon: "The news is often billed as 'stories in the making.' They emerge from nowhere; they live briefly and blend indistinguishably into new emergencies. One-sentence headlines, flecky details, weather, traffic, sports, stocks, compressed catastrophes, affairs of state, revolutions and coups, stabbings, shoot-outs, local fires, fender-benders, the jingle and the sell of endlessly procreating commercials — they drone, they clip (fast, fast, no introspection, no navel) without emphasis, change of pace, or emotional tone in a sort of instant omnipresence, never *to* or *from*, only *at*, the re-creation of a mythical pattern of nowness...

"No one can stay in the all-news world for more than ten minutes at a time. For the lineal mind, instant omnipresence is dreaded nothingness..." [1]

Mobile Units

Vehicles with two-way radios give a radio newscast what the disc jockeys call the "now sound":

"...The men at the levee have been working 16 hours without relief. There with them now is WWW reporter Jerry Jones."

And in comes Jerry Jones, with an on-the-spot, right-this-minute report of the sandbag loading, plus the playback of a tape he got five minutes ago at a place to which he could walk while carrying a portable tape recorder, but could not reach by car.

The mobile radio unit may be as simple as a reporter's private car and a street corner telephone booth, or it can be as elaborate as the radio news car designed for one Midwest radio station. The reporter could transmit sound from either a portable or AC-power tape recorder, or several microphones through a five-channel mixer. He could feed either to the station or directly on the air, using a transmitter mounted on the car. In addition, the car had eight-channel police receivers, one low-band sending frequency, two high band sending frequencies, a typewriter, a desk, and foul weather gear. It transmitted live broadcasts of news conferences, interviews, breaking news, MOS reports. Wireless mikes were fed to the car and "tripped" to relay back to the station on another frequency, so that reporters could work without cords. An inverter provided the necessary AC power. The car was a rolling radio station.

Mobile units run on more than wheels. Some stations use helicopters, not only for those daily traffic reports, but for getting to distant places fast, especially when roads are blocked. Hovering over parades, helicopters advertise their radio stations as they deliver running commentaries heard on portables carried by the good folks below. Mobile unit power boats cover fun or disaster. And at least one radio station uses an amphibian car. The newest kind of mobile unit is the snowmobile. Canadian station CMHL, Hamilton, Ontario, sends its snowmobile out during snowstorms when even police cars get stuck. Radio listeners learn which roads are still open, which are hopelessly clogged. Sometimes people, seeing the snowmobile go by, turn their radios on in a hurry to discover where it is going and what is happening.

The FCC grants remote pickup licenses to licensed broadcasters for two-way radios. The "base station" at the broadcasting station gets an identification of three letters followed by three numbers: ABC-123. Each "mobile station" gets two letters and four numbers: AB-1234. The car's transmitter-receiver usually goes in the trunk, with the mike and controls under the dashboard, and if the car does not already have one, an alternator instead of a generator, in order to keep the battery up to strength.

Sometimes a mobile phone substitutes for a two-way radio. The conversation goes through a telephone operator. The audio quality will probably be inferior to that of a good two-way radio hookup and it may not be possible to patch in a tape recorder for playback, at least without extensive modification. Most radio units can be modified for playback from portable tape recorders.

One manufacturer has developed a remote transmitter-receiver which allows a reporter to send a signal as far as a mile to a radio car, which beams it back to the radio station. It can transmit from inside a building.

For its newsroom, CKOC, Hamilton, Ontario, has created some inexpensive production stations, each consisting of three cassette recorders mounted in a steel cabinet, plus a microphone, a V—U meter, remote starts and a variety of buttons. Remote reports are called into the machine, dubbed onto specially ordered leaderless cassette tapes, so the sound starts at the head of each cassette. To cue up the tape, someone in the newsroom just rewinds to the head. Each recorder is "hot-wired" for instant starting, which solves the problem of getting the recorder up to speed. And the sound from any machine can be fed into any other, so that sound can be mixed on tape.

Tape Recording

With good, inexpensive reel-to-reel and cassette tape recorders now on the market, all radio newsrooms should have at least one portable tape recorder. A cassette will do if it can be patched into a studio tape recorder and is adapted to take a broadcast microphone. A reel-to-reel tape recorder permits the newsman to edit the original tape. Several types of audio tape splicers can be bought. Simplest is the splicing bar, used with a single-edge razor blade. Sliding a fore-finger along the groove holds the tape in place. Each end of the tape is cut at the angled cross groove (to avoid a "pop"), the excess tape falls away, and a bit of splicing tape bonds the two ends firmly. Steel and plastic splicing bars are available for just a few dollars.

A popping sound or any other unwanted noise can be eliminated by splicing or by replaying that segment of tape with the record button down, the volume pot down, and the feed and takeup reels guided by hand past the recording head. A little practice is advisable before trying it on a cut meant for a newscast. A third way to eliminate unwanted sound is to put a magnet on the tape. Again, practice first.

Steps are saved — to say nothing of valuable seconds — if a tape recorder in the newsroom can be patched directly over the air. Regular newscasts need not come from the newsroom, but bulletins should.

Many stations edit on reel-to-reel tape. The edited cut is dubbed to a cartridge. A master control room with many cart machines can play a number of news cuts without having to thread new reels of tape.

For the Student

1. Assume that you are news director of a radio station with one mobile unit and one news wire. A budget increase permits you to add either another mobile unit or another wire. Which would you choose? Defend your choice in class.

2. Suggest ways to promote a radio news operation to the public and to advertisers.

3. Format an hour-long block from 10 a.m. to 11 a.m. for an all-news station. Format the 6 p.m. to 7 p.m. block.

4. Spend a day in a radio newsroom. Keep a log. What surprised you? Write a 200-word summary of what happened.

5. Imagine a *typical* radio news listener. Describe that person.

TELEVISION

The Television Reporter

A Television News Day

The Newscaster

The Television Reporter

7

The best interviews are of people reacting — not people expounding. Joy, sorrow, shock, fear — these are the stuff of news.

— Reuven Frank

At a news conference for a United States senator one day in one of the nation's large cities, local newspaper and wire service reporters were casually asking their questions, which the senator answered perfunctorily. Suddenly the door opened and, making a fair amount of noise, six men strode in. They were a reporter, a photographer and a sound technician from each of two local television stations. With sound cameras mounted on the photographers' shoulder braces, with film in the cameras, with portable lights and with amplifiers and microphones already hooked up, these two television news teams needed only a minute or so to get ready to shoot, not much more time than a pencil-and-paper reporter takes to settle himself and prepare to jot down replies.

The atmosphere in the room became electric. The senator sat up, obviously more attentive. He completely ignored the newspaper reporters present. The television reporters were no-nonsense journalists. The newspaper reporters dropped back as the hot lights went on and the television reporters moved into position. Each television reporter crisply fired three or four questions at the senator, who responded just as crisply. In five minutes it was over. The lights went out and the television news teams departed, hurrying to the next story. The senator slumped back in his chair. The air of casualness resettled through the room. For the remainder of the news conference the senator behaved as if he could not care less whether the other reporters stayed or went, or even what they wrote. For him the most significant portion of the news conference had already occurred in a five-minute blaze of hot lights, because the film would carry his face and his voice to more voters than he would reach in a dozen speeches in that city, to voters he could reach in no other way, even by visiting supermarkets and standing outside factories when shifts changed.

For the reporters, the attitudes and events which had just transpired were by no means unusual, and were remarkable only in their degree of acceptance by all participants. Quite possibly, each television news reporter was not a whit more competent than his newspaper colleagues and, just as possibly, was less versed in the topics under discussion. He and his questions were favored solely because they were the means by which the senator could appear on television.

If from this event, which one can find repeated dozens of times daily across the nation, a lesson can be drawn, it is that the television news reporter should train himself to take advantage of the opportunities the television medium gives him.

Guidelines

In *Creative Interviewing*, Ken Metzler said:

> For better or worse, most of what the public knows about interviewing comes from broadcast: the harsh confrontation tactics of a Mike Wallace, the amiable sensitivity of a Dick Cavett, the aloof hostility of a *Meet the Press* session, the gross tactics of the local newscaster who thrusts a mike beneath the nose of a distraught crime victim. [1]

Some guidelines for a television news reporter's preparation and conduct can be laid down.

A television reporter should have at least a conversational knowledge of the specialized field of every person he interviews.

He should know enough about each specialized field to ask sensible questions.

He should know enough to recognize what is new and interesting and important.

He should not embarrass his station, the person he interviews or himself by asking stupid questions. He may lean on friends who are experts in various fields for the kind of incisive questions that really get to the heart of the story. The best reporter has friends whose knowledge spans much of the field of general information. A fast phone call often is all that is necessary to prepare the reporter for the technical or complicated story.

He should not waste time with sophomoric questions. If he must ask an elementary question, he should be aware that it is elementary, and he should ask it unobtrusively, off camera, before the interview begins formally. However — and this qualification is significant — if his elementary question is likely to produce an interesting answer, he should go ahead and ask it. For instance, it would be amateurish to ask a visiting NASA official on camera, "How many manned flights have there been so far?" But try one like, "Why should my tax dollar go toward sending more men into space?" and he may get the best story on tonight's news. (Or, the reporter may be brushed off with the same reply the NASA spokesman gave to the last ten reporters who asked that question.) Note, too, that the second question is open-ended. Unlike the first, it cannot be answered with a word. The reporter asks for opinion, not facts he himself could easily get by doing his homework. And by asking for opinion rather than facts, he flatters the person he questions. (It should be added that this is not the sort of question ever asked during a space shot, nor is likely to be asked by a veteran science news reporter.)

He should be aware of the interview situation. He should not start an interview with the sort of tough question asked toward the end of "Issues and Answers." A friendly opening question or comment, maybe stated before the camera rolls, breaks the ice.

A somewhat green television reporter accompanied by a photographer and a sound technician, once arrived late for the opening of a candidate's storefront headquarters. The small store was packed with well-wishers. Other camera crews had arrived early and had set their gear up on a platform facing a stand reserved for the candidate, due to arrive momentarily. With no time to shove through the crowd and no space to set the camera up, the photographer suggested setting up on the sidewalk outside, collaring the candidate before he went into the store, and getting a quick statement. Agreed. The crew set up, the candidate arrived, was collared, persuaded, and festooned with a lavalier mike. As the photographer adjusted his focus, the reporter politely told the candidate the question he intended to ask in order to get that quick statement. The candidate was taken aback, for it was a very tough question indeed, the sort a reporter should build up to. The candidate did not know if the camera was rolling (it wasn't), but decided to take no chances. He not only did not want to answer the question, he did not want the question itself used. So he proceeded to destroy the reporter. With one hand he tried to tug the mike off, meanwhile covering it, which muffled the sound. With the other he pointed at the reporter and barked, "I answered that question two weeks ago on your network. Don't you watch your network's newscasts? It was reported in the papers. Don't you read the papers? How come a station sends a reporter out who doesn't watch his network's newscasts or read the newspapers?" Etc. Etc.

The photographer, observing what was going on, stepped away from his camera, waved his arms over his head and told the candidate the camera had not been turned on yet. (Which was really a shame.) He walked up and put a friendly arm on the candidate's shoulder, smoothed the ruffled feathers and asked for a fast 40 seconds on what the candidate thought of having such a nice turnout of nice supporters on such a nice sunny day. The candidate curtly nodded agreement, threw a last dirty look at the reporter, who stood there stunned, and — at the photographer's signal — flashed a warm smile and launched into a "I'm delighted so many of my...." statement. Then off to the storefront. (*The reporter eventually came to appreciate the lessons that day taught, and offers them to you in this book. The candidate went on to become president of the United States, bruising more than one reporter on the way.*)

The Interviewee's Knowledge

The reporter should keep his questions within the field of the interviewee's competence. It makes no more sense to ask an astronomer about the latest military policy than to ask a flyer about the climate of Mars.

For that matter, it is unlikely that the flyer is an authority on military policy. He knows something about air attack, military morale around him, air strategy and the outward condition of the local populace. The reporter should talk to the flyer about what the flyer knows. The story will be more informative, more exciting, and less likely to be misleading. To be sure, Captain Hiram Jones may be perfectly willing — indeed, eager — to spend five minutes of the television station's film giving his views about foreign policy. But the reporter is better advised to save the policy question for the ambassador, the senator or the professor who has spent years of his life studying the complexities of political events in the war-torn region.

Ralph Paskman of CBS News opposed what he calls "indiscriminate interviewing of the so-called man in the street." He asks, "What purpose is served, what information is gained by asking somebody's mother (a complex question)? You are not providing news or information when you ask somebody to be an expert on something they cannot possibly be qualified to discuss. Man-in-the-street assignments are really not valid unless you are asking people questions they are qualified to answer." [2]

Radio news director Gary Franklin disagrees in part. "MOS's won't add to the viewers' basic knowledge of events. But they're interesting. People like to know what others think. It's like a newspaper's Vox Populi."

When astronaut Virgil Grissom, later killed in preparing for Apollo I, made his 15-minute sub-orbital flight in 1961 in the Mercury spacecraft Liberty Bell 7, the entire nation thrilled to the news. Los Angeles television station KABC-TV sent a camera crew out to do a man-on-the-street interview asking two questions: 1. What do you think of the space flight? 2. Who is Virgil Grissom?

Everyone who was interviewed glowed with pride in answering question 1. Some spoke knowingly about its effect on the Cold War. But two-thirds of them did not know who Virgil Grissom was. Someone thought he was a barber.

Fools speak knowingly on any subject. And sometimes their opinions get pride of place in the press and on the air. One reason is that ignorant opinion usually comes across as less stuffy than informed opinion, a generalization supported by considerable observation. But the danger of disseminating misinformation should weigh heavily on a journalist's conscience. Non-expert expertise gets far too much play, at the expense of the thoughtful views of authorities in a field. On a political question, a few views taken at random are an insufficient sampling of public opinion, even with the best of editorial motives and the greatest editorial discretion. Majority opinion exerts considerable influence in swaying belief. Quoting three or four individuals with similar views gives those views an aura of universality.

For instance, *Newsweek* once bannered a non-expert survey as its lead story: "War Over Berlin: The Brutal Question."[3] The question, "Should the U.S. risk a nuclear war to defend Berlin?" was asked of "mother of an Air Force man," "Marine veteran at Harvard," "assistant pastor," "father of four," etc. *Newsweek* used a nice folksy approach, but at a critical moment in our foreign policy, they saw no need to pose this question to a diplomat, a general, a political scientist, or anyone else who was likely to have given more than five minutes of consideration to the matter in his life. Understandably, the folksy replies fell mostly into the "yes" or "no" category, without anyone replying with such an obvious question as: "Do you mean defend Berlin against invasion, or against blockade, or the tactical move of East German police replacing Soviet soldiers at Checkpoint Charlie?" If such a question was asked, *Newsweek* ignored it.

In the hands of a biased and unscrupulous journalist, random interviews can harm a political candidate. In a political sidewalk interview film once made for showing in local theaters, everyone supporting one candidate was pleasantly ordinary. Supporters of his opponent looked odd or were sloppy or stuttered.

The Reporter's Knowledge

It is not unknown to find a reporter who refuses to do homework in advance of an assignment, saying, "It's best if I don't know, because then I'm just like the audience." That argument excuses laziness. The reporter who knows nothing about a subject cannot know what is interesting or important, and he must waste time and try everyone's patience with pointless questions. His sharper competitor at another station reads newspapers, magazines and books, and does his homework in advance of an assignment whenever he can, not to impress anyone with fancy language or esoteric knowledge, but to be aware of the latest research and the flashpoints of controversy.

The interviewee will be more relaxed with the reporter who can speak his language, more confident that the reporter will get the story right. The reporter is likely to be more confident, too, than the lazy fellow who may mask the fact that he doesn't really know what's going on by being pushy and demanding answers as his god-given privilege.

Obviously, a reporter cannot be an expert on everything. Ideally, he will have a broad liberal arts education, a comfortable command of the English language, ability to think quickly on his feet, a friendly manner, a clear voice and an up-to-date awareness of what's going on in the world and in his backyard.

The television reporter should be able, in the course of a morning, to shift mental gears from quizzing a detective about a homicide to a news conference with the visiting Secretary of Agriculture to an interview with a local civil rights leader to a chat with a minister's wife just home from the Congo.

Yet, even this is not enough. The reporter must be a translator. A pencil-and-paper reporter translates the expert's information and opinions into a story the reader of his newspaper or magazine understands. The television reporter leads the expert to do this himself, and to do it with brevity and a measure of excitement, if possible.

Brevity is a factor that must always be in the back of a reporter's mind when his camera is rolling. Words that fall to the cutting room floor represent dollars in the news department's budget. However, in the field the cheapest thing a crew has is film or tape. It is false economy to be stingy with film when the station has invested half a dozen expensive man-hours in the story. Brevity is the soul of television reporting, but it must be tempered by common sense.

Brevity can also be the soul of witless reporting, and chances are it will not be the reporter's fault. Prepared to explain, lucidly, what happened in the state legislature today, he is told by the producer of the evening newscast that he must limit himself to a 25-second wraparound, maybe 15 seconds intro to an interview statement and a 10-second tag. Who can blame him for grumbling?

A television reporter, especially in a standupper, in which he speaks directly to the camera, should communicate the importance and the excitement of what he is reporting. Sam Zelman of CBS News remarked, "The biggest weakness of the beginner, it seems to me, is a lack of urgency in his delivery. News is urgent and exciting. But so many of us are somewhat matter-of-fact and casual about news. This attitude is not designed to attract attention either on the air or across a dinner table. To impart urgency, you needn't talk louder or faster. But you certainly must somehow communicate your own excitement and interest in the material. If you do, you'll look bright-eyed and alert on the air — and that's considered rather attractive." [4]

Digging for Facts

The value of a story sometimes is exposed only when the reporter probes for it. In many interviews, the person facing the camera tries to limit the matters he willingly discusses. When a reporter inquires about matters beyond those limits, the interviewee will fend off the questions. A skillful politician can turn a question so deftly that most reporters will not be aware that he is not answering it. A reporter is well advised to listen carefully to answers. The give and take of questions and answers can produce statements which the interviewee would not include in a speech. Too many reporters pay little attention to answers, devoting their attention instead to the framing of the next question.

A camera and a microphone are not the only tools of the television reporter's trade. The notebook and pencil go along as well. Dan Rather on the subject:

> I am not a note taker in the classic pose of a reporter who whips out his notepad and scribbles furiously. I do carry a notebook and pencil. No reporter worthy of the name can walk out of the house without those articles on his person. But for broadcasting, for my own style, what has

worked best for me is to watch and listen as closely as I possibly can, trying to *burn* it into my head, so that if I have to describe a scene again and again I can. I do take down direct quotes. That is one thing I try to get exactly.[5]

Writer Nora Ephron tells of watching "in dismay as the cameras moved in and the television reporter cornered the politician ('How do you feel about the vote, Senator?') or cornered the man on the stretcher being carried out of the burning building ('How do you feel about the fact that your legs were just blown off, sir?')." [6]

One is tempted to call that second quote an insulting exaggeration, and probably it is, except for the nagging feeling that at some time or other one or two reporters come close to asking a question like that. This brings up the very real practice of asking interviewees how they "feel" about this or that, usually when it is perfectly obvious how they feel.

In *The Living Room War*, Michael Arlen said, "The 'how-do-you-feel' stuff would be okay if it led anywhere, if it were something people could respond to...but in a professional interview what it really amounts to is a sort of marking time while the reporter thinks up some real questions."

A television reporter's qualities should include sensitivity but should also include toughness. He needs a thick hide if he intends to cover more than supermarket openings. A politician who feels a reporter is prying into what the politician prefers hidden may not be above trying to silence the reporter in the presence of others with a scathing personal crack about the reporter's ignorance or amateurishness. If the reporter lapses into blushing muteness — or if he snaps back angrily — the politician wins. If the reporter keeps his head and has confidence in his line of questioning, he may dig out a story in the public interest.

A reporter should leaven his toughness with sympathy. At times he will need both. Every reporter on general assignment sooner or later faces a story he prefers not to cover. It is not easy to shove a microphone near a father whose child has just drowned. No final answer can be given to the question, "Then why do it?" The question and answer fall into the realm of news department policy, and can be debated endlessly. For most reporters, the only answer is, "It's part of my job." This is not a crass, callous answer without ethics. Covering one child's death may save another child's life through a safety precaution that would otherwise have been neglected. Not every distraught father, suddenly seeing a microphone, will turn away or get mad. Many a parent has poured out a heart full of grief, communicating to the television audience more emotion and understanding than will ever come from a soap opera. But be careful. A reporter for one Cleveland television station interviewed a 10-year-old boy who survived a Lake Erie boating tragedy in which his companion, another boy, drowned. The reporter asked the youngster if he was sorry they had gone out on the lake that day. And if that wasn't bad enough, the question was used on the air.

Reuven Frank, in a memo to the NBC News staff, said, "The best interviews are of people reacting — not people expounding. Joy, sorrow, shock, fear — these are the stuff of news. No important story is without them...And no qualified reporter can afford revulsion at random contact with other humans."

It was noted, above, that the reporter must be a translator. He must interpret or have the interviewee interpret specialized information for the public. First, the reporter must understand the topic himself. This point cannot be stressed often enough. A reporter who brings no background of knowledge to the interview is as blameworthy as the photographer who forgets his film. Where the subject is highly technical, the reporter who feels ill-prepared should at the least get some information from the interviewee or a public relations associate (if one comes along) before the cameras roll.

With an awareness of the subject, the reporter must then guide the interview so that it relates to what will be understood by the viewers at home. Suppose the visiting Secretary of Agriculture is in town to give two speeches on new proposals for wheat parity pending before Congress. Wheat parity doesn't mean a thing to the worker who just came home from an eight-hour shift at the Ford plant. An explanation of parity would bore him. So the reporter asks the Secretary of Agriculture, "How much more will I pay for a loaf of bread if this goes through?" "Nothing," comes the reply, "if the bread companies will absorb it. Otherwise, about a penny." Now the reporter has his story in the film can. This, the factory worker will understand. And if he turns his head toward the kitchen and yells, "Hey, Mabel, did you hear that about the bread?" the reporter has done his work well. He has helped an expert to communicate a complex matter across the air waves so that people at home understand and care. And that is what this business of television news is all about.

The reporter could have phrased his question differently. Instead of asking, "How much more will I pay?" he could have asked, "What would be the average cost increase for the quantity of wheat needed for a single loaf of bread?" But then he would not be translating fully. He would not be speaking the viewer's language. The factory worker might not have caught it. Instead of calling to his wife, he might have reached for the television program guide to see what movie the station was showing after this dull newscast.

A reporter's preparation for a story varies with both the reporter and the story. To learn a day ahead that you will interview the Syrian ambassador is far different than being told to rush out to cover a fire. Given a day's notice on the Syrian ambassador, one reporter will spend an hour at the library that night leafing through recent issues of *The New York Times* for the background and latest facets of the Middle East dispute. Another will ask the assignment editor to suggest a couple of questions. Another will go to the interview cold, except for some half-remembered headlines. One reporter will write his questions down on paper and will read them to the ambassador. Another will also write his questions down, but will keep the paper pocketed to refer to only in an emergency.

The reporter who "sort of remembers" headlines probably won't bother writing anything down, or even thinking of questions in advance. He depends instead on his toothpaste smile to charm the ambassador.

As for a decision on whether to read questions from paper or to avoid this crutch, there can be no final answer. What is best is what is most suitable and most comfortable. The only certain rule is that preparation is better than no preparation.

A radio reporter, microphone in hand, once greeted the president of the Teamsters Union with this: "I don't know what is going on. I haven't been paying any attention to the news. But what is the situation?"

Some other questions to make us wince, and then maybe make us wiser:

In New Orleans, a TV reporter asked the head of a teacher's union if teachers should unionize.

In Chicago, a sports reporter asked someone, "Is good physical condition important to success in sports?"

In Santa Monica, shortly after President Kennedy was shot, a TV reporter asked a friend of Pat Lawford, the President's sister, "Does this shock you?"

Besides toughness and sympathy and background information, a reporter should carry a dram of gall. There will be times he will either bluff his way into a story, or he won't get the story. Other times, he will have to elbow his way in, or again, no story. These times are not as frequent as the movies would indicate, but they exist. When gall is required, a reporter may choose to sit outside on his ethics and watch another reporter barge in, microphone in hand, cameraman close behind, grinding away. Or the reporter can do his own barging in. This, too, is part of "the game."

Digging for a story frequently means work away from the camera. Studying an issue is important. Books, old newspaper clippings, public records and telephone calls to knowledgable persons are source material. A rule to remember is that where there is an issue, there are individuals in opposition to each other. Get the arguments of each side, and face the other side with those arguments, preferably on camera.

Politicians and Reporters

Interaction between politics and media is the subject of entire books and not a few doctoral dissertations. Discussion of this subtle, multi-faceted and fascinating topic is clearly beyond the scope of this book, except to state a few facts. Some of the most obvious:

1. Reporters and politicians feed upon each other.
2. Television news is the tastiest meal of all.

The green reporter who is grateful because a politician gives him a statement, thereby fulfilling the afternoon's news quota, soon learns that the politician is as eager for the contact as the reporter.

When the politician runs for office he hires, if he can afford it, one or more media contact people. It is not important to go to the factory gate at 5 a.m. to shake hands. It *is* important for television news that night to show the candidate shaking hands. Increasingly, campaigns are designed to entice cameras out of television newsrooms. The candidate whose budget is not overly pinched may even bring along his own television crew, which later delivers edited videotape to stations.

Into all this warmth and mutual backrubbing a sharp pin has been stuck by two researchers, Thomas E. Patterson and Robert D. McClure, whose book, *The Unseeing Eye*, alleges that television news coverage does not inform the voters about the issues.[7] After two thousand interviews with voters who watched newscasts, the researchers concluded that television news ignores the major issues of a campaign and the candidates' qualifications. In fact, they said, paid political commercials offer a better means of improving the voters' understanding of where the candidates stand on the issues.

The mechanics of the television process and the persons involved in the process represent what we might term a new variable in the equation of persuasion. The other variables have been analyzed for two thousand years, dating back to the *Rhetoric* of Aristotle, which counseled the speaker in the ways to win over his audience, whom Aristotle referred to as "judges."

In our own era, the television medium does more than project the *voices* of ambitious men. Much more. Every nuance of tone, gesture and facial expression is projected into the parlors and even the bedrooms of those whose minds and hearts the politician seeks to conquer. He reaches his audience when they are relaxed and secure, perhaps more receptive than in any other situation — except being in a great crowd hearing martial airs, and seeing flags and uniforms.

Understandably, the politician wants television coverage. He holds a news conference wherever he thinks a camera crew can be coaxed from its station. He allows ample time for the film to "make" the newscast. He sets aside space for tripods at his public addresses, and alerts the television stations. He makes himself available for interviews, and more available for television interviews. If he can afford it, he hires an advance man and a public relations representative skilled in the requirements of television news.

"I know we're being used," David Brinkley admitted. "I simply decide how to handle the story on the basis of who is using us, and how, and why."

The television newscast has come between the speaker and his audience. Without television, the speaker reaches 500 people or 5,000 people. With television, he may reach 50,000 people in a medium-size city or 500,000 people in a metropolis. If the speech is reported on a television network, the politician's good, earnest face and his stern or honeyed words may enter 50 million homes. Even those who hear him in person, if they see cameras present, are anxious to hear him again on television, perhaps curious to learn what television regarded as important. Certainly what they will hear repeated in the newscast will remain with them longer than anything heard in person. Every television photographer and reporter is accustomed to onlookers coming up to ask, "What station will this be on?" and "When will it be on?"

Curiously, television seems to create its own reality. When Robert Kennedy's body was flown from Los Angeles to New York, reporters waiting at the airport were standing just a few feet away when the coffin passed, yet they had their backs to it, choosing instead to watch the event on a portable television monitor nearby.

It has been observed that in television studios, people often prefer to watch the performers on monitors. Billy Graham claims he gets more converts among closed-circuit TV viewers than among audiences who watch him in person.

The role of mass communications in rhetoric should be studied. Today we have a rhetoric of television. We might even call it a rhetoric of television news.

"Don't let him off the hook."

CBS News editor Ralph Paskman pointed out that all interviews are not necessarily interesting: "All too frequently interviewing somebody in the news is used as the easy way out. We are not covering a story if we get somebody to say on camera what has already been published in the press and broadcast on radio." [8]

If the reporter, having asked a pertinent question, thinks the answer is shallow or evasive, he should not hesitate to bore in. Almost invariably the real news, especially in a tense situation where the interviewee wants to stay tight-lipped, comes on the pressing follow-up questions which make it perfectly clear that the reporter will settle for nothing less than a direct answer or a flat refusal to answer.

In the case of a pertinent question, a refusal to answer sometimes is as revealing as a direct reply. As Ed Arnow, a veteran television reporter, put it, "When the fish has important information, don't let him off the hook."

Individuality

Any reporter, and especially a television reporter, needs to keep his own individuality. When Edward R. Murrow reported for CBS, lesser newsmen tried to imitate his deep voice. When David Brinkley came along a few years later, other reporters copied his pacing. This is wrong. The best newscasters, commentators and reporters ought to serve as guides to a reporter who is developing his own manner, but the reporter who apes them appears merely obvious.

Three Case Studies

Three television news reporters who covered City Hall in the same Midwestern city were accompanied for one week each by Dan Drew, who was doing a research study at Indiana University. [9] These are some of his observations:

Reporter A pictured the journalist's main function as informing audience members about "important things" that take place in the community. He described these as "things that affect the welfare, livelihood, and comfort of members of the community." The newsman thought his audience consisted of white, middle-class homeowners who were deeply "interested in the welfare of the community." Since the reporter was middle-aged and deeply entrenched in the community, his audience appeared to be a reflection of himself...

The reporter seemed to pay little attention to what he thought were the policies of his news organization. He said that his editors were interested in "anything that catches the eye or ear" and complained that much of what went on the air was not news...

Reporter A chose most of the nine stories that he covered during the week of observation. He particularly liked stories that showed the city, its police force, or its officials in a favorable light. Of the stories he covered, six were scheduled events, one resulted from a friend's tip, one was the result of reporter initiative, and one was a story that he saw first in the local newspaper.

City officials were used almost exclusively as sources of information. In fact, the newspaper and criminal court records were the only written sources he checked on a regular basis. Reporter A's typical story consisted of a sound-on-film interview with a city official.

The television newsman was on extremely good terms with his sources. He was friendly, cooperative and positive in his interactions with them. The reporter and officials often discussed personal matters, and he sometimes offered advice or suggestions for dealing with either personal or civic problems.

One of the most noticeable aspects of Reporter A's behavior was his reluctance to broach subjects that he thought sources would not want to discuss. He usually began such conversations by going off the record. When they told him not to use certain information, he carefully obeyed. As a result of this he sometimes got information that the other reporters did not have, but would not use it. The newsman seemed to view events through the same frame of reference that city officials used. He explained that both he and the officials were interested in the "welfare of the city."

The television journalist interacted with radio and newspaper reporters several times each day. They traded bits of information about stories and discussed what they were going to cover later in the day. Reporter A summed his relationship with the other reporters saying, "I give a little and get a little..."

Reporter B said that he felt strong pressure from his superiors to produce as many visually interesting stories as possible each day. This appeared to be the major factor that governed his daily activity. The reporter's search for news was rather random. He started at the top floor of city hall each morning and wandered from office to office asking secretaries, "Any news today?"...

In his interactions with sources, Reporter B was careful to be friendly and cooperative. He was afraid that if he offended them, they would not cooperate, and he would not be able to meet his daily quota of stories. After one particularly frustrating day, he told the observer, "I'm tired of kissing ass to get stories." He was shy about asking questions that he thought the source would not want to answer and went off the record before making such inquiries. At one point, a city official said that someone had offered to make it worth his while to vote the "right way" on a municipal land transaction. The reporter ignored the statement. Afterwards, the observer asked if the official had been talking about a bribe. The reporter said that probably was the case. He did not mention it again...

Of the three reporters studied, Reporter C was least concerned about newsroom policy...Reporter C appeared to be more satisfied with his job than the other subjects...

Reporter C made most of the decisions about what he would cover each day. Of the 11 stories he followed during the week of observation, seven were scheduled events, two developed from conversations with sources, one grew from a tip, and one was picked up after the newspaper printed it. The main information source was the interview with city officials, but he checked more written records than the others. Reporter C looked at such documents as zoning filings and city procurement forms.

In his interactions with sources, Reporter C was less cooperative and more tenacious than the other newsmen. In return, sources were more cooperative with him than they were with the others. Perhaps they either respected him or feared him more. The television newsman did not go off the record when dealing with sensitive issues, but he did try to separate himself from the questions. He would be extremely friendly with the source, then suddenly turn serious and say, "Officially I'm here to..." Sometimes he prefaced his questions with phrases such as, "Some would say..."

About all three television journalists, Drew concluded:

It was quite obvious that the newsmen had little time for digging. Each had to cover the same territory that was handled by two or three reporters for the local newspaper. Also, each interview with a government official involved meeting a photographer, setting up equipment, filming, and editing the finished product.

A lack of knowledge about such specialized topics as law and budgets also limited the reporter's effectiveness. The source sometimes took on the role of educator in order to explain basic facts to the reporter about legal or economic matters. Under these circumstances, it seems highly unlikely that the journalist can do much probing.

Covering a News Conference

The television photographer, or the producer or reporter who advises the film photographer when to start and stop, must pace a news conference. Pacing even matters, although it matters less, with a minicam. What is said here applies mostly to the photographer with a film camera. He knows film runs through his camera at the rate of 36 feet per minute, and that his camera has a 400-foot magazine. Even where the cost of raw film stock is not a problem (as it is on most local stations) the photographer should not simply turn his camera on and let it run out because:

1. Precious minutes are wasted developing, screening and removing unwanted film.

2. The film might run out at the wrong time during the shooting. Of course, there is less chance of getting caught short if the camera carries 1200-foot magazines, but these are seldom used for daily news work.

3. The photographer would have to carry many extra magazines. They are heavy. Loading them with film and hooking them into the camera system are troublesome processes.

4. The cost of raw film stock should never be completely ignored.

5. At a news conference it usually is neither prudent nor practical to keep the camera rolling. It is rarely necessary to use up a 400-foot magazine. Half that amount should be ample. This means selective filming. The reporter who misses a good question and realizes it while the answer is being given should not waste film by instructing the photographer to record the remainder of the answer. Instead, he should wait until the interviewee has finished and then, with camera rolling, he should ask for a clarification or extension of the reply. Likely as not, the reply will be much the same, somewhat paraphrased and often tighter, the interviewee now having had a chance to consider his words.

Sometimes the photographers do not pick up the reporters' questions, especially if the reporters are not from their stations, but they listen to each question, and pick up the answers to those questions which they feel may elicit a valuable response. Sometimes, a reporter signals his photographer that he is about to ask a question, giving the photographer the few seconds notice necessary to flip his switch on and get the camera up to speed. The signal may be a wave of the reporter's hand held discreetly behind his chair. This signal is not always possible at a large news conference, where the reporter may be some distance from his camera, or crammed close to other reporters, so that a hand behind a chair cannot be seen in the confusion. An equally discreet wave of a pencil behind his neck may serve the reporter. But in the turmoil of a crowd of reporters and photographers collaring some news figure in a hallway or at an airport, the reporter and photographer must forget about signals. They are busy enough just keeping their balance, getting some picture and some sound, and squeezing in one or two questions. Here more than anywhere the photographer must have his wits about him and, if the impromptu news conference lasts more than three or four minutes, begin to pay attention to what is said, so he can stop using up film if he feels that something being said has little news value. Once again, experience counts, for it brings, or should bring, judgment.

Editing Problems

A television news reporter should know the technical requirements of his medium.

A windy airport creates an audio problem. So does a "boomy" room with hard walls, no windows or rug, and little furniture. So does a school cafeteria at lunch time. A freeway at night creates a lighting problem. So does a cathedral.

The reporter who doesn't know or doesn't care about these built-in problems is likely to be reminded by the photographer, but not by the film editor, who doesn't go along on the assignment. His complaints may be heard too late to help the story.

More good film has been thrown away for want of a two-second cutaway than for any other reason. If the Secretary of Agriculture made two usable statements in the course of an interview, but had his eyeglasses off for the second statement, the editor who lacks a cutaway must use: (a) roll thru film — not seen on the air — while the newscaster bridges on camera (some newscasters don't like this because the rapid switching sometimes works badly); (b) a roll thru or Academy leader (numbered, 10 seconds long, for roll-thrus lasting more than 10 seconds) or a cut to a card in the studio during the show; (c) double chaining; (d) a jump cut, cutting directly from one statement to the other, leaving the audience wondering what happened to the glasses; or (e) just one of those two statements by the Secretary of Agriculture.

Unfortunately, especially when time for editing is at a minimum, (e) may be the choice, and a good piece of film goes into the trash barrel. Many a harried film editor has spent half an hour searching through his cutting room for just two seconds of usable cutaway film. The thoughtful editor will lay aside a stock of indoor and outdoor cutaway shots, but he won't be prepared for every eventuality. And when he's on deadline, he won't have time to look. This might be considered a photographer's concern rather than a reporter's concern, except that a reporter has charge of the crew. Sometimes, a film editor who asks a photographer why he didn't shoot cutaways on a certain story is told that the reporter was in a hurry to get the next assignment, and did not want to spare the time.

A reporter who forgets to allow three or four seconds between the start of a film camera and his opening question will find his first words lost. The camera needs those seconds to get up to full speed. The loss of words is called an up-cut. The reporter is also likely to get into trouble by beginning his second question before the interviewee finishes his first answer. He jeopardizes both question and previous answer, if the editor finds it necessary to cut at that point. The reporter who wants to have the interviewee terminate a drawn-out answer should learn to give the interviewee some meaningful, silent gesture with hand or eye that signals the start of speech (i.e., that indicates a desire on the part of the reporter to say something). This is not as difficult as it may sound.

To avoid an up-cut in the reporter's question — when the reporter begins to ask the question before the camera is up to speed — the pre-question is used: "Governor, a question about the university...." In the three or four seconds it takes to say this, when stated leisurely, the photographer can flip the "on" switch and the camera can accelerate to full speed.

Reverse Angle Questions

The filmed interview may show the reporter asking questions, a technique which gives the interview perspective, gives the reporter visibility, and gives the film editor cutaways.

For the interview itself the best camera position is behind the reporters' shoulder. The interviewee is seen head-on; the reporter is not seen at all.

Commonly, when the interview ends, the reporter sits still and the photographer moves his camera close to where the interviewee sat. The reporter then repeats his questions. The interviewee need not be present. If he is not, the reporter might be asking the questions of the floor lamp a foot to the right of the camera, because the camera does not pick up what he is looking at. To be sure he asks the same questions, the reporter can carry a small tape recorder. Without this he either consults his notes or jogs his memory. Later, the film editor will intercut questions and answers. The reporter should allow three seconds of silence before and after each question for film editing.

Interviewees who are present when this occurs sometimes get confused and start to answer the questions all over again.

If the interviewee remains and is willing to be a silent prop, the photographer should set up behind the interviewee for the reverse angle questions. Now the reverse angle catches the reporter full face and the interviewee one-quarter face.

The reporter has another reverse angle option besides asking questions. He makes a pre-question statement, such as, "That brings up another point" or "Well, let me ask you this..." The film editor bloops this cutaway statement in front of the question actually asked during the interview.

Let us say that the editor wants to splice two statements made by Mayor Jones. The first, at the start of the interview, concerns the new airport site. The second, at the end of the interview, is a response to the reporter's question, "Will you be looking for new taxes?" With a pre-question statement in hand, the editor can put it together like this:

VIDEO	AUDIO
MS, MAYOR	(statement about airport site)
MS, REPORTER	"Well, let me ask you this…"
MS, MAYOR	(reporter's voice): "Will you be looking for new taxes?"
	(mayor replies)

Lack of Alternatives

In the field, the reporter may get a clear, sudden vision about how the story should be edited. The story will be "edited in the camera." Well and good unless, foolishly, no other footage is shot. For example, the reporter may start with a stand-up intro outside the victim's house. Then he'll invite the camera to come inside for a tour of the room where police found signs of struggle, then to the room where the body was found, then to the room where the knife lay, all bloodied. Unfortunately, the reporter's brainstorm may not look so grand two hours later in the screening room. Often as not, the resultant story is too long. A reporter in the field can never know how the flow of the day's news affects the time which can be devoted to his story. If he has constructed an elaborate visual story whose parts are so interwoven that none will stand alone, then the whole story may be junked, or it may be butchered beyond recognition in a desperate effort on the editor's part to salvage something from three hours of work by a reporter and photographer. These worthies, after viewing the wreckage on the tube, will mutter furiously about the clods who call themselves editors.

The solution: give the editor as much flexibility as possible.

The reporter will also be asking for butchery of his footage if he doesn't allow enough time to have the tape or film brought to the station, developed (if film), screened, edited, scripted and put into sequence with other films for the projectionist. All the reporter's care and preparation is wasted if he doesn't give his co-workers back at the station enough time to do their work well, too. The difference between a story being used or not being used, or between a story being well cut or being hastily chopped up, frequently has a direct correlation with the story being tightly conceived and edited in the field, with the addition of shots necessary to give the editor flexibility.

Add a Dash of Humility

Finally, the reporter should retain a sense of humility, of proportion, of his role in the news situation. He is a medium through which news is clarified and imparted. Nothing more. Bill Beutel, newscaster for WABC-TV, New York, stated:

> I think there's a very great danger on the part of television reporters to become drugged by their own power, so drugged that they find themselves developing a mystique — a mystique about television reporting that even they believe. This eventually ends with attempting not only to report but to control what goes on in a precinct station or a city hall. When

we near the point where all of us carry that mystique around in our breast pockets — I think the time then comes for re-evaluation.[10]

The reporter should remember that he is, after all, just one link in the chain that begins at the scene of an accident or a news conference and ends in a viewer's living room. Reporters and all other on-air personnel have been pinned with the designation "talent," a relic from early broadcasting days. No connection exists between "talent" and talent. Some "talent" are talented, just as some non-"talent" personnel are.

The reporter is the representative of the public at a newsworthy event. He is their ears, their eyes and sometimes their conscience. His primary responsibility is to the public. His questions are asked on their behalf. If he ever represents a conflicting interest, he betrays his proper role. There are degrees of betrayal, from the favor to a public relations rep of a free plug to an attempt to shape attitudes toward a candidate for public office because of the reporter's personal views, to doing a thing because "there's something in it for me." A television journalist cannot excuse himself because his ethical lapse is small. A little betrayal of the public trust is, to quote an old joke, like being "just a little bit pregnant." The betrayals are sure to grow bigger.

The reporter's job is demanding, but rewarding. It is the most varied and exciting job in the television news department. Except for the jobs of news director and newscaster, it is the most desirable job on most stations, and one to which a student can aspire soon after graduation, especially at smaller stations.

For the Student

1. Assume that the Secretary of State will hold a news conference in town tomorrow morning. Prepare some questions, based on current news.

2. The new Miss America arrived in town and has scheduled a news conference for tomorrow morning. Prepare some questions.

3. Interview a public official or a professor who has been interviewed by a television reporter. What did he or she think of the interview? Where could it have been improved? Was the reporter well enough informed about the topic?

4. Interview another student on videotape or audiotape. A job last summer, a hobby or some other first-hand experience can be the topic. Prepare some questions in advance and, if possible, bone up on the subject before the interview.

5. Tag along with a television reporter for one day. Report to class.

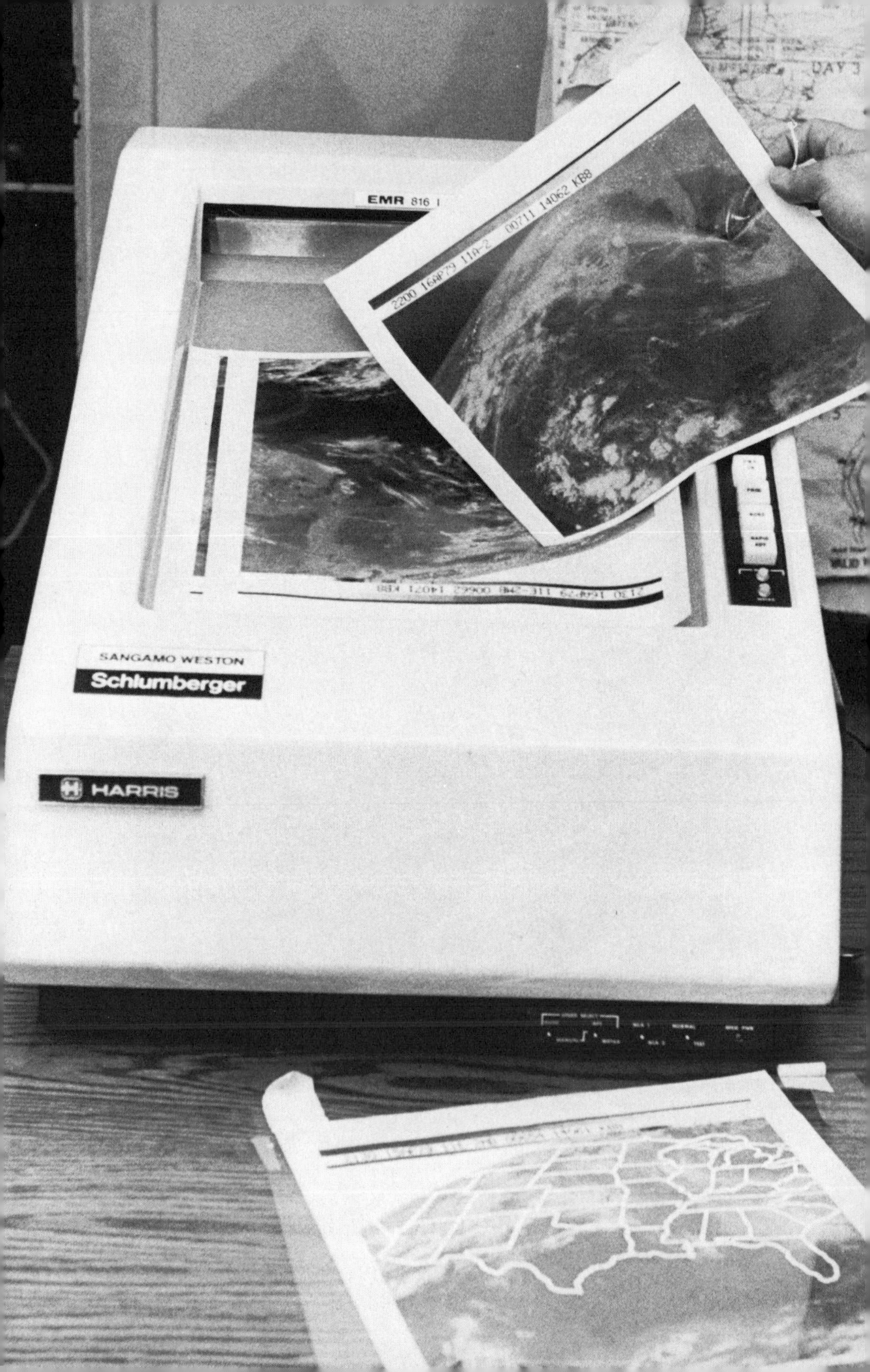
EMR 816 I
2200 16AP79 11A-2 00711 14062 KB8
SANGAMO WESTON
Schlumberger
HARRIS

A Television News Day

8

I never go home totally satisfied.

— *Walter Cronkite*

It is seven o'clock on a weekday morning. The dayside assignment editor at a medium-size city television station arrives at work. Let us consider him and his co-workers, for they are fairly typical of local television news staffs of comparable size everywhere. Even where news staffs are much smaller, most of the same tasks are performed, although on a reduced scale, by employees with combined job functions.

The dayside assignment editor of our typical news staff walks into the newsroom and goes straight to the bank of teletypes, even before he hangs up his coat. In a few seconds, he scans the last 30 minutes of copy transmitted by the AP, UPI and the local news wire (if his city has one). Seeing nothing that will require the immediate alerting of photographers, he hangs up his coat, plugs in the coffee pot, flips the weather machines to "on," and begins his day. For the rest of the day either he or the nightside assignment editor will either rip or glance at the "wires" (all the teletype wires) roughly every 15 minutes. As air time nears, the trips to the teletypes will be increased to every five minutes; this frequency will be maintained until the newscast is done. Throughout the day other staff members will look at the wires, out of professional and personal interest and the knowledge that when a major news story breaks, they will probably learn of it first by teletype.

The Bulletin

The dayside assignment editor is not the first person on duty at the station. At least one engineer begins work before the station goes on the air. An early morning announcer reports in soon after. If the assignment editor sees a bulletin on the teletype which he feels should be broadcast as a bulletin (the ratio of broadcast bulletins to teletype bulletins may be one in a hundred), he will direct the engineer to cover whatever program is being broadcast by a bulletin slide and he will give the announcer bulletin copy to read. A news editor has the authority to interrupt programming at any time with a bulletin. As a rule he will not interrupt a station break or commercial with a bulletin which is not of overriding importance. Of course, when a bulletin is of major importance — the kind which once would have been called a "flash" — anything on the air is interrupted; in the event of a war or the death of a president regular programming does not resume after the news is announced; instead, the available fragments of news are repeated and amplified as new information appears until such time as the network takes over or the local staff can organize its reportage.

A bulletin may read as follows:

HERE IS A BULLETIN FROM THE KLMN NEWSROOM: AUTO WORKERS HAVE GONE ON STRIKE ACROSS THE COUNTRY. 154 THOUSAND WORKERS AT 62 PLANTS ARE IMMEDIATELY AFFECTED. STAY TUNED TO KLMN FOR FURTHER DETAILS.

Brief introductory and tag lines sandwich the bulletin, in order to put the news announcement into the context of the programming situation. The facts are kept to a minimum, and the bulletin is very short, for it is meant only to declare that an event has taken place. Details of that event are reserved for the regular newscast or for a special news program.

Sometimes the significant fact of a bulletin is repeated. For example:

WE INTERRUPT THIS PROGRAM FOR A NEWS BULLETIN: RURITANIA HAS DECLARED WAR ON CARPATHIA. RURITANIAN BOMBERS STRUCK DEEP IN CARPATHIAN TERRITORY, HITTING AIRFIELDS AND RAILROAD DEPOTS. RURITANIAN TROOPS CROSSED THE FRONTIER AT THREE POINTS. TO REPEAT: RURITANIA HAS GONE TO WAR AGAINST CARPATHIA. KLMN WILL BULLETIN MORE DETAILS THROUGHOUT THE DAY.

News may be worth bulletin treatment, but not immediate program interruption. The seasoned news editor asks himself how important it is to viewers to learn this news at this moment, before he commands the television equivalent of "Stop the presses!" He also asks himself if a bulletin reporting a tragedy should be inserted into a comedy program, when the bulletin will be followed by a return to comedy.

Daily Assignments

If the dayside assignment editor has found nothing on the wire requiring his immediate attention, he begins to plan the day's camera schedule for three photographers. One photographer has a sound film camera, one has an ENG camera, and the third not only has an ENG camera but also travels in a remote van with live transmission capability. Each of the three also routinely carries one of the station's old silent cameras in his car. From a box containing 31 consecutively numbered "future" folders, one for each day of the month (after a date has passed, that folder is used to accumulate assignments for the same date of the following month) the editor takes the folder for the present day. In the folder he finds six items:

1. A letter from a viewer discussing a neighborhood problem. Along the margin, the nightside assignment editor has penciled an address and a time, 10 a.m.

2. A handout from a local department store announcing groundbreaking ceremonies at noon for a new store.

3. A typewritten note from the news director, setting up an interview with the author of a best seller at 9 a.m.

4. A wire advisory of a noon news conference for an important out-of-state senator.

5. A wire feature story about plans for a local shopping center financed by a black group dedicated to self-help business enterprise. Undated.

6. A newspaper clipping about an all-day conference on air pollution.

The three photographers are assigned to begin at 8 a.m., 10 a.m., and 2 p.m. Based solely on this future folder, the assignment editor makes this tentative schedule:

	CREW 1 (FILM)	CREW 2 (ENG)	CREW 3 (ENG, VAN)
9 a.m.	author		
10 a.m.		neighborhood	
noon	senator	new store	
1 p.m.	lunch		
2 p.m.	air pollution	lunch	
3 p.m.			shopping center

Any schedule requires some assurance that persons to be interviewed will be ready when the crews arrive. In this schedule, meetings with the author and the neighborhood spokesmen had already been set up. The senator and the store dedication had established their own times. The air pollution conference could be done at any time, although it would be necessary to call ahead if some particular spokesman was wanted for an interview. Only the black shopping center story has to be arranged. However, today's wire file has not yet been read.

The assignment editor rips all the wires. His practiced eye runs down each item, searching for several kinds of stories:

a. A story which should be covered today.

b. A feature story, which can be filmed any time.

c. A future news assignment.

d. An out-of-town, national or international story with a local angle.

e. A story which should be presented with still photos, maps or drawings.

f. A backgrounder or some other story which should be called to some staff member's attention. The editor will send it along with the letters "FYI" (For Your Information) scribbled on top.

g. Out-of-town stories for which tape or film might have been shot — or yet might be shot — by another television station or a free lancer.

h. Hard news: major news stories which can be reported as is. As the day wears on, almost every major story will have been updated several times.

i. A cute "brite."

j. Specialized items of interest to the sports editor and the weather reporter.

As the assignment editor scans the wires, the first news team, a reporter and a photographer, arrive to start their day. (In very large cities, the photographer will be assisted by a sound technician. At small town television stations, the reporter does it all.)

The reporter is given the note from the news director. Fortunately, she has made a practice of thumbing through the future folders, and knew that she would be assigned to interview the author. The reporter has already spent an hour in the public library leafing through the author's latest book, a critical review, and a reference work on the topic covered by the author. This interview promises to be an enlightening and intelligent one, with some wry humor and some sparks flying.

After the first crew leaves, the assignment editor completes his reading of the wire. He adds two more assignments to the six tentatively made:

7. A midnight high-speed car chase after a robbery suspect. Interviews with police and film of suspect.

8. A beautiful starlet in court to seek a divorce. 10 a.m.

The day shift dispatcher arrives and turns on the special band radios tuned to police and fire calls, plus the bandwidths reserved for the highway patrol, the sheriff's department and all other radio frequencies which carry the first reports of emergencies. He also monitors the frequencies on which the other television news departments in the city communicate with their camera crews. In front of the dispatcher sits a microphone to communicate with his station's reporters and photographers. He knows, of course, that other dispatchers might be listening in. In the electronic age, the old fashioned news scoop is harder to come by.

The assignment editor tells the dispatcher to call crew 1 on the mobile radio and wrap up the author story quickly in order to get to court for the starlet. If he cannot reach the crew by radio, the assignment editor will phone the author at his hotel to request that the crew call in when they arrive. If the story is that special event, an important news beat ("scoop" is an old fashioned term, replaced by the confusing word "beat," which has two meanings in news coverage), the assignment editor will not inform the crew by radio for fear of alerting the opposition. Instead he will tell the crew, via mobile car radio, to get to the nearest phone booth and call him back by "land line."

The editor, realizing the crew may be late to the courthouse, also calls a bailiff he has befriended at the courthouse to ask him to inform the starlet that a news crew is on the way, if she will only be patient. Starlets being starlets, she will wait. The car chase story arrangements must also wait. It is a weak story to begin with, and by the 6 p.m. newscast, it will be 18 hours old. The assignment editor notes it as marginal, to be covered only if nothing else develops.

Later in the morning, something unexpected does turn up. A freelance photographer brings in film he shot of the conculsion of the chase and the capture of the suspected robber. The film is sent to the lab. If a writer judges the quality to be good, the later interviews will definitely be scheduled.

The editor phones the neighborhood problem spokesperson to say the photographer and reporter will be almost 30 minutes late. Please be patient. His phone call not only keeps the people there, it is good public relations.

At 10 a.m., a second photographer and reporter arrive. Reporters and photographers often work together, but not always. Some stories may not need reporters; for example, the filming of an art exhibit, a parade, or a circus performance. Photographers are sometimes assigned to non-news tasks such as taping segments of a documentary. On the other hand, reporters may be sent where photographers are not needed (e.g., to search records) or not allowed (e.g., at a trial). Also, photographers necessarily move from story to story more slowly than reporters do. A reporter may be assigned to work with different photographers during the day, either to cover more stories or because he has particular knowledge in a certain subject area. And if a reporter edits his own field reports into story packages, he may have to leave his crew in mid-afternoon. Sometimes the reporter travels in his own car; sometimes he travels with the crew, and takes taxis if he has to break away. When he covers his beats he works by himself.

The second reporter and photographer are quickly briefed about their assignments and sent on their way. Stories of neighborhood problems, such as a demand for a traffic light or objection to a zoning decision, usually require no advance study by the reporter. Sympathetic questioning by a skilled reporter plus intelligent camera work at the scene of the problem usually produce a good story. If both sides to the dispute can be brought in front of the camera, the story is even better, especially when a writer can later intercut the arguments to produce short and punchy statements by each party in turn. Very rarely, a camera is witness to a heated discussion by both sides present at the same time, perhaps brought together by the reporter. One or both parties may grow quite angry at the television reporter off camera. On the other hand, the camera may record an absolutely fascinating argument, either with the reporter or, more properly, between the antagonists. If a tape editor intercuts statements by opposing parties who did not actually confront one another, the newscaster must be careful to point out that a face-to-face debate did not take place, and that the tape was edited this way so that points of view on the same subject could be presented together.

The Day

The first writer to arrive spends his first 30 minutes scanning the day's shooting schedule, the morning wire copy and the newspapers to which the newsroom subscribes. He keeps up with the news events on all levels from local to international for several reasons:

1. He may be called upon to look at film or tape concerned with this news event or a subsequent event related to it.

2. The news event may be mentioned by someone whose words he must edit.

3. He may find in the news event something worth following up. Here, his purpose duplicates that of the assignment editor. It is a useful redundancy. The more staff members who read news extensively, the more depth of coverage the newscasts are likely to have.

4. He may write a non-visual story, an editorial or humorous essay based on a news event.

5. He may refer, in passing, to a news event in his copy or another story.

About 11:30 a.m., the assignment editor receives three phone calls. Crew 1 calls in to say they have finished the starlet story and are now heading for the senator. Crew 2 calls in to say they have finished the neighborhood story and are heading for the groundbreaking ceremonies at the side of the new department store. The assignment editor decides to dispatch a messenger to the senator's news conference to meet Crew 1 and get the film of the author and the starlet, when the dispatcher reports a fire out of control at a paper box factory located just down the street from a paint factory.

The editor immediately contacts each crew by car radio. Their orders are to head directly to the fire, ignoring their next assignments. As the assignment editor speaks to them, he is looking at a large city map over his desk. He learns where each crew is, locates the place on the map and mentally traces two lines to the fire scene. Somewhere along each line he finds a major intersection to use as an intercept point for tape and film pickups. The crews may remain at the scene of the fire for two hours. Between them, they have three stories. He cannot afford to wait until the crews have finished the fire story to get those stories "into the house." Therefore, he tells each crew to drop what they have already shot at an intersection he has selected, and to call him back to let him know at what gasoline filling station or what store they have deposited the tape and film. He and the crews know from experience that filling station attendants and storekeepers are more than obliging in this regard. They tend to become keenly interested in what is going on. They get caught up in the excitement of the news, and they make sure to watch that night's newscast, pleased that they have played a part in making it possible.

A messenger is dispatched to one of the intersections. When he arrives he will telephone back to the office. By that time, the assignment editor should have been given a precise location by each crew. Because he does not wait to hear from a crew before he leaves, the messenger may advance by 30 minutes or even an hour (depending on how far those intersections lie from the station) the time that those three films are available for screening and editing. Back at the office the assignment editor is wishing the station manager would consider buying a jet helicopter capable of sending live pictures from its own camera and relaying live pictures from a photographer on the ground.

The news conference for the senator is now lost for the station. As for the store dedication, there is still a chance that the store itself will have commissioned a commercial photographer to film the event, in which case a print of the film can be given to the station without charge. The editor pulls the original handout from his future file, notes the phone number of the public relations firm which mailed the handout, and telephones. He learns that film is being shot and, yes, it is 16mm color film. However, the commercial photo lab usually used to develop this agency's film could not have it ready before tomorrow. The lab is not geared for the exigencies of news. The assignment editor is tempted to give this story up also, since it is of marginal value at best. However, this experienced journalist discovered long ago that it pays to make an extra effort to get a visual story. It is not up to him to determine by telephone the value of a piece of film not yet shot. A writer has that responsibility, after he sees the film. If the story is worth assigning at all, it is worth trying to get, so long as the getting does not become too expensive and it does not interfere with the getting of better stories. So the assignment editor gives it one last try. He tells the public relations agency man that the station's news lab will develop the film free of charge. A writer will screen it. If it is worth using, the film editor will cut it, then restore it after the newscast. Only a few frames will be lost in the splices, and the film will be essentially in its original condition. If it is not worth using, the agency will get it uncut. With virtually nothing to lose by this arrangement and a chance to get his client's film on a newscast, the agency rep readily agrees.

Both duty crews are now occupied at the fire. The assignment editor telephones the photographer and engineer of the remote van crew and asks them to come in as soon as they can. A call to the home of the third reporter gets no response, so the assignment editor calls Crew 2 by mobile phone and tells the reporter to take a taxi to the air pollution conference, line up a story and wait for Crew 3. The Crew 1 reporter will handle the entire fire story. Crew 3 will tape the shopping center story, then microwave it back to the station.

At noon, the assignment editor's news line-up looks like this:

		CREW 1	CREW 2	CREW 3
In house:	robbery suspect (stringer)			
Completed:	author			
	starlet			
	neighborhood			
noon		fire	fire	
1 p.m.				air pollution
2 p.m.		lunch	lunch	
3 p.m.				shopping center

The News Director

The news director makes his own schedule and keeps it flexible. At 10 a.m. he arrives at the station for a management conference on the news budget. Unlike some television news departments run on a shoestring and producing lackluster newscasts which do little but keep the Federal Communications Commission at a safe distance, his news department makes a lot of money for his station. The twice daily newscasts are interesting and informative. Their audiences represent a large slice of all viewers in the city, and the viewers tend to be faithful. Watching one or both newscasts is as much a part of their day as eating supper. Local advertisers request time within or adjacent to the newscasts, and some segments are sponsored. Station management, aware that it takes money to make money, plows much of the profit back into the news department in salaries, equipment and a budget to cover purchases of film, artwork, rental of helicopters and other costs to improve the newscasts.

At noon the news director goes into the newsroom. As he looks over the line-up of stories, the assignment editor describes the fire story. The fire is still out of control and has spread to the building adjoining the paint factory. Everyone in a three-block radius is being evacuated, and engine companies throughout the city are converging on the area.

The story is assuming major proportions, and the news director elects to exploit its possibilities. The assignment editor phones a helicopter service at the airport and hires a "chopper" and a pilot to fly to an empty field a mile from the fire. He is told to wait for a photographer. At the same time, the assignment editor tries to reach either crew by car radio. He gets no response, as he expected, because both crews are away from their cars, filming the fire. He orders the newsroom dispatcher to keep trying. When a crew member finally returns the call, the assignment editor orders a photographer to meet the helicopter. Only a photographer will go aloft.

The Producer

At some television stations a member of the news staff, perhaps the news director, a writer or the assignment editor doubles as a producer. The producer is responsible for the content and production of a particular newscast. In some news operations there is no producer as such; several staff members share the work and the responsibility for the content of the newscast.

The producer confers with the assignment editor about the day's film and tape stories. As he listens he mentally begins to block out the 6 p.m. newscast.

The Writer

Now the early writer returns from the screening of the car chase film. He reports that the film is excellent, as far as it goes. He recommends sending a crew to the police station to seek statements from the suspect, a detective and, if possible, one of the officers who made the arrest. Learning that no crew is immediately available, the writer calls the detective handling the case in order to get the story and to learn when the arresting officers will begin their duty shift.

The writer then calls the art department of the television station. That department is separate from the news department. The artists print and draw cards for commercials, for the morning children's show, and for every other locally produced program. The writer wants the art department to produce three line drawings showing the chase at various stages. He intends to tell the story "over" cards until it reaches the point where the film begins, instead of trying to cram both the beginning of the story and its conclusion behind the film of the conclusion of the chase. If a camera crew can be freed, he will round off the story with interviews.

With the cards ordered and the later film pending, the writer decides to delay writing the story. Instead, he and an editor view the morning tapes and films: the author, the starlet and the neighborhood problem.

The author has sent along a copy of his latest book. The writer removes its jacket, which will be mounted on a card to be placed on a rack in front of the television camera. At the moment in the filmed interview when the book is mentioned, the director will order a four-second dissolve from film to card, so the viewers may see the jacket. The writer also orders a "super" of the author's name to be stored in the news department's electronic titling machine, the character generator. The name will appear on the air over film or tape at the touch of a button on the technical director's console. Also stored will be the names of reporters doing standuppers that day, plus weather forecast highs and lows, ball scores, the Dow Jones Industrial Average, and the "bumpers," the supered line preceding the commercial which says: STILL TO COME: CITY COUNCIL VOTES.

From the 200 feet of film shot of the interview, which rolls through a projector at the rate of 36 feet per minute, the writer chooses four silent segments totaling

12 seconds for a lead-in to the sound interview, and one minute 15 seconds of sound. His script will have copy to cover the opening 12 seconds, and will indicate to the director when the super and the book jacket are to appear. He will give the times of the various segments and an end cue, so that the director will be able to cut on the closing word. It is his news department's policy to time the super and other internal cues from the start of the SOF. Other news departments prefer to time their cue from the start of the film, so that the super cue, below, would be at 30 seconds into the film (adding 12 seconds of silent film to the 18 seconds of SOF before the super is taken).

author/6   p.m./march   20/runs   1:27

:12 SIL

> William Johnson has written one of the most controversial books of the year, "A Spy in the Department of Commerce." Since its publication, he has been in constant battle with critics. He is here to visit relatives...and talked with Sue Miller.

1:15 MAG

> SOF

AT :18 SUPER: WILLIAM JOHNSON

AT :30, DISSOLVE TO BOOK JACKET FOR 4 SECS.

AT 1:00, AGAIN SUPER: WILLIAM JOHNSON

> ENDS: "...expression will prevail."

The starlet proves to be quite dull. She was only willing to plug her next picture, and would say nothing about the divorce or anything else. However, the photographer, using his sound camera to get natural sound of court corridors and her heels tapping on the marble floors, caught the starlet walking into and out of the courtroom, toward him and away from him, and chatting with her lawyer. From these scenes, the writer constructs a 30-second film story. He ignores the interview.

The neighborhood problem is a demand by residents that a school crossing guard be placed at what they consider a dangerous intersection. When requests to the city and the school district failed to get action, the residents turned to television and newspapers. The television reporter asked the group of neighbors who had assembled in their spokesperson's living room to accompany him to the intersection. There, with the traffic in the background, he interviewed the spokesperson at some length, then took short statements from as many of the other residents as he could coax to speak up. The photographer took establishing shots of the neighborhood, the school and the crossing from several angles. He caught children crossing the street. To further illustrate the story, the writer asks the art department to draw a "pull-tab" map which shows the busy street, the intersection, the school on one side and the houses on the other. A tab is built into the map, with the end of the tab jutting slightly outside the card. The card will be placed on a rack during the newscast and a television camera will focus on it. At a signal, a stagehand will slowly pull the tab out, exposing a line of contrasting color beneath it, showing the path children take from home to school. On the television screen, it will look very effective, establishing the perspective clearly.

At 3 p.m., the nighttime news producer, a writer, an ENG and film editor, and the nightside assignment editor report to work. The fire is under control and all the fire footage is "in the house." Reporters and photographers have finished their lunch breaks. Crew 3 is out on its assignments. Crew 2 is dispatched to the police station after the assignment editor phones ahead to set up the interviews. The Crew 1 photographer is given time to check equipment before going home for the day. News cameras and sound gear get rough handling, yet they are precision built to respond to differing light and sound conditions, so they need attention and frequent maintenance to guard against failure at crucial moments. The Crew 1 reporter returns to the station to help put the fire story package together and, when that is done, to poke through the future folders so that she can try to prepare herself for tomorrow's scheduled assignments and to learn what lies further ahead. (She dreams of becoming a network correspondent, and she knows she won't make it by handing in pedestrian interviews.)

The nightside editor and the writer are assigned to the fire story. The complex film and tape story will be transferred to a single VTR (videotape recording) tape during a pre-newscast taping session, cutting down chances of technical error on the air.

The nightside producer goes to a television monitor to catch a special network videotape feed of international, national and sports stories available for local affiliate newscasts. Most of these stories were done in hopes of a place on the network evening newscast but, for one reason or another, didn't make it. However, they are good news stories, which will be seen by the public on local newscasts, usually as part of the early evening newscast, about 6 p.m. The nighttime newscast, about 10 p.m., will include taped excerpts from the evening network newscast itself.

From some 15 available clips in the videotaped special service, the writer may choose four. He will edit them as necessary. He directs the videotape engineer to dub the clips he wants onto a separate reel in the order he requests, with cue marks in between. He will prepare a script for each videotape clip, so that the director will have timing marks and end cues.

The nightside assignment editor will take over duties from the dayside editor in the space of half an hour. The transfer of responsibility and information must be smooth and complete. If not, the nightside editor may not do what the dayside editor promised would be done: important phone calls will not be made; phone calls that are received will not be understood (e.g., "Say, anybody know why Detective Joe Green was supposed to call us?"); and news stories will not be assigned as they should be.

Building the Newscast

As the afternoon hours pass, a pile of individual story scripts grows on the desk of the producer of the early evening newscast. At 4 p.m. he begins to build the newscast from wire copy, film scripts, videotape scripts and local copy. The nighttime newscast producer who monitored the network feed also rewrites news stories from the wire copy. He chooses the major stories of the day, selects the latest information available and summarizes it briefly, writing in broadcast style. He will continue to watch the wires closely until both the local and network newscasts have been completed. The network newscast may be received from New York one to three hours before it is played back (depending on national time zones). If late news contradicts what has been taped already, or if a bulletin of overriding importance appears on the teletype, the writer will write a script to cover a portion of the taped network newscast with a slide, or with a local newscaster, live, to report it. Besides rewriting wire stories for the local newscast, the writer also chooses a half dozen wire copy stories which he doesn't bother to rewrite. He simply staples the copy to sheets of paper and writes the word "PAD" at the top of each sheet. If the newscaster runs out of copy before the end of the program, he will have these additional items to read.

The producer lists the elements of the evening newscast:

	SLUG	TIME
COPY ONLY	sniper update	:30
	President	:30
	drug hearing	:30
	China	:30
	tax cut	:30
	court ruling	:30
	stocks	:15
	elephant brite	:15
VISUAL	fire	3:00(?)
	robbery chase	2:00
	author	1:30
	starlet	:30
	neighborhood	2:30
	groundbreaking	:45
	shopping center	1:30
	air pollution	2:00
	sniper	1:30
	floods	1:15
	Israeli army	1:00
	Arizona killer	1:30

The total time, as tentatively outlined, is 23 minutes 15 seconds. The 30-minute newscast, of course, does not permit airing 30 minutes of news. Its format includes an opening one-minute commercial, four one-minute commercial periods within the program, a 20-second opening, a 20-second closing and 20 seconds at the end for a "promo" (a promotional commercial for a later television program) and a station break, leaving 24 minutes for the news.

However, five minutes each day is allotted to sports and three minutes to weather news. A sports reporter and a sports writer have been working independently of the main news operation, assembling the items for their segment. They add two tapes to the reels being built by the editors. One clip is of a night baseball game shot the previous evening by Crew 3. The other clip is of an afternoon horse race at the local track, taped by the track and supplied free. For the sports reporter, the race is legitimate news. For the race track, it is inexpensive advertising, and the managers are happy to rush the film to the station each day of the racing season.

Subtracting eight minutes from 24 leaves the news director with 16 minutes of time available for 23:15 of film, tape and copy. The producer now has a chore he must cope with each day: what to cut. He always has more news available to him than he can use. If he did not have more, he would worry, for he would sense a weakness in the overall quality of the newscast material. He would also worry if too much had to be trimmed away, because that would mean a lot of effort and expense was going to waste. Ideally, he wants to trim the script to 15:45, with 15 seconds for leads into commercials. But first he assembles his individual scripts for each story into a newscast script within the framework of the format. Where an individual script is not yet available — for example, the fire script will not be complete for another hour — he simply writes the slug (e.g., "fire") on a sheet of paper and inserts it into his arrangement. In a few minutes, the rundown looks like this:

:20	OPEN
3:00	VTR:fire
1:00	COMMERCIAL
:30	sniper
1:30	VTR:sniper
:30	China
1:15	VTR:floods
:30	President
2:00	VTR: air pollution
:30	drug hearing

1:00	COMMERCIAL
1:00	VTR:Israeli army
:30	court ruling
1:30	VTR:shopping center
:30	tax cut
:15	stocks
1:30	FILM:author
1:30	VTR:Arizona killer
2:00	FILM:robbery chase
:30	FILM:starlet
1:00	COMMERCIAL
3:00	weather
1:00	COMMERCIAL
5:00	SPORTS:1.baseball
	2.racing
1:00	COMMERCIAL
:45	FILM:groundbreaking
2:30	VTR:neighborhood
:15	elephant bright
:20	CLOSE

The producer now has his script. It is, however, 7:00 too long. Many of the times are approximate. Taking out a stopwatch and reading at the pace he knows the newscaster uses, the news director reads the rewritten wire stories, all of which are marked, arbitrarily, as segments of 30 seconds. As he reads, he edits out a phrase here and a sentence there, finishing with a saving of 45 seconds. He knows the three minutes alloted to the fire story is also approximate. He may be able to trim this story, but he does not want to cut anything out that would hurt a major local story, his lead story of the day, one which the news staff covered in depth. He goes to the editing room, where the writer and film editor are now piecing together on paper what they have just seen. The producer asks about the quality of the story and its length. The writer praises the photography and asks the producer how "tight" the newscast is. When he is told, the writer asks for 2½ minutes. The producer returns to his line-up, orders a story here killed, a story there trimmed, and soon the newscast is the right length.

The Director

It is now 4:30 p.m. The newscaster and the director arrive. Each page of the script has been typed in quintuplicate. The producer sorts the pages into five separate scripts, slipping in "slug" sheets where pages are still missing. The top copy goes to the newscaster, the second copy to the director, who circles a word five seconds ahead of each film and videotape. When the newscaster reads that word, the director will order "Roll film" or "Roll tape," knowing that each film clip and each tape story will be physically halted in their machines precisely five seconds of rolling time ahead of the first frame of film or the first videotape picture that is wanted. The director also calculates which of three television studio cameras he will focus on the newscaster each time he appears, which camera on the sports reporter (and, if the newscast used stills mounted on cards, which camera on each card on the two easels in the studio; additionally, he decides which cards go on which easels).

The newsroom set in the studio is fixed. It does not change from day to day. It is never "struck" unless it is redesigned. The set is pre-lit; that is, once the director has arranged the lights, no changes are made in lighting so long as there are no complaints and no changes are made in the set; the single exception is the occasional need to light a prop used to illustrate a story.

The third copy of the script goes to the producer. During rehearsal he will time each story and keep a running time as well, marking these times on the pages of his copy. The fourth copy will go to the audio engineer. Although the audio engineer gets instructions from the director, his copy of the script enables him to cut away from film and tape exactly at the final word of the end cue, so that the studio sound comes crisp and clear, with no unwanted words going over the air or "upcuts" (the loss of words because the sound was brought in a second or two too late). The final copy goes to a TelePrompTer typist, who reproduces the script in large letters on a roll which will fit into a device above a television camera lens, or superimposed in front of the lens to improve eye contact. (Another system, Q-TV VideoPrompter blows up normal size type.) As the newscaster reads, someone will electrically roll this script to keep pace. To the viewer at home, the newscaster seems to be looking right at him, telling him the news. Actually, he is reading. Sometimes, he uses the script in his hand as a prop. Other times, he reads each in turn. That final copy will end up in the producer's hands, and later in the files. On smaller stations there is no Tele-Prompter. In fact, there may be only two or three script copies.

As a rule, except on some smaller stations, the director and other studio personnel are not journalists. They consider a newscast a "show" which is handled much like any locally produced show, except that they get the script very late, feed it live and occasionally accommodate changes while the program is on the air. Otherwise, to them it is just another show using two or three cameras, one or two film chains, videotape, slides, etc. It uses a set which must be lit, and it begins and ends at specified times, with breaks for commercials. Their concern is not with content, but with format. An hour earlier their concern was with Jumbo the Clown and 20 squealing children in the audience. An hour later, they will be concerned with commercials and station breaks during the run of a movie or of network programming. At the network level and at larger stations, directors assigned to news usually do nothing else.

Control Room and Studio

As air time nears, everyone connected with the air production of the program (as distinct from news assembly) gathers in the studio and the adjoining control room. More distant rooms, such as master control, projection and videotape are already staffed. The reels which the film editor has built of the individual stories, based on an order list from the producer, are taken to the projection room and mounted on sound projectors, videotape reels are cued up in the videotape room.

In the control room are the director, the newscast producer and the technical director, who is seated before a panel of buttons and levers called a switcher. Built into the wall in front of them is a bank of television monitors showing what each studio camera sees, what each projector sends, what the videotape room sends, what the control room is sending out and what the television station is beaming. During the rehearsal, if there is one, and the newscast several monitors show the same picture. For example, when the newscaster begins the program, his or her face will appear on a camera monitor, the studio monitor

---

SIMPLIFIED JOB CHART

News Director — Oversees entire news operation and administration, often including documentaries and editorials.

News Producer — Responsible for a single newscast each day.

Newscaster (or *Anchor*) — Reads news on air, introduces film reports and reporters in studio.

Reporter — Reports news stories from the field, either appearing in the visual report or doing a voice-over. May occasionally report from the studio.

Writer — Writes copy, makes video editing decisions.

Editor — Does the hands-on tape and film editing. Shares the editing decisions.

Assignment Editor — Assigns reporters and photographers to news stories.

Director — Has charge of actual presentation of newscast, including studio cameras, film and videotape projection.

and the "air" monitor. During rehearsal, a film may appear on one film-chain monitor and the studio monitor. While one camera monitor shows the newscaster waiting, another is focused on a still photo. The tape monitors and the second film-chain monitor may be blank and the "air" monitor has Jumbo the Clown or an old movie.

In one corner, or in a room adjoining the control room (or "control booth"), is the audio control booth, perhaps with a plate glass wall enabling the audio engineer to see the director and the monitors while shutting out all unwanted sound.

In another room is a booth announcer. He introduces the newscast and the newscaster, gives station breaks, reads "promos" for the later programs, reads some commercial copy and some public service spots, and introduces the next program. The only equipment in his soundproof room is a microphone and a television monitor, except for his headset, consisting of earphones and a tiny microphone, which can be shoved aside. Everyone in the control room has a similar headset, and so do the floor director and each camera operator in the studio. The projectionist and the videotape engineer have either headsets or a two-way speaker system to complete the informational hookup under the control of the director. Sometimes, especially in live coverage of major news, the newscaster will wear an earpiece, called an IFB (Interrupted FeedBack), through which the producer gives him instructions and advises him of upcoming films and switches. (On many stations, the booth announcer has been replaced by an audio cart.)

In the studio proper are the television camera operators (not to be confused with the film and tape photographers or "cameramen" who go into the field to record news stories), a "boom mike" man responsible for all the studio microphones, the fellow who operates the TelePrompTer, an electrician responsible for lighting (he doubles as a cable man, whose responsibility it is that the camera cables trailing along the floor don't snag, which would cause the camera to jerk), a floor director who is both a sub-director and the person who cues the newscaster, and, of course, the newscaster plus others who will appear in the newscast, such as the sports reporter, a news reporter, a feature reporter, the weathercaster or a guest.

Rehearsal

Most local newscasts are not rehearsed. They look it.

A rehearsal brings together for the first time all the elements of the newscast. The headlines or the "tease" film or statement which may precede the newscast gives the audio engineer a chance to adjust his "pots" to get the sound level he wants. He also balances the announcer's mike level during the "open." More importantly, for the first time, the written copy for each story is read against the edited film and videotape. The newscaster paces himself and may edit some more words so that copy matches pictures. If something escaped the eyes of

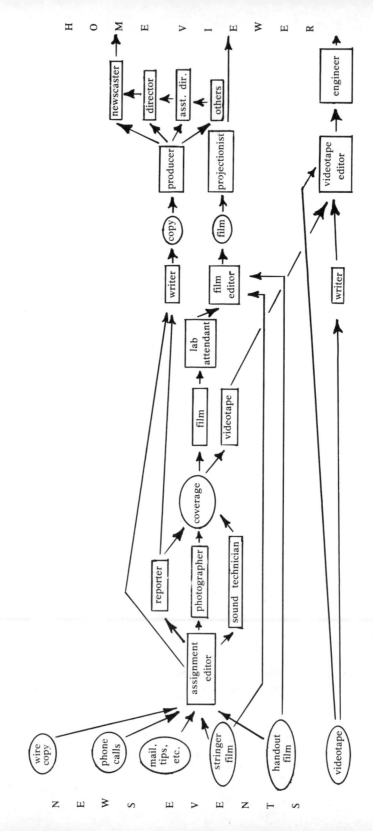

the editor and the writer, a dozen other pairs of eyes will catch it at rehearsal. If the editor has transposed two film stories in a hurried assembling of the projection reel, it will be caught here. Like theatrical rehearsals, a rehearsal of a newscast starts and stops, as the director orders changes. The TelePrompTer operator runs through his script roll.

While each segment is practiced, the assistant director times the segment with his stopwatch, and notes that time on this copy of the script. When the rehearsal is finished he adds up the segment times, and informs the director, producer and newscaster of the total. It may be necessary to cut some copy, or even to excise a film or tape story, which usually means rolling quickly through the film or tape during the program when the reel has reached the point where the particular story begins. Only if the script allows no time for a roll-through, will the film be physically cut. On the other hand, if the newscast runs short of its allotted time, the newscaster will "fill" with "pad" copy, either until the program ends, or a pre-set "backtime" segment is reached, enabling the newscaster to conclude strongly, rather than sloppily with pad copy.

While the rehearsal continues, the technical director glances frequently at the clock. Everything stops when he reports, "Two minutes to air." Now the projectionist and the videotape engineer rewind the reels back to the first cue positions. The television camera operators swing their heavy cameras into opening position, "get on" the suitable lenses, and focus. The TelePrompTer is rolled back to the newscaster's opening words. The director, the newscast producer and the audio engineer stack the pages of their scripts, and leaf through them to make sure all pages are in numerical order. The newscaster does the same with his copy. He straightens himself in his chair, picks up a pencil or whatever prop he uses, and assumes an expression of intelligent seriousness.

"One minute to air."

"Thirty seconds."

The floor director gives a final flip to the trailing cord of his headset and calls out, "Fifteen seconds. Quiet on the set....Ten....Five...."

With his eyes fixed on the sweep-second hand of the clock mounted on the wall in front of him, the director addresses, in turn the technical director, or T.D., beside him and the floor director listening by headset: "Four...three... two...one...Up on one (telling the T.D. to fade in from black to camera number one)...Cue him."

The floor director, standing beside the camera designated as number one, jabs a forefinger toward the newscaster.

And the newscast begins.

For the Student

1. Watch a local newscast for one week. List the things you like about it. How can it be improved?

2. Read an afternoon newspaper before watching a network newscast and

list the stories you think the newscast will cover. Then monitor and compare. Why the differences?

3. Should a reporter edit the stories he or she covers, or should someone else, like a writer, be assigned? What are the advantages of each method?

4. Watch a newscast to see if you can detect the reading of pad copy and the start of a backtime segment.

5. Spend a day in a television newsroom. Keep a log of newsroom activities.

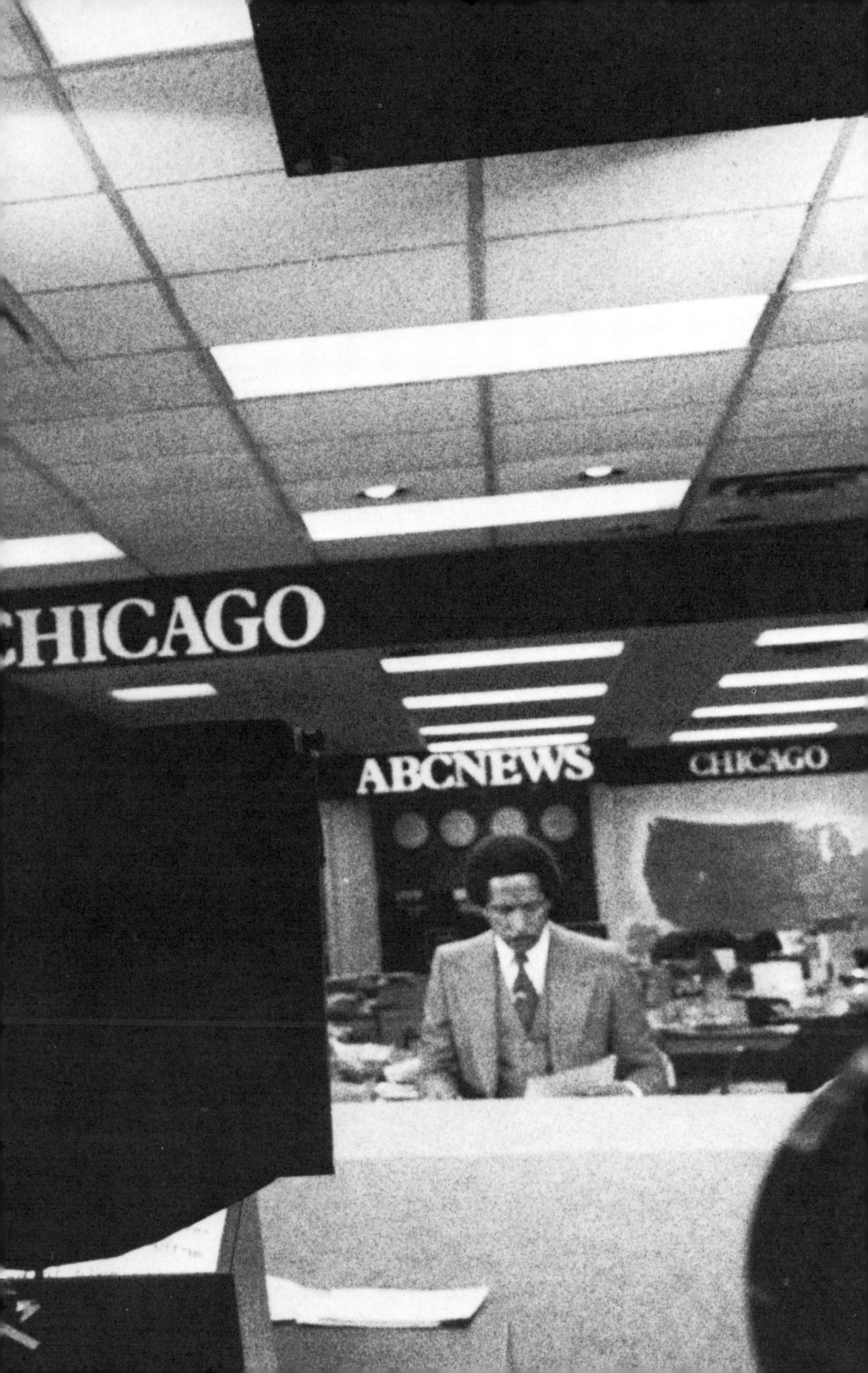
CHICAGO
ABCNEWS
CHICAGO

The Newscaster 9

That's what I remember best, hair.

— *Charles Kuralt*

Kids aspire to be newscasters the way they once wanted to be railroad engineers. The glamour of the railroad engineer went with the steam locomotive, and Walter Cronkite has predicted a day when the newscaster will follow:

There is a canard abroad in our business that television news always will be limited by the simple fact that many, if not the majority, of news stories cannot be illustrated.

Horsefeathers! as the saying goes.

We can't illustrate many stories only because we don't know how. *I* don't know how, or I'd be doing it. But there will be some bright young men coming along who will figure out how, you can count on it...

When all this happens there are going to be some radical changes in news programs. If we can illustrate *all* stories, there is no further need of a news broadcaster to read half the items to the public. Disembodied voices can narrate the film, reporters on the scene will be seen when the situation demands, and there will be no need for a news master of ceremonies in the studio.[1]

The newscaster, or anchor ("anchorman," "anchorwoman"), has the most desirable job in the news department. He is paid more than others, sometimes disproportionately more. To station management, he and reporters are the "talent." To everyone in and out of the station operation the newscaster is the person most closely linked with the newscast even though others spend more time in its preparation. On the network level the viewer says he tuned in to the "Cronkite news," or "Paul Harvey," and on the local level the viewer recalls the "Joe Doaks news" or the "Joe Doaks show" or "Joe Doaks and the news."

The newscaster is the representative of the station and the news department in addressing the Kiwanis luncheon and the Wednesday Book Club. Accompanying the glamour is a measure of insecurity. If audience ratings fall, the newscaster may be the first to go. Chances are he will seek employment in another city unless he chooses another occupation. He feels not only the competition of other newscasters but the hot breath of reporters on his station who want the job.

On some stations the newscaster is also the news director and is the most experienced journalist on the staff. He may go out daily to cover stories. On other stations he is an announcer who was appointed by virtue of his stage presence, his authoritative voice, his delivery or his looks. If he does not immerse himself in the day-to-day news operation but merely contents himself with picking up a finished script, other news staffers scornfully label him "a news reader."

Charles Kuralt and All That Hair

Today the "reader," "the news master of ceremonies" is very much with us, some would say too much with us. In the decade of the Seventies one television news program after the other shifted its emphasis from content to style, seeking to add a profitable rating point or two by giving the program an "image" much as radio stations seek a "sound." At the heart of this image-making sat the newscaster, or team of newscasters, blow-dried hair in place. But listen to CBS News correspondent Charles Kuralt tell it to news directors convulsed with laughter and moved to cheers at an RTNDA convention in Dallas:

I assert fearlessly that I have watched nearly every one of your newscasts at one time or another...I can whistle the Action News theme song, a march. I have got the words Eyewitness News printed across my eyeballs.

I have been dazzled by the technical progress...but my overwhelming impression of all those hours in all those years is of hair. Anchormen's hair. While mine has been going, theirs has been growing. That's what I remember best, hair. Hair carefully styled and sprayed, hair neatly parted, hair abundant, and every hair in place.

There's been a big improvement in hair styles. But I can't remember much that came out from beneath all that hair. I don't think much did. I remember the style, but not the substance. And I fear that the reason may be there wasn't much substance there...

I cannot watch the Mary Tyler Moore Show without a shudder of recognition. I know that sensible professional news director, terrified of what his idiot anchorman might say next. And I know that anchorman, in love with himself and his image, who wouldn't know a news story if it jumped up and mussed his coiffure...

And I don't care what the station managers say, I don't care what the outside professional news advisers say, I don't care what the ratings say, I say this is the continuing disgrace of this profession...

I am ashamed, I think we all ought to be ashamed, that twenty-five years into the television age, so many of our anchormen haven't any basis on which to make a news judgement, can't edit, can't write, and can't cover a story.[2]

"Eyewitless News"

On-air talent are the most visible targets of criticism of consultant-directed newscasts that the *Columbia Journalism Review* savagely called "Eyewitless News." Writer Ron Powers wondered how Edward R. Murrow would react to television news in the late Seventies:

Murrow would have seen rank upon rank of "news teams" in matching blazers and coiffures like so many squadrons of "Up With People" teenagers, all displaying standardized wry smiles behind their *Star Trek* desks. He would have seen news teams that begin their evening's duty by strutting on camera en masse...

He would have been puzzled by full-page newspaper ads that trumpet a news team as though it were a new kind of low-tar cigarette, and by TV "promo" commercials that show anchorman, weatherman, sportscaster, and principal reporters riding around in cowboy suits on white horses or passing inspection dressed up like doughboys...

What the hell, Murrow might understandably have asked, has all this got to do with *news?*...

The on-air men and women look and sound less like their fellow citizens than like some idealized product of genetic breeding. This may be good for viewers' sexual fantasies; it does not do much for a station's credibility. The anchor-gods and -goddesses seldom remain long in a given "market"; they are nomads, their aspirations fixed on New York, whence their loyalty often derives.[3]

One embarrassed member of a news team, Dave Patterson of Cleveland's WEWS said, "The only reason to call the show I'm on 'news' is that the title of it is 'Eyewitness News'. It's really an entertainment program, and what they want of me is to be a literate buffoon." [4]

Many journalists are angry at what has happened to newscasts and to newscasters. Said Eric Sevareid:

The astounding daily story of the astounding human race is apparently now regarded by many local station managers as not compelling enough. Reality itself must be jazzed up...the news is delivered by newsmen turned actors, very bad actors. They grin, they laugh, they chuckle or moan the news. They puff cigars and pipes; they wear pinstripes and carnations or sweatshirts. They kid each other or applaud each other. And any day now, one of them will sing the news while doing a buck-and-wing stark naked.[5]

Not all broadcast news has taken this direction, of course. The intelligent, honest reporter with a sense of dignity who has "paid his dues" in field work remains the role model in the profession. Dan Rather put it this way:

> Walter Cronkite, David Brinkley, John Chancellor, Harry Reasoner, Mike Wallace, Edwin Newman, Eric Sevareid. In looks, voice and approach no two are alike. But there is a common denominator. They are believable. No machine known to science can measure the human waves that come across the screen. But believability is the test.[6]

Doing It Right

For a newscaster, "doing it right" includes: 1) speaking clearly; 2) imparting the sense of the news; 3) convincing viewers that he knows what he is talking about; 4) keeping the newscast moving smoothly; 5) maintaining contact with his audience.

To present information clearly, the newscaster must speak in an understandable manner, enunciating so he does not slur word endings. He should not try to pitch his voice low so as to give it "authority." If he does not naturally sound like Edward R. Murrow, so what? Elmer Davis sounded authoritative with a high voice and a flat Midwestern accent.

He should "woodshed" his copy; that is, he should rehearse it, either aloud or sub-vocally, so that he won't stumble on the air. He may discover unfamiliar words or names. He also comes across tortuous sentence structures.

Because we have been breathing all our lives, it does not automatically follow that we have been breathing correctly for voice projection. Nor does it follow that we place our vowels correctly. Some lessons from a competent voice coach could be the best investment a future newscaster makes today. Repeat: a *competent* voice coach.

To impart the sense of the news, he should, above all, keep up with the news. His rate of delivery should reflect the mood of his copy. So should his inflection. He should know when to pause. And out of the corner of his eye he must observe the gestures of the stage manager.

The studio stage manager uses these signals:
> Two minutes to go: two fingers.
> One minute to go: index finger.
> 30 seconds to go: one index finger crossing another, making a plus sign.
> 15 seconds to go: a fist.
> 5 seconds and count down: a wide open hand, with the fingers dropping as the seconds tick away.
> Cut: a finger cutting across the throat.
> Slow down: palms drawn apart slowly.
> Speed up: an index finger making a fast turning motion.

Watch me for cue: finger pointing to eye.
You're on: index finger jabbing toward newscaster.

A Sense of the News

An intelligent newscaster makes hack writing sound intelligent. A news reader who could not care less makes intelligent writing sound glib, and just plain awful. On the air his attitude, reflected in his voice and expression, will indicate his understanding of the news. One of the leading local newscasters in the United States reportedly began his career by trying to smile his way through every news item, aware that he had a charming smile and pearly, evenly spaced teeth. Luckily for him, the people he worked with got through to him fast.

Psychologist Israel W. Charny thinks newscasters and reporters should go considerably further than a grim expression and a serious voice to present somber views.[7] He feels that objective reporting of violence says in effect, "Well, folks, it's happened before, it's still happening, and there's nothing we can do about it." He said newscasters should develop "a more human language" to get across their feeling of sadness over loss of human life, anger over the wastefulness of violence, and a feeling of hope that man can live peacefully. A story would not begin, "Three persons died today when..." but instead, "A sad accident today claimed the lives of..." The author knows of no newscasters who report news this way. Among the objections to this kind of reporting would be its abrogation of objectivity and its maudlin tone. Also, few accidents are *not* sad and tragedies are *always* terrible.

To convince viewers he knows what he is talking about, the anchor must, of course, keep abreast of current events. He must also know how to pronounce the words and names he uses, including foreign words. As a rule, a foreign term or name should be pronounced accurately, but with an American accent; that is, the stresses should be on the right syllables and the pronunciation of the vowels should resemble the pronunciation a native speaker would give them, but the newscaster should not try to imitate a Frenchman or a Russian or a Spaniard when he refers to their cities or native dishes. A newscaster or reporter who is rattling along in midwestern American, then suddenly purses his lips to form an *umlaut,* sounds as though he is trying to impress someone with his worldliness. He sounds phony. Best bet: a slightly Americanized version of the original.

A smooth newscast requires mental agility when fluffs occur — and they occur in the best rehearsed newscasts. The newscaster fluffs a word, or the wrong tape or film comes up, or the remote switch does not come in, or the audio fails, or a splice breaks. The newscaster must decide on the spot whether to apologize or whether to ignore it, and if he apologizes, what to say. Usually, a short apology with the briefest explanation and no embarrassment is the best way to handle an error. At times a sense of humor helps.

"I'm sorry. We seem to have lost our sound. We'll try to rerun that later."

"My apology. We have line trouble between here and Chicago. But we heard most of that report."

"That is: She sells sea shells."

Rapport

Maintaining contact with his audience is more than just staring at the lens or the TelePrompTer when the red light is on. Certainly a maximum amount of eye contact and a minimum amount of nose-in-script helps in television. (When reading a direct quotation, the reporter should be looking at his script.) Beyond this, the newscaster must realize he is talking to one person somewhere on the other side of that lens. Like the writer, the newscaster should imagine an audience he can visualize, one, two or three people at most who are letting him into their living room so he can tell them what's been going on today that will interest them and may be important to them. The best newscasters have an instinct about this. They go *through* that lens. They talk to *you*.

They also share with you an interest in visual coverage. Notice how often a newscaster will introduce a tape or film, then will settle back and turn his head slightly to look at a camera monitor located beside his desk or recessed into it. After the story ends the camera may catch him still staring at the monitor. An instant passes, then he looks up and continues with the newscast. All quite natural. The newscaster and you at home have shared the experience of viewing that event.

One consulting firm turned down a newscaster who was considered "friend-ly, good looking, casual, objective, knowledgeable, calm, good voice and un-ruffled." He was rejected because he seemed also to be distant, uninvolved, and personally uninterested in the news that he was reporting.[8]

Guide to Pronunciation

The pronunciation of unfamiliar names and places should not be guessed at. Nothing is more likely to irritate a viewer or make him think the newscaster is a rube as much as the mispronunciation of the viewer's home town or the city in Italy where the viewer's grandfather was born. Admittedly, a mispronun-ciation is not the worst of offenses. It's just one of the most glaring.

A guide to the correct pronunciation, in brackets, should follow the un-familiar name: Robert Cholmondelay (CHUM-lee). The stressed syllable is capitalized.

If you are not sure of the pronunciation, use the telephone. Call the source. If you are calling a wire service, better give the local editor an hour to check with the regional or national office.

UPI uses these phonetic conventions:

- A -

AY for long A (as in mate)
A for short A (as in cat)
AI for nasal A (as in air)
AH for soft A (as in father)
AW for broad A (as in talk)

- E -

EE for long E (as in meat)
EH for short E (as in get)
UH for hollow E, or schwa (as in the)
AY for French long E with acute accent (as in Pathe)
IH for middle E (as in pretty)
EW for EW dipthong (as in few)

- I -

IGH for long I (as in time)
EE for French long I (as in machine)
IH for short I (as in pity)

- O -

OH for long O (as in note or though)
AH for short O (as in hot)
AW for broad O (as in fought)
OO for long double O (as in fool or through)
OW for OW dipthong (as in how)

- U -

EW for long U (as in mule)
OO for long U (as in rule)
U for middle U (as in put)
UH for short U (as in shut)

CONSONANTS

K for hard C (as in cat)
S for soft C (as in cease)
SH for soft CH (as in machine)
CH for hard CH or TCH (as in catch)
Z for hard S (as in disease)

S for soft S (as in sun)
G for hard G (as in gang)
J for soft G (as in general)
ZH for soft J (as in French version of Joliet)

Where the pronunciation runs counter to the spelling, use the word "like":
Roger Blough (like NOW)

Among books listing the pronunciation of names or words are the *NBC Handbook of Pronunciation, A Pronouncing Dictionary of American English* by Kenyon and Knott, the *English Pronouncing Dictionary,* and Noory's *Dictionary of Pronunciation.*

Reading the Script

While the director and the assistant director mark their copies of the script for cue words in the minutes prior to rehearsal or air time, the newscaster reads his copy for content and delivery. If he comes across a name or a word that he is not sure he will pronounce properly, he checks it with a writer or looks the word up in a dictionary or a gazetteer. The newscaster also watches for words he feels a writer chose in error.

The newscaster takes his script to a quiet corner and reads it aloud to himself, getting a feel of words, phrases, meaning, and a rhythm pattern. He may pencil slash marks at places he will pause for breath and he underlines words he will emphasize. Here and there he edits words and phrases, eliminating those he considers unnecessary to the meaning and changing others to permit a smoother reading. He may break a series of sibilants or words ending in "th" or "ths" ("The death of a sixth youth in that bus accident..."), or he may remove the word *today,* probably the most overused and unnecessary word in newscasts.

After he is satisfied with the script, the television newscaster either goes to the make-up department or puts some on himself. The radio newscaster is spared this ordeal. Make-up for a newscaster is usually limited to "pancake," to avoid appearing washed out under the hot studio lights. Sometimes features are highlighted or subdued, depending upon the skill with which the make-up is applied. As a rule, newscasters grin and bear this show-biz aspect of presenting the news.

CBS correspondent Dan Rather recalled, hilariously, the day he lost his compact:[9]

> Applying your own makeup in the field is one of the small perils of the trade. It is one thing in a studio. Often there is a makeup person on hand to touch you up but if not, you do it yourself. At least, you have privacy.
>
> It is an entirely different matter to carry around with you a compact of, say, Gay Whisper. Literally. In 1962 I was still getting used to carrying my own makeup when I boarded a Delta flight from Memphis to

Birmingham. As I placed my coat on the overhead rack, the compact fell out and landed with a plop on the carpet.

The stewardess bent down, retrieved it and turned it in her hand. "Mah goodness," she said, in what I guessed was a Savannah, butter-wouldn't-melt accent, "who dropped this heah compact?"

She glanced around at each passenger and I just gave her an innocent, blank stare that said, Well, don't look at me. What would I be doing with *that?*

And the rest of the damned flight, I'm thinking, My God, I have to do a piece almost the minute I hit the ground and I really need that makeup. But I walked right off the plane without it.

Formats

Segmented: Popular in the old radio days and at the start of television, this may no longer exist anywhere in the United States. News, weather and sports are separate programs. One or more may be separately sponsored.

Integrated: What most newscasts are today: news, weather and sports are part of a single package. The newscast leads with the most important story, which might be a weather or sports story. But vestiges of the old segmented format remain in the scheduling of weather and sports at more or less definite times and running the same length each evening.

Traditional or *formal:* A single newscaster reads the news, with no nonsense or chit-chat. Cuts to film, weather news and sports news are straightforward.

Informal: There is some chit-chat between the talent on the set, usually during the introduction by the newscaster of the weathercaster and the sports-caster. Talk is generally limited to the occasional friendly remark or question.

Happy talk: News as entertainment. Lots of light features. Lots of banter among the on-air talent, with in-jokes and the assuming of comic roles (e.g., the weathercaster may be the newscast's clown or second banana.)

Tabloid news: Not much of this yet, and it may not spread beyond a few big cities. The nightly news is drenched in sex, violence and vulgarity, which is matched by the on-air talents' jokes.

Eyewitness News: The station's reporters come onto the set to talk about the news they covered and to introduce their film pieces. The newscaster asks them a question or two to glean still more information about what has happened and what is likely to happen next.

Action News: The reporters become involved in the stories they cover. Because this leads away from objective reporting, "action news" is usually limited to the investigative reports and consumer-affairs reporting.

Television Sets

Sets will vary according to tastes, budget and format. The simplest sets amount to little more than a lectern or two with a rear projection screen behind them.

Some newscasters prefer to stand, others to sit. Ultra-modernistic sets featuring clear plexiglass have been popular in recent years. There seems to be no demand for the traditional set containing books on a shelf, or the appearance of books on a shelf.

Another increasingly popular set is the newsroom itself, with the newscaster seated behind his own desk, other newsroom personnel in evidence in the background, usually pretending to be busy, and the AP and UPI wire machines going clack-clack, punctuated by the occasional ringing telephone.

These days the rear projection screen is likely to be Chromakeyed, capable of showing stills, films, tapes, live action or freeze frames. With the advent of ENG, the reporter at the scene can be Chromakeyed behind the newscaster, who can turn and exchange some conversation with the reporter, before the director cuts fully to the reporter at the scene. An impressive bit of electronic hocus-pocus.

For the Student

1.If you ran a station, would you look for newscasters purely on the basis of their competence? Discuss.

2. Charles Kuralt gave a funny speech, but was he right?

3.Is there anything wrong with taking a couple of minutes in each newscast to let viewers know that their anchor people are human beings with senses of humor and that they like one another?

4. Take turns with other broadcasting students in reading copy while trying to maintain as much eye contact as possible. Criticize one another constructively and frankly.

5. As a class exercise, present brief newscasts using each format.

NEWSCASTS

Getting It Together

News For Everyone

Weather

Sports

ON
OFF
UNITED PRESS INTERNATIONAL
Property of the Associated Press

Getting It Together

10

When I read statistics that show sixty percent of Americans get all or most of their news from television, I shudder.. I know what we have to leave out.

— Av Westin

With few exceptions, everything in a daily newscast — on radio, every audio tape and on television, every film clip, every videotape, every still photo, and every map, and every scrap of news in both media — is prepared and assembled on the day it is aired, all done within the space of a few hours. In a few minutes it is over. The careful work is shelved or scrapped. Tomorrow it must be done again with fresh news, and the tomorrow after that with still other news.

Newscasts are presented so often and, as a rule, so smoothly that all those who have participated in the news operation forget what they may have concluded the first time they saw a newscast from the vantage of a studio control room: an informative news program is an achievement.

The gathering of news and the preparation of a newscast follow familiar paths, despite the diversity of the news itself, so that what may seem to a newsroom visitor near deadline as chaos is actually an orderly haste, an organized system going at top speed.

Sources of News

In theory, radio stations, television news departments and newspaper editorial departments have identical sources of news available to them. In practice, it does not work out this way. One reason for the difference is that the media differ in the kind and degree of news they use; for example, newspapers have no use for motion picture film sources, while television newscasts have no use for the Dow Jones wire.

Wire Services

The wires have always been a mainstay of broadcast news, sometimes too much so. NBC correspondent Tom Pettit, covering the Alabama school integration story in the Deep South, telephoned a producer in New York.[1]

Producer: There's a good story in *The New York Times* this morning.

Pettit: We don't get *The New York Times* down here.

Producer: Well, the night lead of the AP says....

Pettit: We don't have the AP.

Producer: Never mind. The UP's got a pretty good angle on it.

Pettit: We don't have the UP either.

Producer: You don't have the UP?

Pettit: No.

Producer: You don't have the AP?

Pettit: No.

Producer: You don't have *The New York Times*?

Pettit: No.

Producer: Then how do you guys know what's going on down there?

The Associated Press and United Press International offer their subscribers a variety of wire copy, still photo, film and audio services. Wire copy services include:

1) "A" wires, emphasizing international and national news, now available at a computer driven 1,200 words per minute, and within a few years at twice that rate.

2) "B" wires, emphasizing feature stories, reports in depth and texts of speeches and agreements. This wire holds little interest for broadcasters.

3) Sports wires.

4) Broadcast (or "radio") wires, in which news is rewritten in broadcast style, condensed, and arranged into five-minute and fifteen-minute summaries, plus some stand-alone reports. "Rip-and-read" newscasts make heavy use of this copy. AP and UPI have been criticized for the quality of broadcast wire writing. Both agencies have made efforts to improve it.

Note: Garbled wire copy can sometimes be unscrambled using this key:

A B C D E F G H I J K L M N O P Q R S T U V W X Y Z
- ? : $ 3 ! & 2 8 ' ( ) . , 9 0 1 4 ' 5 7 ; 2 / 6 "

So: &99$,32' becomes: GOOD NEWS

5) Still photo machines, such as AP's "Laserfax" and UPI's "Unifax," which reel off still pictures and maps, already captioned.

The AP serves more than 3,000 television and radio stations in the United States alone. UPI more than 2,000 television and radio stations. There are in the United States approximately 728 commercial television stations (516 on VHF), including a handful of satellites which lack their own news departments. There are also 260 non-commercial television stations (102 on VHF). For radio: approximately 4,500 AM stations, 4,100 FM stations. (Approximations are preferable in a book, because new channel licenses raise the totals.)

Taking advantage of new technology, AP, UPI, and Reuters have computerized their news flow. They also offer a 24-hour newswire designed for display on a CATV channel.

Reuters, the British news agency, has expanded its worldwide coverage to include correspondents in a few American cities. *The New York Times* and *The Los Angeles Times-Washington Post* offer news analyses not available on AP and UPI, but excellent as they are for newspaper readers, these wire services have little appeal to television news directors, who prefer to spend budget money in other ways.

Some large cities have a separate city news service, which deals only with local and area events. A city news service provides not only news, but tips, and usually both a news calendar of upcoming events and a court calendar indicating some of the more interesting cases on tomorrow's docket.

Almost all Canadian television stations, radio stations and newspapers receive CP, the Canadian Press wire service, or BN, the Broadcast News wire provided by Canadian Press. UPI exists in Canada as UPC. It is comparatively small.

Other Media as Sources

Metropolitan newspapers contain rich veins of news leads for broadcast stories. The leads may be found in local news coverage, feature stories, items in local columns and nationally syndicated columns.

Suburban and small town newspapers should be regularly scanned for local stories which have potential for development into radio actualities or visual stories.

Other stations ought to be monitored for several reasons: to learn what the competition is doing, to learn what the competition is missing and to learn what the competition has that your station is missing. While a station should never present stories that will have viewers muttering, "Heck, we saw that yesterday on the other channel," it must still be alert to developing news.

Radio newscasts can be monitored at home before a television reporter or photographer starts for work, and on the car radio whenever he is driving. Radio news can alert him to breaking stories, and send him scurrying to grab a camera and head for a major story.

Magazines provide occasional leads to local stories. More often, their treatment of a national event or their reporting of national attitudes can lead a local station to an interesting feature, perhaps by interviewing local residents on the same topics.

Network newscasts may be mined for ideas. One television network news feature showing how easy it is for a burglar to open most door locks led a local station some months later to cover the same subject with a different approach. A locksmith went from door to door in an apartment house corridor. Using the simplest of tools, he flung open each door in turn. It will be instructive to note that, in addition to the useful warning this news feature gave to householders, it angered many viewers who phoned the station to complain that the film was so explicit that it was a lesson, especially for the young, in how to burglarize.

Sources for Visuals

Because television is primarily a visual medium and because it is virtually the only medium which is able to show action (the only other medium is the now extinct movie theater newsreel), the sources of news must include the sources of newsfilm and videotape. Many news programs are built each day around film and videotape. The variety of sources supplying these commodities, film and tape, depends upon the news department's budget.

1. The news department's own camera crew(s) will shoot most of the local film, ENG live and tape stories used, and often will cover stories within the television station's reception area but outside the city. The farther away the stories are from the television station, the more important they must be to merit coverage, not only because of the added expense of sending a photographer and perhaps a reporter to a distant locale, but also because the time required for travel cuts down the number of stories which can be shot in one day, and because their absence may leave the station unprotected in the event of a breaking story close to home.

2. Stringers are free-lance photographers (Note: newspaper stringers are reporters) who are paid per story used. In large cities, stringers may be permitted to sell only breaking news stories. Some big city stations have union contracts with their own photographers which forbid the station to assign a story to a stringer or to buy film of a scheduled event, like a parade, from him. In smaller cities, where such union contract provisions do not exist, the stringer may provide everything up to full coverage for small stations which lack their own camera crews. The stringer uses his own camera equipment, rents equipment or borrows it from the station. Some local stations even equip regular stringers, buying piecework, in effect.

Stringers do it for the excitement and the pleasure of hearing their names mentioned occasionally, if that is the station's policy. Some do it in hopes of breaking in as staff photographers. Anyone who does it for the money must be hungry, for there is little of that, and there is risk in trying to reach a scene of disaster faster than anyone else. In Los Angeles a stringer who had filmed a nighttime accident in which a woman pedestrian had been run over was himself struck by a car a short time later, giving him two broken legs and a concussion. A second stringer came along and coolly filmed him lying there. The second stringer sold his film to a television station, which thereupon sent someone to visit the barely conscious first stringer in the hospital to. learn if he had film of the woman. The station wanted to tie the stories together! [2]

3. A regional network of stringers or of television stations which interchange VTR stories or film clips will effectively extend the reach of any television news department that takes the trouble to set up such a network and keep it functioning smoothly and fairly. If done strictly on an exchange basis, the cost of a regional tape and film network can be very small compared to the coverage — and protection — gained. Even where film stories are bought, a stringer system can be relatively cheap, costing only the agreed fee if the clip is bought on speculation (or if the story was assigned by the station to the stringer), plus the film replacement whether the clip is purchased or not (certainly an inexpensive way to maintain goodwill), plus the cost of shipment (usually by Air Express or by an airline's own freight service). Taped stories can be shipped or fed over rented phone lines.

4. Special network videotape feeds of news clips reach subscribing stations daily: CBS Late Afternoon News, ABC Daily Electronic Feed, and NBC Network Program Service.

5. A videotape or film feature service adds variety. Newsweek Broadcasting, for instance, offered such syndicated features as "You and the Law," "Cartoon-a-torial," "Today's Woman," and the "Newsweek Feature Service." A video library service, "Time Capsule," was also available to subscribers.

6. Videotape is taken from network newscasts by affiliates for use on late local newscasts. It is a common practice of local stations affiliated with a major network to pepper their late night news reports with videotape lifted from the early evening network newscast. Film which appeared in the dinner hour CBS Network newscast will reappear in the 10 p.m. or 11 p.m. newscast of many local CBS affiliates.

In Canada, the English-language network news is broadcast at 11 p.m. in each time zone by both CBC, the public network, and CTV, the commercial network. Many Canadian viewers can pick up the ABC, CBS or NBC network newscasts in the early evening. Late night broadcasts use segments taped from these newscasts, with voice-over translations for the French-language newscasts.

Stations in the Pacific and Mountain time zones sometimes delay network newscasts until 6 p.m. or 7 p.m. local time, which may mean that a videotape of the evening newscast will be on a shelf for three hours before people in Los Angeles or Seattle see it. A news editor must monitor that incoming feed in case breaking news requires that it be updated. Not only must he know what each news item consists of and where in the feed it is located, so that a videotape engineer will be able to fast-forward to the right spot, but the editor must also know what news items near the top of the newscast can be blocked out if a totally new event requires reporting. Updating a network feed consists of writing copy which will exactly cover an existing news segment, allowing a smooth transition into and out of the network videotape. The local update copy can be read by a newscaster on camera or by an announcer over a bulletin slide. In 1979, CBS decided to do its own updating, feeding West Coast affiliates a newscast in which a CBS reporter stationed in Los Angeles updated the CBS Evening News as needed.

7. A news VTR service which competes with the networks, UPITN, United Press International Television News, feeds more than two dozen stories each weekday over leased lines to subscribers. On weekends a little more than half that comes down the line. A daily story lineup like those provided by the networks is also fed to subscribers, giving them timings and suggested intro scripts, plus a brief description of each videotape story.

8. The news department's own library can often supply just the right footage to illustrate a story. When aired, library footage should incorporate a super identifying its date. The news department should be aware of specialized libraries in the United States which sell news film.

9. Handouts are produced by local or national companies and public relations firms with something to sell or a name to keep before the public. When handouts are well done and based on genuine news, they can be a useful addition to visual sources. The fact that they are non-exclusive (everyone gets the same scenes) is a minor drawback. The fact that they are free should not be a drawback either, nor an inducement. When used, they should be labelled, "SUPPLIED BY...."

10. AP's Laserfax and UPI's Unifax II come by wire, approximately 20 hours a day.

11. AP and UPI photo slide services each provide a basic package of slides, plus a monthly update of some 20 news and sports pictures, maps and graphs. Television stations use them mostly for rear projection.

12. The station has a slide library.

13. Stills are given out by a police agency, loaned by a family, or arrive in the mail from any number of sources hoping for publicity.

14. The television station's own artist turns out maps in the art department and sketches in the courtroom.

The Community

1. Notices of scheduled events, either mailed or telephoned, help an assignment editor plan his day.

2. Public relations representatives, either making the original contact to the television newsroom or receiving a call from the newsroom, ease the work of setting up stories involving their clients.

3. Politicians are sometimes their own best "PR men." They or their secretaries will call stations "just to let you know" what they will be doing or where they will be speaking later that day. Politicians are almost always cooperative (unless they are being indicted for something). When election time rolls around again, they may have to pay cash for the exposure.

4. A disgruntled or concerned expert will sometimes call in to draw the news department's attention to something of public concern.

5. An angry citizen will do the same.

6. A neighborhood representative (e.g., for a group of mothers protesting the lack of a traffic light near an elementary school) will do the same.

7. Colorful characters will do the same. Every town has them. They may be hermits or cat collectors, and they may be delightful interview subjects when they are in trouble with the law or come to public attention in some other way. But a word of warning: the colorful character on Tuesday's newscast may become Wednesday's nuisance when he tries to talk the news department into another appearance, and Thursday's pest, and Friday's pain....

8. A traffic dispatcher employed in the newsroom will alert camera crews and reporters to fires, accidents and crimes reported over the special police and fire department radio bands. Dispatchers are hired by many stations in lieu of a full-time assignment editor. The student preparing for a career in broadcast journalism should consider applying for a part-time job as a traffic dispatcher at a station near the university.

Covering Beats

PBS journalist Robert MacNeil said, "Television news is not set up to gather the news routinely but to disseminate news which other organizations gather. There are few beats. For the most part, television news is reactive: it goes out to cover stories which others have developed through original reporting."

News directors have been more reluctant than newspaper city editors to restrict reporters to specific beats, with the result that broadcast reporters tend to be general reporters. One reason is that the reporters are spread thinner. Newspapers usually hire more reporters than radio and television stations do, and that's a shame. Television stations can certainly afford better.

Still, some beat coverage exists. One reporter may get the state legislature, another city hall and the police beat, a third the university and the suburbs north and west of the city (for the logical reason that he lives northwest of the city, where the university is also located). Still another reporter has the responsibility of checking the hospitals, police and fire stations.

Here are some other sources of news, "beats" in the familiar sense that they are places where newsworthy events occur:

Courts: municipal, county, state and federal; jails.

Law enforcement agencies: local police, county sheriff, state highway patrol, F.B.I., plus other federal law agencies like Post Office detectives and Treasury agents.

Government administrative offices of all kinds and at all levels.

Hotels, airport, convention center.

Chamber of Commerce, major industries, big union local headquarters.

Colleges, school district offices.

Churches, clubs, veterans organizations.

Ball teams, theaters, film distributors, museums, zoos.

Processing the News

To a visitor, a big city newsroom around air time on a busy day is a place of shouting and confusion. People seem to be running into each other in wild dashes. Wire machines clack. Half a dozen employees yell at once. Journalists are familiar with the stranger's wondering comment, "How do you get anything done in this madhouse?"

In fact, a great deal does get done, and in a very short time. These daily feats appear even more remarkable when we consider the penalties of making errors of one sort or another: dead air, the wrong tape coming up, film splices that break in the projector, the embarrassment resulting from bad judgment and bad taste, and even libel suits.

Errors seldom occur in competently managed and staffed news departments because journalists and studio personnel know their jobs thoroughly and care about doing them well. In creating and processing the written, audio or graphic materials which comprise a newscast, experienced personnel have learned what it is possible to accomplish within any given span of time.

Processing written and graphic materials can be broken into a series of steps. (Note: not every news operation takes all the following steps.)

Processing Film

Shooting. A good local newscast depends upon good visual stories, especially those breaking news stories covered by camera. Of course, important news without visuals should take precedence over film of minor news value, but the producer structures most segments between commercials around a core of film or videotape.

Transporting. As each deadline approaches, the problems of getting film to the lab loom large. Even early in the day, assignment editors scan maps to keep camera crews moving from story to story without constant trips to the lab to drop off film. Means must be devised to bring the film in.

Developing. Most television stations own their own processing machines. A few rely on commercial agencies in town. The newsroom should alert the lab technician when film is due to arrive, to make sure the chemicals have been heated to the proper temperatures and that someone else's film is not in the way.

Screening. A writer or the reporter on the story and a film editor may view the film together. The writer holds a stopwatch or follows a timer wired to the projector in order to locate the scenes he wants.

Editing. The film editor cuts and assembles a film clip from the developed reel. He must constantly watch for frames which should be removed and for scenes which should not be spliced together. As deadline nears, he often finds himself rushing to finish a clip in time, but never rushing so much that he does not tug lightly at each splice to be sure it will hold. Films, especially complex stories, are often pre-taped.

Scripting and integrating with other visuals. While the editor builds the film clip, the writer builds the film story, which is based on all the copy available, phone calls if needed to garner added facts, and other visual elements, such as maps, photographs, super cards and other films.

Projecting. Finally the finished clip headed by numbered leader goes to the projection room as part of a reel containing several clips in the sequence determined for the newscast. The story may actually be on two reels mounted on two projectors, if it is to be double chained. At the command "Roll it" from the director in a studio booth — the command coming over a loudspeaker or through a headset — the projectionist flips the switch that starts the projector, sending the film through the film chain and out over the air. If the director has transferred the film stories to tape during a special pre-newscast session, they will be handled like any other taped stories.

Videotape

Recording. An ENG crew's live feed will be microwaved and received on tape or it may broadcast live. A taped feed will be microwaved or physically brought in. Likewise, film or live programming transmitted from another television station or from the network is either broadcast live or taped for later replay.

Playing. The network newscasts are replayed just as they were recorded unless in the intervening hours either a major news event occurs or a story reported in the newscast has been significantly altered by subsequent events.

Editing. ENG tape is edited on three-quarter-inch cassettes. It may be transferred to two-inch quad tape or rolled directly from a ¾-inch playback machine through a time base corrector. Evening newscasts on tape and network news interview programs, such as "Meet the Press," are often raided for short segments to be used in local late newscasts. Segments are sometimes also extracted from library tapes. A writer "screens" tape cassettes just as he screens freshly developed film using a stopwatch or a built-in counter, then edits electronically.

Scripting. Writing to videotape is just like writing to film. In each case, the writer must cover a five-second cue with an "intro" lasting at least five seconds. When the director gets the script, he will circle the word which comes five seconds before the tape is to begin. If there is no on-camera intro, the director puts his roll cue five seconds from the end of the preceding item.

Feeding. When the newscaster reads that circled word, the director will order the videotape engineer to "Roll tape" or the projectionist to "Roll film." Newer videotape machines allow dissolves into and out of tape. Older machines allow only cuts. Some cassette or cart machines feature "instant start" and need no roll cues.

Audio Tape

Audio tape is used in television, but only in connection with visual elements.

Sometimes the newscaster on camera holds a telephone or headset to his ear, as if he is joining the audience in listening to a live report. An alternative to this bit of staging is to play the tape behind a visual, such as silent film (fresh or stock footage), silent videotape, or a series of cards. The film or a live camera might show a tape recorder with the tape rolling. Tne film or videotape often has sound already on it, but this sound is suppressed in favor of the audio tape. The writer determines which elements will be used in conjunction with which other elements, and outlines what he wants in a story script.

The audio engineer shares space in the studio control room with the director and the technical director, sometimes in a closed cubicle of his own, while the projectionist and the videotape engineer are off in other rooms (other studio control personnel, such as the video shader, may also be in the control room). The audio engineer gets a copy of the script to guide him, but he still awaits the director's command to "Roll audio tape."

Graphics

Cropping. Photographs arrive at a newsroom in all sizes and height-width relationships. But a television receiver shows pictures in a relationship of three units height to four units width. To fit square photographs or tall and narrow photographs — both of which are sometimes transmitted by AP Photofax and UPI Unifax — into television's 3 x 4 aspect ratio, it is necessary to crop them, trimming top and/or bottom, or to extend them by drawing additional background on either side.

Outlining. Sometimes background must be removed. For instance, when two dignitaries meet, lesser officials are likely to be present. An air brush, a dark pen or a pair of scissors can remove these unidentified and unwanted figures from the photograph. It is also necessary sometimes to use a pen to outline a figure in order to bring it into sharper relief. Such jobs fall to a news staffer in a small station. Large television stations have graphic arts departments.

Drawing maps, graphs and cartoons. A higher degree of drawing skill is required here. However, anyone using a little care can draw a serviceable map or graph. When a map is needed, nothing else will do so well, and television newsrooms need maps often. A good world atlas and some state, county and city maps are a worthwhile investment for any television art department.

Studio cards. A simple way to prepare a photograph or Laserphoto for air use is to trim it artistically, such as outlining a person's head, then fasten it to a colored card with double-stick tape or glue. Rub-on letters complete the job. When a personal picture is borrowed from a private citizen, use masking tape if it must be attached to a card, in order to protect the picture. Better yet, make a slide.

Slides. The disadvantage of cards is that they tie up a television camera. When a script calls for a sequence of cards, two cameras are needed. On the other hand, slides require only a slide projector which can share a chain with a film projector. Both cards and slides can be Chromakeyed. Any newsroom staff member can learn to make such slides.

Supers. Character generators or white lettering on black cards identify persons, places and dates, appearing over film, videotape, persons in the studio or in live remote situations. Super cards can be made of block type run on a proof press with white ink, small white cardboard letters pasted on a black background, white plastic letters on a cafeteria menu sign, rub-on letters, or some similar device.

Copy

Selecting and Sorting. Newsrooms receive far more copy than they can ever use. The bigger the newsroom, the more teletypes and the more copy. One or more staffers may have no other job than controlling this flood of information. From it, the day's file of significant and visual news must be pulled, some likely features must go into a future folder, and fresh leads must be attached to stories already selected for use. Additionally someone must open and at least glance at the news releases arriving in the mail, for some of these are also useful.

Script Information. All information pertaining to stories to be included in the newscast must go to the writers assigned to those stories. The information may be in wire copy, handout (mailed news release) copy, the photographer's dope sheet, the reporter's notes, facts garnered by telephone or captions on photos.

Writing. The writer combines all pertinent factual information with his own scribbled notes about visual elements which will form part of the story. His resulting story script is essentially a unit which can be placed anywhere in the overall newscast script. He rewrites wire copy into short news items, tightening and simplifying the stories, phrasing them in broadcast style, emphasizing local angles and altering them to include new information.

Late News. Television, like radio, offers immediacy of information. This sometimes means that carefully constructed visual stories must be redone or discarded at the last minute. The newsroom also has a responsibility to the public every moment the station is on the air. General programming must sometimes be interrupted for bulletins. A mark of a station's quality is the willingness of station management to put bulletins and live news switches on the air, and the ability of a newsroom to cope with major news breaks quickly, smoothly and informatively. This responsibility includes covering ("updating") delayed network newscasts with later news.

Script Assembly

Arrangement. Some newscasts begin with international and national news, move on to state news, then to local news, then to stocks, the weather, and sports. Others restrict themselves to local news, weather and sports. Some stations lead off with local news, unless a world news story is of unusual importance, and end with a feature. In every newscast there is a segmented organization according to some pattern, or format. Within each segment, stories are usually arranged in order of news value and, in television, according to visual elements (e.g., so that all of it is not in a block).

Commercials. Whether a newscast is unsponsored or partly sponsored, it is often the preferred place for commercials known as "spots" — commercials from companies which buy time rather than programs. Most newscasts are profitable endeavors, a highly desirable state of affairs when some of the profit is plowed back into the news operation to improve quality of coverage.

Timing and Back-timing. The newscast's assistant director times individual stories and segments. This makes it easy to tell if a program is running late and permits a quick decision about what items may have to be dropped. During the commercial break of 90 seconds or two minutes, a director is busy checking timing, consulting with others and reaching decisions about the balance of the program. Newscasts are often "back-timed," that is, timed to a closing segment whose time is known, so that the end of the newscast will be clean and strong. The raggedness of reading short pad items is much less obvious when a script is back-timed, because these items are in the middle of the program, just before the back-timed segment.

Pad Copy. If a program runs less time than expected or if film breaks in the projector (or similar minor catastrophe), the newscaster fills the gap with pad stories. These are short news items which have no news connection to other news items in the program. They are delivered on camera without visuals. In most cases, pad is simply wire copy edited with a pencil and stapled to 8½" x 11" sheets.

Protection Copy. Every so often, even in the most carefully managed news programs, something goes wrong mechanically or electronically. Telephone line troubles interrupt a live switch to a remote truck or another city. A videotape machine quits. A projector bulb goes out. On local stations there is usually no provision for such calamities, and the newscaster apologizes as gracefully as he can, although he may feel he has been left "with egg on his face." Networks provide their anchors with "protection copy," summaries of what was said or shown in the remote feed. Reporters phone these summaries to New York.

News Values

As newspaper readers we can scan headlines. If a headline interests us, we read the lead. If that interests us, we read the second paragraph. And so on, breaking off as soon as the story ceases to matter. As radio news listeners and as television news viewers, we lack this option. If a story does not interest us, we have two choices: we wait it out or we reach for the dial.

The newspaper editor need not care if a story lacks wide appeal. The broadcast journalist must care. If a long, dull story in the middle of a newscast sends one per cent of his viewers station hopping, the effort and expense in producing the rest of that newscast is lost on that one per cent.

Therefore, stories are chosen, written and organized into a newscast with as broad interest as possible within the framework of news value and good taste. Stories of limited concern are either omitted or are left until the end of the newscast.

For example, sports news is awaited by many men and a few women. They want very much to hear the scores, and will leave any newscaster who ignores these daily doings. But other listeners could not care less. They would leave a newscaster who wasted their time with scores when they want to hear today's solution to yesterday's global crisis. The newscaster lifts himself from the horns of this dilemma in a way familiar to us all. The sports report follows the news and weather. Those who wish, may stay. Another subject of only partial interest is the stock market's activity. The newscaster solves this problem by giving a very short report after the bulk of other news has been delivered. Sometimes he describes the market's activity in one sentence, the behavior of the Dow Jones Industrials in the next, and he is done. Still a third subject getting cautious treatment is the weather forecast. While everyone is affected by the weather, not everyone is willing to spend four minutes of his time learning that the stationary high front over the city is likely to remain for another day, and that tomorrow's high will be 86 after an overnight low of 52, while today's high was 85 and this morning's low was also 52, except near the airport where it was 51.

If any of these normally routine stories becomes extraordinary — if its news value increases sharply — the story moves into the general news section. A world's series score, a sudden drop in the stock market, a blizzard — all these stories have wider appeal and move toward the front of the newscast.

This might lead us to the conclusion that the top story of the day is read first, followed by the second most important story, and on down to the least interesting story, which ends the newscast. However, this is not the usual arrangement, although short radio newscasts often follow this pattern.

The most frequent arrangement of stories — or line-up — in a television newscast begins with the top story of the day, whether local, national or international. This might be followed by world news, with stories being melded into one another, tied with a verbal bridge, or at least put in proximity because of similarities of subject or region. Within this world news section, there might be such subsections as world and national news, or hard news followed by feature stories. The world news section is likely to be followed by a local news section. Here, the same connections and separations prevail. Stories that can be linked are linked. Features follow hard news. Political news may be separated from murders and accidents. Finally, a visual feature story or on-camera "brite" may wrap up the report.

Another consideration in arranging stories is the avoidance of the monotony of having too many on-camera stories following each other, or too much film without the appearance of the newscaster.

The guidelines for a newscast in a metropolitan area may be partly based on audience analysis. With several stations to choose from, urban news audiences tend to sort themselves out according to such demographic factors as occupation, age, education and race. Young city-bred university professors and retired farmers may live side by side, but their tastes differ in many ways, including preferred news programs. Station executives know this.

In television news, what is on videotape very often determines whether a story will be used, and this is always weighed in determining the time allotted to the story.

Yet another consideration is what is uncharitably called "jiggle" on the screen. A newscaster on-camera for long stretches can be tedious. What television news does best is to present action, showing the viewer what happened, visiting the place it happened, watching and hearing the people involved giving their sides of the story. Certainly, a newscaster can sum up the bare facts of any story in less time than it takes to show it, and at much less cost, but if he just talks he will lose his audience. Here a balance must be struck. Editorial judgment comes into play. Film for the sake of "jiggle" is as wrong as eliminating film to squeeze in as much hard news as possible. The test — within the bounds of good taste — should always be: what will our viewers get out of this? What will they remember when the program ends? The answers to these questions form the framework for practical news judgment.

For the Student

1. Spend a few hours with an assignment editor on shift. Observe how he processes information: where he gets it and how he uses it.

2. Write a list of guidelines for stringers.

3. Spend a few hours with a reporter covering a beat. Would you do it differently?

4. Go through a copy of *Time* or *Newsweek* for stories which can be given a local angle.

5. Arrange the stories on the front page of today's newspaper into a newscast running, say, two or three minutes. Compare your organization with what other students put together.

News for Everyone 11

It is we who make the community weather, and sound the notes of the day.

— Eric Sevareid

Is broadcast news fundamentally different from newspaper news? If we strip format and technique away, are they not just the same? Certainly any lively discussion of the merits of broadcast news raises comparisons with the printed medium.

The answers are not simple. Fundamental differences *do* exist because of the fundamental differences between Man as Reader and Man as Listener. Yet the similarities are just as fundamental, because Reader and Listener are frequently the same person, whose interests, desire to comprehend and standards of taste are indivisible in terms of differences in media.

It's Still a Small Town

A veteran Los Angeles television newscaster managed for years to give viewers the comfortable feeling that they lived in a small town, sort of. The neighborhood squabble over whether to replace a stop sign with a street light at one corner does not seem to be "worth" two or three visits by reporters and camera crews plus several minutes of air time in that megalopolis with its million street corners, but the crews from his news department were dispatched nevertheless. Maps helped the newscaster explain how the neighborhood kids must now walk three blocks out of their way if they want to cross at a traffic light.

This story *ought* to have no importance to 99% of the viewers, but curiously it *does* matter. Ignored by the viewer is the fact that the corner is located in Long Beach, while the viewer lives in Van Nuys or Malibu or Whittier. All that matters is those kids, whom we see dodging through traffic. The newscaster localized this story by treating an urban sprawl of eight million people as if it were

North Platte, Nebraska.

A more familiar way to localize a story is to feature a local angle in a national story:

> *"Three St. Louis area residents were on the airliner which crashed...."*
> *"Like the rest of the nation, Missourians this morning found...."*
> *"The President announced he'll make an airport stop in St. Louis as part of his 15-state...."*

In our electronic age, the time of what McLuhan calls "the global village," such a provincial approach seems anachronistic, out of date. Mobile and upwardly mobile viewers who lack a strong community feeling may not be turned on by localizing. But for the majority of listeners, the newspaper city editor's hoary admonition that names make news and his testy demands for local angles have a meaning even in the global village.

Broadcast News vs. Newspaper News

Broadcast news writing is not newspaper writing read aloud. Broadcast news differs from newspaper news in content, arrangement, style and delivery. The receiver of the information is different also, although in many cases, the radio news listener and the television news viewer are also daily newspaper readers. They are different because the media require different degrees of attention and participation. Print is a medium in which the reader must be actively involved to get the message. The reader must concentrate. He must focus his attention on the printed word, and he must let his imagination, his mind's eye, fill in the picture the text describes.

Quite opposite demands are made by the broadcast media. The listener or viewer sits passively. He doesn't come to the news, as he would by turning the pages of the evening paper. The news comes to him. It follows him around the room if he gets up from his chair. It follows him into the kitchen when he goes for a snack, until he is out of earshot. While he watches the tube, his sense of sight is captured, so his imagination is not called forth. However, television news does not demand the viewer's full attention. His mind may wander. The newspaper reader is not likely to be doing much else while he is reading that occupies his attention, but when hearing or watching the news, he may also be carrying on a conversation, building a model airplane, or even glancing through a magazine, depending upon his degree of interest at any moment.

The result is that the broadcast news writer has a more elusive target at which to aim his information than does the newspaper writer. The news writer who offers the audience nothing but newspaper news read aloud will not keep his audience.

A 15-minute radio or television newscast gives the audience approximately the same number of stories as does a newspaper front page and a local news page, each at a depth of one to three paragraphs. For a 30-minute newscast, add page 3 of the newspaper and a few more paragraphs of depth from the front page. That's all.

It has been repeated often that television news will never replace newspapers. Television news and radio news cannot provide the number of facts a newspaper provides. Actually, they should not try. The audience would not absorb that much detail, and would soon grow bored.

David Brinkley said:

> The basic reason we are different is that in a newspaper you can skip around, read what is interesting to you, and ignore the rest. While on a news broadcast, you have to take it as it comes, in order.
>
> We all know that, and what does that mean? What it means is that a newspaper can print items most of its readers don't give a damn about, because those who don't give a damn about it can skip it, and go on to something else. We can't.
>
> So what does that mean? In my opinion, it means we should not put a story on the air unless we honestly believe it's interesting to at least 10 percent of the audience. Preferably more. But at least 10 percent....
>
> If news is something worth knowing that we did not know already — (as it is) — then the appropriate test is: worth knowing to whom? And to how many? The right question to ask is: who really cares about this? Does anyone care and should anyone care? [1]

Let us consider what a newspaper tells its readers. A story about a day's fighting in a distant war goes into considerable factual detail. We learn the identity of the battalion and the number of miles it pierced that day and how far it is from some city we use as a reference point and how many enemy soldiers it encountered, how many it killed as against its own losses. We learn who the officer is who gives us this information, and what he has to say about the battle and the battle which is likely to follow. The story gives us similar information about the activities of a regiment a certain number of miles (we are told how many) away (we are told which direction). The same story also tells us about the day's bombing, which means learning how many bombers left from where to what targets to drop how many tons of explosives how far from what referent points, and to what degree of success according to what air force source. The same story may also tell us of the day's political activities in that distant country, the internal maneuverings, the attempts to control or the attempts to get out from under. We learn the names and titles and assignments of the visiting political officials and where they are going and who is meeting them and how long they intend to remain, and what they say about what they have seen so far.

Detail after detail, fact after fact. Furthermore, this is just one story, or at least it is wrapped up under one dateline. Ten other stories on the front page carry just as many names, places, quotations and numbers. If there is any characteristic which makes newspaper writing unique, it may well be its use of numbers.

To try to duplicate this detail in a broadcast not only would be hopeless. It would be foolish. It would be wrong. Television and radio news are not good·

vehicles for carrying great volumes of little facts. As a test, read some newspaper stories to a friend. Read one story or several. Wait five seconds, then ask your friend to repeat what he heard.

The News vs. What Really Happened

Plato's allegory of the man in the cave, in Book VII of *The Republic*, pointed to the difference between what we think exists and what really exists. We also have Herbert Spencer's tragedy of the murder of a Beautiful Theory by a Gang of Brutal Facts. Walter Lippmann discusses the difference between reality and "the pictures in our heads" in *Public Opinion*, which should be must reading for every journalist. Lippmann cites opposing French and German military communiques in February, 1916, about the "battle of Fort Douaumont."[2] The Germans announced they had taken the fort by assault. The French Staff knew nothing of such a battle, but they felt impelled to say something because the German communique was being flashed around the world. So the French issued the following communique, which was translated and published in The New York *Times*, Sunday, Feb. 27, 1916:

> LONDON, Feb. 26 — A furious struggle has been in progress around Fort de Douaumont which is an advance element of the old defensive organization of Verdun fortresses. The position captured this morning by the enemy after several fruitless assaults which cost him extremely heavy losses, was reached again and gone beyond by our troops, which all the attempts of the enemy have not been able to push back.[2]

According to Lippmann, what actually happened was that the position somehow had been forgotten in a confusion of orders during a shifting of front line troops. Some German soldiers saw the door open, crawled inside, and captured the few French soldiers they found. There had been no battle and no casualties. Nor had the French troops advanced beyond it.

We may be sure the French Staff would not have printed the truth even if they knew it: the position was taken because of the stupidity of a French officer in issuing orders. And probably a news correspondent, had he known this truth, would not have cabled it, because he depended on the French headquarters for information, and he would have offended them by telling the truth. Or, military authorities might have censored the cable.

Lippmann also reprints the following dispatch:

> WASHINGTON, Dec. 23 — A statement charging Japanese military authorites with deeds more "frightful and barbarous" than anything ever alleged to have occurred in Belgium during the war was issued here to-day by the Korean Commission, based, the Commission said, on authentic reports received by it from Manchuria.[3]

Of this dispatch Lippmann comments, "Here eyewitnesses, their accuracy unknown, report to the makers of 'authentic reports'; they in turn transmit these to a commission five thousand miles away. It prepares a statement, probably much too long for publication, from which a correspondent culls an item of print three and a half inches long. The meaning has to be telescoped in such a way as to permit the reader to judge how much weight to give to the news."

As factors standing between reality and report, Lippmann includes censorship, the desire for privacy, limited public interest in current affairs, the superficiality of news reports, and the restrictive stereotype patterns into which most of us fit the news we read and hear.

Unwrapping the Truth

A story selected at random from the Associated Press radio wire reads as follows:

THE SOVIET AND YUGOSLAV FOREIGN MINISTERS HAVE ANNOUNCED THAT THEIR NATIONS' POSITIONS ON MOST INTERNATIONAL PROBLEMS COINCIDE. THE STATEMENT WAS ISSUED AFTER A WEEK-LONG VISIT TO MOSCOW BY YUGOSLAV FOREIGN MINISTER KOCA POPOVIC (POP-O-VICH'). THE ANNOUNCEMENT INDICATED RELATIONS BETWEEN THE 2 NATIONS ARE THE WARMEST IN A LONG TIME.

A listener might fairly conclude that Yugoslavia is, after all, a Communist country. Its break with Russia does not really amount to much, certainly not enough to keep the Yugoslavs from presenting a united Communist front against the West. If the listener should hear later that his congressman intended to vote for something that would improve relations between the United States and Yugoslavia, he might be inclined to write a wrathful letter to Washington.

Actually, the story is meaningless. Discovering why is a little like playing detective:

1. The story says not a word about the purpose of Popovic's visit to the Soviet foreign minister or the subject of their conversation. Two sophisticated, skillful, busy diplomats do not meet to decide that their governments agree on "most international problems."

2. The story contains only one fact taken *from* the official statement issued jointly by the foreign ministers: "positions on most international problems coincide." The rest of the story contains facts *about* the visit and an inference.

3. That one fact is a pleasantry. Joint statements always mention areas of agreement. Two foreign ministers would hardly emerge from a meeting to say that positions on a *few* international issues *do not* coincide. Yet this statement is a corollary of the other.

4. No support is given for the inference that relations were the warmest in a long time. With heightening tension over Berlin, Russia might have preferred Popovic's agreement to a joint statement about solving that crisis.

5. The foreign ministers would certainly agree on one matter: what they talked about was none of our business. Not only are diplomats close-mouthed, but Communist government officials do not feel that the public must be kept informed via privately owned newspapers and broadcasting stations in the West.

6. The one fact, "positions on most international problems coincide," is given from an obviously longer official statement. Such statements are carefully worded. Taking one phrase out of its context might be a gross simplification.

7. Even that sole phrase might bear little relation to the original joint statement after going through the hands of one translator and several editors.

8. It would be difficult to reach a higher level of abstraction than the three words, "most international problems." These are "words cut loose from their meanings."[4]

9. The words "announced" and "announcement" connote something new being disclosed. People "announce" an engagement or the arrival of a baby. But there is nothing new in the phrase quoted by the AP. The two governments' foreign policies have not suddenly veered so that their positions on most international issues now coincide, where they did not hitherto. If either government had shifted its views on just one issue, and had revealed this, the story would have been far different. No, it was not an announcement. It was just a statement, as we understand the term.

To sum up, the AP story actually says nothing except that the Yugoslav foreign minister spent a week in Moscow, during which he met with the Soviet foreign minister, and that Popovic's name is pronounced pop-o-VICH' — which Yugoslav-speaking radio and television listeners might conceivably dispute.

The likes of this news item can be found day after day on the news wires, leaving vague, yet perhaps indelible impressions of states of affairs which do not exist. This particular item may have reinforced a stereotype about Yugoslavia: that it is strongly pro-Russian and anti-American, whereas Yugoslavia has actually pursued neutralism avidly and has provided the inspiration for other Eastern European nations to try to break the embrace of the Russian bear.

Local Stations Try Fresh Approaches

A number of television stations have developed special segments or unusual kinds of news coverage in a continuing effort to give meaning to the news, to tap audience interest. Some of the ideas were abandoned after a time and some became popular, permanent features that have been imitated by other stations. Here are a few:

KVII-TV, Amarillo, Texas, created a feature called "Secret Witness." The newscaster sought tips on unsolved crimes. Audience members who knew something were encouraged to send in clues. Their anonymity was protected and, if their clues solved the crime, they were rewarded.

In Youngstown, Ohio, WKBN-TV's "A Child is Waiting" feature interviewed adoptable children on the air. Families who were moved by what they saw and heard,called in. Adoptions were arranged. Instead of a foster home or an orphanage, the child now had a home of his or her own and parents.

"Detroit Adventure" told WWJ-TV viewers about cultural events.

An interesting feature, "Commentary," was used to explain to KMBC-TV,

Kansas City, viewers those complicated stories that were presented too quickly on the news.

Several stations decided to take a reporter off general assignment to become a full-time investigative reporter. KTTV, Los Angeles, said it had a team of four investigative reporters. They presented a segment called "On Target."

In Portland, Oregon, KGW-TV followed 90 minutes of network and local news with another 30 minutes nightly called "Evening," filled with human interest features and opinions which the newsroom felt did not belong on a regular newscast. Many of the features were light, but not all. Film was heavily used. One of the more successful segments was of a secretary who wanted everyone to know just what it meant to be a secretary. (This segment suggests the possibility of a feature along the lines of Studs Terkel's best-seller, *Working*. What does, say, a bus driver think of his job? A surgeon? A bottler at a soda pop plant?)

In Cleveland, WEWS tried a local version of *Today* called *Morning Exchange* and beat the network opposition on the other channels with a mix of consumer tips, news, classified ads, contests, weather updates and, its main staple, interviews.

A few stations have physicians covering a medical beat. Dr. Ted Castele of Cleveland's WEWS and Dr. Charles Berry of Houston's KPRC-TV, who gained fame as the astronauts' doctor, are working physicians who do television reports as a sideline. Dr. Michael Breen of Minneapolis' WTCN and a Chicago dentist, Dr. Barry Kaufman at WMAQ-TV, chose to become full-time journalists. (Having an M.D. reporting medical news is not something that a publicity-conscious television station is likely to hide.)

Stock Market Reports

Some people tune in mainly for the stock market report. For them, the movement of the Dow Jones Industrial Average is a gut issue. If the Dow drops, their stomachs churn, because the value of their 100 shares of A.T.&T., their 17 shares of I.B.M. and their 40 shares of American Zinc may have eroded the equivalent of a week's pay. If the Dow soars, so do their spirits. An extra week's pay! The morning newspaper will give them the grim or delightful specifics, but they can't wait, so they watch the evening newscast for a clue.

Most newscasts limit themselves to a minimal report, the rise or fall in the Dow Jones Industrials. Sometimes other indices appear: the closing Industrials average, the Dow Jones Rails, the Dow Jones Utilities, *The New York Times* index, the rise or fall of the American Stock Exchange. Except for arrows on the stills of RP's, the report consists totally of numbers. Like baseball scores, the stock market numbers intensely interest some of the audience, are of passing curiosity to others, and bore or irritate the rest.

But economic news can be considerably more than this. Inflation, especially food prices, wages, taxes, and mortgage rates affect us all. Some large stations and all the networks assign reporters to cover the economic or consumer "beat."

The quality of their reports depends on clarity: how clearly can the reporter explain to each listener what a 0.3% rise in the cost of living index actually means to us all? Visuals help, provided each still contains only a little, easy-to-absorb information. For example, a photograph of a lamb chop with the words: UP 15¢ IN JUNE tells it like it is to everyone. Graphs are not quite as effective, but better than just a newscaster or a reporter on camera. Rule: *For economic news, get away from the "talking heads."*

KOMO-TV, Seattle, shot a daily report on stock market activities at a local brokerage office. News director Jack Eddy said: [5]

> We feel the secret is to avoid, like the plague, a recitation of quotations. If that's what people want, they can get them from the financial page of the newspapers. Secondly, most people don't care. What they are interested in, is how will "what happens on Wall Street" affect them, and we approach it from that angle.
>
> We also look for the news peg. When the President eases the freeze of Federal construction, who will it affect? The construction industry and the money lenders. How did specific stocks respond to such news, particularly those with local ties?
>
> You can almost always find a news hook. We also look for the human interest angle. For example, we came up with a chart showing the relationship between hemlines and the market. It's great for the slow day.
>
> Also the unusual. Ever hear of stock called McIntyre Porcupine? Or do you know what gold stocks seem to go up when the rest of the market declines? Or what in the heck is ex-dividend?
>
> The other element for television is making it visual. Instead of doing a straight talking head interview, we are able to utilize some of the electronic equipment in the Merrill Lynch office, to punch up and read market figures, the hi's and lows, the trading on a particular stock, any number of things that give the report a little pizazz.
>
> In the morning on our 8:00 a.m. TV news program, it's a little different. The newscaster is connected by telephone patch to Keith Patrick at Merrill Lynch; and with some general film of the board room, we get a report on the market at that moment, in an informal, conversational manner.

A UHF station in Los Angeles, KWHY-TV, simply transmitted the New York Stock Exchange ticker from the time it opened until it closed. Small brokerage houses which could not afford their own tickers tuned in. So did investors, many of them retired and elderly, who could sit at home and watch their fortunes diminish.

Radio stations can get access to several financial reports. For instance, the American Stock Exchange offers a Radio Amex service, including a 90-second hourly stock market report, free of charge. Radio stations subscribing to the Associated Press audio service, APR, may receive 60-second national stock market reports. Regional grain and livestock reports are also available.

Of Tenors, Turnips and Teachers

Audiences for plays, concerts and art shows are large and enthusiastic. The little theater production of "To Kill a Mockingbird" generates at least as much excitement as the Broadway road show import of "Annie," but both rate a big yawn in many newsrooms. KPRC-TV, Houston, news director Ray Miller noted, "People regularly send me little memos pointing out how many more people attend operas and symphonies than basketball and hockey games. I think they're right. The fine arts have been neglected....Most sports are designed for coverage. And it's easy to tell who won."

A symphony also has a score. So does each opera. You just have to learn how to report them.

Covering a farm beat presents a challenge to the journalist raised in the city, but many have learned to cope. Larry Hatteberg, KAKE-TV Wichita photographer offers this advice:

> The farm community must be able to trust the television reporter. But getting that trust isn't always easy. First, they must believe that the reporter at least understands the farmer. They're not looking for sympathy —just what they believe is a fair deal.
>
> They want the television reporter to know what he's talking about. They want questions that show forethought and insight....
>
> Many times on a farm story I'll leave the camera in the car for a while. We'll discuss the price of wheat, the farm strike movement, anything that keeps them talking. Afterwards, I bring in the camera. At this point I'm not a stranger and they are much more at ease in front of the camera.[6]

Television stations located near major universities may find it prudent to assign one reporter full time to the education beat. WBRZ, Baton Rouge, Louisiana, for instance, concluded that covering two universities, a board of regents, five state education boards, schools for the deaf and the blind, plus a local school system was more than a part-time beat. Sometimes it's more than one reporter can handle. News director John Spain said, "We find many of our stories not in university handouts, but in specialized publications. For example, university professors working on new fuel systems to aid in the energy crunch published their results in a local refinery's magazine...

"While the universities are a ready source of feature stories, we have also found them to be full of experts ready to discuss breaking stories and to translate government double-talk...We found an economics professor who can boil down the cost of living figures, the government's first quarter inflation figures and current unemployment numbers to what it will mean in terms of buying power to your wife at the local grocery store."

The Older Audience

An audience that one does not seek, does not particularly want, and usually ignores is a "shadow audience." For example, U.S. armed forces radio stations in foreign countries broadcast only for American servicemen and their families, yet attract a much larger "shadow audience" of English speaking nationals and American civilians abroad. In the United States, some program directors place little value on the elderly because they are not "buyers." You don't program for them; the "demographics" are "wrong." Those program directors are just doing their jobs, callous though they must seem, but it is unlikely that news directors ape such a policy and ignore such a sizeable segment of the audience, if for no other reason than that the old are heavy news consumers. They are also buyers of some products whose manufacturers advertise heavily in newscasts.

An Indiana study of the viewing habits of the elderly showed that people watch more television as they grow older but see friends and relatives less.[7] News is a particular favorite, perhaps because with fewer direct human contacts, the older person must rely on media to find out what's going on. There is also some evidence that many of the modern entertainment shows, aimed at the demographically desirable 18 to 45 year olds, lack appeal to the older audience. The majority of the older viewers sampled in the study felt that television news covers most subjects adequately, but would like more features, and less time spent on crime, politics and sports. Three out of four also thought that television news is "usually fair and accurate." Newspapers and radio news were rated lower.

The Younger Audience

Another study showed that one out of four six-year-olds watches a network newscast "almost every day" and the percentage rises as the kids grow.[8] The study also showed that the more they watch the more they know about current events. No surprise there.

World and national news bewilder many adults. When the economy dominates the headlines, reporters do more explaining and clarifying than straight reporting for their adult listeners. But who tries to communicate with kids?

Happily, quite a few newsrooms do. CBS-TV for one. *In the News* on Saturday mornings consisted of three minute spots sandwiched between the cartoons and the commercials every half hour. Many of the spots were soft features or news features (the difference is that a news feature has a specific time-event reference), but the *In the News* producers tackled the hard stories, too. The producers also used techniques not employed on the evening newscasts. A story of school violence was illustrated with animated film of students smashing desks, plus news film of the results of the violence. In other stories, introductory titles were supered and so were hard words. In a story about the U.S. embassy in Moscow being bombarded by radiation, "microwave" was supered. Narration was slower paced than on regular newscasts and more attention was paid to matching copy to film.

CBS has also produced *What's It All About?*, a three-minute feature news program; *Closer Look*, three-minute spots following the evening network news; and *Razzmatazz*, a Saturday afternoon magazine show.

At the time of publication, some 74 stations were carrying the award-winning syndicated *Kidsworld*, with three pre-teens anchoring and local reporters chosen from among kids who send in the story ideas. Some of their Super 8 film is also shown.

WNBC-TV, New York, tried Mason Reece, a gravel-voiced child actor, in its weekly half-hour news program for youngsters. WRC-TV, Washington, also tried young anchors in its weekly *Youth News*, and did not quail at reporting such stories as rape, race problems and Watergate, along with gentler news. In Provo, Utah, the KBYU-TV half-hour weekly children's newscast was not only anchored by elementary school children, they also did the writing and the still photography. WNCC, Lansing, Michigan, created a *daily* half-hour children's show, of which news was an important part. KOLN-TV, Lincoln, Nebraska, presented *Children's News* two afternoons a week. In Chicago, WMAQ's weekly *Bubble Gum News* was an ambitious newscast using a magazine format.

It is not necessary to hire a couple of nine-year-old newscasters to reach youngsters, but it is necessary to write clearly enough so that children can understand what the newscaster is saying, to illustrate the news with maps and other graphics so that a youngster can differentiate between the Middle East and the Middle West, and to relate a news event to a youngster's frame of reference. In short, it is necessary to do for children what the journalist ought to do for adults.

When KRON, San Francisco, premiered *Kidswatch*, formatted like an adult newscast, opposite a regular newscast on another station, *Kidswatch* came out with a higher rating! That may not say something about kids, about adults, about promotion, or about San Francisco, but it certainly does say something!

For another delightful use of what local children produce, around Christmas get some of their letters to Santa from the Post Office and read them on the air, if possible over silent footage of the children who wrote them. This feature would be welcome on the regular evening newscast as well as on a program for kids.

Kids are hard to deal with. They cut up and stare at the camera. One photographer gets kids to cooperate by carrying a small roll of adding machine paper. When she wants to film children, she first shows them the adding machine paper and tells them the film looks like this, and if they look at the camera, "I'll see it on this film (pointing to the paper) and I'll tear it up and throw it away — like this." After the children watch a crumpled strip of adding machine paper being tossed into the waste basket, the photographer reports that they settle down and do not look at the camera lens. Says she, "It really works."

For the Student

1. How does the television or radio audience differ from the newspaper readership?

2. Rewrite a newspaper's local story leads for broadcast.

3. Quietly observe people watching a television newscast. What can you say about their behavior and degrees of attention?

4. If you were a news director, in what ways, if any, would you take your audience of older people into account?

5. Based on today's newspaper, write six stories for a newscast aimed at third graders.

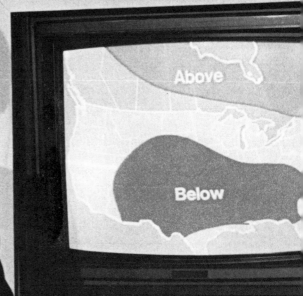

Weather

12

What does "barometric pressure" mean?
I don't know.
What is a "high pressure system"?
I don't know.
> *— two out of three viewers sampled in a study*

WJW-TV, Cleveland, gives a daily "solar reading," telling how much the heating needs of an average home can be met by the sun. Times are changing.

Live video lets the weather reporter say, "This is how things look right now." The reporter is in the studio. A photographer meanwhile is capturing a scene in a park or on a freeway or outside an office building.

The Nightly Report

A weather report has two parts, the actual report of what has happened and a forecast of what is likely to happen. When either of these becomes especially important to the community, as in the report of storm damage or the prediction of a tornado, most newscasts will move the report to the "hard news" segment, with the report given either by the regular weather reporter or by the newscaster. On average news days, when neither the weather nor anything else in the news is likely to make the radio or television audience's pulse race, the weather report is tucked unassumingly between news and sports with — on TV — what passes for a humorous exchange between the newscaster and the weather reporter leading into a commercial which precedes the weather report. The report begins with a look at what has happened in the nation, then the region, then the city. Sometimes the forecast — what may happen — will be given "right after this message." After the forecast, the newscaster appears in a two-shot for a final friendly exchange, and then it's off to another story or two before the set-piece is repeated for sports.

Value of Weather News

In cities large and small, mothers want to know what weather to expect before they send their children off to school. Commuters want to know what the day will bring.

When winter comes to the northern states, people want to know what schools are closed for the day, what roads are out. When smog hangs over Los Angeles, everyone, especially the elderly and parents of school age children, want to know how bad it will be today. Along the Florida and Gulf Coasts, folks anxiously tune in for news of the tropical storm which is spinning itself into a hurricane. In the Plains States, people wait to learn which way a tornado is moving. Downpours, snowstorms, hail, drought. These matter. To a farmer, any one of them can mean the ruin of a lifetime of hard work and dreams.

Scottsbluff, Nebraska, did not have a radar station within sixty miles until radio station KOLT paid $10,000 for a second-hand radar unit designed for a jetliner. In the spring of 1979, the radar unit picked up a funnel cloud west of Scottsbluff. The news was broadcast and then, as news director Larry Cooper related, "KOLT phone lines began to hum as those living within sight of the twister watched it pass from farm to farm. One caller would tell our listeners he had the funnel in sight as he stood at the window of his home 20 miles to the southwest. It was moving east, he reported. A few minutes later another listener was reporting on the air that he had picked up the storm, and it was 17 miles southwest of the city, moving east..." [1]

Weather Jargon

Weather reporters and news directors assume that viewers understand what weather news is all about and get some useful information from it.

That assumption was challenged in a study (done under the author's direction) that found that most viewers can remember nothing of weather reports they had just heard, and furthermore have a foggy notion of the meaning of such commonly used weather jargon as "high pressure system" and "barometric pressure." [2] Three out of four television viewers who were called during the 75 minutes immediately following a newscast could remember nothing of national weather conditions. The research team concluded:

> Despite the evident lack of retention and understanding of weather information, the audience appeared to be satisfied with TV weather reports in general. Perhaps this could be attributed to apathy; many respondents said they just had not thought of it before.

The results of this study raise interesting questions:

1. If most viewers remember little about the weather report, why is so much time devoted to weather in local newscasts?

2. Is it possible that many television news directors and weather reporters are unaware that some of the weather jargon is not understood by most viewers and much of the weather report is not absorbed?

3. What can be done to make weather news more meaningful?

4. Should weather reports on television be reduced to the few basic facts and figures most likely to be retained by most viewers?

Television journalists have long realized that television news cannot match newspapers for detail in the reporting of hard news. They do not attempt to load the viewer with names, numbers, and other data. Yet this basic limitation of the medium is apparently ignored during the weathercast.

Meteorologists' jargon has crept into the weather report like Carl Sandburg's famous poem about fog coming "on little cat feet." Take the word *activity*, as in *thunderstorm activity* or *shower activity*. Why does a weather forecaster tell a television news audience, "Shower activity is expected tonight," when he means "We might have showers"?

On the other hand, if we don't get "shower activity" we'll have "zero precipitation," which means that *it won't rain*.

Weather forecasts need not sound so dreadful. Steal a line from H. Allen Smith, and say, "The weather forecast calls for snow, followed by small boys and girls on sleds." Better yet, use your own imagination.

Said one ABC News journalist, "I like words like rain, mild, snow, sunny, cold, hot, thunderstorms, tornadoes, nice, etc. I like forecasts that tell the viewer how to dress for the next day and how to plan for the weekend. Down with the H's and L's. Boo to the isobars and inverted, occluded troughs. Up with good old easy to understand American."

CBS News essayist Andy Rooney opined, "Anchormen and weathermen, with nothing much to say about the weather, get involved in a lot of cute smalltalk. The weatherman gives us some pseudo-technical talk about high- and low-pressure areas just to reassure us that he knows more about weather than we do. All we want to hear is whether we ought to take along a raincoat or not, and he's telling us that something has dropped from 31.2 to 31.1 and is headed our way from Canada."

Sources of Weather News

The National Weather Service provides a weather wire to subscribers at no charge except for machine rental and drop charges. In some communities the Weather Service even pays the phone line charges. The information itself comes free to everyone. Television stations, radio stations and newspapers have benefitted from this arrangement for years. The public is the ultimate beneficiary. At first only the larger cities got the service, but in the early Seventies it was extended to media outlets in smaller communities through what is called the NOAA (for

National Oceanic and Atmospheric Administration) weather wire. The feed is identical to the major city weather wire.

Stations without a weather wire get some weather news from the AP and UPI radio wires. Telephone calls to the local National Weather Service office garner still more information. Radio stations sometimes take a telephone feed from a weather bureau meteorologist just for the sake of having a feed from someone who sounds as if he knows what he is talking about.

Professional Meterologists

More and more stations are hiring trained meteorologists as weathercasters. What the station pays him may represent just part of his income. The trained meteorologist may be in business for himself, offering a tailored weather report to private industrial and agricultural clients who need specific kinds of information which the National Weather Service does not supply. The meteorologist skilled in broadcast techniques is a plus to a station. The American Meteorological Society grants its Seal of Approval to meteorologists who meet its standards, the only certification of competence by a board of peers in the news industry.

"Happy" Weather

At the other end of the spectrum is what might be termed "happy" weather. At one TV station the weather reporter did a report from the field, measuring the depth of a new snowfall. The camera crew threw snowballs at him. At another station, the weather reporter was shown standing up to his neck in a barrel of water, an illusion done with Chromakey. At WLWC, Columbus, Ohio, the weather reporter brought a bear onto the set one evening, and on another evening was followed around by someone dressed as a leprechaun. The times have indeed changed, but have they improved at every station?

"Weather is not hard news, and a weatherman is not a newscaster," was the view of one Chicago news director, who said the weatherman could "yuk it up, but only when the weather isn't serious." And his weatherman did in fact stand on his head one evening and throw wads of paper around on other evenings.

Why this childish behavior? The answer is the "happy talk" format which some stations present as newscasts. On these the weatherman has a comic's role as a "fall guy" or "second banana." What this has to do with news is open to question.

Illustrating the Weather

Weather news may offer the only bit of lightness in a television newscast filled with disasters and dire forebodings, giving this segment of the newscast a personality, a quality of its own, a digression from the usual severe run of news.

Illustrating the weather report and the forecast adds measurably to the product. Much can be done, and done cheaply, to relieve a tedious recital of numbers and details. Here are just a few ideas:

1. Maps of the United States and the local region are painted on glass or on a blackboard, or are printed on big sheets of paper tacked up on a board and replaced each newscast. The weather reporter uses chalk for the blackboard, Magic Marker or crayon for the paper or glass, in order to outline the weather pattern, with its fronts, highs, lows, and movements, and to write all those numbers.

2. A magnetic map board is a handsomer alternative to a blackboard. When designed in relief, its mountains stand out. Front movements are indicated by iron arrows which hold fast wherever they are placed. Numbers slapped to the wall cling. Miniature suns and rain clouds join the display. By using a rotating polarity filter over the lens of the television camera, in combination with numbers and symbols responsive to polarized light, whatever the weatherman sticks to the board pulsates. Mystified viewers telephone the station to inquire what the trick is.

3. Another mystifying trick depends upon reversing the camera scan, which is difficult to do in a color camera and therefore would require a station to reserve one camera solely for the weather. The trick is done with a large, clear Plexiglas map. The map is placed between the weatherman and the camera. The map faces him and he sees it in its proper East-West perspective, and he writes on it normally, from left to right. The camera sees the map backward. But with the scan reversed, the audience sees the map in proper perspective, the weatherman is not blocking any of the map with his body, and it appears that he is writing backwards. Of course, this could still be done without reverse scanning if the weatherman would actually learn to write backwards. [3]

4. A large pad of blank sheets is placed on an easel. The weatherman, a quick and clever cartoonist, ad libs his weather report while he draws a child in rain gear hurrying to school, a smiling sun shining down and so forth. The viewer is delighted by the rapid movements of the charcoal across the page and the effortless patter of the weatherman.

5. Stock slides are used to illustrate predictions. Because interest in tomorrow's weather is so often child-centered, the slides are pictures of children in various quantities of clothing, from thin cotton play togs through light sweaters to boots and snow mittens. The slides fill the screen, so the weatherman — or whoever reports weather news — does not appear on camera at all, unless the slides are used for rear projection.

6. A huge thermometer forecasts the weather. The weatherman makes changes on camera by means of a pull tab.

7. Each day the weather information is prepared in advance on cards. They show outline maps, names of states on a national map or towns on a local map, plus numbers.

8. A few feet of film or tape are shot each day of scenes around town: children going to school, people shopping, a couple getting in their car to drive to work,

ducks in a park lake, an oil heating truck, a thermostat being turned up. Arthur S. Harris, Jr., of WRGB, Schenectady, N.Y., suggests:

Have a station's photographers bring back during the course of their work a few feet of film which captures that day's weather. In Washington, weathercasts are enhanced with 16mm footage of children sailing boats, of joggers in Rock Creek Park....On the first day of summer vacation from school the photographer brings back a few feet of film of children playing in mid-morning; and if the next day there is a sudden summer shower with inches of rain falling in a few hours, he shoots footage showing the rain sweeping down onto the streets, rushing off into the sewers — just enough footage to capture the beauty of it all.

The next day is a scorcher. The temperature is in the high 90's. Using his imagination, the photographer produces a series of little vignettes. Children gathered around a street corner ice cream vendor, youngsters with a Kool-Aid stand, a taxicab company installing signs on its cabs that say "Air Conditioned." These little vignettes appear on TV as the weather-caster talks about the high temperature of the day instead of having nothing more imaginative than a gigantic 97 on the screen...

So we visualize turnpikes shrouded in fog, snowblowers clearing air-port runways, rushing streams of springtime, splashers and swimmers and sunners at a placid country swimming hole in mid-August. We see early morning wintertime scenes of people trying to start their cars in sub-zero temperatures, overhead shots of a five o'clock downpour and workers streaming from offices with umbrellas, newspapers, magazines over their heads rushing for hard-to-get cabs and crowded buses. We get soft evening scenes of summertime haying.[4]

The list is endless. After use, the film clips or tapes are kept in a library, but camera crews remain constantly on the lookout for new scenes to illustrate the weather. The weatherman or the newscaster gives the weather report and forecast over the film, sometimes with the help of super cards or super slides containing a single number. The cards or slides, of course, are kept on file. Each time the forecast predicts a high of 51 degrees, the proper card or slide is at hand.

9. Permanent maps are built with block holes for numbers. The numbers are display digits, controlled electrically by an off-camera panel. The numbers change on camera. Display digits are also used in television news to report scores and standings, election results and stock market averages. Each number breaks vertically or horizontally in half while in view. The visual effect is like a staccato burst. It is fascinating to watch.

10. Satellite weather maps, now available, give a weather report a scientific and up-to-date appearance.

11. Children's drawings show the weather today and the outlook tomorrow. In London, the commercial channel, THAMES, came up with a delightful idea, using children's drawings. The news department contacted several elementary

schools to ask if children, age 6 to 11, would draw weather pictures. The channel supplied cards, measuring 24″ x 12″, colored felt drawing pens, and a list of 18 different weather conditions: light showers, cloudy and cold, etc. Each school's drawings were used for a week or two, and the weather reporter always mentioned the school. Two cards appeared nightly, one illustrating today's weather and the other illustrating tomorrow's forecast.

12. The weatherman uses an illuminated pointer, with an on-off control, at rear projection maps.

13. Short animated films illustrate outdoor conditions. Animation Techniques, Inc., produced a series of 10-second cartoons of animals. Example: a frog under a lily pad, with the rain coming down. Fairman Productions of Milwaukee offered 16-second animations of a cartoon character named Freddy Forecast.

14. At KOTV, the weathercaster explained matters to a puppet.

15. Through ENG and Chromakey an outdoor scene is shown live as a rear projection.

16. An actual radar system is displayed by a meteorologist who gives the audience a few seconds of basic instruction in what it shows.

Radar

The classiest, most expensive weather operation uses color radar hooked to a frame storage unit, so that viewers can see the intensity of a storm and how it has been moving through the region. Light precipitation might be recorded in a pale blue, medium precipitation in green, and heavy precipitation in red. The multi-color picture is automatically recorded every few minutes and stored. Played back on the air, it is time-lapse photography on a disc of the movement and changing intensity of the storm.

The radar, operating over a range up to 250 miles, easily picks up hail and rain, but has more difficulty detecting snow, which is ten parts air to one part ice crystal. The radar beam passes through the flake rather than bouncing back. Present radar systems cannot detect clouds or fog.

A station owning its own radar system should hire a meteorologist trained in radar to interpret the data. For Weather Service radar drops, training is a must.

Stations which do not want the expense of a radar system can tap into the nearest radar-equipped National Weather Service station by means of a dedicated phone line. A picture will be sent over that may be printed on recording paper or put directly on the air. A number of National Weather Service stations have a system which permits stations to tap in by dialing up the signal over a *WATS* line, so that a dedicated line is not needed, but the picture quality is subject to noise on the phone line.

For the Student

1. Think of one more way to illustrate weather news besides those listed.

2. Trace an outline of the United States from an atlas onto a large sheet of white paper or light-colored construction paper. Using the newspaper weather forecast, draw a weather map.

3. Do the same to make a regional weather map.

4. Now, without a script, videotape or audiotape a television weather report. Review the tape. What did you do wrong?

5. Is it necessary that most people understand what is meant by barometric pressure, or should a weathercaster report it even if just a few viewers understand it?

Sports 13

There is no way to measure the destructive effect of sports broadcasting on ordinary American English, but it must be considerable.

—Edwin Newman

Back in the days of the segmented news format, before our present integrated format became popular, sports were reported in separate programs with their own sponsors. Radio listeners or television viewers who wanted to hear the latest scores or the latest news or some gossip about an athlete tuned in; others did not.

Today, not too much has changed. In a half-hour newscast, the sports segment begins about 23 minutes into the newscast. Those sports fans who care little about hard news or the weather, but are anxious to learn how their beloved Braves did this afternoon, can tune in at 23 minutes after the hour to find out, while those viewers who don't care what the Braves did will tune out, knowing that all the hard news that will be told has already been told, and nothing will follow sports except perhaps a humorous "kicker." Those viewers who want to hear everything will sit out the entire newscast.

ABC News research showed that 25% of viewers were very interested in sports news, 40% were somewhat interested, and 35% were completely uninterested. An ABC News executive commented, "In truth, most statistical material should be dumped. Good action footage interests the viewers, whether or not they are sports fans...not a talking-head of a coach or a jock." He advised stations to cover participatory sports like tennis and fishing, including how-to segments.

The Sports Reporter

When the director tells the T.D., "Fade up on 1," to start another television newscast, the camera is likely to reveal the familiar triumvirate of newscaster, weather reporter and sports reporter. Of the three, only the sports reporter may be exactly where he wanted to be ever since he was a teenager. Other journalists tend to drift in and out of jobs, dreaming of becoming foreign correspondents but settling for the next train. Sports reporters seem to have been born to be sports reporters, a job they consider the next best thing to being an offensive quarterback.

On a local television news staff the sportscaster may also be the only sports reporter on staff, aided by a photographer who is part of the regular news staff and a high school or college student who volunteers his free hours for the fun of being part of the sports coverage and who is sent, joyfully, from time to time, to cover a game. Larger cities will have a paid reporter or two in addition to the sports anchor. In small towns and at many radio stations the sports reporter doubles on regular news assignments.

Filling the last five or seven minutes of the TV newscast, the sports reporter will lead off with his top news story, the one he headlined at the start of the newscast. A typical evening may include three short films or tapes, maybe highlights of a game, plus an interview plus a feature. The sportscast will include a few scores from important national games, some local scores, some hard sports news both national and local, and an announcement or two about upcoming games or where the best powder snow can be found for downhill skiing.

Thanks to videotape, sports coverage is less of a hit and miss affair. The photographer can turn the video camera on for an entire ball game because the tape is reusable. With live video facilities, portions of an important local game can be fed live into the newscast, which combines nicely with edited tape of previous action, provided, of course, that the ball teams do not object to unpaid live coverage. Some pooling arrangements may also be worked out between stations.

Sports News Ethics

Objectivity is virtually ignored by the sports reporter as it is by the weather reporter. The weatherman smiles when he can forecast a pleasant day, the sports reporter is jubilant when the home team wins, and no one thinks twice about it. But objectivity has much more meaning when the news concerns not the results of a game but the sports business. If we stop to think about it, sports reporting deals not only with the games themselves, an entertainment like the movies, but also with its economic structure, which is a business just as a department store is a business.

Things can get sticky when a reporter who treats the games as entertainment insists on treating the rest of sports news as news. For example, in late 1976, two reporters for the Oklahoma City *Times* who reported on an impending NCAA investigation of alleged misconduct involving the University of Oklahoma football program were threatened by angry football fans for "disloyalty" to the team. The reporters requested police protection for four nights because of bomb threats and other intimidation by telephone, including thirty calls in one two-hour period.

Yet the plain fact is that a reporter owes no "loyalty" to a team any more than he owes loyalty to a supermarket or a steel factory because they are located in his city, or than the city hall reporter owes loyalty to the mayor. Aside from the harmless and universally accepted cheerfulness when the local boys win, the sports reporter's "loyalty" should belong to the community alone. He has no writ to protect the team's owners or coaches or players by his silence. His job is news, not P.R. The sports reporter should never be simply a cheerleader, no matter what blandishments are offered. And there are temptations, ranging from the steady stream of insider's tips and the entree to the locker room for interviews to the "freebies" — the free tickets, free dinners, free trips, even free bar tabs and gifts and extra money for doing a commercial or writing a column for a home game program. The more responsible television stations and newspapers put strict limits on what a reporter may accept. Examples of the temptations were cited in a Columbia Journalism Review article:

> When a reporter covers one of the twenty-four major league baseball teams, he is given the team's card admitting him to private lounges in stadiums. He sits with other reporters and team executives as he hears information that the club wishes to reveal and enjoys complimentary liquor and/or dinner. If... he avoids the free meals, he still can find it extremely difficult to socialize repeatedly with a team and then be the only journalist to report its faults or present a true characterization of a tough-talking coach. [1]

The publisher of *Sporting News*, C.C. Johnson Spink, once noted that a reporter "and his family socialize with the players' families. He goes out to movies, breakfast, or to and from the game with the players. Many reporters' wives are in social events with players' wives. What you have is a big, happy family....A reporter should avoid this situation...."

Of course, sports reporters are feted by the managements of well-known teams because the reporter provides free advertising. In a sense the management of, say, a professional basketball team based in a large Eastern city competes for precious television time with the managements of baseball, football and hockey teams in that city. Air time means popularity and that translates into dollars at the box office.

Sports Jargon

No other area of news has such a wide gulf between those who want to know and those who do not. The dyed-in-the-wool sports fan cares more about how his team is doing than about what the city council is doing with his taxes. When he (more sports fans are male) tunes in, he wants most of all to hear the scores, so each day sportscasters reel them off.

But because there is a sameness about reading off lists of names and numbers, sportscasters follow the practice of newspaper sports reporters by pepping up the English language. Instead of learning what's happening in *baseball*, we learn what's happening in *baseball action*.

Instead of one team *beating* or *defeating* another, a litany of similes tells us that a team was *downed, dumped, crushed, creamed, slaughtered, smashed, walloped, wiped out, flattened, floored, blocked, sneaked past,* or *taken care of*, all by the score of 3 to 2.

The sports reporter gets away with what is simply bad English, stuff that no editor would permit in news of politics, business or any other endeavor, a style that one newspaper editor called "the most horrendous mess of gibberish ever set before the eyes of a reader."

A lot of sports writing is also limited to numbers: "It was their first win in a best two-out-of-three series after four straight losses, with Robinson going 0 for 3 before homering in the seventh to bring his R.B.I. to 76 and his average to .308."

Is this really any different from: "The Dow Jones Industrials closed up 3.42 to 904.56. The average price per share rose six cents on the New York Exchange and two cents on the American."?

The Wider World of Sports

ABC's *Wide World of Sports* discovered an audience for sports which many television station sports reporters largely ignore in their concentration on the big teams in spectator sports, an audience less interested in the head-to-head competition of one team against another than in the art, the skill, the courage, and the fluid grace that is the essence of all sports. So *Wide World of Sports* used its time not to reel off a series of scores, names and batting averages but to show how all kinds of sports are played, and in doing so built an audience of tens of millions and put itself into the broadcasting history books.

The sports reporter for a local station cannot duplicate *Wide World of Sports*. He must attend to the demands of the fan who wants the scores, but there is time in the evening's sports reports for an interview and a feature, and it is then that the sports reporter should be aware that there is more to sports than the big names and the big teams in *spectator* sports.

People of all ages enjoy a great variety of *participant* sports. They play sandlot softball, go bowling, swim, jog, take whacks at tennis balls, handballs and golf balls, ice skate and ski. Some lift weights and some learn karate. They're not watching, they're out there doing it, however awkwardly, and the television station which takes pride in thinking that it shows the community to itself may be neglecting this rich part of the community life. The sports reporter who sneers at jogging as a soft feature which the news side can handle if it wants to not only does a disservice to the community but also dismisses a potential audience.

Another kind of sports coverage usually ignored in large cities is high school and small college competition, not the scores but the contest itself. With video-tape a sports reporter might choose to cover "the game of the week"; this week, why can't radio listeners or television viewers get highlights of the game between the Washington High School Patriots and the Roosevelt High Tigers?

Wide-ranging sports coverage in newspapers and on the air gets into other areas as well: the growing role of women in sports, accusations of racism, accusations of violence, labor disputes, gambling, and business deals. All this has not come without objection, as writer David Shaw noted:

> There is, in fact, considerable resistance to the new school of sports journalism — from fans, from athletes and from longtime sportswriters themselves. These critics see the sports page forsaking its traditional role as an essentially escapist medium — a purveyor of information and entertainment — and becoming, instead, a forum for haughty cynicism and gratuitous sociology.

> These criticisms are not without merit. Even the most *avant garde* sportswriters admit that in their zeal to eschew the old scores-and-statistics approach, they often have overreacted and provided a surfeit of offbeat, interpretive, sociological stories at the sacrifice of solid news and analysis of daily happenings in the sports world.

> ...unlike other reporters, sportswriters are not generally — by instinct or by training — skeptical, questioning, probing. They have tended to shy away from asking the difficult question — and they have too often automatically believed, and written, whatever they were told.

> Again, there have been exceptions. Many great newspapermen and novelists and writers for the stage and screen began their careers as sportswriters — men like Ernest Hemingway, James Reston, Damon Runyon, Westbrook Pegler, Heywood Broun, Gay Talese, Jimmy Breslin, Paul Gallico, Ring Lardner and John Lardner.[2]

For the Student

1. Reread the section on illustrating weather news in Chapter 12. Is there anything that can be applied to illustrating sports news?

2. Should a sports report be prepared for the widest possible audience or for the dedicated sports fan?

3. Most sportscasts today are aimed at the follower of major spectator sports, not the participant of such sports activities as jogging and raquetball. Should that be changed? Discuss in class.

4. What "freebies" should a sports reporter accept? For example, should he accept free passes for his friends to the games? Out of town trips to cover games, expenses paid by the home team? Or should his station pick up every

expense, including his own ticket to local events? In short, where should the line be drawn?

5. Does sports jargon give a sports report a unique and desirable flavor? Send that around the infield horn for a few minutes.

CONSTRAINTS
AND CONCERNS

Speaking Out In Editorials and Documentaries

The Law

Mike and Camera in the Courtroom

The Profession

Show Biz

The Round Events Peg and the Square News Hole

Speaking Out in Editorials and Documentaries

14

> (**Regarding a free press**) *To many, this is and always will be folly, but we have staked upon it our all.*
>
> — *Judge Learned Hand*

In Seattle, KING-TV used its program *Newservice* to run a series of half-hour reports called "The Burned Child." What happens to children whose clothing catches fire? Viewers stared in horror as the camera looked for eight unflinching minutes at a little girl enduring a change of dressing on the burns which covered most of her body. Reporter Don McGaffin told them to write to the Secretary of Commerce in Washington, D.C., demanding new standards for children's sleepwear. And write they did. More than 4,000 letters. And soon there were new standards, despite the textile industry's dragging feet. KING-TV's programs, said Sen Warren G. Magnuson (D.Wash.), were "the one single factor" which led to the tougher regulations.

To begin *and* end this chapter on such editorials would be to indulge in wishful thinking. When it thinks about the life around it and is willing to act upon its conclusions, a radio or television station or a network can be powerful. At times, even magnificent.

We have seen the maturing of the first generation over which television has had a substantial influence, and we have seen that television editorials and documentaries have more than once exerted a change that bettered our society.

The Reluctant Broadcaster

Unfortunately, when some broadcast station owners think, they think only of fattening their purses. Safety lies in saying as little as possible. Many choose to say nothing. And the record of presentation of editorials and documentaries is, nationally, spotty. Survey after survey, including one taken by this author, shows little enthusiasm for controversy at a lot of stations.[1]

Former FCC Chairman Newton Minow once complained about television stations that editorialized for "canoe safety, milk for children," and causes just as daring. And Dr. Frank Stanton came out of retirement in 1974 to criticize broadcast editorial writers for "either a failure on your part to fully understand your opportunities and responsibilities as broadcast editorialists, or a failure on the part of your management to give you the support that you need." [2]

A 1972 survey showed that nearly a third of all television stations ran no editorials at all.[3] At least that is better than the 1958 situation when, nearly a decade after the Fairness Doctrine, only one third of the stations ever editorialized and only 5% editorialized daily. FCC Chairman John C. Doerfer wondered then if the right to editorialize was proving too much of a shock. "Ten years," he noted dryly, "is a long time to stand in stunned silence."

The Radio Television News Directors Association annually awards prizes for the best television editorials. The quality of editorials has been improving but, as a category, editorials lag sadly behind spot news coverage.

Editorials from many stations pop out devoid of technique or artistry, and consequently devoid of impact or charm. It seems as if all concerned, including viewers, grit their teeth, mutter "FCC," and suffer the editorial. This despite evidence that people want stations to take editorial stands on public issues. And in fact, a 1975 study by Dr. Herschel Shosteck reported that two out of three regular editorial viewers believed stations should "take a strong editorial stand on the issues."[4] That percentage rises to three out of four among the younger audience and those with more income and education, the people stations are most anxious to attract. The study showed that most of the audience wants editorials which present facts and not just opinions, which present both sides of an issue, take a strong editorial stand, editorialize "for" rather than "against" an issue, and suggest specific improvements.

Broadcasters Who Speak Out

That, of course, takes research. WTVJ-TV, Miami, the nation's first television station to run daily editorials, realizes what its editorials have accomplished. Said station owner Mitchell Wolfson, "We do our homework. Our editorials are like icebergs. The research and thought that goes into them is hidden from view. The public sees only the minute-or-so of delivery. But behind each one... supporting each one...is easily two or three days of painstaking research. And even then, it is not our purpose to move people to blindly parrot what we have to say. The single purpose of our editorials is to stimulate thought."[5]

After a reporter and photographer followed health inspectors around restaurants, WTVJ-TV ran a series, "Not on the Menu," every night for twelve weeks on both the 6 p.m. and 11 p.m. news. Viewers were treated to film of dead mice, live cockroaches, and techniques to recycle half-eaten salads. The result: new sanitation regulations. WTVJ-TV also turned its cameras on police corruption and organized crime in Dade County, forcing the county sheriff to resign. Indictments, including one with the sheriff's name on it, followed. WTVJ-TV's campaign included 85 consecutive editorials, surveillance film shot at risk, and an anti-crime telathon.

WTVJ-TV displays national awards for its editorials. In 1962, the year Minow made that crack about canoe safety, WTVJ-TV successfully fought city hall to force the rehiring of the city manager. The station editorialized that the city commissioners fired him because he was "too good for his own good."

Another oft-praised station, WDSU-TV, and its companion radio station, WDSU, of New Orleans, dared to speak out for a responsible civil rights policy at a time when local newspapers shrank back.

WDSU-TV became the first television station to use political cartoons. It has since been joined by stations in Chicago, Atlanta and Indianapolis, among others.

John Chase, editorial cartoonist for WDSU-TV New Orleans, concluded:[6]

> Graphic humor belongs on a graphic medium like television...Response from viewers in our area has been more than encouraging, although some would like the cartoon to stay on longer. I'm more pleased that no one has written in grumbling that it stays on too long. A more general complaint is the inability of the cartoon fans to cut out a favorite cartoon to send to — well, whomever they send them to.
>
> I have many of our efforts on film. Most of them have musical accompaniment; some have narration, all have some kind of movement, and...all (are now) in full color. We still can't figure out how to reprint them on paper for those who write in for copies.
>
> Although my cartooning on TV has been but a few years of the number I've been a published cartoonist, I've never had so much response and so little privacy as these past few years on television.

Chase devised several techniques to take advantage of the medium. Among them: two cameras, music, multiple panels, multi-segment overlays, and signature wipe-in. Presenting the cartoon from start to finish takes about 45 seconds. It is pre-taped.

Newsweek Broadcasting offered to television stations 15-second animated editorial cartoons in color, drawn by well-known newspaper cartoonists.

Documentaries

There are reasons to do documentaries and reasons not to, and the arguments were going on long before Edward R. Murrow tusseled with the CBS front office.

Motivating forces are:

1. Pressure from news personnel
2. Desire for prestige

3. Pressure from citizens' groups
4. FCC's public service criterion
5. Appreciation by broadcasters of public service responsibilities.
Working against these motivating forces are inhibiting forces:
1. Production costs
2. Inadequate staff
3. Lack of advertiser support
4. Low ratings
5. Fear of legal tangles
6 Fear of stirring up hostility
7. Fairness Doctrine requirement for response time.

In a sense, to be in favor of documentaries is to be on the side of the angels. Unfortunately, the angels have not been winning. Instead, with humankind's genius for covering a bad situation with a nice word (e.g., *inner city* for *slum*), the old television news feature story has now become a "mini-documentary." The problem with the two-minute or three-minute "mini-doc" which typically runs each day for one week is that by the time the subject is re-introduced, there isn't time enough to say anything, let alone create the mood that is so important to successful documentaries.

All this is not to imply that the half-hour and one-hour documentaries have had their day. Each year thousands are produced, and a number of these deservedly win awards. What can be said with some certitude is that the longer documentary has never been as popular in the front office as it has been in the newsroom, and consequently the making of documentaries — their authorization, budgeting, production and scheduling — has ever been a source of conflict.

If a mini-doc is too short and a half-hour or one-hour documentary is too long, maybe the solution lies somewhere in between. The success of *60 Minutes* has led the other networks and a number of stations to develop magazine format programs. One or two host-reporters usually offer two or three investigative reports or light features that run from ten to twenty minutes each. An electronic letters-to-the-editor segment rounds off the program. Fred Friendly, who did those excellent *See It Now* documentaries with Murrow, has predicted that within a few years a magazine show would be on the air every night of the week. "Entertainment programming is bankrupt," Friendly said, rather hopefully. "Television is beginning to see that real life, which is constantly fresh and renewing, is the answer."

What's Your Viewpoint?

Audience opinion is always popular with audiences. Newspapers and magazines run letters to the editor. Radio and television stations run what used to be called Man-on-the-Street, or MOS, reports, and now may have a more neutral gender designation like Person-on-the-Street or, better yet, Your Viewpoint, for that is what it is.

A few broadcast stations have used a console for public opinion polling. Equipped with three "stations," each consisting of a tape recorder with a pre-taped outgoing message hooked by special circuitry to a tape recorder for recording incoming messages, the console enabled a single telephone operator to make 100 to 125 calls an hour. The first recorder asked the question of the day, the second recorded the answer. WDAY-TV, Fargo, N.D., has conducted polls on everything from the Russian wheat deal to a proposal to raise the mayor's salary. The console can also be used by the sales department to measure audience.

WCVB, Boston, had a question-of-the-week which reporters asked of everyone they encountered while they were filming. A weekly feature, it offered the faces of the well-known and the unknown, all having a crack at the question of the week.

Other stations regularly run letters to the editor in response to editorials with a reporter reading portions of the letters with permission of the writers. To stimulate letters, a station may send out copies of the editorial before and after it is delivered. The letters go to individuals and groups likely to reply.

Under the terms of the Fairness Doctrine, responsible individuals and representatives of groups have a right to reply either by letter or in person, and these feedback editorials can be audience builders.

A four-day sequence prevailed at KFBB, Great Falls, Montana. Tuesday saw the editorial. On Wednesday, viewers' response was given in the form of letters to the editor electronically supered. On Thursday the station ran person-on-the-street interviews about the issue. On Friday a guest editor responded to the Tuesday editorial.

Consumer Problems

Many television stations now run regular consumer advocate segments, an ombudsman service which may be called "Direct Line," "Action Line," or "Action News." These regular features are so popular that viewers will wait out news segments they find dull just to listen to someone's problem and to learn how the news department solved it. The service is quite simple. The "Action Line" reporter invites letters from viewers who have a problem "we can help solve," which translates to problems involving some level of government or a private business firm. The letters pour in from the woman who is wakened by garbage trucks at 6 a.m., the man who can't get a replacement part to fix a broken lawn mower, the woman who sent money to a mail order firm and has not heard, the youth who sent three job applications to a distant company and got no response, and so forth. The news department establishes a policy of answering every letter, knowing that this alone may require someone's full time attention. One or two letters of particular interest become part of the newscast. After a problem is solved, the letter is read on the air. The steps taken by the news department to help and the eventual outcome follow.

News departments also show their concern for consumer issues by documentaries and specials. "Not on the Menu" and KING-TV's series on children's sleepwear are two of dozens, even hundreds, of examples that could be given of consumer issues which became documentaries and effected change.

Consumer's Union, which publishes *Consumer Reports*, offers 90-second television reports on the products it tests, sent out twice a week.

WFAA-TV ran a four-part report on hamburger sold in Dallas and Fort Worth supermarkets. The title of the series, "Germburger?" was used in newspaper and magazine ads with a picture of a juicy hamburger to catch the attention of viewers.

At WCCO-TV, Minneapolis, *Consumer Inquiry*, a newscast feature, discovered that 40 percent of Grade A potatoes were actually Grade B. The Minnesota Department of Agriculture ordered 125,000 pounds of potatoes recalled. *Consumer Inquiry* reporter Larry Schmidt also identified by name the auto dealers who had turned used car odometers back. Several dealers were taken to court. And Schmidt saved some poor families a total of $30,000 in hospital bills when he discovered that 123 Minnesota hospitals failed to provide some free care to patients, which was required under a Federal hospital construction program.

In Jacksonville, Florida, WTLV-TV discovered that private ambulance services were using unethical tactics, even to the extent of mutual sabotage, and successfully pressed for a single city service run by the fire department.

KABC-TV, Los Angeles, learned that people were paying up to $300 for contact lenses that cost $10 to $18 to manufacture, and attacked state fair trade laws that forbade price advertising.

WTTG-TV, Washington, D.C., used George Washington University law school students to field consumer complaints. They reportedly solved four out of five, and some were heard on the 10 p.m. newscast. Across town at WTOP-TV, a woman reporter got complaints from several women who had mailed $9.95 to a post office box number for an advertised "breast developer." What they received was a jump rope plus instructions for jumping. WTOP-TV managed to develop refunds for all of them.

Of all the consumer affairs reporters in the nation, perhaps the most interesting was Herbert S. Denenberg, who first came to national attention as Pennsylvania's insurance commissioner. With impressive credentials as a former college professor, a lawyer, and the author of several books, Denenberg went on Philadelphia's WCAU-TV to become what *Time* called "one of the funniest, roughest consumer-affairs reporters ever to read fine print on a label."'One of his typical on-air statements: "I make sure I get my exercise, get enough rest, and eat healthy food. So I don't need Geritol."

Denenberg, at the time of this writing, had not been sued. He is both knowledgeable and careful. However, other consumer reporters have not been so fortunate, nor have their stations.

Consumer affairs reporting bridges the gap between objectivity and advocacy. It is both. In theory, at least, the reporter approaches each question objectively and dispassionately, investigating the cause of a complaint and the remedies available. When the reporter concludes that the remedies are inadequate and that those responsible choose not to apply remedies which, in the reporter's view, would remove the problem, the consumer affairs reporter moves from objective examiner to advocate. He presents the matter on the air as the problem he feels it is, and urges solution.

Editorials, Not Editorializing

It mattered not that NBC's Howard Tuckner was revolted by the sight of Saigon's police chief pulling out a revolver and calmly shooting a bound Vietcong prisoner through the head. He was there to report, not to opinionate, and report he did in a few lean words. But the impression the story made was stronger for Tuckner's restraint.

Between "editorials" and "editorializing in news," a clear line of demarcation exists. Editorials are statements of opinion by the station management or a commentator, usually with the word "editorial" or "commentary" announced in advance or in plain view. Editorializing in news is a more or less covert expression of opinion through choice of words or film or subject matter or even gesture.

A more subtle difference exists between editorializing in news, which might be sneakily intentional, and the honest reaction to a news event. In the latter case the journalist, admitting that perfect objectivity is neither possible nor desirable, tries to be fair. In the former case, he probably denies that he is not being objective, but really has no intention of being fair.

If a station speaks out courageously on local matters, almost by definition it will generate some community ill will which arrives through the diligent labors of the postman and the PBX operator. The timid station manager or news director avoids this ill will by several means:

1. Dullness — a lack of wit, of bite, of impact will mitigate criticism;
2. The "Mom's apple pie is good for you" approach — as noted, canoe safety and milk for children also work;
3. "Afghanistanism" — say what you like about the Communists, but don't knock anything in this town;
4. Balance — "Side A has excellent arguments. So does Side B. We hope this healthy and spirited community dialogue continues";
5. Escape — "We don't want to inflict our opinions on you. We want to reflect what our community thinks. So we have invited the people of this city to do the talking."

Washington Post columnist Nicholas von Hoffman said of broadcast editorials, "Strong points of view illuminate information, give it shape and meaning, and from the clash of many strong points of view come new understandings and validations of old ones. This is one reason for having free speech, and no amount of balanced and bland fairness can substitute for the struggle of competing advocacies.''

As for #5 above, *vox populi* has strong merit, but only in addition to regular editorials, not instead of them.

Who should write the editorials? Who should deliver them? The answers depend upon station policy. For example:

1. The station manager writes and delivers the station's editorials. They are not aired during the newscast, but possibly adjacent to it.

2. An editorial writer researches and writes them. The station manager delivers them.

3. A news writer does the research and writing. The station manager delivers them.

4. The news director delivers them. Either he or a news writer prepares them.

5. A staff "editorialist" prepares and delivers them within the newscast. The station manager approves them.

6. A staff commentator writes and delivers opinions within the newscast. These are commentaries representing the views of the commentator, not editorials representing the views of the station.

The Fairness Doctrine requires opportunity for reply. In some cases, especially where an individual has been attacked, equal time may be demanded under the "personal attack rule" (see RED LION). Where a viewer disagrees by letter with a station's editorial viewpoint, it has been customary for the person who delivers the editorials to read from the letter a portion which gets to the heart of the viewer's disagreement. For added clarity, a television station may, like CBS' *60 Minutes*, print a sentence from the letter for use as a rear projection while the letter segment is read aloud.

It has also been customary at the end of each editorial to invite viewer response.

Ralph Renick, WTVJ-TV vice president for news, bases his daily editorials on these standards:[8]

1. One person must be the sole, final authority.

2. The editorial should be restricted almost wholly to local and state issues.

3. The station must be able to conduct "research in depth" in a speedy manner.

4. The one who delivers the editorial must be well known and respected, and he must know his community well.

5. The editorial must be clearly defined on the air, and carefully separated from the news reporting segments.

6. Courage is important — to take a definite stand and then stick with it.

7. No editorial should be a "blast" — a course of action must be presented.

8. Editorials should be clearly on the side of righteousness and betterment. If it is necessary to delve into politics, or truly double-edged issues, then the station must be immediately prepared to air the opposing side of the issue on which it has taken a stand.

A typical editorial will run two to three minutes. Whether the TV viewer sees only the person delivering the editorial or visuals as well depends upon the station. Of course, there is no limit to the visuals which can be used: political cartoons, stills, film, etc. Detroit's WJBK-TV neatly turned a SOF news feature, about a woman trying to raise money to run a local charity, into a fine editorial by offering to match, dollar for dollar, all money raised to reach the goal she had set.

From Carl Zimmerman, news director of WITI-TV, Milwaukee, here is still further expression of the need to use the television medium fully: "If we criticize our city, county or state officials, let's show those officials in action at their meetings, at their public hearings. Let the viewer *hear* and *see* them on sound film. What better way to know the kind of men they elected? If we cry out for correction at the dangerous intersection, let's show the driver that traffic hazard, that congested bottleneck. If our expressway construction is proceeding too slowly, let's take our sound cameras right there and show where and how county officials are failing to keep construction humming along. If we ask for greater speed in wiping blight from our central city, again our cameras should film the editorial right there where the problems are the greatest." [9]

The Fairness Doctrine

One of the hottest controversies in broadcast journalism in recent years has been the Fairness Doctrine. Was it fair? Did it make television and radio stations stepchildren of the First Amendment, not enjoying the full rights of free speech?

As of 1980, the proposed revision of the Communications Act would totally deregulate radio: no Fairness Doctrine, no Section 315, not even a requirement for news or public affairs programming. For television the Fairness Doctrine would be replaced by the "equity principle," a concept similar in many respects to the Fairness Doctrine but not requiring stations to actively seek out controversial issues of public importance. Section 315 would be retained for television, with exemptions for presidential, vice presidential, senatorial, gubernatorial and other statewide elections. But 315 would still cover congressional and local elections.

How did all this begin?

By the Mayflower Decision, in 1941, the Federal Communications Commission ruled editorials off the air, stating, "A truly free radio cannot be used to advocate the causes of the licensee. It cannot be used to support the candidacies of his friends. It cannot be devoted to the support of principles he happens to regard most favorably. In brief, the broadcaster cannot be an advocate.''

The FCC gradually changed its attitude, and, in 1949, reversed itself with a report which came to be known as ''The Fairness Doctrine.'' The Commission not only said that broadcasting stations *could* editorialize, but they had a *duty* to discuss controversial issues. In all cases, they were obliged to present all sides of a controversy.

The Fairness Doctrine states:

> ...the needs and interests of the general public with respect to programs devoted to news commentary and opinion can only be satisfied by making available to them for their consideration and acceptance or rejection, of varying and conflicting views held by responsible elements of the community. And it is in the light of these basic concepts that the problems of insuring fairness in the presentation of news and opinions and the place in such a picture of any expression of the views of the station licensee as such must be considered....

> This affirmative responsibility on the part of broadcast licensees to provide a reasonable amount of time for the presentation over their facilities of programs devoted to the discussion and consideration of public issues has been reaffirmed by this Commission in a long series of decisions....This duty extends to all subjects of substantial importance to the community....The licensee must operate on a basis of overall fairness, making his facilities available for the expression of the contrasting views of all responsible elements in the community on the various issues which arise....

> These concepts, of course, do restrict the licensee's freedom to utilize his station in whatever manner he chooses but they do so in order to make possible the maintenance of radio as a medium of freedom of speech for the general public....

> We do not believe, however, that the licensee's obligations to serve the public interest can be met merely through the adoption of a general policy of not refusing to broadcast opposing views where a demand is made of the station for broadcast time....Broadcast licensees have an affirmative duty generally to encourage and implement the broadcast of all sides of controversial issues over their facilities....a conscious and positive role in bringing about a balanced presentation of the opposing viewpoints....

> The Commission believes that under the American system of broadcasting the individual licensees of radio stations have the responsibility for determining the specific program material to be broadcast over their stations. This choice, however, must be exercised in a manner consistent with the basic policy of the Congress that radio be maintained as a medium of free speech for the general public as a whole rather than as an outlet for the purely personal or private interests of the licensee. This requires that licensees devote a reasonable percentage of their broadcasting time

to the discussion of public issues of interest in the community served by their stations and that such programs be designed so that the public has a reasonable opportunity to hear different opposing positions on the public issues of interest and importance in the community. The particular format best suited for the presentation of such programs in a manner consistent with the public interest must be determined by the licensee in the light of the facts of each individual situation.

A complaint to the FCC by attorney John Banzhaf asking, under the Fairness Doctrine, for anti-smoking messages to offset cigarette commercials led to an extension of the scope of the Doctrine to commercials. The FCC and the courts, however, have since pulled back from that position. In its 1974 Fairness Report, the FCC argued that the Fairness Doctrine was not an appropriate vehicle for the correction of false or misleading advertising, saying that Federal Trade Commission sanctions are available and that false ads should be banned, not made the subject of debate. The FCC refused snowmobile opponents the automatic right to reply to snowmobile commercials.

The Fairness Doctrine: Pro and Con

Has the time come to scrap the Fairness Doctrine? Here are some arguments on both sides:

> Former NBC president Julian Goodman: "Nobody is telling anybody else what can or cannot be broadcast. Yet a form of censorship does exist — censorship after the fact. The peril to the American public is that with time, it can become self-censorship before the fact, inducing caution and blandness."

> Former ABC News president Elmer Lower: "My personal feeling... is that the fairness and balance doctrine is not inhibiting. I always found that one good way to deal with a controversial subject is to present a lively clash of differing opinions. Dramatists use it effectively. So can broadcast journalists.

> NBC reporter Bill Monroe: "There are stations that don't do investigative reporting. There are stations that confine their documentaries to safe subjects. There are stations that don't editorialize. There are stations that do editorialize but don't say anything...My opinion is that much of this kind of caution, probably most of it, is due to a deep feeling that boldness equals trouble with government, blandness equals peace."

> Professor Fred Friendly: "It may be your frequency, but it's everybody's Bill of Rights. To demand the First Amendment protections without providing free speech for those who seek to talk back and to attempt to

stunt the growth of all new channels of communications is to impugn broadcasting's credibility."

Sen. William Proxmire: "The Fairness Doctrine has stifled professionalism. On the other hand, newspapers, operating without government regulation and with full constitutional freedom, have improved vastly in fairness, objectivity, accuracy, and relevance."

ABC News executive Av Westin: "The Fairness Doctrine is used by too many station managers and news directors as an excuse to avoid controversial programming and to prevent aggressive newsmen from performing their jobs well."

In his book on the subject, Friendly argues against abandoning the Fairness Doctrine until more channels are made available through cable and satellites, developments that the television industry has lobbied against. When this happens, he contends, the Fairness Doctrine will wither away.

Jerome Barron, dean of the National Law Center at George Washington University, would go beyond the present Fairness Doctrine:

The basic defect of the Fairness Doctrine is the primitive level on which it functions. Only if someone says X may someone else say anti-X. This hardly leaves room for the spontaneity that gives excitement to the clash of ideas. There should be some less ponderous way to stimulate discussion of fundamental social issues and problems....

The performance of broadcasters should not be judged just on how meticulously or generously they apportion reply time. They should also be judged on how well they meet an affirmative obligation to give access to controversial issues of public importance in the first place....

If vital issues are not broadcast or given attention as a consistent policy, it doesn't matter whether the reason is commercial avarice or ideological prejudice. Consistent denial of access for such views should be as much a factor in consideration of the license renewal application as the Fairness Doctrine now is.[11]

This brings up the subject of licensing itself, a topic beyond the scope of this text although often connected with arguments over the Fairness Doctrine. Monroe, arguing for permanent licenses, said, "Some critics argue peevishly against permanent licensing on the basis that a broadcast license is a permit to mint money. But on this point, what is the distinction between renewable and permanent licenses? All that the present perverse system manages to achieve is to turn broadcast profits against the public interest because it motivates broadcasters not to jeopardize those profits by offending the government."[12]

In summary, both supporters and opponents of the Fairness Doctrine agree on one thing, the record of many broadcasters is rotten in this area. Opponents have faith that broadcasters will do better if the shackles of the Fairness Doctrine are broken, and better still if licensing is extended, and best of all if current license holders are granted those licenses in perpetuity. Supporters of the Doctrine see scant reason for optimism, and less for a blanket reward. If a hospital were run with as little concern for public service as some stations are run, the townspeople might critically confront the administrator. Yet, as the examples cited in this chapter indicate, there are many fine television stations with proud records of service. The problem is to distinguish good from bad in terms of public service. A station's news programs, documentaries and editorials are obviously a significant part of its public service record. The Federal Communications Commission has the authority granted by Congress and affirmed by the Supreme Court to reward with renewals the stations with good records and to deal more strictly with those stations which flagrantly violate their promise to operate in the public interest, convenience and necessity.

Experience has not shown the Fairness Doctrine to be adequate as a guide to public service *as it is applied by the FCC*. It has large loopholes and it rubs against the First Amendment. Yet until someone comes up with something better or until the FCC chooses to enforce the Fairness Doctrine more rigorously as regards the "affirmative duty generally to encourage and implement the broadcast of all sides of controversial issues," what we have is the only game in town. The Supreme Court has declared that the FCC "is not powerless to insist that (licensees) give adequate and fair attention to public issues."

Red Lion

Is The Fairness Doctrine constitutional? That question was asked many times, but was not answered until the Supreme Court ruled on a Fairness Doctrine case in 1967, *Red Lion Broadcasting Co. v. Federal Communications Commission*. We refer to it as the *Red Lion* decision. It stemmed from a radio broadcast, over a station owned by the Red Lion Broadcasting Co. of Red Lion, Pa., in which the Rev. Billy James Hargis attacked Fred Cook, author of a book, *Goldwater — Extremist of the Right*. Cook demanded equal time to reply, under an aspect of the Fairness Doctrine called the "personal attack rule," and wanted the time supplied free of charge. The station agreed on condition Cook warranted that no paid sponsorship could be found for a program carrying his reply. Cook refused. He complained to the FCC, which supported him. The matter went to the Supreme Court. Cook won.

Like Section 315, the personal attack rule exempts newscasts, news interviews, and on-the-spot coverage of news events, but includes editorials. It requires that the station notify the person or group attacked within a week, provide a script or tape of the attack, and offer time to reply.

In its decision on *Red Lion*, which it coupled with a decision on the *RTNDA* case concerning the FCC's rules on personal attack and political editorializing, the Supreme Court stated, "It is the right of the viewers and listeners, not the right of the broadcasters, which is paramount. . . .The First Amendment confers no right on licensees to prevent others from broadcasting on 'their' frequencies and no right to an unconditional monopoly of a scarce resource which the government has denied others the right to use."

On the question of whether a station might be able to keep silent on issues, the Court declared, "That this will occur now seems unlikely, however, since if present licensees should suddenly prove timorous, the Commission is not powerless to insist that they give adequate and fair attention to public issues."

The FCC ruled that an NBC documentary, "Pensions: The Broken Promise," was too one-sided, meriting an opposing view for balance, but a federal court reversed the ruling, saying that a licensee had a "wide degree of discretion." That court decision was later declared void. Because of changed pension laws the matter was dropped, so that the case did not become the constitutional test of the Fairness Doctrine that many hoped it would. Judicial opinion on both sides pointed up the fact that documentaries, while they need not be balanced, do not totally escape the Fairness Doctrine.

Redefinitions of the Fairness Doctrine are likely to continue for some years, quite possibly in the direction of greater access by various segments of the public to air time. Most broadcasters oppose what amounts to a lessening of their control and any movement toward "common carrier" status for broadcasting stations. The National Association of Broadcasters has resisted efforts to widen public access under the Fairness Doctrine. Broadcasters have pointed out that if they cannot control what is said, they cannot be legally responsible for it. Conceivably, uncontrolled access to a broadcast medium could open a Pandora's Box of obscenity, libel, expressions of racial and religious hatred, and calls for riot or revolution. Of course, through recording or tape delay, such statements *could* be censored. But what *should* be censored and *who* should do the censoring are some of the problems which must be faced. Some Fairness Doctrine problems are also problems of what is widely known as the Equal Time Provision of Section 315.

Section 315

When an outspoken racist named J.B. Stoner ran for the U.S. Senate in Georgia, Atlanta stations were forced to sell him time for his 30-second spots to urge people to "vote white." Stations had no choice but to accept the ads, although many of them ran editorials and disclaimers explaining their obligations under the law.

Section 315 of the Communications Act of 1934 states, "If any licensee shall permit any person who is a legally qualified candidate for any public office to use a broadcasting station, he shall afford equal opportunities to all other such candidates for that office..." Then it goes on, under a 1959 amendment ("Lar Daly Amendment") to exempt candidate appearances in newscasts, news interviews, bona fide news documentaries in which the candidate's appearance is incidental, and on-the-spot news coverage such as political conventions.

The trouble with Section 315 is that, by granting equal time to every minor candidate, broadcasters surrender the use of their facilities to anyone who paid the filing fee, including bigots, revolutionaries and publicity seekers. But simply repealing Section 315 might lead to the effective silencing of important third or fourth parties. Unable yet to discover a compromise, Congress knows it can suspend the equal time provisions of Section 315, so that major candidates for major offices may buy or receive free the television and radio time they want.

Congress suspended the equal time provisions to allow the Kennedy-Nixon and Ford-Carter debates. Such debates can also be turned into bona fide news events if they are sponsored by a third party, such as the League of Women Voters, and conducted in a neutral forum. The broadcaster then covers the debate as a routine news event.

Over the years the FCC ruled on some Section 315 matters relating to news. Among their decisions:

315 does not apply to news conferences or political conventions.

315 does not apply to particular political issues, which must get balanced coverage under the Fairness Doctrine.

Write in candidates who make a "substantial showing" that they are bona fide candidates are entitled to equal broadcast opportunities with candidates whose names appear on the ballot.

A newscaster who becomes a candidate must leave the newscast, or else his air appearances are considered a "use" and his opponents are entitled to equal time. Anyone who broadcasts falls under this decision, a state of affairs which led comedian Pat Paulsen, a semi-serious presidential candidate, to go to court to argue that "a single class of citizens (is) required by the government to abandon their livelihoods in order to offer themselves for higher office." Even showing old Ronald Reagan movies would require equal opportunities for his political opponents.

315 does not apply to normal news program coverage of a candidate. It does apply if the candidate provides the film clips.

315 does not apply to regular news interview programs, such as "Issues and Answers" or "Meet the Press." It does apply if a candidate is interviewed on a talk show.

A station may not censor a candidate's words, but it is absolved from all liability for what the candidate says.

Because so many questions about Section 315 fall into a gray area, any news director puzzled about what constitutes a "use" should inquire directly of the FCC.

Broadcasting and the First Amendment

Allegations that network television news is biased have sometimes been accompanied by the claim that radio and television newscasts do not share First Amendment protection with newspapers, magazines and books because the government must assign broadcast frequencies and because the Federal Communications Commission regulates broadcasting as a whole.

That is not true. The United States Supreme Court has consistently held that broadcasters are protected under the First Amendment.

Ruling on the case of the *U.S. v. Paramount Pictures* in 1948, the Supreme Court said, "There is no doubt that...moving pictures, like newspapers and radio, are included in the press, whose freedom is guaranteed by the First Amendment."

In *Superior Films v. Department of Education*, in 1954, the Supreme Court noted, "The First Amendment draws no distinction between the various methods of communicating ideas."

In *Farmers' Education and Cooperative Union v. WDAY, Inc.*, in 1959, the Supreme Court said, "Expressly applying this country's tradition of free expression to the field of radio broadcasting, Congress has from the first emphatically forbidden the (Federal Communications) Commission to exercise any power of censorship over radio communications."

Some qualification was expressed in the *Red Lion* decision in 1969, "Although broadcasting is clearly a medium affected by a First Amendment interest, differences in the characteristics of the news media justify differences in the First Amendment standards applied to them."

However, the Court also stated in *Red Lion*, "The people as a whole retain their interest in free speech by radio, and their collective right to have the medium function consistently with the ends and purposes of the First Amendment."

Ex-FCC Commissioner Glenn O. Robinson, has stated, "Virtually everyone accepts the proposition that the First Amendment does apply to radio and television."[13] A media scholar, William A. Hachten, stated, "As the news and public affairs activities of the broadcasters increase in scope and importance, so has the First Amendment protection they enjoy. In fact, the FCC has encouraged broadcasters to editorialize on the air, provided they give an opportunity for opposing views to be aired later. For all intents and purposes, the broadcast journalist enjoys the same freedoms as does the pen and pencil journalist."[14]

In 1949, the FCC said, "We fully recognize that freedom of the radio is included among the freedoms protected against government abridgment by the First Amendment."

Yet the FCC indicated that this freedom is not absolute:

> The basis for any fair consideration of public issues, and particularly those of a controversial nature, is the presentation of news and information concerning the basic facts of the controversy in as complete and impartial a manner as possible. A licensee would be abusing his position as public trustee of these important means of mass communication were he to withhold from expression over his facilities relevant news or facts concerning a controversy or to slant or distort presentation of such news.[15]

And Congress, in 1959, included newscasts in its concern for the public interest when it amended Section 315:

> Nothing in the foregoing sentence shall be construed as relieving broadcasters, in connection with the presentation of newscasts, news interviews, news documentaries, and on-the-spot coverage of news events, from the obligation imposed upon them under this chapter to operate in the public interest and to afford reasonable opportunity for the discussion of conflicting views on issues of public importance.[16]

The gist of all these statements appears to be that a broadcaster does indeed share with a newspaper, magazine or book publisher the First Amendment freedom of the press to report any news event as he chooses without fear, but unlike the publishers, who may do almost as they please, the broadcaster's total news and information output concerning public issues should be fair. The broadcaster is under an obligation of "decency" which is not demanded of a publisher.

For the Student

1. Interview the commentator, or editorialist, of a local station.

2. If a local station refuses to present editorials, should a concerned citizen do anything?

3. Monitor several local editorials. What are their strengths and weaknesses? Consider controversiality, quality of arguments, willingness to gore local oxen, and visual appeal.

4. Write and deliver an editorial on a local subject. Does your writing style or your delivery differ from the manner in which you handle news?

5. Discuss the Fairness Doctrine in class. Should it be kept? Removed? Changed?

The Law   15

Congress shall make no law...abridging the freedom of speech, or of the press.

— The First Amendment

A reporter who totes a tape recorder or camera into a courtroom is likely to be hustled out by the bailiff. If he tries next at a committee hearing, the door may be slammed in his face.

City council meeting? "No!"

Public records? "You can't look!"

School board meeting? "Sorry. Executive session."

He's not sure he can use this tape without running into obscenity laws. He's not sure he can use that quote without running into libel laws. What if his outtakes are subpoenaed? And can he get some private information without fearing he will be forced to testify and name the person who gave it to him?

Fenced by laws, judicial decisions, rulings, recommendations, and some legal question marks, the broadcast journalist who wants to perform his duty to inform the public of matters they ought to know, and to perform that duty professionally, honestly and ethically, must at times agree with Dickens' Mr. Bumble. "If the law supposes that," said Mr. Bumble, "the law is a ass, a idiot."

What follows is not a law text, which lies beyond the scope of this book, but an introduction to where things stand as of this writing. For a fuller understanding, the reader is directed to *Mass Communication Law: Cases and Comment* by Donald M. Gillmor and Jerome A. Barron (St. Paul: West Publishing Co., 3rd ed., 1979), *Law of Mass Communications* by Harold L. Nelson and Dwight L. Teeter (Mineola, N.Y.: Foundation Press, 3rd ed., 1978), *The First Amendment and the Fourth Estate* by Marc A. Franklin (Mineola, N.Y.: Foundation Press, 1977), and *Regulation of Broadcasting* by Douglas H. Ginsburg (St. Paul: West Publishing Co., 1979).

Nine of Canada's ten provinces have legal systems based on British common law, but that law has developed differently. A good reference is *The Law and the Press in Canada* by Wilfred Kesterton.

Libel

Until recent years, a person who felt he had been libeled in print or on the air expected, if he could show defamation, identification and publication, to collect a lot of money in general and punitive damages. But in 1964 the Supreme Court ruled that a public official had also to prove actual malice, which means knowing a statement is false, or having reckless disregard for the truth. This landmark decision in reporting news was based on a suit brought by City Commissioner L.B. Sullivan of Montgomery, Alabama, against *The New York Times* over an advertisement paid for by a civil rights group. Subsequent extensions included public figures as well as public officials.

Then, in the *Rosenbloom* decision of 1971, the Supreme Court further broadened the freedom of the media to report. Now, not even a private citizen, a "little person," could successfully sue if that person became involved in a public issue, unless he or she proved actual malice or reckless disregard for truth. George A. Rosenbloom, a Philadelphia magazine distributor arrested on charges of criminal obscenity, was described in a WIP radio newscast as a "smut distributor" and "girlie book peddler." Rosenbloom was acquitted. He sued WIP and was awarded damages in a lower court. A court of appeals reversed this decision. The Supreme Court agreed, 5 to 3, holding for WIP.

The majority decision stated, "If a matter is a subject of public or general interest, it cannot suddenly become less so merely because a private citizen is involved, or because in some sense the individual did not voluntarily choose to become involved."

In an oblique reference to the *Red Lion* decision, the Supreme Court added, "If the states fear that private citizens will not be able to respond adequately to publicity involving them, the solution lies in the direction of insuring their ability to respond, rather than in stifling public discussion of matters of public concern."

In another 1971 decision, the Supreme Court ruled that the private lives of public officials are also protected from libel suits, because their private activities often give clues to their qualifications to hold public office. However, this protection is not as strong for defamatory news about the private lives of private citizens. (See also The Right of Privacy.)

In 1974 the Supreme Court, in *Gertz v. Welch*, turned away from the *Rosenbloom* decision in a 5 to 4 vote, and found in favor of Elmer Gertz, a prominent attorney who did not fit the definition of "a public figure" in the circumstances of the case. He had been libeled by the John Birch Society magazine *American Opinion*. Until Gertz, the Supreme Court had become increasingly liberal in stating what could be published without fear of libel. But, said Justice

Powell in *Gertz*, "The need to avoid self-censorship by the news media is....
not the only societal value at issue....Absolutist protection for the communications
media requires a total sacrifice of the competing value served by the law of
defamation."

Truth and fair comment on public matters are defenses against libel. Where
a libel is committed, a full and prompt retraction and apology will lessen the
severity of the damages awarded.

Section 315 of the Communications Act, requiring "equal opportunities"
for all candidates, also prevents a station from censoring a candidate's remarks.
What if such remarks are libelous? In *Farmers Union v. WDAY*, the Supreme
Court ruled that a broadcasting station, barred from tampering with a candidate's
speech, cannot be held responsible for what he says.

Libel is written defamation. Slander is oral defamation. Broadcast defamation
if it stems from a written script is libel, writing-read-aloud. If the defamation
is ad-libbed, the law may regard it as slander. A legal gray area exists here,
but the difference is important because libel victims usually can collect more than
slander victims.

Laws of defamation protect the individual's good name. A communication
libels or slanders someone if it exposes that person to "contempt, aversion,
disgrace, or induces an evil opinion of him or deprives him of friendly intercourse
in society."

A broadcaster (or newspaper, etc.) can offer three main defenses: truth,
qualified privilege (a news medium may publish a fair report of public proceedings), and fair comment (on a subject which invites public controversy). But
the primary defense is *The New York Times* defense, where the burden is on
the *public person* plaintiff to show that the publication was made with actual
malice; that is, with knowing falsehood or with reckless disregard as to truth or
falsity. A *private person* must show that publication was made with negligence.

The Right of Privacy

Surprisingly, not every state recognizes a law of privacy. But 39 states and the
District of Columbia do, although there are sharp differences from state to state,
and even from court jurisdiction to court jurisdiction on how privacy is defined.
The differences represent the results of the conflict from place to place between
the individual's right to be let alone and the public's right to know. The right
to be let alone includes not only publication of material, but physical intrusion.
Reporters who use telephoto lenses and shotgun mikes to enter forbidden areas
could be inviting a lawsuit.

Much remains to be clarified. When in doubt, consult a lawyer who has some
experience in privacy matters. Here are seven general guidelines:

1) News of legitimate public interest is privileged (it may be published).

2) A story about a person involved in the news is privileged, as long as what is published deals with the news event.

3) News about a public figure is generally privileged.

4) Matter taken from a public record is privileged.

5) Fictional accounts of real events may not be privileged. The James Hill family of Whitemarsh, Pa., sued *Life* for connecting them with a novel and play (later a movie), *The Desperate Hours*, about a family which, like the Hills, was held prisoner in their home by three escaped convicts. (The Supreme Court narrowly — 5 to 4 — supported *Life*, but left questions unanswered. The losing attorney was Richard Nixon.)

6) It is unsafe to show pictures of individuals in stories not involving them; for example, using "stock footage" as a substitute for a story the photographer missed. One Miami, Florida newscast showed an innocent bystander being questioned during a police raid on a hotel cigar shop. The bystander sued the station and lost. The judge ruled that the film clip was not an unreasonable invasion of privacy. Yet he said journalists should "make a reasonable effort to portray persons who are thrust into an event of public interest in a manner which will not subject the person to false and harmful inferences."

7) Truth is no defense if a story is not newsworthy. [1]

A Southern California plumber who practiced healing with clay, herbs and minerals won an invasion of privacy judgment against *Life* after it sent two reporters to his home carrying a hidden camera and microphone, pretending to seek medical help. The team was working with law officials who arrested the plumber. Even though the plumber pleaded no contest to the medical charges, he still sued and collected, not because *Life* published the story, but because the reporters entered his home under false pretenses.

On the other hand, when employees of Senator Thomas Dodd of Connecticut rifled the senator's files and turned incriminating documents over to Jack Anderson, who published them, the court ruled that no intrusion was involved.

A television camera crew went to a hotel where a fire had killed a hotel worker. The hotel manager refused to let the crew in. They phoned the news director, who told them to figure out some way to get in and shoot the film. The camera crew decided not to follow orders. They may well have been right, although this type of case has not yet come before a court.

Journalists' Privilege

Reporters and editors of all media have been bothered and angered by the use of subpoenas to extract information, especially names of sources. District attorneys, defense lawyers, grand juries and others have demanded that journalists reveal who gave them information and also hand over film outtakes and notebooks. To refuse has meant going to jail, sometimes for indefinite periods. Several reporters did just that. Walter Cronkite wryly commented, "Advice for a modern lawman: let the reporters do it for you."

Journalists have claimed privilege under the First Amendment. The issue went to the Supreme Court in three separate cases, *Branzburg, Pappas* and *Caldwell*, and the Court in a single opinion in 1972 ruled 5 to 4 that no absolute privilege exists under the First Amendment. *New York Times* reporter Myron Farber fared no better in 1978. He spent 40 days in jail and the *Times* was fined $285,000.

A journalist summoned before a grand jury must answer at least some of the questions asked. For example, if he witnessed criminal activity, he must certainly testify. And if testimony is required before a grand jury, it may also be required in a public trial. Tapes and documents may have to be surrendered to grand juries.

The Supreme Court was less clear about whether any qualified privilege exists, but suggested that it would honor state or federal shield laws if such were passed. As of 1980, twenty-six states had passed shield laws, and many jurisdictions recognized a qualified privilege.

Journalists have expressed concern that the requirement to testify has a "chilling effect" on the reporting of information because news sources dry up. Recent years have produced quite a number of "Deep Throat" sources, especially in government, who have revealed corruption in high places.

Pressure has been applied in various directions. Federal officials concerned about leaks went to A.T.&T. with subpoenas and got the telephone records of reporters and news organizations. A WGR-TV, Buffalo reporter was told he lost his privilege to withhold eyewitness information on the Attica riots because he had already given it to the grand jury.

In *Zurcher v. Stanford Daily*, the Supreme Court permitted searches of newsrooms by police who are armed with warrants and are looking for criminal evidence.

And in the *Herbert v. Lando* decision in 1979, the Supreme Court by a 6-3 majority required a *60 Minutes* producer, Barry Lando, to testify about his "state of mind" at the time of his preparation of a segment. The Court ruled that public figures who sue for libel may, during the pretrial proceedings called "discovery," investigate the "editorial process" that led to the alleged libel.

CBS News has been the principal target of government attempts to secure information and outtakes. A 1967 report of a soldier trying to cut off the ear of a dead Viet Cong soldier, a 1969 film report of the stabbing of a Viet Cong prisoner in the presence of a U.S. officer, and a 1970 film showing South Vietnamese soldiers nearly suffocating a Viet Cong prisoner during interrogation, all brought efforts by the Defense Department to acquire additional information and outtakes. In each case, CBS News refused. To disprove charges that the stabbing incident was a "cut and paste" job, CBS News replayed it twice, once in slow motion.

Other examples: the Justice Department acquired from CBS News some film which was never broadcast of Mike Wallace interviewing Eldridge Cleaver and other Black Panthers in Algiers. CBS News also handed over film of a planned, then abandoned, documentary on preparations to invade Haiti.

Matters grew considerably more serious when a House investigation sub-committee chaired by Rep. Harley O. Staggers (D.-W.Va.) subpoenaed the outtakes and notes used in the documentary, "The Selling of the Pentagon," which alleged that millions of dollars were being spent annually on propaganda in support of the Vietnam War and the military services. CBS refused to surrender the material and was supported in its refusal by broadcast and press journalists and journalistic organizations throughout the nation, including a few, notably the Chicago *Tribune*, which argued that the documentary itself was distorted. *Barron's*, the financial weekly, editorialized that CBS should lose its O & O licenses.

The FCC took the position that it would consider the "fairness" of the CBS documentary in terms of the Fairness Doctrine, but it refused to consider the matter of distortion, stating:

> ...action by this Commission would be inappropriate — and not because the issues involved are insubstantial. Precisely to the contrary, they are so substantial that they reach to the bedrock principles upon which our free and democratic society is founded...
>
> Lacking extrinsic evidence or documents that on their face reflect deliberate distortion, we believe that this government licensing agency cannot properly intervene. It would be unwise and probably impossible for the Commission to lay down some precise line of factual accuracy — dependent always on journalistic judgment — across which broadcasters must not stray...
>
> What we urge — because we believe it will markedly serve the public interest — is an open, eager and self-critical attitude on the part of broad-cast journalists. We urge them...to examine their own processes, to subject them to the kind of hard critical analysis that is characteristic of the best traditions of the journalistic profession... [2]

The position of many members of the journalism profession is that no government or individual has the right, where controversial news is presented, to demand anything beyond what is presented, for this amounts to harassment and violates the rights of free speech and free press.

In the case of broadcast journalism, the principal counter argument, as stated by Rep. Fletcher Thompson (R.-Ga.) is that, since stations are licensed, Congress has a responsibility to be certain the American public is shown "a balanced news coverage." This cannot be determined unless there is an opportunity "to see what is the unedited picture as related to the edited picture . . . because it gives us, supposedly an impartial body, the right to determine whether or not there is any slanting of the TV coverage through editing and deletions of items." [3]

"The Selling of the Pentagon" involved no court trial, a crucial point. Broadcast journalists have surrendered outtakes many times upon being handed a subpoena signed by a judge.

With the courts offering little comfort except a cold jail cell, journalists have turned to Congress and state legislatures for shield laws. Aside from the twenty-six states' laws, Congress in recent years has seen the introduction of bills referred to by the general heading of "newsman's privilege," the best known bill being one introduced by former Sen. Sam Ervin (D.-N.C.) and co-sponsored by Sen. James B. Pearson (R.-Kan.). None has passed. A law of this sort is no simple matter. In the first place, who is a "journalist?" Does Congress or anyone else have the right to say who is and who is not? There are those, and former CBS News president Richard Salant is one, who argue that if Congress can give a right to the news media, Congress can also take it away. "The moment the press has to start asking the government for favors, it's asking for trouble," Salant contends. "I'd prefer to stand on the First Amendment."

ABC News executive Richard Wald disagreed, "It's clear to me that to say 'I'll stand on the First Amendment' isn't going to get William Farr (a California reporter who spent many weeks in jail for refusing to give a judge information in the Manson case) or any of the other reporters sentenced for contempt out of jail."

In seeking protective laws, some journalists argue that the journalist-source communication deserves the same legal umbrella, absolute Constitutional privilege, given to attorney-client communications, or the qualified privilege given to doctor-patient, priest-penitent, and husband-wife communications. Opponents point out that in all these other communications, the source of the information is known and the information is confidential. Only in the journalist-source relationship is the source confidential, while the information may travel on every wind. Therefore, they argue, this particular analogy breaks down.

Court Gag Orders

In 1979 the U.S. Supreme Court ruled, in *Gannett v. Pasquale*, that if prosecution and defense agree, the judge may hold a pretrial hearing in secret. Several years earlier, in Baton Rouge, a black civil rights worker, accused of murder, claimed that the state was just trying to harass him and he asked for a federal hearing. Two local newspaper reporters were sent to cover the hearing. The judge ordered them not to report the details of the evidence presented at this public hearing. The reporters felt that the judge was wrong, that this was prior restraint, a "gag order," and went ahead with their stories. The judge fined them each $300. They appealed. The Court of Appeals ruled in 1973 that even though the judge was wrong in issuing the gag order, because it violated the First Amendment, the reporters were wrong in disobeying the judge. They should have appealed his order, not ignored it.

Yet it is plain that a judge can use gag orders to hold back news reporting when it is most timely, even though his order will be struck down on appeal. The Supreme Court recognized this in a 1976 decision (*Nebraska Press Association v. Stuart*) striking down a Nebraska gag order blocking reporting of testimony in a mass murder case. The Supreme Court called prior restraint "the most serious and the least tolerable infringement on First Amendment rights."

Another blocking technique is the sealing of records. Judge John Sirica did this in the trials of the Watergate defendants. He not only sealed documents and tapes, but when the Reporters Committee for Freedom of the Press wrote the judge a letter asking him to unseal the material, Judge Sirica even sealed the letter!

The best advice to a news director faced with a gag order or sealed records is to appeal the order immediately if he feels it is unconstitutional. He has a reasonable chance of winning.

Access to Public Meetings

In what may be a historic statement on prior restraint, the freedom of the press and the public's right to know, U.S. District Judge Murray L. Gurfein declared, *"A cantankerous press, an obstinate press, a ubiquitous press must be suffered by those in authority in order to preserve the even greater values of freedom of expression."*

In mid-1971, in *U.S.A. v. The New York Times*, Judge Gurfein considered the publication of Pentagon-classified papers on how the United States became deeply involved in the Vietnam War. He said, "These are troubled times. There is no greater safety valve for discontent and cynicism about the affairs of government than freedom of expression in any form."

Yet all times are troubled. Some degree of discontent and cynicism always stalks the land. And, although he may not be confronted as the *Times'* reporter was with the "Top Secret" stamp, the journalist will meet public servants who would prefer to have certain things kept from the public.

The right of a journalist to inspect public records or attend public meetings varies from state to state, depending upon what are known as access or open meeting and open record laws. The laws not only differ from state to state, but they are often interpreted differently within a state from one public body to another, and from one public office to another. For example, a city council may welcome coverage, while the school board resists at every opportunity, holding executive sessions and private meetings to transact its real business and holding public meetings for little more than show. A full discussion of access laws lies beyond the scope of this text.[4] Concern here is with broadcast news access to public meetings.

The House of Representatives began in 1979, using government personnel and its own broadcasting system, to record and transmit video and audio signals for distribution by television and radio stations. Cameras fixedly point to the front so that no congressman needed to fear being caught with his chair empty or, even worse, dozing. The method of coverage compromised between the broadcast journalists' wishes for total freedom to move in with their own gear to do what they liked, and the cautious traditionalism expressed by Sam Rayburn with the pithy comment, "Things are bad enough as they are. Keep the cameras the hell out of here." The compromise may yield in time to more journalistic freedom rather than a concerted effort by congressmen to dismantle the experiment. The Senate may one day follow the lead of the House.

Coverage of certain House and Senate committee hearings have been hallmarks of television news history and have left an imprint on American history of this century. Among them were the Kefauver subcommittee crime investigations, which turned an unassuming Kentucky senator into a national personage; the Army-McCarthy hearings, which helped swing the national mood against Sen. Joseph McCarthy; the Fulbright Foreign Relations Committee hearings on the Vietnam War, during which Fred Friendly created a *cause célèbre* by resigning as CBS News president; the Senate Watergate hearings and the House Judiciary Committee debate on the impeachment of President Nixon, which captured the attention and may have helped to unify a badly shaken and divided nation; and the Senate debate on the Panama Canal Treaty, another nation-dividing issue.

Cameras and microphones transmit, live, sessions of the United Nations during world crises. Millions of people hear the debates. Most state legislatures now permit coverage of their sessions.

Urging the opening of all Senate, House and Supreme Court sessions to television and radio, former CBS president Frank Stanton said, "There is no reason why we cannot do it with regard to critical sessions of the highest legislative and judicial bodies in the land — bodies whose actions and determinations influence our lives, our pocketbooks, our present, and our future."[5]

Obscenity

The Nixon tapes threw broadcast journalists into a tailspin. Just how in the (*expletive deleted*) do you report a (*expletive deleted*) story like that??? When the tapes are made available, what can you play? The deleted words are as newsworthy as anything else on the tapes, and the tapes had so much force that they helped to end a presidency and an era. Those obscenities, hinted at but not revealed, those unexplicated expletives, have left their smudge on history.

Yet it is unlikely that we will hear them in the United States. Maybe the British will hear them. Maybe the French or the Canadians or the Germans will, but Americans probably won't. The reason is, in part, the FCC's objection to "indecent" language, especially when children might be listening. Interestingly, the use in the print and broadcast media of the bracketed phrase — (expletive deleted) — may have led a lot of readers and viewers to imagine the foulest term that could fit the context, when the actual expletives may have been much milder.

There are several kinds of "dirty words." *Obscene* means indecent, usually sexual or excretory. *Pornographic* refers to writing, drawing or photography, with the intent of arousing sexual desires. *Profane* refers to irreverent cursing. *Vulgar* refers to crudities, "toilet humor."

Broadcast journalists flee all of them.

The six o'clock newscast at one Twin Cities station in 1974 carried filmed interviews with automobile workers who had been laid off. One angry worker said "bullshit." In the ten o'clock newscast, the film was shown again, but the word was gone.

The FCC ordered seven specific "barnyard" terms, used to describe sexual and excretory functions, barred from the airwaves. The U.S. Circuit Court of Appeals in the District of Columbia, which rules on many broadcasting matters, threw out the FCC order in 1977.

In a celebrated 1979 case involving a Pacifica radio station and the comedian George Carlin, the U.S. Supreme Court upheld the FCC's "indecency" standard, a standard making broadcasters more liable than other communicators to punishment for obscenity.

During a WINS, New York, radio newscast in 1970, newscaster Lee Murphy quoted former Soviet Premier Nikita Khrushchev as calling President Richard M. Nixon "a son of a bitch." On another newscast sometime earlier, Murphy quoted California Governor Ronald Reagan as referring to a political opponent by the same epithet. As a result of the Reagan quote, nothing happened. As a result of the Khrushchev quote, Murphy was fired and so was the news editor. Murphy fought to get his job back. Through arbitration, he was reinstated, but the news editor chose to take another job.

If these examples seem to prove nothing, it may be because obscenity exists in a legal fog.

Section 326 of the Communications Act of 1934 forbids government censorship of broadcast content. But it also says "No person within the jurisdiction of the United States shall utter any obscene, indecent, or profane language by means of radio communication." And Section 1464 of the Criminal Code states, "Whoever utters any obscene, indecent, or profane language by means of radio communication shall be fined not more than $10,000 or imprisoned not more than two years, or both."

Legally, obscenity over the air is as elusive as obscenity in print. And that's pretty elusive these days. In practice, broadcasters must be more careful than publishers. The FCC maintains a vigil of sorts. Frank J. Kahn wrote:

> On occasion a commissioner's speech or a proposed (but not enacted) FCC rule will stimulate program decisions in the industry. This phenomenon is known as "regulation by raised eyebrow," and is often as imprecise as it is subtle.

Nor are governmental pressures the only ones that affect the output of radio and television stations. Audience ratings, sponsor needs, and the temper of the times all exert their influences on what is broadcast.[6]

In a KPFA, Berkeley (Pacifica radio station) case concerning non-news programs, including homosexuals discussing homosexuality, the FCC declared, "We recognize that as shown by the complaints here, such provocative programing as here involved may offend some listeners. But this does not mean that those offended have the right, through the Commission's licensing power, to rule such programing off the airwaves. Were this the case, only the wholly inoffensive, the bland, could gain access to the radio microphone or TV camera. No such drastic curtailment can be countenanced under the Constitution, the Communications Act, or the Commission's policy, which has consistently sought to insure the maintenance of radio and television as a medium of freedom of speech and freedom of expression for the people of the nation as a whole." But just to play it safe, the FCC issued KPFA a one-year renewal instead of three.

In the FCC's view, freedom of expression does not extend to songs which overtly or covertly sanction the use of drugs. The FCC generated considerable heat with a notice in 1971 warning licensees of their responsibility to be aware of the music they play. While drug lyrics are not obscene in the more restricted sense of that troublesome word, they might be regarded as indecent.

The outer limits on what is obscene were vaguely defined by the Supreme Court's *Roth*, *Fanny Hill (Memoirs)* and *Miller* decisions, as to whether the material as a whole, by local community standards, is patently offensive and appeals to prurient interests.

Broadcast material stops far short of these outer limits. Most newsrooms follow the rule, "When in doubt, don't." (Or, to state the actual practice more precisely, "When in doubt, splice it to the stag reel instead.") Material considered blasphemous, obscene, or on the borderline of obscenity almost always reaches the newsroom on film or tape.

Yet, "When in doubt, don't" is too easy an answer today. It is simplistic in a complex time when some extremists wield obscenities like weapons, at times speaking softly, at other times letting fly in all directions. To report, "A policeman hit a demonstrator who cursed him," is a guarded truth which may be only a half truth. In a day when breasts and buttocks, bare or barely draped, fill our newspaper and magazine ads, our billboards, and even — with slightly more cloth — our television commercials, newscasts retain a modesty resembling prudery.

Contemporary journalistic standards reflect "the temper of the times." Remember when journalists could barely bring themselves to write the words "social disease"? When nobody was "pregnant"? Today, television newscasts and documentaries tell the community about drugs and venereal disease and divorce and unwed mothers and the pill and ex-priests and abortion and pornography and a dozen other matters of community interest and concern that a generation ago would have been left in the closet.

One news editor in North Carolina reported that standards for the 6 p.m. newscast were tighter than standards at 11 p.m. An editor in Georgia said he was convinced that listeners were understanding about profanity on film but would resent the same words coming from newscasters, even as quotations.

A newspaper reporter named Gary Cummings struck a blow of sorts against hypocrisy. When Chicago police arrested a number of prostitutes, WMAQ-TV reported that the arrest was made at the Ambassador East. Cummings' newspaper and one other paper simply referred to "a near north hotel." So be it, said Cummings, and thereafter wrote about all events in hotels in that fashion: a speech in a Loop hotel, a dinner in a near north hotel, and so on. His city editor, patient at least for a while, routinely changed the copy to identify the hotel.

In 1979 a few television stations carried in prime time the Academy Award winning documentary "Scared Straight," narrated by Peter Falk. Teenage boys and girls who had committed minor crimes were taken to Rahway Prison, New Jersey, where, for two hours, they were verbally abused by convicts who tried to convince them that prison is a living hell. The language was filthy and the homosexual references explicit, but stripped of them the documentary would have had little impact. The words were hammers which cracked the teenagers' shells of toughness. It is not at all unlikely that these obscenities might also have convinced some young viewers to scrap any thoughts of commiting a criminal act.

A television news director in the Midwest was faced with a decision about obscene language and gestures in a filmed story. His cameraman had shot a police raid at a roadhouse. As a prostitute caught in the raid was being led away, she addressed some choice language to the camera, accompanied by some equally choice gestures. What was on film was clearly obscene by contemporary standards, by what might be called the standards of Middle America. He did not use the film, but as he later described it during a panel discussion on obscenity, he sounded upset that the girl's words and gestures forced him to kill what would otherwise have been a most desirable segment of film, a lewd girl being taken away by the police. This is hypocrisy. If a news director wants to uphold standards of community morality, those standards begin at the assignment desk. The assignment editor should not have sent the photographer on a roadhouse raid in the first place.

No area of news judgment is as touchy as determining what is too obscene to be aired. The news director and all the journalists involved must summon up the best that is within them, that intelligence and skill and experience which from time to time elevate the craft of journalism to the level of professionalism.

The student may ask, how do I decide what to use? Indeed, he *should* ask it. He is either a fool or a Solomon if he does not, and our universities turn out few Solomons. To answer the student's question, one is tempted to say, don't decide, because you are too young and too green. Give the problem to someone older and more experienced in news editing. But this answer is not really an answer at all. It is an evasion of the question, although it shall serve as one of the guidelines set down here concerning judgment in matters of propriety:

1. Remember that editing is art, and not science. Outside the legal strictures, few absolutes prevail.

2. When in doubt, seek counsel and, if possible, consensus.

3. Consider the intent of the questionable word or act. Consider its possible effect. If either is prurient, do not broadcast it.

4. At the same time, do not guide your decisions according to the imagined response of every little old lady in tennis shoes. You are reporting the news of a real world. The sight of blood, the sound of pain, and the gesture of defiance are part of the real world.

5. Don't overdo it. A four-second shot of the victim of a fatal accident is usually acceptable in a long shot. Fifteen seconds of the same footage, or a four-second close-up is not acceptable.

6. Be cautious about intruding into private lives of citizens thrust into the news, especially when publication would distress them. For example, never name or show film of a rape victim. For such news coverage, live by the Golden Rule.

7. Learn by observing, and don't forget. Sensible decisions are based upon common sense and experience. As you grow older, experience is the best commodity you provide in return for a paycheck. The experience of the veteran is worth more than the energy of the beginner. Their comparative paychecks reflect it.

Lotteries

The courts ruled in 1976 that news about a state-run lottery — any news at all — may be broadcast by a station located within that state or adjacent to it, provided that the adjacent state has its own lottery.

Beyond that, a station must be careful about what it says. It may report that a state has a lottery, that a state legislature is debating a lottery, or that an unemployed bus driver named Joe Glotz won the big one, but it may not report anything which may be construed as advertising a lottery and it may not report winning numbers. Live ENG of the drawing is also forbidden by FCC guidelines. In summary, news is all right but the promotion of gambling is not.

For the Student

1. Visit the law library at your university. Browse for an hour.

2. Interview a working reporter (any medium) about restrictions he has encountered in getting information that he considers to be in the public sector.

3. Interview a criminal lawyer on the subject of publicity before and during a trial.

4. Where should "the right of the public to know" end? Where should "the right of privacy" end? Give some examples of how you would like to see the laws framed.

5. Should journalists get the same shield protection as doctors, lawyers and priests?

Mike and Camera in the Courtroom

16

Proceedings in court should be conducted with fitting dignity and decorum.

— Canon 35

For forty years the sturdy wall of Canon 35 kept radio and television equipment out of the courtroom. Here and there, in Colorado or Texas, fissures allowed a microphone and a camera to peer through, but the wall held. Now it is crumbling. Canon 35, renamed Canon 3(A)(7), is slowly breaking under the pressure of responsible broadcast journalists bearing modern video cameras, helped by attorneys and judges who sense that the arguments for permitting broadcast coverage of a trial may be more compelling than the arguments against it. The wall of Canon 35, while it still stands in most states, now has breaches wide enough to drive a remote truck through. Yet journalists cannot simply dismiss criticism, including the cogent argument of St. Paul district judge Hyam Segell, "Thirty to 45 seconds of coverage at 10 p.m., squeezed between Stay-Free Maxi Pads and Arby's Roast Beef, can hardly be classified as coverage, nor is it likely to prove to be informative..."

Hauptmann

Let us consider why the wall went up in the first place. In 1935, Bruno Hauptmann was tried in the Flemington, New Jersey courthouse for the kidnap-murder of the Lindbergh baby. Tourists took snapshots of each other on the judge's bench. Guides ran sightseeing trips. Hawkers peddled little wooden ladders, souvenir reminders of the ladder the kidnaper used to climb to the second story nursery. Reporters and photographers crammed into the tiny courtroom each day. Their stories heaped contempt upon Hauptmann. The lawyers told reporters who the witnesses would be, what evidence was coming up, what was wrong with the other lawyers' tactics, and how guilty or innocent Bruno Hauptmann really was, all of which the reporters eagerly printed or aired. (One young radio reporter instead twanged the heartstrings in sympathy for the dead baby, and began to build a national reputation. His name was Gabriel Heatter.) The judge finally barred cameras, but one photographer in the balcony used some special equipment to snap dramatic photos surreptitiously at the end of the trial. His pictures made the front pages coast to coast. If all this weren't enough, it was rumored that the jury was seriously considering an offer to go into vaudeville.

Canon 35

Two years later, the American Bar Association adopted Canon 35 of its Judicial Ethics:

> Proceedings in court should be conducted with fitting dignity and decorum. The taking of photographs in the courtroom during sessions of the court or recesses between sessions, and the broadcasting of court proceedings are calculated to detract from the essential dignity of the proceedings, degrade the court and create misconceptions with respect thereto in the mind of the public and should not be permitted.

The A.B.A. amended Canon 35 in 1952 to include television but to exempt broadcasts of naturalized citizens taking their oaths. It was amended again in 1962 to take out the phrase "are calculated to" and added that broadcasting distracted people involved in the trial.

In 1972, Canon 35 was replaced by Canon 3(A)(7), which permitted mikes and cameras in courtrooms provided that they do not distract anyone, that everyone involved in the trial consents to their presence, that nothing is shown until the trial is finished and all appeals are exhausted, and that the presentation should be for educational purposes only, presented only at schools.

At the federal level, broadcasting on criminal cases was flatly forbidden after 1946 by Rule 53 of the Federal Rules of Criminal Procedure.

While Rule 53 was the law of the federal court system, Canon 35 and 3(A)(7) were only recommendations of the Bar Association, but in one form or another they were accepted by nearly every state in the Union. Colorado, Texas and Oklahoma were exceptions. Some states gave judges a little leeway, but the force of custom was strong. In 1956, television cameras covered the Graham trial in Colorado, a man accused of blowing up an airplane with 44 aboard in order to collect life insurance on one of the passengers, his mother. Naturally, the trial received national attention. When it was over, the judge, the jury foreman, attorneys on both sides and the defendant's wife said the broadcasts had not distracted anyone, as far as they knew, and had not interfered with the fairness of the trial. "Frankly, I had forgotten that it was there," said the jury foreman.

Sheppard

Dr. Sam Sheppard, an osteopath, was brought to trial in Ohio on charges of bludgeoning his wife Marilyn to death. After he was sentenced to life imprisonment, he appealed, charging that newspapers attacked him so viciously that he could not get a fair trial. As for broadcast news he charged, among other things:

On the evening before the trial began, journalists from the Cleveland *Press* and the Cleveland *Plain Dealer* debated over radio station WHK on the question of which paper deserved more credit for indicting him.

One day on the courthouse steps, while jurors were arriving, there was a television interview with the judge, the prosecutor, a city detective, and Inspector Fabian of Scotland Yard, then retired and working as a Scripps-Howard stringer.

All available rooms on the courthouse floor were taken over by television, radio and newspaper journalists, who filled the rooms with equipment.

In the halls outside, television lights and photographers were constantly present.

Sheppard's objections to being photographed were ignored. Cameras were everywhere, although not in the courtroom itself.

One juror and her family were interviewed for television in their home.

Bob Considine, in a radio broadcast, compared the Sheppard trial to the Alger Hiss trial.

Walter Winchell, in a radio broadcast, quoted a woman as declaring she was Sheppard's mistress.[1]

Sheppard's conviction was reversed by a U.S. District Court, reversed again by the U.S. Court of Appeals, and finally, in 1966, was reversed again by the U.S. Supreme Court, setting Sam Sheppard free.

The Chicago *Tribune* editorialized, "The purpose of the courts is not to provide the populace with entertainment or even with instruction. The purpose is to do justice." (The *Tribune* did not recall that the first trial ever broadcast was the Scopes monkey trial on the teaching of evolution, over *Tribune* radio station WGN in 1925. Photographers were also permitted in the courtroom as famed lawyer Clarence Darrow faced aging William Jennings Bryan in a trial that electrified the nation. Apparently no one complained about the broadcasts, made possible by WGN's leasing of telephone lines from Chicago to Dayton, Tennessee.)

But the Supreme Court's majority decision in the Sheppard case also included this:

The priniciple that justice cannot survive behind walls of silence has long been reflected in the Anglo-American distrust for secret trials. A responsible press has always been regarded as the handmaiden of effective judicial administration, especially in the criminal field...The press does not simply publish information about trials but guards against the miscarriage of justice by subjecting the police, prosecutors, and judicial processes to extensive public scrutiny and criticism.

Estes

Proponents of Canon 35 argued that the presence of television cameras disrupted judicial proceedings during the trial. And they pointed to the 1962 preliminary hearing for Billie Sol Estes, the Texas wheeler-dealer, on charges of swindling. According to *The New York Times*, "a television motor van, big as an intercontinental bus, was parked outside the courthouse and the second floor courtroom was a forest of equipment. Two television cameras had been set up inside the bar and four marked cameras were aligned just outside the gates. A microphone stuck its 12-inch snout inside the jury box, now occupied by an overflow of reporters from the press table, and three microphones confronted Judge Dunagan on his bench. Cables and wires snaked over the floor."

Estes objected to the coverage. After he was convicted he appealed, partly on the basis of the presence of television, and the Supreme Court voted 5 to 4 to reverse his conviction. So he was tried again, this time with television kept at arm's length. He was convicted again. But the Supreme Court decision on *Estes* was a benchmark in the matter of broadcasting that goes on in courtrooms. Here are some opinions by the justices on both sides of the decision:

Justice Clark, speaking for the majority: "The heightened public clamor resulting from radio and television coverage will inevitably result in prejudice. Trial by television is, therefore, foreign to our system. Furthermore, telecasting may also deprive an accused of effective counsel. The distractions, intrusions into confidential attorney-client relationships and the temptation offered by television to play to the public audience might often have a direct effect not only upon the lawyers, but the judge, the jury and the witnesses."

Chief Justice Warren: "So long as the television media, like the other communications media, is free to send representatives to trials and to report on those trials to its viewers, there is no abridgement of the freedom of the press. The right of the communications media to comment on court proceedings does not bring with it the right to inject themselves into the fabric of the trial process to alter the purpose of that process...On entering that hallowed sanctuary, where the lives, liberty and property of people are in jeopardy, television representatives have only the rights of the general public, namely to be present to observe the proceedings, and thereafter, if they choose, to report them."

Justice Stewart: "The suggestion that there are limits upon the public's right to know what goes on in the courts causes me deep concern. The idea of imposing upon any medium of communications the burden of justifying its presence is contrary to where I had always thought the presumption must lie in the area of First Amendment freedoms."

Justice Harlan: "The day may come when television will have become so commonplace an affair in the daily life of the average person as to dissipate all reasonable likelihood that its use in courtrooms may disparage the judicial process."

Looking back on their decision, Justice Brennan said *Estes* was "not a blanket constitutional prohibition against the televising of state criminal trials."

In Camera or **On Camera**

For four decades the wall of Canon 35, held after *Estes* by the mortar of Supreme Court decision, stood against the grape shot occasionally fired by often dispirited broadcast journalists. Only here and there at rare intervals did we read about the broadcasting of a trial. In 1956 a judge permitted radio station KLPM in Minot, North Dakota, to broadcast a murder trial in an effort to end some slanderous talk against one of the principals; the judge later praised the station for its coverage. In 1957 a judge permitted KOMU-TV, Columbia, Missouri, to cover a murder trial in Tuscumbia; silent film only was shot of testimony on the grounds that sound-on-film would add weight to any testimony aired, but SOF was shot of the judge's instructions to the jury, the attorney's summations, and the delivery of the verdict. Afterwards, Circuit Judge Sam C. Blair told news director Phil Berk, "Hardly anyone knew you were there...I hope you come back again."

In 1970 an entire trial was shown over the National Educational Television network on four consecutive evenings, a trial that had taken place in Denver, Colorado in 1969. A Black Panther had been arrested by a white policeman on charges of "resisting a police officer in the discharge of his duty." The defendant, in his turn, accused the policeman of harassing him with shouts of "white power." A woman judge, Zita Weinshienk, presided at the first documentary study on American television of an entire courtroom trial. A Harvard law school professor commented on each day's events. Selection of a jury came during the first day of "Trial — the City and County of Denver vs. Lauren R. Watson." On the second day, the policeman took the stand. On the third day, the defendant did. The fourth day brought the verdict. Judge Weinshienk later said she felt the trial brought out deep feelings blacks have toward the police, and their mutual fears and distrust. She also felt it was an excellent way to show viewers, many of whom have never been inside a real courtroom, how an actual trial is conducted. Her only concern was that a more experienced judge should have had the honor of presiding for this television first.

Again in 1971, a camera went through the courtroom doors. A 17-year-old girl in Wichita, Kansas was charged with incorrigibility, shoplifting and being a runaway. A KAKE-TV reporter and phtographer got permission from the judge, the girl and her parents to film the juvenile court hearing for a documentary. Said Judge Michael Corrigan, "We must be smart enough to be able to establish a system whereby the public can be informed and the judicial decorum maintained...We had a message in the approach that the court takes and in the type of young people that come before the court.''

Such exceptions to the general ban were few and far between, yet in an era where American television viewers could see men walk upon the moon, it seemed quizzical and arbitrary that their television sets could not also take them inside an American courtroom, when the Sixth Amendment to the Constitution called for ''a speedy *public* trial before an impartial jury.''

Sirhan

It remained for the development of new technology to crack the wall, and then not until it had proven itself in non-broadcast situations. A case in point was the trial of Sirhan Sirhan for the assassination of Robert F. Kennedy. More than one hundred reporters and correspondents from around the world applied for credentials to enter a courtroom in which only forty seats were set aside for journalists. Judge Herbert Walker, over some objection from his colleagues, set up a closed circuit television system. Planned by KNXT technicians, the system used a camera hidden in a dummy courtroom air conditioner to feed three monitors in another room assigned to the overflow of reporters. The quality of the picture was rather poor, but the system worked without disrupting the proceedings. Although news about the hidden camera was reported widely, people inside the courtroom seemed unaware of its presence. A Norelco black-and-white vidicon camera about the size of a cigar box, noiseless, using normal interior lighting, was placed behind the air conditioner grill. The fixed lens got its image through the louvers at first. Later, the louvers were removed.

Sound was transmitted separately, utilizing the courtroom's own audio amplifier. In the course of the trial several changes were made in sound transmission. Five microphones were spaced along the counsel table. Lavalier mikes later replaced witness and bench table microphones. When attorneys began to question prospective jurors, the jurors could not be heard, so they were asked to hold a table microphone. Later, a lavalier mike was used.

It takes little imagination to recognize that it would be just a short step from a hidden remote camera with an immovable lens to a hidden remote camera with a zoom lens. Even less obtrusive than some of the microphones employed would be one or two remotely controlled highly directional shotgun mikes.

One of Sirhan's defense attorneys said the public as well as accredited reporters should have been permitted to view the trial in the television room; the public was, of course, permitted in the courtroom itself. From the public in a courtroom to the public in a television room is really a small step. From the public in a television room to the public at home is just another step. And that step is now being taken in several states, among them Alabama, Colorado, Georgia, Nevada, New Hampshire, and Montana. Most of the states in the United States are either testing or considering plans to permit cameras and microphones to attend trials.

The Alabama Plan

Judge Robert E. Hodnette, Jr., of the Thirteenth Judicial Circuit of Alabama, drew up a plan for broadcast and photo news coverage of trials which is being used as a model for other states. Written in consultation with journalists in his district, it was submitted to the presiding circuit judge, the district attorney, the president of the local bar association, the president of the county commission, and finally the state supreme court, all of whom approved it. Adopted in 1976, it included the following limitations:

1. Coverage must be requested in advance of the trial.

2. Lawyers and all parties to the trial must consent in writing. Any witness who will be recorded must also give consent. The jury must consent. Minors must have parental consent.

3. If anyone withdraws consent, coverage stops, and it stops for everyone (except, of course, pencil-and-paper reporters who are not considered in these guidelines). The judge may stop coverage at any time if he thinks it is distracting.

4. No one connected with the trial could be interviewed until the jury reaches a verdict.

5. Members of a jury should not be photographed so that they can be individually identified. A grand jury could be photographed if members consent.

6. No juvenile proceedings may be covered.

7. Reporters and photographers must avoid distracting behavior, must keep to designated areas, and must not use flash or change lighting during the trial.

8. No more than two cameras and two tape recorders may be present. Cameras must be blimped to block out sound.

9. Pooling of a signal is permitted.

10. The media must furnish their own equipment, and must keep cables, microphones and cameras as unobtrusive as possible.

11. Instant replay and stills are restricted.

12. If a reporter comments during a trial, he must use a hooded microphone.

13. The news media agree to report a trial impartially, and not to make speculative comments.

14. Attorneys must observe the state bar's rules of discipline as regards trial publicity.

The 1978 Conference of State Chief Justices recommended that state supreme courts allow television, radio and photographic coverage of their own judicial proceedings. The following year, however, the American Bar Association voted to continue its opposition to all camera and microphone court coverage as expressed in its canon.

Judges Use Video

Even where broadcast coverage of trials remains forbidden, the video camera is entering *as a tool of the court.*

An Ohio judge ordered testimony in every injury claims case videotaped, then permitted the opposing lawyers to present the testimony in any order they wished. One lawyer moved a physician's testimony from lead-off to closing witness. The judge was absent during the questioning. He watched the tape in chambers, considered objections while being free of courtroom pressures, and erased everything he regarded as objectionable. Only then was the testimony, via television, presented to the jury. Afterwards, the jury heard the lawyers' summations live, then retired to consider a verdict. Among other advantages, this method shortcircuits the lawyers' well-known trick of saying something they know will be overruled, but saying it in hopes that jurors will remember it anyhow.

In a federal personal injury case, which involved an automobile falling off a hoist, videotaped experiments with the hoist — impossible to duplicate in a courtroom — were admitted into evidence and impeached an expert's testimony. In another case, videotaped testimony was admitted from a person suffering a mental disability which prevented him from being questioned for very long. [2]

A Pittsburgh judge, Joseph F. Weis, said, "I find it hard to justify the taking of a confession by a police department by any means other than videotape. It is so much superior to the painfully typed question and answer statement and reveals so much of demeanor, hesitancy or spontaneity that many of the hearings on voluntariness could be eliminated or drastically shortened." [3]

Wisconsin, Iowa, Colorado and Illinois are among states in which videotape of drivers arrested for drunkenness may be introduced as evidence in court.

The spreading use of the tools of broadcasting negates one of the basic arguments against broadcast coverage of trials, namely that the presence of the equipment is distracting and disruptive.

In fact, NBC-TV quietly televised a meeting of the District of Columbia Bar Association while members debated the merits of Canon 35, some arguing that television coverage disrupts and degrades. No one present realized that the entire meeting was being recorded.

New court facilities are being wired for television. For instance, the Los Angeles County Criminal Courts Building was designed with the advice of KNXT editorial director Howard S. Williams, in cooperation with several criminal court judges, although courtroom broadcasting is still forbidden. If it was desired, a television signal could be fed from any of sixty courtrooms to an antenna on the roof for beaming to a broadcast transmitter. The signal could also go to auxiliary courtrooms to handle an overflow of reporters, as in the Sirhan case; to a room where a disruptive defendant is kept, perhaps solving some of the legal implications of preventing a defendant from witnessing his own trial and hearing his accusers; to classrooms, where law students and other students can watch actual cases and discuss them while the trial is in progress, just as medical students discuss surgery they watch on closed circuit television; to the offices of the district attorney and the public defender, who may want to watch a trial deputy in court; to the presiding judge, so he can see what is going on in any courtroom; to the sheriff for security reasons; and to videotape and audiotape machines, replacing or supplementing the court stenographer.

Common Sense Conduct

For the television journalist, the opportunity to report fully what goes on in court-rooms is available as never before, but it is an opportunity that must be grasped gingerly. Coverage ought to be for the best of reasons, not for sensationalism. Editing should be as judicious as the conduct of the trial itself.

Reporters and photographers should dress and comport themselves with as much dignity and respect for the court as attorneys do. It is a shame that this needs to be said, but it does. United States Information Agency general counsel Richard Schmidt, Jr., explained:

> You know the cameraman who walks in with no tie, no coat, and barrels right across in front of the judge. The lawyers are aghast, so is the judge and everyone else. The judge raps for order and the cameraman looks at him like, "Well, what did I do?"...This is the thing that lawyers see, and....they say keep the newsmen and the cameramen out.[4]

The walls of what is now Canon 3(A)(7) have been breached, but they still stand in many states, and even where breached, some lawyers are waiting with brick and mortar to erect them again. What happens next depends a great deal on the broadcast journalists themselves.

Justice Oliver Wendell Holmes, in an often quoted opinion, stated:

> It is desirable that the trial of causes should take place under the public eye, not because the controversies of one citizen with another are of public concern, but because it is of the highest moment that those who administer justice should always act under the sense of public responsibility, and that every citizen should be able to satisfy himself with his own eyes as to the mode in which a public duty is performed.[5]

For the Student

1. What useful purpose could camera coverage of a trial serve?
2. What harm could be done?
3. Should reporters and photographers dress and behave as circumspectly as lawyers at a trial, even though this is not their usual behavior?
4. Find out what situation prevails in your state as regards bringing cameras and microphones into courtrooms.

5. If coverage is barred and you think it should be permitted, what could you personally do to encourage change?

The Profession

17

The price of liberty is eternal competence.

— Anonymous

Anybody can be a journalist. All he needs is a job. Although he may be in a position to *inform* millions of his fellow citizens, no law requires that he have so much as a fourth grade education. He may be in a position to *influence* millions of his fellow citizens, who can vote governments into and out of office, yet if he is incompetent, unscrupulous, or even provably unethical, no law can remove him and no body of his fellow practitioners can deny his right to practice.

Is It or Isn't It?

Is journalism a profession? David LeRoy put the question this way:

> When Walter Cronkite states, "I am a professional," what does he mean? If I understand him correctly, he means that he controls his emotions and biases in performing his duties. Stories are selected for their news values and reported in as fair and as objective a manner as possible.
>
> Another cluster of values commonly associated with this usage revolves around the idea of the "old pro." In this instance, the term indicates that a person can perform well under stressful conditions. It is the elan or style under pressure which defines the criterion of judgment.
>
> Is this the meaning commonly associated with professionalism as it is employed by social scientists? The answer, of course, is no.[1]

The National Labor Relations Board ruled that journalists are not professionals and therefore can be organized into one union with clerks and other non-journalists. The NLRB declared that journalists do not meet the test because they are not "engaged in work requiring knowledge of an advanced type in a field of science or learning customarily acquired by a prolonged course of specialized intellectual instruction and study...as distinguished from a general academic education."

One analysis of professionalism concluded that it includes the use of the professional organization as a major reference group, a belief in service to the public, a belief in self-regulation, a sense of calling to the field, and autonomy in one's work.[2] The question, according to LeRoy, is not: Is broadcast journalism a profession? Rather, how professional is broadcast journalism? Clearly, the answer will vary from journalist to journalist.

Broadcast journalism, and indeed all journalism, seems to be improving with the years. Listen to Eric Sevareid in 1976:

> Let me say now only that we are not the worst people in the land, we who work as journalists. Our product in print or over the air is a lot better, more educated, more responsible than it was when I began some forty-five years ago as a cub reporter. This has been the best generation of all in which to have lived as a journalist in this country. We are no longer starvelings and we sit above the salt. We have affected our times.[3]

A 1976 Louis Harris poll reported that more Americans had confidence in the people running television news than in any other institution, including higher education, the military, the press, business, unions, the White House and Congress. Even Ralph Nader ranked lower.[4]

Standards

Groups such as Sigma Delta Chi and the Radio Television News Directors Association set ethical standards, but they cannot enforce them because of the First Amendment to the Constitution. Freedom of speech and press may not be abridged. Journalists might wish enforceable standards existed, but not at the expense of freedom of expression. We cannot cheerfully contemplate the licensing of journalists, even for such a laudable reason as enforcing the standard of a trifle of education or skill. We may envy physicians and attorneys for being able to set up standards of competence, but we cannot agree on a way to emulate them.

In 1966, the Professional Development Committee of Sigma Delta Chi reported to the national convention:

> It is the opinion of many newsmen, although perhaps not shared by all members of our society, that the time has arrived — it is long overdue, in fact — for the profession of journalism to establish its minimum standards, announce them to the public, and begin enforcing them.

This idea has not been adopted.

When Dr. W. Walter Menninger of the Menninger Foundation proposed certification for journalists, perhaps by a board of their professional peers, he received little support and considerable opposition. He said:

> Freedom of the press is the only guarantee of the Bill of Rights which cannot be exercised by each individual citizen. Practically speaking, this privilege can be exercised only by those in the journalistic profession. Thus journalists and broadcasters hold an important trust as guardians of democracy. How does the public have any guarantee of the quality and integrity of these guardians?
>
> In other professions with a public trust — medicine, law, education — laws for licensure and certification assure the public that the practitioner has fulfilled minimum standards, met certain requirements for training and demonstrated competence in the profession. The public is entitled to similar safeguards in the quality of the practitioners of this most important cornerstone of our democratic society, the news media. [5]

Peter Hackes of NBC News declared:

> Journalism to become one of the true professions must set minimum standards with which its adherents must comply. Journalism, for example, has yet to specify uniform educational and professional requirements for all of its would-be professionals. In the meantime, misfits, ill-fits and don't-fits daily bring down whatever nebulous standards we set for ourselves. And the business of journalism — which it is — continues to be just that, having great difficulty emerging into the profession it should be.
>
> One of the worst offenders in this area, I feel, is my own field of broadcast journalism. Why shouldn't someone who is giving the news over radio or television be required to have as much of a news background as the average cub reporters on a newspaper? Why should a young fellow whose major qualification is a resonant voice be given the responsibility of relating events to thousands of people — as if he knows what he's talking about — often without a shred of preparation, either in covering news events or in pre-professional schooling? [6]

Instead of statute law, the law of supply and demand works more or less, and it can work to the benefit or the detriment of the journalist. Some station owners care little about news coverage or community affairs. To them, news is a dead loss. They will hire almost anyone who agrees to work for a depressed wage. On these stations, reporters with university degrees earn little more than clerk-typists. Congress or the FCC could give these station owners the motivation to upgrade their news operations, but have not yet done so, nor have they even raised an eyebrow at stations which have no full-time news staff at all, and present little if any news.

Other station owners relish their news department's position in the community. Journalists on the staff receive salaries reflecting their education and experience, salaries matching those of pharmacists, accountants and engineers in the community, professions which compare with journalism in the years of needed education and the dependence for employment upon a businessman whose training may lie in other fields and whose present interests are basically business-oriented. The skilled journalist is valued and sought after. The beginner is expected to get his training elsewhere. On the network level, top news salaries are quite handsome.

The young journalist will learn more on a small television or radio station than he cares to know. But learn it he must. The small radio station newsman "not only gathers the raw material for a story, but he writes the copy and broadcasts it. He must edit and rewrite wire copy, make telephone checks, answer the telephone, change ribbons on teletype machines and keep the machines supplied with paper. The newsman must record telephone reports, edit audio tape, monitor police and fire receivers, file news scripts, keep stringer and tipster logs, and do a host of other chores."[7]

Ethics

A journalist takes no Hippocratic Oath in order to work at a newspaper, a radio or television station, or anywhere else. To perform his functions he never promises objectivity or even honesty. He does not swear that he will not prostitute his art. Indeed, the history of journalism finds its roots not in reporting events as they happened but in the burning desire to express points of view.

Edward R. Murrow once said, "A communications system is totally neutral. It has no conscience, no principle, no morality. It has only a history. It will broadcast filth or inspiration with equal facility. It will speak the truth as loudly as it will speak a falsehood. It is, in sum, no more or no less than the men and women who use it."

The American journalist is, by and large, an honorable person. He is often fiercely honest, and sometimes so objective that he will surrender his job rather than play a story in a way he thinks is not right. His pen is not for hire, although outside the major cities he is often badly underpaid for someone with his education, experience and responsibility, to say nothing of the hours he is asked to work and the risks he must sometimes take.

Not all journalists are so scrupulous. Not all newspaper publishers or broadcast license holders are objective and aboveboard. But the majority of them seem to be decent people with a sense of ethics.

Objectivity never comes easily to a responsible journalist. It comes because he wills it so, although he personally has developed strong political views on many subjects, based on an intelligent appraisal of news events daily and even hourly during all of his professional years. He forces these views to the background. If he lets them take over, he becomes nothing more than a hack, a flack or a propaganda mouthpiece.

Sometimes a well-meaning journalist will compromise his independence a little in order to acquire or present the story he wants. The NBC network was given a demonstration of such a compromise when an outside producer brought in a documentary he had made about American missiles. Robert E. Kintner, then NBC president, related what followed:

> It was a good job. The producer assured us that it was ready to run, that he had already made the changes demanded by the Department of Defense.
> "Oh," said Bill McAndrew. "Security?"
> "No," said the producer. "Editorial."
> We turned down the program. [8]

In another matter involving ethics, a cameraman for a San Diego television station moonlighted for the FBI in covering news about radical organizations. *Time* quoted him as saying, "It's just that I'm in the wrong occupation. If I had been a construction worker or a ditch digger, none of this would have mattered." *Time* added, acidly, "Precisely." [9]

Several national organizations concern themselves with journalistic ethics, most notably the fifteen-member National News Council, which examines complaints against the national news media. Headed by a respected jurist and including journalists among its members, the Council was born amid howls from a number of editors who felt that the "watchdog" news media did not itself need a watchdog. Despite being a professional review board, the National News Council has none of the powers of review boards in other professions. It can only make public its findings, but that in itself carries weight in an image-conscious society. Britain, West Germany, Denmark, Italy, the Netherlands, South Africa and India also have national news councils. In the United States the Minnesota Press Council was the first statewide news council.

The Radio Television News Directors Association has a committee to examine professional standards and ethics. It has considered, for example, guidelines on coverage of airline hijackings.

The Joint Media Committee on News Coverage Problems speaks for journalists. Founded by RTNDA, the American Society of Newspaper Editors, Sigma Delta Chi, and other national media groups, the Joint Committee published a booklet for mayors, police chiefs and other community officials on a program for emergency cooperation with the media on major news. It has also challenged the American Bar Association in the continuing fair trial - free press debate.

A few television station managers insist that the "word from our sponsor" be delivered by the newscaster. If he wants to hold his job, the newscaster, after he has informed the community about the horrors of a disaster, must smilingly inform them about the delights at the local furniture store. If his gorge does not rise every time, he can be sure that some members of his audience are not so lucky. The practice is self-destructive, because the newsman's credibility wanes. He becomes a huckster who also happens to read news.

Walter Cronkite expressed the feeling of many of his colleagues in these angry words:

It is beyond me to understand how anyone can believe in, foster, support or force a newsman to read commercials.

This is blasphemy of the worst form. A newsman is nothing if not believable. And how can he be believed when he delivers a news item, if in the next breath he lends his face, his voice and his name to extolling a product or service that the public knows he probably has never tested?

...It is difficult if not impossible for the individual newsman who wants to feed his family to stand up to a management that demands that he indulge in this infamous, degrading and destructive practice. But I fail to understand why our professional organizations...should not take a firm stand and help enforce an ethic that should be fundamental to our craft.[10]

In Minneapolis a millionaire businessman and sometime politician bought an all-news radio station, which he soon switched to a music format, and promptly sent reporters out selling advertisements as part of their jobs. Several quit in anger. The businessman professed to see nothing wrong.

Education

Journalism has been called a "with it" major. It is attracting a lot of students.

A journalist is a translator, not of language but of complexity. He writes for laymen, and we are all laymen in fields outside our own.

At 10 a.m., reporter Bill Jones talks to a local heart surgeon for an explanation of a transplant technique announced yesterday in Houston. At 11 a.m., Jones talks to an architect about plans for a bridge. At noon, Jones learns from an economics professor what the latest Federal Reserve Board action is all about.

If Jones works for a newspaper, he must write his stories so that they are not only accurate, but clear to everyone. The surgeon and the economist must be able to understand what the architect is talking about. Experts in their own fields, they know nothing about architecture. If Jones works for a radio station or a television station, his concern for clarity is even greater because his audience has only one chance to understand the ideas rushing by. And if reporter Jones is filming or taping interviews with the surgeon, the architect and the economist, he must guide these experts to explain their complex information themselves in a few simple words.

Jones cannot expect his audience to understand what he himself cannot understand. Words and ideas are not hot potatoes to be passed quickly to the audience. Rule: *If you don't understand something, don't expect anyone else to understand it. Insist on an explanation until you can understand it without any nagging doubts.*

What kind of an education should Bill Jones seek in college if he intends to become a television reporter or news writer?

Many of the stories he covers--maybe a majority--will deal with government in some form. Should he take political science courses? Covering what areas?

It is easy to bog down in the jargon of the stock market, international trade, and banking. Should he study basic economics?

Urban and racial crises could be the most important news of the coming decades. Fools see simple cause-effect relationships. Reporter Jones does not want to be a fool. Should he delve deeper through some sociology classes?

Pollution remains major news. So does space. Breakthroughs in physics, medicine, and biology make headlines. The search for alternate sources of energy will be with us for our lifetimes. Should Jones study science?

Even on a local station, Jones cannot escape international news. Should he study geography?

With what other fields should he have familiarity? Law? Psychology? Music? Sports? Meteorology?

Surely, young Jones cannot go through a university catalog and take every course, or even every introductory course. And if he tries to become a modern version of a Renaissance man, he must still consider how much he should learn about techniques.

The Profession

Should he learn how to cover a news story? Should he learn how to write? Information writing is an art, taught and learned. Should he be taught to edit tape and to write copy to film? Should he learn to use a camera? Should he learn to speak clearly and comfortably? Should he know anything about sound? optics? broadcast electronics? production? Should he learn anything about communications research? After all, motivation studies, public opinion polling methods, and propaganda techniques are all used in television. Finally, what should he know about mass communications law, in addition to knowing that too much enthusiasm in getting a story can result in a million dollar invasion of privacy suit?

Student Bill Jones will not learn all this in the four years it takes him to get a B.A. or the five years or even six years it takes to get an M.A.

Ideally, he will prepare himself with a broad education in the liberal arts. He will certainly take some political science and history courses, plus electives in other social sciences, in the physical sciences and the behavioral sciences. In areas where he does not take formal class work, he should retain enough curiosity to read magazine articles and an occasional well written book. He need not plow through thick textbooks to acquire a rudimentary grasp of a subject.

Besides his general knowledge, he should take classes in broadcasting which teach him techniques. The most useful technique is learning how to write. Classes in speech fundamentals, reporting, film editing, motion picture photography, and television production will teach him other techniques.

At the university, a professor may tell him that learning techniques is time wasting, because he will learn them on the job. Quite true, he can learn techniques on the job. But Jones may not get the job in the first place if he is not prepared to hold it from the day he walks in. Let's say an employer who must hire a reporter to start Monday is faced with a choice between a college graduate who has never held a piece of film or heard his voice on a tape recorder and a high school graduate who spent two years as a reporter at another television station. It is the author's guess that the employer will hire that high school graduate as surely as a flush beats a pair of sixes. Now let's say the college graduate submits a videotape of an in-class newscast plus a half-hour radio documentary. Depending upon how skillfully the newscast and documentary were prepared, the job should go to the college graduate, and will go to him if the employer recognizes his potential.

The Resume

Some advice is in order:

1. Keep your resumé short. Less than one page, if possible.

2. List your broadcasting and journalism education and employment, including internships.

3. List all your university degrees and the jobs you have held for at least a year. List awards and honors.

4. List professional or university references rather than personal references, or offer references upon request.

5. Keep your personal information brief. For example: "22 years old, married, no children, 5'9" tall, 160 lbs., excellent health." It is not necessary to add that you have brown eyes or that your hobbies are reading, traveling and bridge.

6. Be sure your resumé is letter perfect and sharp looking.

7. Include a good photograph.

8. If you are applying for a radio news job, send an audio tape. If you are applying for television, prepare a videotape and offer to send it upon request.

9. Send out a limited number of resumés, to stations where you would like to work and where you believe you have a reasonable chance to be hired. Remember that the good affiliate stations in major markets receive dozens of resumés weekly and seldom hire inexperienced staffers.

10. If you have just graduated from college, consider following up your resume with a trip which takes you through the towns and cities where you have sent resumés. In a cover letter, very short, tell the news director that you would like to drop by for a *brief* chat. And when you do drop by, keep your promise. News directors are busy people.

If things don't go well in the first round, examine what you are doing. Seek some unstintingly critical advice. Try again. Don't despair.

Town and Gown

A favorite topic of discussion in any news shop is what's wrong with journalism schools. (As a working journalist the author participated wittily before he had taken any journalism classes.) It's not quite as good a topic as sex, but it's pretty good.

The embarrassed and hard-pressed journalism professor might well wonder a) how much these critics know about journalism schools, and b) whether the quality of their newscasts gives the critics the right to be critical of anything. Nevertheless, the proof of the pudding is in the eating, it is said, and without a doubt a fair share of sluggish minds emerge from the journalism schools of the nation. (It might be argued that the best brains do not enroll in journalism schools in the first place because of the low salaries at the other end, but such an argument leads to a self-examination too painful to contemplate.)

These are typical criticisms: "I've had journalism graduates in here who can't write a simple sentence." "Why don't you teach those kids how to spell?" "We had an applicant in here with a master's degree who wouldn't know a news story if it bit him." "Too many college grads that we have talked to are looking for a big title, a big office, and a big pay." "They come in here and want to change the world." "Don't you teach them how to fill out a resume?" "Quit giving them all that so-called theory and teach them how to cover a story, if you know how yourself." And so forth.

Another criticism is that journalism schools are bursting with students. Unlike medical and law schools, there are few controls, and many schools follow the logic that bigger is better, or at least that more students may eventually mean bigger budgets, which may improve the faculty or the facilities. The only real solution to all this would be Draconian and no doubt unenforceable–a very sharp limitation applied nationwide on who can enroll in any journalism school, or perhaps some certification upon graduation from a university which was willing to give such certificates only to the very best students. But journalism has been too free-wheeling an enterprise for far too long to choose the rigorous examples of law and medicine in its education.

The sharpest criticisms are reserved for those journalism faculty members with little or no media experience and those who worked for a newspaper in some dimly remembered past and have hardly set foot in a newsroom since. They are criticized for teaching theory instead of practice. Within the journalism schools there may be an echoing conflict between the "chi squares" (the theorists) and the "green eyeshades" (the practitioners). The disagreements center around the function of a journalism school, or to be more precise, to what extent a school should commit itself to the training of journalists and to what extent it should commit itself to research and to a study of the media.

It would be wrong to leave the impression that relations between stations and universities are poor. Probably they are very strong in most places. Apprenticeship programs send students into newsrooms as workers, not observers. News directors patiently hold still for interviews. Reporters and newscasters find their way to classrooms to swap answers for questions. Classes tour studios. More than one hard-pressed news director has been grateful that a school of journalism nearby is able to send at least half-trained students to him as apprentice writers and reporters. Some relationships go even further. For instance, WMTV, Madison, Wisconsin, provided film stock, cameras and advice to broadcast journalism students at the University of Wisconsin. The students, in turn, produced news segments and documentaries for the station.

Research

Sadly, it must be admitted that the gap between the university and the practitioner is wider in journalism than in most professions. Unlike so many architects, engineers, pharmacists, economists, lawyers, systems analysts and so many professionals in other fields, journalists generally do not look to the universities for advances in their profession. A university department of journalism or school of mass communication is regarded firstly as a source of manpower, secondly as a place to give occasional speeches, and thirdly as a pleasant, ivy covered substitute for the daily rat race late in the working newsman's career.

Along with everything else, research suffers. In broadcasting, almost no published journalism research is done outside the university, and what is done within the university appears to have no effect outside the university.

Networks and large television stations maintain sales research departments. News consultants do private audience surveys. The networks and some large stations also do some election coverage research, with the help of university experts. This research includes writing and programming probability equations, drawing up samples and preparing information flow systems. As a result of *this* use of research, coupled with journalistic skill, television election coverage has become so *efficient* that people complain about its efficiency: "You've taken all the fun out of sitting up all night listening to elections." Networks also work with polling firms to explore the opinions of the American people, resulting in some interesting reports ranging from newscast inserts to hour-long programs.

Vanderbilt University videotapes newscasts of all three networks, the only library of its sort in the United States.

Networks and large stations ought to engage in basic and applied mass communications research, using university facilities where needed. And the results of their research should influence their work. Other professions benefit from their own research. So should journalism. Harry J. Skornia has contended that broadcasting can no more exist without real research than can medicine or science.

Millions of dollars have been spent in the United States on research into "market" effects of the mass media. But little has been done to develop significant research by the broadcast industry into learning theory, and the many kinds of effects which broadcasting has on different kinds of individuals, under different circumstances. A great profession would conduct such research, and would develop information theorists who would guide operators of these media in their wisest and soundest uses....[11]

The Library

Every newsroom should have a reference bookshelf. At a minimum, it should contain:

1. Dictionary, preferably of recent vintage. An unabridged dictionary is not necessary.

2. Almanac, no earlier than last year's model.

3. World atlas.

4. U.S. state-by-state road guide, if the atlas does not have it.

5. Thesaurus.

6. Telephone directories of all cities in your broadcast area, plus the state capital.

7. City street map. Keep a few handy. They tend to stray.

If the man with the purse strings will loosen them for *these* books, you should thank him:

1. Pronouncing gazetteer.

2. Biographical dictionary or *Who's Who in America*.

3. Cross-listed phone directory (by street addresses) or current city directory.

4. Book of famous quotations.

5. State government manual ("Blue Book") (who has charge of what, and how you reach him).

6. Maps of nearby counties.

7. *Congressional Directory*.

8. *Statistical Abstract of the United States*, fairly current.

9. *U.S. Code.* (Note: each congressman and senator gets four sets a year to give away free.)

10. Style guide, or book of modern English usage.

11. One or more practical texts in the field of broadcast news, not only as a reference for present employees, but also as a guide for less experienced newcomers.

Besides a bookshelf, you should also keep:

1. All scripts.

2. Films and tapes used on air.

3. Outtakes, for at least 30 days.

4. Notes, handouts and wire copy used as the basis for scripts. File them for 30 days.

5. Stills which might be used another day, especially head shots and well-known public places (e.g., the city hall, the airport, the New York skyline).

Your newsroom should subscribe to:

1. All local city newspapers.

2. At least the larger suburban and small town dailies in your broadcast area.

3. At least one national news magazine.

4. *Broadcasting.*

5. *RTNDA Communicator.*

6. *Quill.*

7. *Journal of Broadcasting.*

These last named publications are concerned, at least in part, with our profession. The techniques, standards, research and news developments of broadcast journalism are reported and discussed for your benefit. Take advantage of them.

For the Student

1. Should a news department be independent of station management except for budget and the hiring of a news director?

2. If your answer is "yes," write an argument to convince a station manager. If "no," write an argument to convince a news director.

3. Ask a working broadcast journalist to speak to your class about his problems in "learning the ropes." (Be sure to talk to your instructor first.)

4. List ten approximately comparable occupations, including radio reporter and television reporter, then take a straw poll at a shopping center or around campus, asking people to rank them according to desirability. (e.g., "Would you want your son or daughter to become a....?")

5. What is the biggest block to professionalism in broadcast journalism? Discuss in class.

Show Biz 18

Consultants have made TV news as predictable as a Big Mac.
— TV Guide

Do you give people "what they want" or "what they ought to have"? The question has tickled at broadcasting almost since it began, and at newspapers long before that. There is no answer except on an individual basis. The question is now confounded by another question: What if "what people want" is mindless trivia or sordid gossip?

In terms of broadcast journalism, "what people want" may be defined as those elements that would tempt enough viewers to tune into a newscast to give it the coveted "number one" rating in its market. "What people ought to have" may be defined as the experienced journalist's perception of news that is important to his community. Life would be simpler if they were the same, if people wanted the kind of news journalists thought they ought to have. Some people do, of course, but apparently not enough to avoid an issue that, going into the 1980's, was as sharp as any in broadcast journalism.

Edward R. Murrow once said, "If television and radio are to be used for the entertainment of all of the people all of the time, we have come perilously close to discovering the real opiate of the people."[1]

But his is not the only quotable quote.

The Other End of the Tube

"The public didn't buy their TV sets to get news," said Philip L. McHugh, president of the McHugh & Hoffman firm of news consultants. "They didn't buy their sets with any idea that they would have to do the work....they want to be entertained....they want you to do the work" of presenting news in a way most convenient to them.[2]

273

Those who would argue that the public has limits to its patience or interest can find plenty of support for a bread-and-circuses approach. You amuse, not inform; divert, not educate; soothe, not upset. The majority may be content and never mind the clamors of the news-hungry minority, who probably read newspapers and news magazines anyway. The same reasoning would put fast-food hamburger chains in charge of school lunchrooms, on the not unreasonable grounds that french fries taste neater than green beans, and mothers who insist upon nourishment can send bag lunches.

Walter Lippmann argued that the mass media oversimplify, but that the public is simplistic, wanting issues in black and white, not digesting very much, and not willing to be bothered for very long. (He also asked what the national priorities for printing would be if there were only three printing presses; however, that is another discussion.)

"I have never read anything serious about inaccurate listening," Eric Sevareid said. "If you read through one week's supply of my mail I think you would be appalled. I am constantly denounced—or sometimes praised—for saying things I never said at all; sometimes I had said the very opposite; sometimes they had me mixed up with Brinkley or Smith."[3]

Dr. Mark R. Levy, a sociologist and former NBC News editor, concluded after a two-year study that television news audiences do not watch news primarily to be informed. "Being informed is only a secondary motive for most viewers," he said. "Most people watch TV news to be amused and diverted, or to make sure that their homes and families are safe and secure."[4]

Two out of three viewers in the study said that newscasters' jokes "make the news easier to take." Three out of four liked television news because it is often very "funny," and more than half said watching the news "helps them relax." Fewer than one viewer in ten said "news quality" was his or her prime reason for tuning in. "I am sorry to say it, but having Merv Griffin or Johnny Carson on your channel, or having a 'celebrity' news reader appears to be a stronger guarantee of higher ratings than doing a good job of journalism," Levy concluded.

The "Show Biz" Issue

The veteran CBS correspondent Alex Kendrick told his young replacement in London, Dan Rather, "You are the next wave and you are here partly because you have a pretty face."[5]

"I would hate to anchor the news opposite Paul Newman," Rather wrote.[6]

Much has been written and said on both sides of what might be called the "show biz" issue. When Charles Kuralt concluded his much quoted speech about newscasters' hair, news directors gave him a standing ovation, yet when the convention ended they returned, as they had to, to those ratings and cans of hair spray.

It is very hard to consider this issue without hypocrisy. Everyone would like to say, "Yes, we can have high journalistic standards and still be number one in our market." Evidence exists to support this argument, but ample evidence exists to contrary. When the 11 p.m. news on KGO-TV, San Francisco, became one of the highest rated local newscasts in the nation on a diet of "happy talk" and "tabloid" sex and sensationalism, the station manager of rival KRON-TV, C.E. Cooney, confronted the issue squarely and said that his station "is not going to bastardize its news for ratings." [7]

The contrary argument was stated by news director Jim Van Messell of another competitor, KPIX, which, reported Mike Wallace, "followed KGO-TV's lead in going tabloid." Van Messell said his ideal for a local newscast would be a local version of the CBS Evening News with Walter Cronkite, but he was "absolutely convinced no one would watch it." He added, "You can't save souls in an empty church."

In at least some cities at least during some periods, Greshman's law that bad money drives out good could be *bad news programming drives out good*. Certainly not all cities have "tabloid" news stations. At the time of publication, very few did. Nor did all stations have "happy talk," but many had settled into some version of it. Hair spray was everywhere.

Ratings can be improved in many ways, a point which cannot be emphasized too strongly. The thrust of this book and every other text on broadcast journalism is to examine ways to make the news more meaningful and more interesting to viewers, thereby increasing ratings.

KSAT-TV, San Antonio, increased its 10 p.m. ratings sharply by abandoning blood-and-guts coverage. Said news director Doug Ramsey: "We still chase breaking news, and we cover it well. But violence is no longer our staple. A triple fatality on Interstate 37 is an important story. But it doesn't begin to compare in importance with the rampaging cost of utilities, the danger to the San Antonio economy from job cuts at the military bases, redistricting for city elections, pollution threats to the area's unique underground water supply."

Those stations that prefer to entertain than inform and those that pick up rating points by pandering and shocking are following the lead set by some newspapers. The New York *Times* is often held up as a model by journalists, but the *Times* has never sought to be number one in the ratings. The New York *Daily News* has tried to be number one in its market, and has succeeded, but it is a far different newspaper.

A television station can certainly increase the number of its viewers by more attention to local news, by sharper writing, and by better use of film and tape. However, the experience of television stations in New York, San Francisco and other cities has shown that against "happy talk" or "tabloid" news, a good, solid product may not be enough to propel a station into the first place in its market. A station can have standards or it can "take the money and run," in which case new standards can be supplied like new paint.

The issue, faced squarely, is painful.

Consultants and Show Biz

Can consultants be blamed for much of what is wrong with local television news today? Do they deserve credit for improvements that have been made in recent years? To both questions, the answer is a firm, "Well, yes and no!" Consultants have recommended courses of action and procedures which have been both praised and blamed, and to the extent that they have made the recommendations, they deserve responsibility. But it is the station manager and the news director who accept or reject the recommendations, and the ultimate responsibility for what goes over the air belongs to the licensee.

News directors who oppose the hiring of consultants are galled by the money lavished on a consultant by an otherwise penny-pinching station manager. Lee Hanna, vice president of news for NBC's owned-and-operated stations, said, "A client of one of these consultants will spend $40,000 or $50,000 for one of these reports. If they would spend that much on just their news operations, think about how much more they could accomplish."

Some of the excellent suggestions by consultants, for example advising a news staff to write more clearly, are so obvious that one must wonder why a news staff needs to be told, unless a suspicion arises that not everyone hired to prepare or deliver television news is adequately trained or experienced, which is a regrettable state of affairs in the permanent "buyer's market" existing for television news personnel. (At a regional conference of news directors, a young man came up to the author to thank him for writing *Television News* because, the young man said, a television station hired him without training or experience right out of college, where he majored in English lit. and never took a journalism course. He was hired to run a one-man newsroom, he said, and the textbook helped him to survive. I suppose I could have felt flattered, but I did not.)

The Consultants

The television news consultant arrived in the Sixties and became a major influence during the Seventies. Two of the earliest firms, McHugh & Hoffman and Frank Magid, dominated the lucrative market, with a half dozen other firms also active in the business of advising television stations how to increase audiences for newscasts, and thereby increase profits not only for news but for the rest of the viewing schedule because a station is known primarily by its newscasts. The consultants were sometimes called "news doctors."

After signing a contract with a station, the consultant sends interviewers into the community served by the station to elicit from a sample of viewers what it is about a newscast that they like or dislike. The results presumably form the basis of recommendations to the station, although critics contend that the consultants are "giving every patient the same nose." The recommendations cover news format, "packaging," presentation of stories and personnel changes. Services provided by the consultant include finding new on-air talent and even helping to get rid of a successful newscaster on a competitive station by finding a television station somewhere else that will make the newscaster a more attractive offer! Since that distant station is likely to be another client, the consultant kills two birds with one recommendation! The consultant also hires people, usually with prior news experience, to give newsroom personnel advice on writing and film editing. The consultants themselves are for the most part audience researchers with no journalistic experience of their own, but as business prospered they were able to hire former journalists.

The impact of the consultants was remarkable. Television journalism, heretofore grudgingly tolerated by a lot of station managers as an expensive but necessary nuisance, overnight became wonderful. Like so many fairy godmothers, the consultants touched the Cinderella news departments with the wand of computer printouts. The Prince Charmings who sat behind the station managers' desks were smitten. Pumpkin sets became Lucite coaches. Money poured in for on-air talent and for abundant promotion. There was often money for new equipment and sometimes for an expanded staff and for daily coverage. Enthusiasm swept newsrooms. Giving viewers the news "they need" was replaced by giving viewers the news "they want." Peppy features replaced sedate political coverage. News stories shrank in length, and more stories squeezed into the time available. Billboards and the sides of buses carried the message to the viewers: tune in to our bright new news team. Newsrooms rediscovered what Paul Harvey knew all along, and Walter Winchell before him.

The viewers hearkened to the call. KGO-TV, guided by McHugh and Hoffman, vaulted into first place in the San Francisco market. WPVI-TV, guided by Magid, went from fourth place to first in Philadelphia in one year. The story repeated itself in city after city. The "news doctors' " patients glowed with golden health. Their unadvised competitors languished in the never-ending quest for viewers. Television stations came flocking to the doors of the consultants, and once in the fold, most chose to remain.

But not all. After WNAC-TV, Boston, cancelled its contract with a consultant, general manager James Coppersmith said, "Consultants are not in there to improve journalistic ethics. They're there to get your audience up. And anybody who says he hires a consultant to help with First Amendment responsibilities or for any other reason is pulling your garter." [8]

Ralph Renick, vice president, news director and anchor of Miami's WTVJ-TV, which also cancelled a consultant contract, said, "Consultants are a little bit like the Soviet army in World War II. They come in to liberate and end up like an army of occupation, and often, to remove the consultant's grip, a news director must wage a counterattack, with the results all too likely to be similar to the Hungarian revolt of 1956."[9] One might recall Thoreau's warning that men were becoming "the tools of their tools."

Supporters were as firm as detractors and just as quick with hyperbole. Ray Miller, vice president and news director of Houston's KPRC-TV, said,

"Frank Magid is the greatest thing that ever happened to broadcasting." From Jerry Danziger of KOB-TV, Albuquerque: "There is no question that Magid made us number one in the market. I attribute the success directly to him."

Consultants' Research

Controversy swirled around most of what the consultants provided. Frank Magid seemed to bear the brunt of the criticism and to lead the attack upon the critics. A group of mass communications researchers at Florida State University, Tallahassee, led by Dr. David LeRoy, director of its Communications Research Center, called the Magid research techniques "primitive," potentially misleading, "ambiguously worded," "biased" and "inadequately supervised." Magid replied that the critics' own research was "so full of holes....it's like a plumber trying to critique the work of a neurosurgeon."[10]

Settling this argument by letting competent neutral mass communication researchers examine the data was difficult because consultants do not release their data. "There are practically no methodologically competent people allowed to see the reports," LeRoy declared, adding that the effect of presenting "a horrendous amount of data" is to "bludgeon the poor news director with this data he's ill-equipped to understand, challenge or even interpret."[11]

Consultants depend upon three kinds of research:

1. Telephone surveys. They are a cheap, quick way to reach a lot of people, especially just after the newscast. Some listeners and viewers are not willing to allow an interviewer into the home, but are willing to talk on the phone.

2. In-home interviews. The interviewers can go into greater depth than is possible by telephone. Greater sensitivity is also possible provided that the interviewer is skilled, a significant provision because not all interviewers who can be hired to go door-to-door are competent.

3. Focus groups. A few people are invited to the station to chat about what they see and hear on the air. A trained interviewer conducts the sessions.

Advice on News Content?

The consultants were also criticized for giving advice about news content, an accusation they hotly denied. "We do not in any shape or form recommend the content of what the news should be," Magid has said. Added WPVI-TV news director Mel Kampmann, "Magid does not get involved with journalistic content; he gets involved with the presentation of journalistic content."

Yet a study of 43 stations, 22 of them "Magid stations," reported what might be thought of as contrary findings.[12] Among them: 65 percent of the consultants gave advice on the number of films to be used, 79 percent on their length, 72 percent on how to handle film interviews, 60 percent on the kinds of news to emphasize, 58 percent on the kinds of news to de-emphasize, 84 percent gave advice on feature stories, 79 percent gave advice on investigative reports, and all of the consultants, 100 percent, gave advice on informal on-air conversation.

In addition, the Magid organization has proposed more than forty ideas for continuing features, including "Action Reporter," who seeks and deals with viewer's problems with government and business; "Greengrocer," a report on produce; "Dollars and Sense," which shows ways to save money; "Backyard Vacation," about places to visit near the city; "Newsreel," which consists of film of silly things and humorous events around the town; "Friends and Neighbors"; "Out and About", and many, many more, all of which eat into the available news time.

The difference may be semantic, depending on how the word "content" is defined. It is unlikely that a consultant would advise an assignment editor not to cover the mayor's news conference or tell a reporter not to pursue a certain line of questioning or tell a writer not to use what the mayor said about street repair. On the other hand, a consultant might tell a news director to spend less time reporting politics. "Hell, in Boston, politics is a spectator sport," was the comment of WNAC-TV's James Coppersmith, who rejected the consultant's advice. The consultants themselves point out that their advice is just advice, not a demand, and it need not be followed.

"Basically what we do is make the stories that they do cover more interesting and understandable to the viewer," said Suzanne Sell, director of personnel resources for the Magid firm. "Our premise is if the viewer doesn't understand, there's no point to the story."

"Happy Talk" and "Tabloid" News

Still another criticism is that consultants trivialize the news. "The real test of success is the daily 'look' of the station's newscasts, for it is here that the viewer forms his impression," states a Magid brochure. Radio clients received a regular newsletter containing jokes which can be used on the air. Critics called the "happy talk" newscasts, developed by both news directors and consultants, "the best comedy show in town."

Where "happy talk" has been replaced by "tabloid" news, according to *Time* critic Thomas Griffith, viewers are treated to:

> ...a constant trafficking in emotions, like closeups of people in pain being lifted into ambulances. This nightly distorted accumulation of police-beat misfortunes makes any city look like a disaster area. Items are tailored to the attention threshold of the least patient viewer. That is what happens when entertainment values outweigh news judgment.[13]

Few consultants recommend "tabloid" news. And it is not usually recommended outside of the larger, "more sophisticated" cities. However, it is part of "giving people what they want."

Walter Cronkite said:

> There is no newsman worth his salt who does not know that advisers
> who dictate that no item should run more than forty-five seconds of the
> newscast and that it must have action in it (a barn burning or a jackknifed
> tractor trailer truck will do), that calls a ninety-seconds film piece a "mini-
> documentary," that advises against covering city hall because it is dull,
> that says the anchorman or woman must do all voice overs for "identity" —
> any real newsman or woman knows that sort of stuff is balderdash. It's
> cosmetic, pretty packaging — not substance....
>
> And I suspect that most station operators know that, too. But I think
> they've been sold a bill of goods; that they've been made suckers for a
> fad: editing by consultancy.[14]

An article in *TV Guide* said, "Eyewitness News is as much a fixture in most
television markets as the golden arches of the fast-food industry. And just as
motel and fast-food chains have made all cities look alike, consultants have made
TV news as predictable as a Big Mac."[15]

A news director who told a consultant that part of the news department's
job was to educate viewers said the consultant replied, "Show me a news director
who wants to educate somebody and I'll show you a station in third place."[16]

A contrasting view was stated by former CBS News president Richard Salant
to a CBS affiliates meeting. "Our job is not to please people," he said simply,
"but to inform them."

Finding "Talent"

Suggesting that broadcast journalists be hired or fired is part of the consultant's
services. Said consultant Philip McHugh, "Yes, we do recommend sometimes
dropping anchorpeople. If you hire a plumber and he can't plumb, you're going
to get rid of him."

What makes a good "plumber"? Critics say that news consultants have
caused competent and professional journalists to lose their jobs to make way
for slick, attractive news readers. "Reporters have become human microphone
stands," said Dick Gottschald of KBJR, Duluth.

Walter Cronkite asked CBS affiliate station managers:

> Why buy somebody else's idea of an ideal anchor person or news
> editor for your market? Your anchor person is the most intimate contact
> you have with your community.
>
> Don't you know what sort of person your neighbors like? Don't you
> know better than any outsider the tastes of your friends and acquaintances?
> If not, I suggest that maybe you ought to be the one to move along.[17]

Suzanne Sell, director of personnel resources for the Magid firm, told an interviewer, "It's very, very sad that a person's credibility can be decided by what he wears. We have a lot of older people who aren't exactly pretty, but may be good communicators or reporters. Their appearance won't matter." She added, "We don't recommend a person be fired if there's any hope. We always try to save a person's job if we can." [18]

Stations that turned to the Magid organization for screening applicants received a service which included a file of newsroom personnel working all over the nation, plus air checks, plus psychological testing and, as needed, talent coaching and the development of new talent. The psychological testing service "is an entire battery of scientifically designed explorations of an individual's aptitudes and desires," according to a Magid brochure, designed "to assure station management that the selection process of screened applicants is 'profitable' in every respect."

Another news consulting firm, ERA Research, wired the fingertips of one hundred members of a test audience with electric sensors to test their galvanic skin response to videotapes of newscasters. Sweat glands open up when people are frightened, angry, guilty or sexually aroused. As a result of this test anchorman Patrick Emory and anchorwoman Sandy Hill were fired by KNXT-TV, Los Angeles.

News or NEWZAK?

After a Jacksonville, Florida, station did an expose on pollution, a few community leaders reportedly complained that the job had been done "too well." The reporter was fired.[19]

At the other end of the spectrum was Boston's WCVB-TV, the station that in 1972 replaced WHDH, which lost a long and celebrated battle to keep its FCC license. WCVB-TV daily aired an "Eye Opener" newscast, midday news, early evening news, late evening news, and a sign-off news final, plus regularly scheduled weekly half-hour reports that at one time included a science program, a report for young people, a sports magazine format program and an investigative report, plus non-scheduled specials and political debates. It did not sell political advertising, giving away free time instead. A survey by the Columbia Journalism Review placed WCVB-TV at the top of the list of television stations in the time it devoted to local news and public affairs.[20] News director Larry Pickard said the number of awards the station has won in just a few years was "astonishing."[21]

There are stations like WCVB-TV and there are the other kind, which thrash about in a desperate and doomed effort to catch everyone's eye and make no one mad. There are never enough of the former and far too many of the latter.

"So much of television news these days is not news," said KNXT newscaster Joseph Benti, after learning about the skin tests which led to the firing of two KNXT colleagues. "It's NEWZAK, like the music heard in elevators and airports, and it's all over the country."[22]

Why Consultants?

Asked why a station needed a service like his, instead of doing it for itself, Frank Magid replied that his consulting organization provided an additional resource to a station which would be impractical or impossible for a station to duplicate for itself; for example, traveling the nation to discover new ideas that could be adaptable to many markets. [23]

WAGA-TV, Atlanta, news director Pat Polillo said as early as 1974:

> Nobody ever dreamed the consulting thing would come as far as it has already. What happens on the day that all three TV stations in a market have switched consultants, and everybody's got their rating book in front of them, and they each know everything about talent, attitudes, news, films, content, format, pacing? Then everybody will start thinking for themselves. [24]

How did consultants manage to get their foot in the door in the first place? The answer is clearly that they filled a need that news directors did not fill and that the broadcast journalism profession as a whole did not fill, and that includes the universities, where applied research is conducted for many other industries, but seldom for broadcast news. A consultant can hardly be faulted for sensing a business opportunity.

Former RTNDA president John Salisbury commented:

> ...it must be stated that over the years, Management has been dragged kicking and screaming into its present enlightened concern for public interest. And it must also be stated that the News Director, knowing this, has developed a touch of superiority complex where Management is concerned. Not in every instance, but in enough to give us pause.
>
> The basic problem, therefore, is the familiar failure of Management and the News Department to fully communicate with and understand one another. The "bundling board" rises ominously between those who share the same bed under the same roof. [25]

"I'm firmly convinced that America seems to be filled with news directors who are somewhat frightened about learning what the public actually thinks about them," said newscaster and former news director Ron Magers of KSTP-TV, St. Paul. "Journalists of all people have some great abhorrence of research."

"News directors themselves caused consultants to come in," said Jim Marshall, news director of WBAY, Green Bay. "Perhaps lack of initiative or inability to change or find out what audiences wanted opened the door for consultants."

Shuffling on-air talent from station to station is of no value in communicating information. Ultimately it may prove of little value in holding audiences. As Shakespeare put it, the fault, dear Brutus, lies not in our stars but in ourselves.

For the Student

1. To what extent should a newscast give viewers "what they ought to have" instead of "what they want"?

2. If you ran a station, would you hire a consultant? Discuss.

3. What's wrong with a consultant advising on news content?

4. If research showed that a "happy talk" format would bring your station higher ratings, would you adopt it? Discuss.

5. If research showed that "tabloid" news, featuring plenty of violence, sex and sensationalism, would make your newscast number one in the market, would you switch over?

The Round Events Peg and the Square News Hole 19

If every television camera went blind, not one problem in this country would disappear.

— Julian Goodman

Senator Larry Pressler of South Dakota was asked by a reporter to explain, in 30 seconds, the significance of the non-military space program. He knew he would fail, but he tried. He wasn't happy about it.

"This approach may be adequate for eruptive news, such as an airplane crash or a flash flood or a bank robbery," remarked *Saturday Review* editor Norman Cousins, "but it doesn't necessarily lead to an understanding of complex events."[1]

Told to keep his report to a minute fifteen, a reporter replied, "Yeah, but when do I get to tell what happened?"

Time is not the only constraint between the event and its broadcast report.

The Ayatollah Khomeini, despite his atavistic, medieval appearance, handled media with sophistication. Particularly, he used the broadcast facilities of the United States and other nations to transmit his cold hatred of the United States and his determination to be revenged on the exiled Shah.

Street demonstrations in Teheran in 1979 and 1980 perked up at the sight of a television camera. American network television correspondents and photographers who tried to report the tension over the capture of the U.S. embassy and the taking of American hostages discovered that they were, in a real sense, being used by the organized street mobs to send anti-American messages to the United States. Just out of camera view of the clenched fists, just out of earshot of the chanting slogans, the people of Teheran went about their ordinary daily affairs. And when the cameras were turned off, so was much of the excitement of the demonstration.

"Public figures the world over are becoming increasingly adept at (television's) use for their own purposes," observed Charles B. Seib of the

285

Washington *Post.* "...television is extremely susceptible to manipulation and, by its very presence, influences events. To recognize that, one has only to watch the Teheran demonstrators shift into high gear when they see the cameras."[2]

We know now that Vietnam was not a war with a lot of visual action. A few people knew it at the time, but they also knew that the producers in New York wanted "visual" coverage, action, drama. At CBS they called it "shooting bloody." The violence of the world's first televised war came nightly into the nation's living rooms in neat packages that ran 1:30. Some psychologists contend that the violence eventually lost its power to shock; it tended to dehumanize us. Others saw an opposite effect, that people began to realize that war was not a John Wayne movie. Quite possibly both effects were at work.

A Harris poll, at the height of the Vietnam War, reported that 64 percent of television viewers said that the war coverage they saw made them more supportive of the war effort, while 26 percent said it intensified their opposition.[3]

Another constraint of television news is its linear nature — a viewer unable to choose the stories he wishes to see — and the consequent desire in the newsroom to make each story as interesting as possible to as many people as possible. One way to do that is to see events as conflicts, to find the controversial element and feature it in the story. Sander Vanocur commented that network news stories tended to consist of a limited number of story plots. Tongue in cheek, he labelled some of them "Black vs. White," "War is Hell," "America is Falling Apart," "Man against the Elements" and 'The Generation Gap."[4]

Other constraints are described throughout the pages of this book: constraints of deadline pressure, budget, skills, knowledge, law, audience interest. Working against these is the journalist's wish to tell what happened, to tell it so that people will understand, and to tell it right.

"That story right after this...."

Punctuating the scenes of war and diplomacy and natural disaster and political wrangling are the commercials, also in neat packages. Robert Lewis Shayon commented:

> On one track ran the tragedy and the solemnity, the heartbreak of the war, while on the other — darting in and out like a lunatic Toonerville trolley — chortled the monadic, machined happiness of the consumer in a paradise of food and drug products, and bar bells for the paunchy man in the family, courtesy of S&H....[5]

News departments and sales departments tend to regard each other as necessary evils. They have little to do with one another or the other's products. The result is, for the most part, healthy--at least healthier than either collaboration or interference. Yet commercials and news stories share the same half hours two or three times each evening, and what their juxtaposition does inside viewers' heads is ignored by the producers of each. Perhaps the viewer compartmentalizes them as neatly as networks and television stations do. Perhaps not.

Just as a newspaper's editorial department fits the news into page dummies that have the ads already blocked out, so too does a television newsroom fit the news around commercials already scheduled. Neither medium's journalists care the least what is being advertised or how, with the exception that airline commercials are dropped on the day of an airline crash and car ads are sometimes moved away from car accident film. Both are done out of concern for the advertiser. No commercials are dropped or moved out of concern for the viewer except in the case of overwhelming disaster. When President Kennedy was killed, all commercials and all programming except news were cancelled for three days.

Simply put, broadcasters are in the business of delivering audiences to advertisers. While newscasts exist to serve the public interest, which broadcasters are required to do, the newscasts are expected to attract audiences in sufficient numbers to attract advertisers. The two goals usually harmonize but sometimes conflict, as the spread of "happy talk" newscasts demonstrates, at least to unhappy critics.

"Why do you want to show that stuff?"

Somebody once said it may take a page of the finest print to convey the effect of one piercing scream. One hundred pages will not do it.

When recalling television news reports that left a lasting impression, what comes to mind is film and, now, ENG tape, often showing confrontation.

The television photographer who sees drama in front of his lens films it. He would be dishonest to do less. The news reporter or writer who screens the dramatic film will choose to use it. He, too, would be dishonest to do less. But he tries to put what the viewer sees into perspective. Herein lies one of the dilemmas imposed by the medium of television: *the impact of strong film is not neutralized by words.* (In the context used here, "dilemma" means only that a solution has not appeared, not that a solution is impossible.)

No matter what the television journalist tries to say or do to put his exciting film into perspective, its impact may outweigh and outlast everything. Equal impact may not be possible, but if 95% of the students at a university did not riot, if 95% of the strikers did not throw bricks, if 95% of the ghetto residents did not loot, the reporter should emphasize this, and the photographer should shoot film of these people behaving peacefully, for these TV journalists have a responsibility to give perspective to the violence that took place. However, journalists will and should show the violence, too. Otherwise, they are guilty of censorship. A newscaster cannot paraphrase the thwack of a police billy club on the head of a demonstrator. He cannot quote glass shattering. No substitute exists for exciting actuality film. And no television journalist worthy of his profession would refuse to show civil unrest erupting into violence.

These pictures touch the emotions more than the intellect. They rub nerves raw as nothing else can. They *move* us. Yet by choosing the exciting over the unexciting, the dramatic over the dull, the moving picture over the "talking head," the television journalist often is also choosing the action over the thought, the event over the issue, the effect over the cause, the personality over the idea.

BBC-TV commentator Robin Day put it this way:

> Man's supreme gift is seen in terms of what the eye sees on that wretched little screen: "a talking head"...
>
> Words on television tend to have their own limitation. They tend to be put into the background by the pictures, especially if these are extremely dramatic...The vivid impact of the picture remains in the consciousness longer than the words of interpretation or qualification. The sight on a TV screen of a person being brutally injured will linger in the emotions far longer than the accompanying words.
>
> The insatiable appetite of television for vivid, action-packed pictures has wide and profound implications. It means that television has a built-in tendency to present issues solely or mainly in terms of their immediately visible results. Wars on television are seen almost exclusively in terms of casualties and combat, (or) in terms of the starving children who were seen with sickening regularity on our television screens...Television does not always take sufficient trouble to ask "who is responsible," "why is it happening," or "what is the alternative."
>
> Television's proud motto is "see it happen," but seeing is not necessarily understanding and the sights selected to be seen may not be the whole picture.
>
> When people are horrified by the sight of bloodshed and mutilation they are not easily convinced that a cause may be at stake. The sight of a dead child, a burning home, a dying citizen-soldier — all these may have a much more powerful impact than abstract concepts like "liberty" or "collective security." [6]

"You can pass by a headline, even if dramatic, but you cannot close your eyes to a dramatic picture that appears on TV," Walter Cronkite said. "We take the troubles of the world and we transfer them to their (the American people's) homes, nightly, and we oblige them to watch. But they don't want to watch. They want to escape such troubles, they want to hide their heads in the sand. And they are brought up to agree with politicians who would like us to shut up." [7]

Because violence horrifies many of us, it does not follow that we do not want to see it, and it certainly does not follow that we ought not to see it, let alone that we should not be permitted to see it. Violence is often a political fact which helps a citizen reach a political conclusion.

As Hollywood has long known, violence does not horrify everyone. Quite the contrary. Robert Ardrey noted:

> We enjoy the violent. We hurry to an accident not to help; we run to a fire not to put it out; we crowd about a schoolyard fight not to stop it....I myself may have no great taste for Molotov Cocktails; it is because I am timid, not because I am good...

Action and destruction are fun. The concerned observer who will not grant it indulges in a hypocrisy which we cannot afford. He who regards a taste for violent action as a human perversion will not likely make any great contribution to the containment of our violent way.[8]

Another dilemma of the medium is that the television journalist cannot always see the violence committed by both sides. A camera crew traveling with soldiers can film the unpleasant acts of these soldiers. The enemy's violence goes unobserved.

NBC reporter Ron Nessen, later President Ford's news secretary, recalled his tour of duty in Vietnam, "We were shunted by helicopter from one operation to another by military press officers who wanted to show off American initiative."[9] That "initiative" usually took the form of search-and-destroy patrols, air bombings, and military sweeps, measured in terms of the daily body count, which always reported much, much higher numbers of enemy dead than South Vietnamese or American dead.

Camera crews filming riots are advised, warned or ordered by police to stay behind police lines, which the crews may be glad to do for their own personal safety. But so shielded, the violence they will witness and film will be mostly what police do to rioters. Even if police do nothing, most of the people filmed from the vantage of police lines will be policemen. And in a tense, angry riot, the likely lasting impression will be of tense, angry policemen.

As might be expected, some members of the general community react negatively to any television riot coverage, arguing that riots feed on television exposure. Television journalists have had to give serious thought to their policies on reporting riots, and particularly violence in the ghettos.

Here is another dilemma, stated succinctly by *TV Guide* reporter Neil Hickey: "Arabs, prison inmates, students--and scores of other identifiable pleaders–have absorbed with bewildering and unerring canniness the first lesson of the electronic age: calculated illegal behavior gets results. The formula, by now, is a proven one. It really works."

Kidnapings, Hijackings, Riots

In 1977, a frustrated, failed Indianapolis businessman named Anthony Kiritsis chose to draw attention to his plight by holding a mortgage company executive as a public hostage, using a sawed off shotgun connected to a wire around his victim's neck. Television and radio news were more than observers of the event. They were the kidnaper's means to communicate to the world his sense of having been cheated. Sensing a major story, television news cooperated as fully as any demented kidnaper could wish.

Expressing remorse later, WIRE-AM news director Steven Yount said that by airing everything the kidnaper wanted aired, his colleagues became hostages, not reporters, and further surrendered their independence by agreeing with a police request not to report anything that would upset Kiritsis, thereby becoming part of the police effort to fool the kidnaper. "We have to cover kidnapings as kidnapings and murders as murders," Yount said. "Those crimes cannot be written off as excusable forms of social protest." [10]

National coverage of the Kiritsis story was soon followed by another nationally reported hostage case, which also ended without bloodshed, and after that, a bloody mass slaying in New Rochelle, New York, when a neo-Nazi gunned down four employees of the furniture company where he worked, then killed a cop, then himself.

There are no easy answers to the ethical and professional questions raised when someone seizes hostages and threatens their lives unless he gets what he wants, including mass media announcements. Like it or not, television news is part of the establishment.

Television coverage of a hostage story in Cleveland led news director Virgil Dominic to conclude that another incident was almost guaranteed. "We are glorifying lawbreakers, we are making heroes out of non-heroes, we are being used."

Washington, D.C. Deputy Police Chief Robert Rabe said the media were definitely part of the problem. He saw no evidence that newsmen were concerned for the lives of the hostages. U.N. Ambassador Andrew Young went so far as to suggest that the First Amendment should be clarified to take account of media "advertising to neurotic people that the way to get attention is to do something suicidal or ridiculous."

What does a news department do when, shortly before air time, an anonymous caller telephones to take responsibility in the name of a group or a cause for some act of violence that had just occurred? Too often this claim is taken at face value and a few minutes later the newscaster solemnly announces, "A group calling itself the Committee of Concerned Anti-Nuclear Irish Zionists has taken responsibility for the explosion." Perhaps there is such a group and they did it. Perhaps their enemies did it. Perhaps neither did it but some high school kids out for fun or a sick mind wanting the thrill of making news. A lot of *perhaps*, but no effort to withhold the report until the unidentified source was checked out.

News directors should plan in advance how such coverage should be handled. They should not be taken by surprise each time. They should not have to patch responses together while wondering what the competition is doing. Television and radio news directors and newspaper city editors could meet on the matter, and it could be the subject of workshops at annual conferences.

Former CBS News president Richard Salant said his network would not hold back reporting assassination attempts against a president on the grounds that some mentally unbalanced person might get the idea of trying to kill the president. "Once you start applying standards other than newsworthiness, you start to play God," Salant said. [11]

Hijackings and bomb hoaxes are two other problems requiring advance thought by journalists. Again, the media, and especially television news, are not always the invisible observers that journalists wish them to be. As the principal means of communicating with all the people out there, television news is willy-nilly a participant, and as such ought to establish guidelines for action rather than invent on-the-spot solutions in the form of a compromise to get the story and please the authorities without angering the hijackers or bombers.

Psychiatrists, police and others who have studied the bomb hoaxer agree that his reward comes in the form of mass media coverage of his threat. The hoaxer's own investment may be no more than ten cents for a phone call from a public booth.

Some stations have already adopted guidelines. Air Canada proposed a set of guidelines which RTNDA of Canada received favorably. They are broken into four categories:

1. (Obviously to be reported; Air Canada will do everything possible to assist):

Live bombs found on airplane.

Simulated bombs found on airplane.

Emergency evacuation of passengers by way of escape chutes or emergency exits.

The return of airborne flights with VIPs on board.

Actual use of emergency equipment such as bomb detectors or fire hoses.

Disruptions of special flights such as inaugurals, charters carrying Olympic teams or NHL teams.

When a person is actually charged as a result of planting a bomb or giving a false warning.

When someone is injured either on the aircraft or as a result of the bomb scare.

When cargo, mail or baggage is damaged as a result of the bomb scare.

2. (Borderline: a judgment matter whether to use or not):

When passengers are told of the bomb threat and the flight is delayed by inspection of checked baggage.

When a passenger is prohibited from boarding or expelled from the aircraft because of utterances but is not charged.

When a flight returns to the gate for inspection before being airborne.

When emergency equipment escorts the aircraft but is used for no other purpose.

When luggage or cargo is searched on the tarmac.

3. (Should not be used, unless circumstances are exceptional):

When the aircraft is delayed briefly for a pre-flight inspection of the aircraft.

When the aircraft is delayed by a pre-flight inspection of hand baggage boarding with the passengers.

4. (Should not be used):
When the aircraft or flight is non-existent.
When the call is obviously a joke.
When a call is received in sufficient time to permit a pre-flight inspection without delays.

The problems of television coverage of riots extend beyond the techniques of filming them. The presence of a camera crew at the scene of an unruly demonstration may incite participants to acts of mischief or violence.

The camera in a demonstration catalyzes what it sees. At work is a kind of Heisenberg Principle of Uncertainty, in which by observing, we alter.

ABC News correspondent Don Farmer put it this way:

Television can report the action better than any medium, but with the same cameras that are required to report the action, we get ourselves involved in the story, whether we want to or not.

When television newsmen are going to cover a demonstration, a march, or a rally on film, they obviously have to know about it ahead of time, whereas a newspaperman needs only enough time to get himself there before it is over. The television people must have more time because of the equipment and the extra manpower needed to do the same job the newspaperman does with a pencil and a telephone.[12]

And a few years ago, someone called the WMAQ-TV newsroom in Chicago:

"We're going to stage a sit-in at the Main Loop post office."

"When is it going to start?" asked the reporter.

"As soon as you get here."

The television journalist's rueful amusement at his predicament in a demonstration gives way to concern and sometimes fear in a riot. Nothing about a teenager wielding a brick is funny. The young rioter in the ghetto wants the world to know his feelings. He sees a television camera crew, and he thinks that through them he can reach beyond the ghetto to tell it like it is. He knows from his own television watching that other young men in other city ghettos spread the word this way. And so he picks up a brick and shouts to attract the photographer's attention.

Even if he does not see a photographer, the rioter senses that he and his friends are making news, and that the more lawless they become, the more news they make.

In several cities, television journalists from competing stations have met to formulate guidelines for riot coverage. They were concerned not only with their responsibility to their community and to their professional standards of reporting the news without fear or favor, but also with the safety of the camera crews sent into the ghetto streets. Some photographers, reporters, and film couriers have been abused, injured, even hospitalized. Plainly marked television station cars have been singled out for burning. Expensive equipment has been smashed.

Television news crews must face the hostility of rioters resenting any whites, and the hostility of those policemen who contend that television reporting, especially live reporting, worsens and lengthens a riot. Some police also feel that the television reporters concentrate too much on police action in controlling the riot and arresting suspected troublemakers, leading to allegations of police brutality from the general community.

Among some guidelines generally accepted:

1. Riots are to be fully covered.

2. Militants without a substantial following are to be regarded as publicity seekers, and are to be ignored. Reporters subjectively determine what constitutes a substantial following.

3. Camera crews should stay out of neighborhoods where trouble seems to be brewing, but violence has not yet broken out.

4. Wherever possible, camera crews are to remain inconspicuous.

5. News personnel who go into riot zones must wear hard hats and, weather permitting, padded jackets.

6. News personnel are to say and do nothing to encourage further depredation. They must not linger, waiting for something to happen.

Other advice for camera crews:

Don't be a hero. Run scared. Stay close to police or national guardsmen when you can.

Dark clothing is advisable. Avoid wearing a coat and tie.

Travel in pairs if possible. If it is safe to drive into the area do it with two men — one driving, one taking the pictures.

Be mobile. Keep your equipment to a minimum so that you can move fast if a mob starts after you. Strap an extra lens to your belt and stuff extra film in your pockets.

Don't carry firearms or Mace.

Use telephoto lenses whenever possible so you don't have to get too close to where the danger exists.

Tape windows of your car to avoid being cut by flying glass. Tape down the light switch on your car door so that when you open the door the light doesn't go on.

Never use flash....you'll become a target from both sides.

Avoid getting involved in a dispute with anyone. Treat everyone with respect.

Keep in touch with your office.

A clever photographer for Britain's Visnews emptied the works from a transistor radio whose case was just large enough to contain a flat Bolex silent camera with a two-turret lens. He walked through riot areas with the "radio" perched on his shoulder against his ear and a bland smile on his face as he listened to the music of 16mm film clattering through the gate.

"Why can't you be objective?"

Suppose a casual acquaintance told you that someone you loved and respected had done something horrible. Even if the casual acquaintance showed you some snippets of film of the deed or its aftermath, you are likely to doubt the story. If you have heard that this acquaintance is occasionally inaccurate, your doubts will grow. And if you believe this casual acquaintance is maliciously inspired and is probably influencing others with his story, who can blame you for becoming furious?

For many television viewers this set of responses occurs when a newscaster, the "casual acquaintance," reports unpleasant news about a person or cause the viewer admires. Reuven Frank reviewed coverage of the 1968 Democratic convention in Chicago, when police went on a rampage:

> The important thing is that a large number of people who watch television for information saw information which disturbed them and which they resented. To one degree or another they refused to allow themselves to believe it. It bothered closely held values. Understandably and naturally, they clung to their values and rejected the information. The only possible explanation for what they saw in this frame of mind would have to be that what they saw was false, and then that it was arranged to be false, and then that it was arranged by a conspiracy to be false.[13]

"The public reaction to TV coverage of the '68 convention riots in Chicago was a perfect example of people reacting out of their pre-set feelings about rioters or cops," Eric Sevareid said.[14] "Thousands of people hundreds of miles from the scene, having no independent source of information of their own, knowing only what they saw on the little screen, immediately declared that what they saw was distorted, slanted. How could they possibly know?"

A study reports that many viewers, by selected or distorted recall, tend to restructure what they see in a film to support their biases.[15]

The Des Moines speech by Vice President Agnew encouraged a sizeable segment of the American people to express the feeling that television news is presented in a biased way. A Gallup Poll taken soon after the speech reported that 42% felt that TV network news tends to favor one side, many (but not all) of the respondents saying it was the liberal side; 40% thought the network newscasts dealt fairly with all sides (18% had no opinion), and--among other findings--45% thought that newspapers tend to favor one side.[16] Those who supported Agnew's viewpoint generally thought the television news bias was leftward, liberal. Most television journalists who have written on this subject disagreed, but ABC news commentator Howard K. Smith, agreed, saying network news departments were almost exclusively staffed by liberals. "It evolved from the time when liberalism was a good thing, and most intellectuals became highly liberal. Most reporters are in an intellectual occupation."

Such a statement, levelled by a respected colleague, ought to concern television journalists. So, too, expressed opinion that some television journalists, especially on local stations, are conservatives. The concern is not that journalists hold political views, but that for some listeners, expression of these views gets in the way of the flow of information, breeding justifiable resentment and suspicion. Any citizen, including a journalist, may hold any political views. Indeed, the journalist who failed to reach political conclusions would not be worth his weight in warm tapioca.

Smith's observation that most reporters are in an intellectual occupation should please reporters, not disturb them. After all, being intellectual, which the dictionary defines as having a notable mental capacity, being extremely rational, and pursuing things of interest to the intellect, is more desirable than being *unintellectual*.

Can a newsman work as a political neuter? Maybe not, but he must always try. To the degree he succeeds, he is an ethical professional. To the degree he fails, he is a propagandist. Reuven Frank put it this way:

> The newsman's prime responsibility is to the news business itself, with its standards and traditions. Put that way, it might seem a simpleton's view of life. The alternative — the only alternative — is the newsman as a conscious instrumentality of social control. To me, that is a frightening and abhorrent idea. I hope it is to you. But in one form or another, it is often suggested. Those who suggest it are rarely aware of this implication of their suggestion. In my experience, it is always suggested for the highest unselfish motives by people who sincerely want a better world and want news to help them achieve it. News doesn't do it. News doesn't know how. News which knows how isn't news.[17]

Strangely, complete uninvolvement by a knowledgable journalist almost defies common sense, for it would mean, as an extreme example, that a newscaster could not look unhappy if the stock market averages skidded, or smile if they recovered, because the stock market short sellers are delighted with a price collapse. Storms would bring no frown, sunshine no smile. And if perfect detachment were possible, it would be too dull and wooden for interest or enjoyment.

David Brinkley on the subject:

> A person presumably is expected to go on the air and be objective, which is to say that he is to have no likes, no dislikes, no feelings, no views, no values, no standards, to be a machine. Well, if I were objective, or if anyone was, he would have to be put away somewhere in an institution because he'd be some sort of vegetable. I'm not objective, make no pretense of being objective. There are a great many things I like and dislike, and it may be that at times some indication of this appears in my facial expression...or anyone else's. If it didn't, we'd be in a pretty sad, indeed pitiful, condition. Objectivity is impossible to the normal human being. Fairness, however, is attainable, and that's what we strive for — not objectivity, fairness.[18]

Edward R. Murrow said, "It is not, I think, humanly possible for any reporter to be completely objective, for we are all to some degree prisoners of our education, travel, reading—the sum total of our experience." Kenneth Stewart, a newspaperman, stated, "If you mean by objectivity absence of convictions, willingness to let nature take its course, uncritical acceptance of things as they are (what Robert Frost calls the 'isness of is'), the hell with it. If you mean by objectivity a healthy respect for the ascertainable truth, a readiness to modify conclusions when new evidence comes in, a refusal to distort deliberately and for ulterior or concealed motives, a belief that the means shape the end, not that the end justifies the means, all well and good."[19]

In workaday terms, the ethical journalist should follow these guidelines in newscasts:

1. Film and tape should be shot and edited, and copy should be edited and written solely because of his perception of its importance and interest to the viewer, never because it puts a political cause or a politician in a good or bad light.

2. No viewer should be able to guess a journalist's political party or candidate preference from the way he reports a news story. However, his attitude toward an individual news event may — and perhaps should — on occasion be made plain, depending upon the event. Common sense and common decency should guide him. Labelled commentary and documentaries give the journalist latitude for political expression, but he must be accurate and he must always be fair. Documentaries are part of the long American tradition of investigative journalism, which seldom pleases the subjects.

3. The journalist's primary goal should be to report what exists, let the chips fall where they may. In a totalitarian society, the primary goal is different.

Howard K. Smith, who saw a liberal slant in reporting, does not advocate blandness. "I find an almost excessive lack of bias on television. We are afraid of a point of view. We stick to the old American belief that there is an objectivity. If a man says the world is round, we run out to find someone to say it is flat."

In an effort to appear objective to someone whose views the reporter finds distasteful or simply in an effort to keep an interview rolling along, the reporter may give the impression of agreeing with what the interviewee is saying. Beware of doing so. Dan Rather recalled the time that he, a young television reporter, interviewed a spokesman for white supremacy. His photographer said later that Rather sounded as if he sympathized with what was said. "That was a mistake," the photographer told him. "You're just starting and you're going to run into this sort of thing all the time. You've got to think through how to handle these situations."[20]

Evidence of Bias

It's as easy to shout "bias" as it is to cry "wolf," though actual bias might be as scarce as actual wolves. Instinct can lead the viewer astray, for if the nature of a news story scores a point or two against, say, a dam that the Army Corps of

Engineers wants to build, the pro-dam viewer may feel the story is biased and so is the reporter.

But actual bias exists and here are signs of it:

1. A run of stories on one side of an issue with little or nothing on the other side, although some real news is being made on the other side. Any allegation that the imbalance is a consistent bias should be buttressed by a careful content analysis of the newscasts, certainly not random impressions from memory, because the viewer is more likely to remember what irritated than what pleased.

2. Loaded language, especially adjectives and adverbs which paint either a glowing or a black picture of the issue. News writing thrives on a lean diet of nouns and verbs. It doesn't need carbohydrates of adjectives and adverbs.

3. The absence of newsworthy controversy which is reported elsewhere. The theory is that ignored news is not really news at all. "News is what I say it is," said the old city editor.

4. Making much ado about nothing, the opposite of #3. These two points refer to what is called "salience" or the "agenda setting function" of the news. That is, events become prominent and take on added meaning by the fact of being reported, and lose meaning if they are not reported.

5. Out-and-out lies about what really happened. The viewer who makes this accusation had better know what really happened, and not what ought to have happened or what some source of questionable veracity said happened.

Checkbook Journalism

The practice of paying for interviews, an old one in Britain, is new in the United States. Many would like to nip it in the bud. The National News Council, asked to consider the CBS payment to H.R. Haldeman, refused to take a stand on the ethics of paying for interviews, but called for an announcement to inform audiences that the interview had been paid for. The question came up again when David Frost paid a large sum to former President Richard Nixon, but those complaints were less forceful on the grounds that Frost, although his interviewing technique won praise from critics, was not strictly a journalist.

It seems most journalists oppose the practice on principle, but unless television networks, stations, organizations of broadcasters and broadcast journalists declare themselves firmly on this issue, checkbook journalism could pour through like water finding cracks in an earthen dam.

"Why don't you put on some good news for a change?"

Most news, or at least most *hard* news, is a report of change. Change disturbs the usual state of affairs which, considered broadly, is more pleasing than not. Where the usual state of things is displeasing, change might be for the better, which results in "good news." More often, especially when the change is unexpected, change from the ordinary is change for the worse. It is ordinary that buses and planes reach their terminals safely and that cats get out of whatever they get into. When a bus or plane crashes or a cat gets stranded in a tree, that's news. With this concept, journalism reflects human nature. A working newsman who admitted that he could devote more space to good news than to crime said people wouldn't remember it. "I go home at night and my wife doesn't say, 'Gee, the neighbors got along swell today.' But if the wife threw her husband out the window, I hear about it."

The late NBC newscaster Chet Huntley said, "Journalists were never intended to be the cheer leaders of a society, the conductors of applause, the sycophants. Tragically, that is their assigned role in authoritarian societies, but not here."

A different attitude, expressed by the Rev. Jesse Jackson, is that journalists often seem obsessed with the sensational—war protests, riots, burning ghettos, crime, immorality, drugs—all the nation's fractures and cancers, yet say little about quiet progress, small decencies, the things that go right. Essentially, Jackson asked for balance and perspective, two commodities not always to be found when the teletypes clack out bad news from a dozen datelines.

Television news, limited in time, focusing on what matters to and/or interests many viewers, must deal with information many viewers find troubling. For network audiences, troubling information all but crowds out pleasant information. The more troubling the news is, the more unusual it is, the further it is from normal activity. For example, no story was as upsetting to many Americans as the My Lai massacre. Seldom has news been so bad and unwelcome. A congressional committee investigating My Lai stated, "In fact it was so wrong and so foreign to the normal character and actions of our military forces as to immediately raise a question as to the legal sanity at the time of those men involved."

The choice of a totalitarian society would be to suppress such news "in the interest of the nation." The choice of a libertarian society, such as that of the United States, is to look at itself openly, warts and all. That we don't like this news, that it is not good news, must not matter in reporting the news. Former CBS president Frank Stanton stated, "The troubled pages of this century's history are writ dark with the death of liberty in those nations where the first fatal symptom of political decay was an effort to control the news media."[21]

Unfettered television news has had, is having, and will continue to have an effect on history. Consider television coverage of the war in Vietnam, the world's first televised war. The London *Economist* declared, "The United States is the first free country that has ever tried to fight a televised war under the rules of democracy--free reporting, opinion polls, the lot—and if the result has been the unsurprising discovery that people loathe war, that is something that all democracies will have to chew over in the future." To which, BBC-TV's Robin Day added, "One wonders whether in the future a democracy which has uncensored television in every home will ever be able to fight a war, however just...The brutal details of military action may be there on the television screen to shock and to horrify, sapping perhaps the will of the nation to resist the forces of evil or even safeguard its own freedom.''

To say that people prefer good news to bad is to state the obvious. So, too, to say that people are distressed by bad news. But it is quite another matter to guess that people will choose good news programs to the usual run. From time to time, one hears of newspapers devoted solely to good news. Their circulations are reportedly minuscule. (The author once worked for a newspaper which, each Christmas, printed an edition with only good news on page one. I observed that readers glanced quickly at the pap on the front page, then turned to page two for the news which mattered to them and really interested them.) To prefer good news is not necessarily to prefer to read good news, to hear it on radio, or to watch it on TV.

However, television stations sometimes go far in the other direction. Their newscasts feature every minor traffic accident, every one alarm fire, and every shooting they can film. ''Fender benders'' matter to few viewers and cannot interest many others. Then why are they shown? Perhaps because the news director lacks imagination. Five minutes of daily reflection would yield story ideas containing, potentially, more action film than two month's worth of crumpled bumpers, and many of these stories would fall in anybody's category of ''good news.''

News director Richard Buddine, WSLS-TV, Roanoke, Va., said, ''If there is a million-dollar fire in the middle of town, all of the stations in the area will have film of it that night, and it will all look pretty much the same — unless somebody had processor trouble. And chances are most of the reporting will be pretty similar. The same thing is true if there's a plane crash at the local airport, the mayor resigns or a local bank is held up. The flashy, obvious stories are easy to cover. So the station which is determined to be outstanding in news coverage... must push above this common level and press for a higher standard of excellence.''

''What can *we* do about what *you* show?''

This question is raised less often, but it is more thoughtful and it is harder to answer except to admit that current television news practice leaves something to be desired. The question is: ''How can we cope with your emphasis on our abnormalities?''

This question may be directed at a television news department by a university president who senses that many citizens have formed an impression of a university dominated by dirty, bearded, wild-eyed hippies egged on by nutty or politically radical professors. Consider the recollections of the then San Francisco State College president S.I. Hayakawa:

> The first thing they asked me was do I expect any violence the following day? It's as if there is an abnormal interest in violence on the part of the networks and when there's violence there are hundreds of cameramen

around and reporters and so on and when there is no violence, when normal operations of the colleges are going, there is nobody in sight except to come around and ask the question, when do you expect more violence.

Now I understand this. In many ways television is a medium that requires action and motion in order to keep interest focused on the screen. On the other hand there are many other things that involve action and motion in a college or university, like pictures of education classes dealing with handicapped children, pictures of the dance programs, pictures of athletic programs, poetry readings, therapy sessions. All sorts of things involving human interaction could just as well be shown as the riots on a campus...[22]

According to the Scranton Commission Report on student violence, "Again and again the cameras focused on what was most bizarre, dramatic, active or violent. Few television or radio and newspaper reporters had the time or knowledge to explore the causes."

A story may be accurate in detail yet add to a distorted picture of reality. It is not enough for the journalist to say it is not his business to be concerned with the effects of his reports upon the public, that his business is simply to report the truth. As a result of this operating philosophy, Monday's accurate and truthful report of campus violence, followed by Tuesday's accurate and truthful report of campus violence, followed by Wednesday's and Thursday's and Friday's accurate and truthful reports of campus violence, followed by a week and a month and a year of total silence about the campus when there is no violence—as a result of all this, elderly Aunt Margaret, who has never visited the campus, has been deeply convinced by television news that the campus is too dangerous a place for her niece, and old Mr. Peabody, who made a fortune in hardware, changes his will to cut out the university where he got his degree.

"Why blame me?" asks the television reporter. "I just told the truth."

Said Berkeley philosophy professor John Searle, "I watch television news not to find out what's happening, but what *other people think* is happening."

The Pseudo-Event

Historian Daniel Boorstin coined the term: *pseudo-event*. It means an event which would not occur if not for the media. *An event created because the media will cover it.* Every news conference is a pseudo-event.

"There are two main entrances to the news," Ben Bagdikian wrote, "One is reserved for conventional established voices. The other is for melodrama. Groups denied access through the front door come in through the back door of spectacular physical acts....It is not just the crazies and the radicals who stage pseudo-events."

One of the Chicago Seven defendants, Abbie Hoffman, declared, "So what the hell are we doing, you ask? We are dynamiting brain cells. We are putting people through changes....The media is the message. Use it! No fund raising, no full-page ads in the New York *Times*, no press releases. Just do your thing; the press eats it up. Media is free. *Make news.*"

Former FCC Commissioner Nicholas Johnson wryly observed, "Demonstrations are happening, and the news media—like moths to a flame—run to cover them."

Two Washington, D.C., lawyers, Rick Neustadt and Richard Paisner, offered the following advice to candidates who want free time on television newscasts:

1. Assignment editors determine most of what we see on local TV news. If you get to know them and can sell them on your story, a reporter will be assigned to it. Reporters always want to please the assignment desk; it isn't wise for them to flub an assigned story, so the reporter will do his or her best to bring back a usable report. Don't call a reporter about a story; call the assignment editor to make sure he or she remembers who you are so the next story will be easier to sell. Don't be embarrassed. Remind this editor how important your story is and that everyone else will be covering it.

2. Schedule the event you want publicized at a convenient time for TV to cover it. The best time is any weekday between 10:00 a.m. and 2:30 p.m. Night and weekend shows have skeleton crews — although if it's a poor news day and most weekends are, Saturday and Sunday may have some possibilities. Don't worry about the late news — the majority of what you see on the Eleven O'Clock News is a rehash from five and six o'clock. Make sure coverage of your story can be completed by midafternoon. Find a site as close to as many stations as possible — no assignment editor likes to waste valuable crew time driving long distances. In this age of live minicam events, it doesn't hurt to consider scheduling an easy-to-cover and important (important, meaning it affects a lot of people) event during the news broadcast. You may convince some stations to cover the event live, and you have a good deal of control over live coverage since it cannot be edited.

3. Think up good visuals. But make sure your visuals contain the message you want to get across. A poorly thought out picture that conveys the wrong impressions can hurt more than help. A political candidate surrounded by smiling children says one thing; a picket line of clean-cut pickets offers a different impression than a picket line with bearded protestors. Make sure the visuals you choose say what you want them to say.

4. If the television station has no time to cover the event, cover it yourself. Hire your own camera crew; then film or tape the event, edit the tape into one-minute to two-minutes packages, attach a script to be read, duplicate the entire package and ship it off to all TV stations (and radio stations, audio only) in the affected area. Many stations, especially the smaller ones, will use the preproduced packages as part of their local

news hour — and few will bother to identify the source of the story; thus, audiences will view the preproduced package as part of the regular news program.

5. If TV is definitely going to cover the event, wait until the crews arrive. They are often late — TV crews cover several stories each day and cannot get everywhere on time. Never ask the camerapersons to hurry; that will produce just the opposite effect. If print reporters resent the delay, remember: most people get their news from TV. Your event has been set up primarily for TV coverage. Placate grumbling reporters with conversation (gossip), coffee or something stronger.

6. Keep your speech or statement short and simple. A prepared copy of it (press release) should be handed to reporters — more often than not, TV reporters will simply put that press release on the air as if they originated the material. If you're reading a statement, keep its duration to less than two minutes. You can always pass out more information but do not read anything to the cameras that runs longer (90 seconds is ideal). You can control what TV will use by limiting what you say. Confine yourself to a single theme — more details confuse the audience. Pause every 20 seconds or so after making an important point. That makes for easy editing — a pause is a perfect cutting point. Do not pause, however, unless you feel you have reached a conclusion that will make your point. If you are forced to make a statement that you do not want to make, then make it long, convoluted and sprinkled with complicated phrases. Do not pause. It probably won't be used.

If you are asked tough questions while the cameras are running — usually you can tell when they're on by a red light on the camera (tape) or a loud, whirring noise (film) — make sure you do answer the question: but ramble on, making the tape or film unusable. (A few years ago you could use profanity and that would make the statement unusable, but in these more liberated times, that can be a dangerous ploy.)

7. End the press conference quickly. The longer it goes on, the more likely the chance for error. Cameras can film or tape something unhelpful; reporters become more aggressive on camera. Say what you want to say; then leave.

8. Don't worry too much if you said something you didn't want to say. If it's buried inside an answer to a question, chances are it will stay there and no one will hear it. TV reporters, unlike newspaper reporters, know little about the stories they are covering; many stations hire glib, good-looking men and women who sound good but have little experience. They get little help from their assignment desks — often the TV reporter is given an address and a two-line description of the event. It may be only one of many stories a reporter covers during the day. There is little time to bone up on background, think up interesting questions or look for any angle other than the one you are prepared to give the reporter. Few in the

newsroom will even see the story before it goes on the air — and if it's a live report, it will be even more to your liking, since the reporter's main job is getting on and off the air with a semblance of a story. Followup questions are seldom asked or used. With only 90 seconds allotted to the story, the reporter simply wants to get the basic information in quickly; and if you've done your job, it will be in your prepared press release and two-minute sound statement.[23]

If *Time* was accurate, the American Indian Movement's takeover of Wounded Knee was a case study in manipulating the media. Reported *Time*:

> Wounded Knee had become a kind of trap, particularly for television. It was obviously a major event that demanded thorough coverage. AIM leaders were so successful in getting their side of the story across, and so enthralled by the attention they were receiving, that they seemed willing to prolong the deadlock for the sake of still more publicity...
>
> Indeed, AIM's Russell Means, for example, cannily orchestrated events within Wounded Knee for the press's benefit. "Cameras over here," he called out one afternoon, directing photographers to where bunkers were being enlarged. Then AIM forces "arrested" four men attempting to enter their compound. Released a few minutes later, the men were paraded at gun point with their hands up past whirring cameras, then let go. Learning that one photographer missed a shot of one of the men leaving, AIM guards forced the "prisoners" to re-enact their release....
>
> (ABC producer Bill) Brown recalled, "I put the question to them: 'Are you setting up a provisional government?' " Shortly afterward, AIM leaders declared Wounded Knee the Oglala Nation.[24]

In Austin, Texas, Chicano strikers outside the Economy Furniture Factory were frustrated by management's refusal to negotiate and the media's lack of interest, so on the first anniversary of the strike they held a demonstration march, despite city council denial of a parade permit, across the state Capitol grounds and public parks. That brought out the riot police and, as the strike leaders anticipated, the media. But the strike leaders felt that the media ignored the basic issues, so they took other action, including an open letter to the FCC. Now television and radio reporters showed up. Lencho Hernandez, a union leader, recalled:

> All of a sudden they all wanted to talk with us about why we were striking. We started having press conferences about once a week, and the press would cover them. We were invited on talk shows. I was taped (for TV) in front of the factory several times.[25]

The union went on to win the strike. Among the things its leaders learned was how to create pseudo-events and how to get broadcast news to cover them. The lessons have been learned by others, too. People are using the levers of influence. Broadcast news may be one of the best.

For the Student

1. Why might a news director send a crew to where violence is brewing but has not erupted--for example, at the main gate of a struck factory? Defend or criticize these reasons.

2. Can news be presented objectively? Fairly? Discuss.

3. Should newscasts have more "good news" than you usually see now?

4. Should a demonstration be covered if the news department feels it is being staged for microphones and cameras?

5. For several weeks, watch and analyze one news program's coverage of one controversial topic. Report your conclusions about the news department's objectivity.

PICTURES

Shooting the Story
Electronic News Gathering
TV Photography
Sound
Film Editing
Stills

Shooting the Story 20

A riot described in a newspaper is a riot described; a riot shown on television is a riot entire: the whole bone-crunching, stomach-wrenching mess.

— Richard Wald

Accidents, fires and crime figure significantly in most local newscasts because many news directors believe that viewers never flag in being interested in these events, particularly when they occur close at hand. It may be disputed that television news features too much crime and violence, but that opinion must be argued within the framework of defining how much is "too much." Meanwhile, some evidence that people are curious about these out-of-the-ordinary events in life's daily routine can be seen in the slow-up of cars passing an accident as drivers become gawkers even at the risk of causing their own accidents. However, the journalist must be aware that this passing curiosity may not include watching "fender-bender" footage on the nightly newscast.

If these violent events appear to dominate local television newscasts, it may be that the assignment editor lacks imagination or it may be because the medium of television is uniquely adapted to showing them. The photographer takes the viewer to the scene, usually showing him the aftermath of the event, but sometimes — when the photographer is fortunate enough to be there when it happens — showing the event itself. The fledgling television journalist learns early how to cover fires, accidents and police business. But he may not learn to cover them well, if he has no model to rely on other than his own past experiences and the films of older members of the staff. He should study techniques used beyond the confines of his own station.

One place to learn them is the annual National Press Photographers Association TV newsfilm workshop, usually held at the University of Oklahoma in Norman each spring. The Defense Department co-sponsors the workshop, which is open to photographers who have at least one year's experience. News directors, producers, assignment editors and film editors may also attend. For information, write to the university.

Let us consider some ways to cover spot news using an ENG camera or a silent camera, with or without wild track sound from a tape recorder.

A Fire

The photographer got the tip by car radio telephone from his office. It took him 20 minutes to reach the site, on the other side of town. He parked his car a block away, and at that point began filming. His first shot was an establishing shot, for by the time he arrived the fire was blazing out of control. With his lens wide open, the photographer caught only the flames themselves and the blinking red lights of the fire trucks.

He then ran toward the fire, stopping to shoot again about 30 yards away. The lens remained wide open for every shot except a few close-up cutaways of firemen, because portable lights outdoors at night are useless beyond a range of a few yards. From a distance of 30 yards, the photographer filmed firemen at work, with flaming lumber behind them, so that the firemen were silhouetted against the flames. At that distance, a medium long shot, he filmed piles of burning lumber.

He moved still closer, shooting individual piles of burning wood. He then shot his first pan; he began with a medium shot of a fireman struggling with a hose, panned along the flow of the water, and stopped at the water's target, a pile of burning wood. The camera held steady on the fireman for eight seconds, panned for 4 seconds over a sweep of 45 degrees, and held steady for 12 seconds on the fire at the end of the pan. This scene shot this way would later give the film editor the option of: a) using the entire 24 second shot; b) using any portion of the pan down to as little as six seconds (one second hold at start and finish plus four seconds of pan); c) the fireman alone; d) the flames alone.

By panning, the photographer was also able to establish the relationship of the fireman to the fire. Under the extremely poor lighting conditions, there was no other way to establish this relationship, except to silhouette the fireman against the flames.

The photographer took a reverse shot — nearly a 180 degree turn — of the fireman. The pan began with the camera looking at the fireman in profile. The reverse was a shot of the fireman almost head on with the water from the hose streaking past the camera. Naturally, the photographer did not "cross the line," the imaginary line which maintains directional continuity; if his profile shot was of the fireman's right side, the reverse was of his right front.

The photographer now began to wander around the lumberyard, getting medium and close shots of firemen, flames, spectators (one more example of public interest in such spectacle), policemen diverting traffic, fire engines, snaking hoses and signs (including street signs to identify the location and a sign identifying the lumber yard). He was also alert to any action, such as firemen battering down a door, or a structure tumbling. If a fireman had been injured, the photographer would have given full attention to his rescue and treatment.

A Collision

The photographer, cruising in his car, got the tip from his police radio band. He reached the scene within moments of the arrival of the ambulance. Had he arrived ahead of the ambulance, the film he turned in would have included a shot of the ambulance arriving. Instead, his first shot was the usual establishing shot, showing both automobiles and their relationship to the street intersection. This shot was filmed as soon as the photographer parked his own car, and took just a few seconds of his time. Had the establishing shot required more time, the photographer would not have taken it until he filmed the focus of the story at this moment, a driver trapped inside one of the cars. The photographer ignored all other possible shots and ran to the side of the car where firemen were trying to extricate the driver by prying open his door with crowbars.

As quickly as he could, knowing that the scene might change in a matter of seconds, the photographer took a medium shot of the side of the car with the firemen working on the door. He then swung about for a reverse of the firemen, remembering (actually, this becomes instinctive) his camera axis ("crossing the line").

The photographer got a single close-up of the victim with an unwavering aim for 15 seconds. One mark of a professional is his ability and willingness to hold a steady shot for what might seem to the amateur to be an interminable time. One mark of the amateur is his seeming inability to hold a camera in one position; he is forever panning, trucking, dollying, and taking a variety of short, quick shots, usually of the same subject from the same distance at almost the same angle. The professional also learns to hold his breath while he holds his camera. The amateur's camera breathes when he does.

The photographer moved back to "re-establish" the scene, another medium long shot of both cars and the surrounding street, but from a different angle. Then he positioned himself so that when the firemen successfully pried open the car door, he would have a clear shot of the door being opened and the victim being pulled from the car.

After the ambulance took the victim away, which the photographer recorded at several stages with cutaways of the faces of firemen, spectators, and ambulance attendants, the photographer turned his attention to the damage done to the cars. Later he showed, again at several stages, tow trucks hauling away the wrecked cars, and again he made sure he had cutaways of spectators.

Perhaps no single element of a film story is so keenly missed as the useful, meaningful cutaway, and perhaps no single shot is so frequently neglected. Cutaways have already been mentioned, but the subject deserves repetition. A piece of wreckage is not a meaningful cutaway between two shots of a victim being loaded into an ambulance, but a spectator's face is. Actually, it does not really matter what the spectator was looking at when the photographer took his picture, as long as it *appears* that he was watching the victim being put on a stretcher. Many experienced photographers make it a standing practice to film some spectators on every story, including news conferences. The photographers ask the spectators to look straight ahead, perhaps at a lamppost across the street, perhaps at a wall. Two seconds of an expressionless face looking to right or left can be a most desirable piece of film! It is important to note that a cutaway shot must be unrelated physically to the scenes immediately preceding and following it; that is, what is seen in the cutaway must not be seen in the shots which it separates except for general setting.

After the filming of any story is completed, the photographer working alone lays aside his camera and picks up pencil and pad. From the police or other public officials on the scene the photographer-turned-reporter gets as many details as he can. What happened? What were the names, ages, addresses of the people involved? What was the extent of their injuries? To what hospitals were they taken? How much is the estimated loss or damage? What is the name and station house of the officer giving the information (he might be needed later to supply some overlooked details).

A Murder

The photographer got a call from a detective friend (such friendships are not uncommon and they are professionally valuable and often mutually rewarding, provided that the television journalist does not surrender his professional standards in return for police cooperation). The tip was that two elderly women had been murdered in their home.

The photographer arrived to find the bodies still lying on the floor, just as they had been discovered. Because the bodies were mutilated and had not been covered, the photographer did not film them. He chose this course of action not only because the police might have objected to filming, but because gory scenes are almost never used on responsible television newscasts. Instead, he filmed the disarray in the house, the murder weapon, and policemen and detectives searching for clues to the identity of the killer. The rooms of the house afforded no space for long establishing shots, and so the photographer panned and trucked (here, a walking shot on tiptoe to avoid jiggling the camera) in order to establish relationships between rooms and objects. Later, when the bodies were covered by sheets, the photographer filmed them, and also took shots of the coroner's deputies lifting the bodies onto stretchers.

Shots of objects, such as the window through which the killer gained entry, are usually better if a person is in the shot; for example, a policeman inspecting the window (if they are not pressed for time, policemen are often willing to cooperate by posing for a shot, but they should never be asked to do anything they do not normally do).

Outside the house, the photographer filmed a long, establishing shot showing police cars around the house and spectators (there they are again) gathered along the sidewalk. Shots were taken of the nearest street corner signs and of the house numbers, either on the house or on the mailbox. Medium shots of the spectators could provide cutaways between a shot of the bodies being carried out and the coroner's ambulance driving away.

One freelance photographer who regularly shot crime and accident victims carried his own sheet for those occasional times when a murder victim lay uncovered and the photographer did not have time to wait for the coroner's ambulance. He talked an obliging policeman into covering the body with the sheet just long enough for some footage. The photographer then retrieved his sheet and went on his way. *This photographer once, arriving after the body had been removed, talked another photographer into posing under the sheet. Unfortunately for the wily photographer and fortunately for the cause of ethical journalism, the "victim" was so fat that the writer who viewed the film (the author) caught the deception and chewed out the photographer for trying to pull a fast one.*

A Riot

The photographer knew in advance that teenagers planned to gather for a protest meeting against what they alleged was police brutality. He showed up early, to avoid traffic congestion, and to get close to the center of action. However, he was not as early as several hundred demonstrators in their teens and twenties who quickly turned themselves into a rampaging mob, trying to turn over cars and a city bus. There was no time to plan. Disregarding any peril to himself (a man holding a large camera is always a target in a mob), he shot quickly wherever he saw action, mixing long, medium, and close shots.

There was no time for pencil-and-pad questions, no time to fool with unessentials, no time to spend on anything he might acquire later when events quieted. He moved on the run. He crouched, climbed, shot, moved, and shot again: long shots of rioters and policemen, medium shots of struggle, close-ups of emotion-charged faces.

The total product of this unplanned collection of shots was not a mass of unrelated confusion for two reasons: a) the photographer was astute enough to shoot a variety of shots and to follow the main action as it occurred; b) an editor and a writer were able to thread the scenes along the story line — and to weave the story around the best scenes.

The photographer who filmed these scenes was a freelancer. He watched with pleasure — and growing profit — as his film was used on two local newscasts, a network newscast and, later, a network documentary.

A Parade

The morning newspaper told the hour the parade was to begin, its staging area, its route, the location of the judging stand, a reasonably accurate listing of participants and the usual wildly optimistic guess of the number of spectators.

With the newspaper story in her kit bag for reference, the photographer drove to the staging area, timing herself so that she would arrive just as the parade was due to start, allowing a walk of several blocks if her press pass was unable to get her any closer to the route than that. She did not park at the staging area. Rather, she chose a spot near the tallest building along the parade route, because she intended to climb to the roof for her final shot, to film the parade marchers strung along the route, a segment which could be used as either the opening or closing scene, or both. Then she walked along the parade route to the staging area, occasionally stopping to film clumps of spectators, children seated along the curb, a child perched on his father's shoulders and an infant asleep in his baby carriage. Sometimes, as she filmed these patiently waiting spectators, she balanced her camera with one hand while she waved her other hand high in the air and shouted, "Howdy" and "Hi, there." Invariably, the bored spectators perked up. Some shouted back and some waved. For all the world, it looked as if they were watching a parade.

At the staging area, the photographer wasted no footage on paraders lounging about waiting to march. Instead, she threaded her way through them, looking for groups, individuals, horses and floats she might want to film en route, to make sure she did not overlook them later. Then she walked back along the parade route and stationed herself two blocks away, estimating that the marchers needed about two blocks to straighten their formations and march in step.

Here she stayed for as much of the parade as she wanted: long shots of marching bands, medium shots of ranks of band members and marchers, close-ups of two or three musicians, medium shots of flag bearers, ranks of horsemen and floats, medium and close shots of a few of the drum majorettes. She followed a drum major's baton as it flew high in the air and returned, then as an afterthought asked two spectators to look up, and filmed that as a possible reaction shot. She filmed all of the marchers head-on, approaching and coming parallel to her, never of their backs, with the single exception of two Cub Scouts who couldn't quite keep up with their fellows and were dropping behind.

The photographer always remained on the same side of the street. Marchers moved past her camera from right to left. Had she crossed the street, the marchers would have moved across the film from left to right also, which would have been totally confusing. She always filmed movement in the same direction — a man walking, a car driving — unless she specifically wanted to show confusion of movement, such as masses of homebound traffic or pedestrians rushing to work. Showing a man going first one way, then the other, or cutting from one view of two people talking to the opposite view, is called "crossing the line" or violating the "180-degree rule" or "180 principle."

When the photographer heard a good band, she left her position and walked along with them, at a distance far enough away to hear the band as a whole with no instruments close enough to dominate, yet not so far away that general crowd and parade noises interfered. When she saw the bandmaster prepare to begin a fresh march, she pointed her microphone at the band. She stayed with them until the final note. She was less concerned with video now than with audio, because the audio she was recording would be used with a variety of pictures. This "wild track" sound — sound which is not connected to a specific piece of tape or film — could later be used with any combination of scenes. She had filmed no marching feet, except at a distance, because it is virtually impossible in the pressure and haste of a news video editing situation to match the fall of marching feet to the beat of a drum.

After she filmed her final scene, on the rooftop, she was able to reach her car in a hurry, escape the mass of people and cars which would soon cause a traffic snarl, and have her film screened, edited, scripted and presented on the evening newscast just about the time the spectators, the paraders and the paraders' mothers and fathers — altogether a sizeable news audience — had wended their weary ways homeward, and had tuned in the local news, fully expecting to watch the film which they saw the photographer take. In this expectation, they were not disappointed.

It is a capability of television news — unique among all media — to show the community to itself in a moment of time, to let the community see itself in tragedy and in joy, to let the community hear its own ragged music, and to present these sights and sounds either at the moment they happen, through ENG live transmission, or very soon after, through film. In this capability television news cannot be equalled.

Lost Child at Police Station

The photographer heard on the police band of his car radio that a three-year-old girl had been found wandering along a street in her pajamas at four o'clock in the morning. A passing motorist saw her and took her to a police station.

At the station the photographer found the child sitting quietly in the care of a policewoman summoned from downtown headquarters. He knew that the child's mother was likely to claim her soon after she woke up to find her daughter missing. If no one came by mid-morning, the little girl would be put in the care of juvenile authorities.

Knowing that a parent could arrive at any moment, the photographer quickly shot a minue of film: a long shot showing the child appearing rather forlorn in a room of the station, a medium shot just of the child and a big close-up of most of the child's face, concentrating on her eyes. He held the close-up for a full 30 seconds. These were his "protection" shots, and with them out of the way and some cooperation from police officers, he next staged some scenes. With their help, he coaxed the child to wander around the police station, curiously poking about the desk sergeant's area. He did not, however, show the child near any guns, for this would offend viewers as being not only risky, but overly cute, obvious and stagy. Many viewers must realize that scenes of a lost child in a police station are staged, but the audience enjoys the show and suspends belief. A bright news item is a different commodity than a hard news story with political overtones. Some news directors now balk at any staging. Others follow the old practices. The photographer filmed the little girl playing with a policeman's hat, but did not place it on her head. He would have shown her licking an ice cream cone, had there been ice cream in the well-known cartoon tradition, but just before dawn there was no ice cream to be found, and if there had been, the policewoman might righly have objected to feeding it to her. However, there was milk and there were a couple of toys lying about to entertain an occasional lost tot. The photographer used these props to full advantage. He had no intention of waiting for a tearful mother to come rushing in, because she might not arrive for hours. However, after taking all the pictures he wanted of the child, he was not through. Why not?

The shots in his camera were all of *the child* in different situations. Now she was smiling, now she was not. Here she was holding a hat, there a toy. In this shot she was running, and in that one sitting quietly sipping milk. In one shot a policeman was holding her, in another she was squirming out of the grasp of a different policeman. In the edited film, how does the editor go from one scene to the next? Obviously, by using cutaways.

In recent years, some feature motion picture editors have broken away from the cutaway, particularly in montage editing. With this convention now established to some degree, the news film editor could adapt it to film stories like this, either with quick cuts of the child or, using a double chain, with quick dissolves. Here, the photographer shot cutaways and the editor used them.

He proceeded to film every officer in the station, singly or in groups. He asked them to look to the left or to the right. He asked some to smile. He filmed the sergeant looking up after writing in his log and two officers arriving from patrol duty, smiling as they discovered a camera trained on them and a photographer saying, "Why don't you smile?" Those smiles would later be cut to appear as smiles at seeing a pretty child in the station. The child herself was in none of these cutaways, for they would not have been cutaways if she had appeared. The photographer had enough scenes of the child alone and the child with officers. As he left the police station, he turned for one last shot: the exterior of the police station.

He departed with what information was available on the police report about where the child was found and by whom. To this he added a description of the little girl. He knew that several hours later, a news writer would call the station for information that was not yet known, such as her name and address, how she managed to get out of the house, how far she traveled before she was found, and whether she had ever done this before, plus an eyewitness report from an officer of the reunion of mother and child, including any talk of a later spanking.

News Staging

The photographer who shot film of the lost child in the police station behaved a bit like a Hollywood director, asking police to look right or left, shoving toys into the child's arms, and getting everyone in sight to do something. People unfamiliar with the daily realities of photographic coverage by newspaper still photographers and television newsreel photographers might object to all this managing of events, for newsmen are supposed to record events, not stage them. If a spectator is not actually looking at the subject of a story, why ask him to look to the left or look to the right? If a child is not playing with a policeman's hat, why thrust one into her hands?

Scenes are set up for two reasons:

1. The presence of a still or motion picture photographer injects an external element into any situation. He himself becomes a focus of attention. If a photographer could will himself to be invisible, he would do so. He cannot hold a camera four feet from a man's face without attracting that man's attention. And, because he needs that man's picture, he must instruct that man to do something, even if only to "keep looking where you were just looking" or "keep doing what you were just doing."

2. Most stories would take far too long to film and be far too dull to use if a photographer simply waited around, camera poised, for someone to do something interesting. So the photographer stage-directs. But he issues his stage instructions only to bring out the inherent value in a news story. He does not try to strike a false note, to make people behave in a manner contradictory to the natural story value, to their own interests or to their own values. A photographer or any journalist who deliberately sets out to harm the people he encounters on a story would not last long in any responsible news organization. A journalist who tries to make a news event seem to be what it is not should seek another profession.

The Federal Communications Commission agreed that some staging is within reason, provided the television journalist does not overstep the legal boundary:

> In a sense, every televised press conference may be said to be "staged" to some extent; depiction of scenes in a television documentary — on how the poor live on a typical day in the ghetto, for example — also necessarily involves camera direction, lights, action instructions, etc. The "pseudo-event" describes a whole class of such activities that constitute much of what journalists treat as "news." Few would question the professional propriety of asking public officials to smile again or to repeat handshakes, while the cameras are focused upon them....
>
> The licensee's newsmen should not, upon arriving late at a riot, ask one of the rioters to throw another brick through a store window for its cameras. First, if the window is already broken, it is staging a news event — one which did not in fact occur but rather is "acted out" at the request of the news personnel; the licensee could fairly present such a

film only with the full disclosure of its nature. In any event, whether or not the window is broken, the licensee cannot encourage or induce the commission of a crime. [1]

The photographer and the reporter walk on shaky ground when they cover a news story showing people breaking the law. The camera is not an invisible presence. The law breakers know it is there, filming the action. Somehow the crime seems less a crime then. And perhaps the crime might not be committed if it were not being covered by television. For example, the FCC came down hard on WBBM-TV, the CBS Chicago station, on grounds that its newsmen "induced" Northwestern students to hold a marijuana "pot party," which it filmed. CBS News was censured by the House Investigations Subcommittee for filming a group of men in Florida planning to invade Haiti and overthrow the government. CBS spent about $170,000, some of which went to the would-be-invaders, before CBS grew skittish and dropped the story, calling it "the non-adventures of a ragtag crew . . . a gang flouting U.S. law to no purpose." The House subcommittee called for a new law to "protect the public against falsification and deception in . . . news programing" and to "prohibit the practice of news media involvement in criminal activities." No law was passed, however.

As for creating news or staging news for political purposes, a television news operation should, like Caesar's wife, be above suspicion, if for no other reasons than: 1) a newscaster and/or news operation is a tempting, visible target, a scapegoat, a means by which a politician can take the heat off himself; 2) some people are politically paranoid, seeing every unpleasant news story as a lie, part of a conspiracy to discredit their side. There are, of course, many other reasons for not staging news for political purposes. They come under the heading of professional ethics. Rep. Harley O. Staggers (D.-W.Va.), regarding the falsifying of a television news report to be a national disgrace, sent investigators to collect examples of staging. They did not have far to look.

ABC filmed a report in Seattle on a program to acquaint policemen's wives with their husband's work in hopes of lowering the divorce rate among police. Wives rode along in police cars. As part of the report, a woman in the Community Relations Department was asked to dress like a police wife and sit in the front seat of a police car that was instructed to make some high speed runs past a camera. The road was wet, the car went out of control and nearly struck another car.

An ABC field producer hired actors in Las Vegas to pose as gamblers for a story on gambling. The film crew also asked a minister to repeat a prayer he had made earlier before a business group, a prayer to increase tourism. The crew wanted close-ups.

CBS did a story about how easy it was to buy dynamite in Oregon, posing a friend of the reporter as a customer.

A CBS story about pop wine included a lot of staging: customers in a grocery asked by the camera crew to pick up bottles of wine, a clerk posing as a customer, young people asked to drive around a parking lot so they could be filmed drinking and driving.

Two female sheriff's deputies, not undercover agents, were posed as undercover agents, dressed in white clothes so they would show up in night filming outdoors. Later, the same two women were shown in a story about venereal disease, with the implication that they were infected.

A story about the pollution of tidal pools in southern California included pickled octopi and starfish borrowed from a nearby college to be filmed around the edges of the pool as pollution victims.

A CBS crew arriving too late to film a speech by the governor of Indiana asked him to repeat parts of the speech after the crowd had left.

WPIX, New York, worried about the loss of a license worth tens of millions of dollars after it was accused of several deceptive news practices which went far beyond news staging in the field. It was accused of telling viewers they were hearing "our man in Prague" when viewers were really hearing a UPI stringer in Vienna during the Czech spring of freedom which was crushed by Soviet tanks. That story allegedly had the words "Prague" and "via satellite" supered over the film of the Budapest uprising a dozen years before. The station was also accused of pretending that film of an army tank in Virginia was shot in Vietnam.

The list runs longer, ranging from the apparently mild and harmless to outright fraud. Former ABC News producer Bruce Cohn said a distinction must be made between hard news and feature news, which by its very nature may be nothing but staging. "It can and should be honest staging, not altering any facts or circumstances," he added.

CBS News policy is that there should be no staging or re-creation that gives a viewer an impression of any fact other than the actual fact, no matter how minor or inconsequential. Its policy also bans the use of reverse questions and composite editing to tie two statements together.

The Times of London has observed, "It did not require the prophetic writings of Marshall McLuhan to uncover the fact that press and television are not passive recording instruments, with or without distortion, of the events they observe. Their presence, and still more the prospect of what they will make of their presence, may effect objective alterations in the events themselves...The reason is that these observers are on the lookout for 'news,' a specialized and competitive commodity, which it is to some extent within the power of the actors in the event to supply or withhold according to their judgment of their interests."

For the Student

1. In your opinion, what is permissible stage managing? What is not ethical?

2. Interview a working reporter on the subject. Interview a photographer.

3. Spend a day with a reporter and a photographer. How much stage managing went on?

4. List the shots which should be taken of a demonstration by a dozen pickets

in front of city hall, aside from any statements.

5. Suppose you are covering the funeral of a well-known person and one of the mourners comes over to whisper that the presence of a camera on this solemn occasion is disrespectful. How should you reply or what should you do?

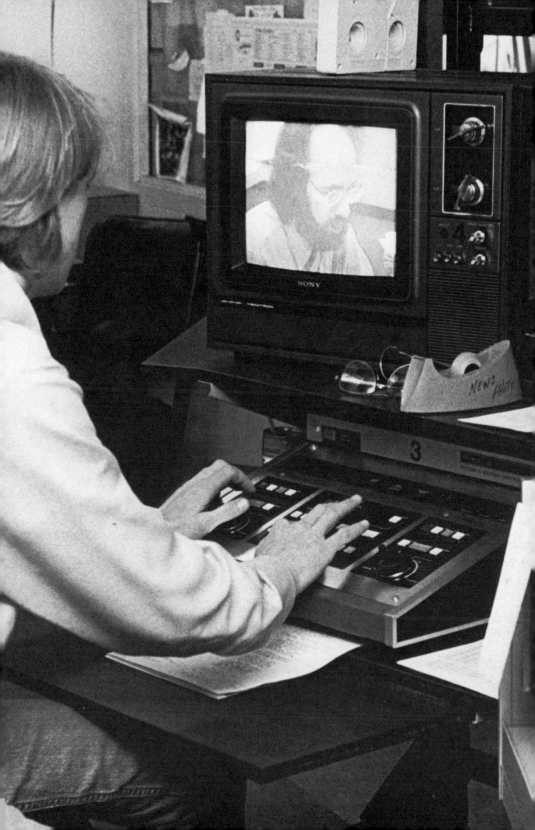

Electronic News Gathering

21

One of the most important ingredients for any news department is live, local coverage. Yet it amazes me how many stations never seem to learn that.

— Dan Rather

On a wintry afternoon in St. Louis, a KMOX-TV news crew in a mobile van was stranded seventeen miles from the station as a snowstorm and icy roads tied up traffic. They were carrying two videotaped stories for the 6 p.m. newscast and it was already 3:30 p.m. They would never make it. At least not in the usual way.

The van pulled off the road, the videotape engineer got out and raised the microwave dish on the roof while the reporter alerted the station via mobile radio. Within a few minutes the first of the two videotaped stories was beaming its way through the snowstorm. Meanwhile, the reporter, using the mobile radio, was calling in editing suggestions. A writer-editor, aided by a computer which marked incues and outcues, quickly whipped the stories into finished packages. Total elapsed time: 20 minutes.

The reporter, Betsy Bruce, decided to stay where she was, stuck in traffic in a snowstorm. After all, the storm was probably the biggest story of the day. When the six o'clock news began, she broadcast live from the van, reporting on weather and traffic.

A new technology has taken hold. It is the age of "Minicam" and "Live Action Cam," "Accu Cam," "Rapid Cam" and "Live Eye," the age of instantaneous reporting, but in its bag of electronic marvels hops a truth-telling Jiminy Cricket who chirps that instantaneous reporting is sometimes really not reporting at all, for part of journalism is the ability to edit, to make judgments, and that is not always possible.

It is still a nervous time, with reporters not always sure about what they should be doing with this new tool. One reporter began his live feed by saying,

"Wait a minute!" San Francisco reporter Kathy Tong did a little dance of joy when her first live broadcast had gone well. Trouble was, she was still on the air.

How It Developed

The history of videotape is almost as instantaneous as its present transmission capabilities, and that history is still being written as manufacturers compete to produce lighter, cheaper and more sophisticated equipment, and television news departments compete to use the technology in more imaginative ways. In 1956, Ampex sold the first practical black-and-white videotape recorder, a machine which converted pictures and sound into electrical signals and recorded them on a spool of polyester tape.

Sony introduced ½-inch black-and-white portable videotape cameras and recorders in 1967. Three years later Japanese manufacturers agreed to standards permitting a tape recorded on one company's machine to be played back on another's. In 1971 CBS News, which pioneered electronic news gathering — ENG — sent crews out with a color-capable Norelco PCP-90 camera married to an Ampex VR-3000 videotape recorder, a barely "portable" outfit ("mobile" would be more accurate) which gave CBS News several scoops. When Secretary of State Henry Kissinger forbade live coverage in a news conference called to announce that "peace is at hand" in Vietnam, CBS News had the taped recording on the air in 25 minutes, leaving rival networks flat. Now, for the first time, videotape was being used in actual news coverage instead of serving only to record and play back programs and special news feeds, plus providing that marvel of sports coverage, the instant replay.

By 1972, some CBS crews had Ikegami color cameras and Sony ¾-inch recorders. Picture quality was going up as weight was coming down, thanks to such items as the small Plumbicon picture tube. NBC was soon pushing a German company, Bosch, to manufacture a good, lightweight news camera, and by 1974 their Fernseh cameras were in the hands of NBC photographers. In the spring of 1974, CBS News ENG crews accompanied President Nixon to the Middle East and Moscow. The satellite relay from Moscow was the first time that ENG material was relayed halfway around the world. A spontaneous cheer went up in the CBS New York offices when the sharp picture came beaming in. ENG had provided a stable, sharp picture, portability, and immediacy, hurdling one problem in international news coverage, a lack of film processing facilities in many foreign bureaus. By the end of that watershed year of 1974, all three networks were able to send ENG gear to Martinique to cover President Ford's meeting with French President Giscard d'Estaing.

But it was in Los Angeles on May 17, 1974, that ENG captured the nation's attention. Police looking for Patty Hearst located a Symbionese Liberation Army hideout in a small house. The SLA decided to shoot it out. As bullets whizzed, a KNXT-TV crew crept to within 150 feet of the house and transmitted a live picture which KNXT pooled. Local stations and then the networks picked up the feed.

Millions of viewers watched reporters and police duck gunfire and saw the house go up in flames, not knowing whether Miss Hearst was inside:

Television reporter Bob Simmons: It's a bad time to talk to you, I know, but just tell me what you have seen here....(*Gunfire*)

Police sergeant: You've got as close as I have.

Simmons: Look out there. That's bad. Get back, guys. (*Confusion, many voices*) We just took...we just took a ricochet or direct...I don't know which.

Television reporter Bill Dietz: "We just got missed by a bullet. Ooh, that's as close as I ever want to get.

Simmons: It went through the house right beside us here. I can see a hole in the screen, I believe....(*Noise, more gunfire*).

Simmons: Let's see if we couldn't still get this picture, but from a little better location, huh?

Dietz: I don't know if it's a good idea to interview someone right now. (*Burst of gunfire fills the air.*)[1]

Many companies now had engineers working on video equipment for television news coverage, as station owners and news directors began placing orders. Akai came out with an inexpensive ¼-inch color system. Sony improved its ½-inch black-and-white system and created a ¾-inch color cassette system which became widely popular. RCA built a portable color camera.

Fresh ideas turned into salable hardware of many kinds. Besides tape, portable cameras allowed for direct transmission of signals, so vans were being equipped with transmitting facilities which could send microwaves directly to stations after locating a clear line-of-sight transmission path, or bounce them off helicopters. "Uplink" and "downlink" joined the television news jargon.

ABC News moved more cautiously into ENG than CBS News, and many local stations hesitated to move at all. Cost was the big factor. Not only did ENG equipment cost far more than a 16 mm camera, but prices kept dropping every year as new portable electronic equipment reached the marketplace. The new equipment was also better, lighter in weight, more rugged in construction, containing more features, and better able to operate with low light levels.

A rumor was always floating around that the Army or the C.I.A. was using a palm-sized video camera which could see in the dark. In fact, the latest round of ENG design is coming very close to these rumors, with an 8 lb. Thomson-CSF "microcam" camera hooked to a 4 lb. electronic pack, and the promise of still smaller, lighter cameras not far off, so that television news can match radio news in mobility and speed. General Electric is trying to develop a wallet-size camera weighing less than one pound and producing images at extremely low light levels.

All ENG

The first station to abandon film entirely in news gathering was CITY, a little UHF station in Toronto, in 1972. Two years later, a major station, KMOX-TV, the CBS owned-and-operated television station in St. Louis, redesigned its news operation to be totally electronic. Other stations followed, either partly or completely. "Minicams" dotted the land. News crews equipped with lightweight cameras and recorders traveled in vans or station wagons fitted with microwave transmitters. A small battery-powered microwave link could be set up near the camera to transmit the video picture to the van, or other support vehicle, permitting live broadcasting from such remote locations as an upper floor of an office building, as long as a line of sight was available from the van to the station or to an auxiliary receiver. Otherwise, the van might tape the story and move to a better location to transmit it to the station. Stories could be fed live from the scene of an event, transmitted from the field to be edited in the newsroom for a scheduled newscast, or physically brought into the newsroom on tape. A lot of flexibility was possible. For example, video could be fed early for editing into a B-roll, while the reporter did a standupper or provided voice-over live during the newscast.

ENG forced a restructuring of traditional newsroom roles, with the jobs of assignment editor and executive producer combined into the executive news coordinator, who sat at a console where he could monitor the pictures being received by each field crew and could decide whether the story merited breaking into regular programming. In direct radio contact with each reporter, he was able to suggest questions during interviews and could feed the reporter late breaking information from the news wires or from other crews. In actual practice, this seldom happened. A 1977 survey of news directors asked who made the key editorial decisions in field coverage:

> It's the same person for ENG as for newsfilm. The "reporter" was checked by 81 percent of the ENG and 79 percent of the newsfilm operations. Six percent in each category checked "producer." At only two of 108 ENG stations...was it "someone back at the station." The advent of an "electronic news coordinator" sitting in a control center at the station and calling the shots for electronic news coverage on the field has not arrived.[2]

Without the need to drive to the station to deliver film for processing, news crews covered more stories each day. With microwave links, assisted occasionally by helicopter links, crews could travel further for news stories. And with videotape of earlier stories available for immediate playback, it was less easy for someone being interviewed to duck a response through the familiar escape route, "I can't comment. I haven't heard the statement."

Television newsmen boasted of what ENG enabled them to do. In New Orleans, a WWL-TV crew discovered a fire, called the fire and police departments, taped their arrival and their efforts to put out the fire, and had the story on the air, all inside of 15 minutes.

At KOOL-TV, Phoenix, covering a fire may have taken twice as long, but in those 30 minutes if air time was fast approaching, reporter Jerry Foster, flying his own traffic helicopter, left the station, flew to the scene, taped the story, returned to the studio, and did a quick edit.

The newscast had already begun at WBBM-TV when two elevated trains collided on Chicago's South Side. Live pictures were on the air in 22 minutes.

WCBD in Charleston, S.C., pulled the neat trick one election night of calling a congressional candidate the winner at 7:20 p.m., and at 7:35 p.m. airing a tape which showed the candidate at home listening to the newscaster declaring him a winner and then being interviewed.

KPRC in Houston taped an important vote on a state constitution by legislators in Austin, several hundred miles away, rented time on a common carrier microwave, then transmitted the tape back to Houston for editing and airing one hour later.

And WSVA-TV in Harrisonburg, Va. used its portable video camera and recorder not only to tape a surprise nine-inch snowfall but to tape a commercial for snow tires, which was aired two hours later. The pleased local tire dealer sold a lot of tires before the snow melted.

Tool or Toy

A danger exists that ENG equipment will be regarded as a kind of expensive toy, a gimmick to hype ratings rather than a versatile tool to help the journalist perform his job. Sometimes ENG has been used that way. Upon acquiring the costly equipment, stations have taken ads in newspapers, on billboards and on the sides of buses to promote "live minicam action." When two stations in one large city made the investment, a promotional war ensued and one station sued the other for advertising its "exclusive live Action Cam report." The suit was later dropped.

Some stations have gone so far as to promise a live report each evening, a surrender of news judgment which has led to such nonsense as watching a reporter having his teeth cleaned. Fortunately, news values tend to reassert themselves before the manufacturer's parts warranty expires. Few stories merit live coverage during regularly scheduled newscasts, and the pledge to provide a live story a day must lead both to triviality and to manipulation by outsiders who want news coverage and who realize that an event scheduled during a newscast is more likely to be covered because normal journalistic defenses have been weakened. We might also hear a standupper like this, strained to give it a "now" sound: "I'm standing outside the conference room where tomorrow morning negotiators will assemble to begin to thrash out..."

According to a survey by Vernon Stone and John DiCioccio, "Live ENG generally has not been used to make the viewer a regular witness of shoot-outs, fires and other police news. Indeed it is being used more often to bring the public live reports of government-related news."[3]

Timeliness, an important consideration in judging news value, ought to be distinguished from mere availability or from the creation of an event for the camera, the "pseudo event." The litmus test is whether a story would be used if it had been filmed a few hours earlier. Nor should the value of live ENG be based on its frequency of use. Rather, now it is a tool in news coverage, which, like any tool, should be brought out when needed, and only when needed. As Mitchell Charnley once put it, "News...is news, and reporting--through any medium--is reporting."

Ethical Questions

Depending upon what it is used for, live coverage can make a newscast crackle with excitement. Being able to telecast almost any event while it is happening forces reporters and editors to make decisions they never faced before.

For example, does the station air a race riot while it is happening, knowing that the telecast may send viewers spilling out into the streets, some of them to get into the action, some merely curious, at a time when police are anxious to calm things down and get everyone off the streets? No responsible news director wants to exacerbate a riot, but is not a riot a legitimate story which will be a front page headline tomorrow morning? And if a riot is a legitimate story, is it not legitimate to present it in the most timely way, by interrupting regular programming for live coverage? Is live coverage unethical whereas delayed coverage is ethical? If so, how much delay? One hour? Eight hours? When the streets cool off? When?

Another example of the ethical questions which must be faced occurred on May 23, 1975, when an airliner with 300 aboard was having problems landing at Minneapolis-St. Paul International Airport. WCCO-TV and KSTP-TV sent ENG crews to the airport. WCCO-TV decided to carry the landing live. KSTP-TV decided it would not, for reasons news director Ron Magers argued:

> How do you break into the soap operas and show a plane crash and people dying? What have you accomplished? But if we tape it, when do we play it back? In the context of the newscast it wouldn't bother me.... We're all going to learn. I think what's interesting when we talk about ethical situations is that it's impossible to rely on old values.

The airliner crash landed safely, but the answers to the questions have remained airborne. Among them are the right of privacy and the right to private grief. Is it ethical to show someone being maimed or dying, either alone or in a packed airliner?

The essence of journalism is judgment, but once the judgment is made for live coverage, no other judgments are necessary, or in some ways even possible.

One news director considered the matter realistically, if cynically, "Who knows, my boss might fire me if I didn't carry a story like the S.L.A. shootout in Los Angeles...I don't know. We'll all stumble around and in the end, if our competitors are out there, I suppose we'll be there."

Live coverage of people speaking carries the danger that they will say or do something vulgar or slanderous or inflammatory. Radio talk shows use a tape delay of a few seconds to catch the crudities, but live ENG reports operate in real time. Responsible journalists in the past have taken it upon themselves to filter out obscenities, although the role of self-appointed censor of the public morality has not been much discussed. Live coverage virtually takes the matter out of the hands of the reporter, who can do little but murmur, "Sorry, but that's life." Television news can show the community to itself, but the community isn't always nice.

WCCO-TV news director Ron Handberg observed, "Sure, there's an argument for delayed broadcasting. No doubt we'll get stung a few times. Someone will streak across the scene or make an obscene gesture. We could get stung very easily." Handberg then recalled a live report on a competitive station on the last night to mail income taxes, when a reporter outside the post office asked a driver, who was not identifiable in the dark, for some comments: "What a perfect opportunity for someone to let the world know how he felt. It didn't happen but one of these days it will. If that had been our reporter, I would have warned him. There are precautions you have to take live. I suppose like everyone else we'll have to get burned before we do something."

How does a television news department respond to the demented man who seizes hostages and wants to negotiate with authorities through live television? It has already happened more than once. The answer to that question seems easy enough at first glance: the station goes along with the situation, willingly acting as a catalyst while the drama plays itself out before a large and fascinated audience, life imitating art. However, like the popularity of the Golden Gate Bridge for suicides, live television coverage may become the medium of choice for the violent paranoid schizophrenic, and one day one of them may face a news department with demands which will cause anguish to accept and anguish to refuse, a situation which will arise because live coverage is ready at hand.

You Can Let the Camera Run

One of the best things about videotape is that it is reusable. When covering a news conference or a speech, the photographer can let the camera run, unlike the film camera, where nickels, dimes and dollars flow quickly through the gate. The reporter using a film camera to cover a speech, if he fails to acquire an advance copy of the speech, must guess when the speaker will say something interesting. On many stations a limited amount of film is allotted to a routine story such as a speech. Even the most generous stations put some brakes on film usage. Therefore, the reporter must "go with what he's got." His selectivity is limited.

When radical attorney William Kunstler, in the middle of a speech to Vanderbilt students, was hit by a pie, the video camera had it on tape. A film camera might have missed it.

News conferences provide some leeway for the reporter using film if he is clever enough to rephrase a question which brought an interesting answer when his own camera was turned off, but in news conferences, too, the reporter dependent upon film is sometimes at a loss, for he cannot always coax an interviewee to repeat an inadvertent admission. In any case, a measure of spontaneity is lost the second time around. Tape is better.

Many kinds of news stories benefit from the camera crew's leeway to over-shoot. Consider, for instance, coverage of storm damage. The photographer limited to 200 feet of film shoots five minutes of film and rushes off to the lab. The video photogrpher may shoot five minutes of tape and then continue to poke around, knowing that five minutes or ten minutes of extra shooting costs very little more, and knowing also that no time is needed for developing. The tape photog-rapher can shoot almost until air time, especially if he can microwave the story to the station. The film photographer trying to "make" the six o'clock news will quit shooting about 3 p.m. or 3:30 p.m. The video photographer's advantage is obvious. If the story is still breaking in late afternoon, there is all the difference between a verbal report and a visual report.

Other Advantages

Most television sound newsfilm is shot with a single system camera, which presents the editor with the disadvantage of cutting where sound precedes picture. Videotape records the image and the sound together. It is all sync sound. Some newsrooms send video camera crews in vans from reporter to reporter. Unhampered by the need to return to the station for film processing, tape crews can cover more stories than film crews can. Nashville's WLAC sends a van out at 6 a.m. daily. It returns at 11 p.m. after one crew change. On any station that uses video cameras in the field, reporters can spend more time developing a story and gathering information with less concern for the dynamics and the daily rhythm of news photography. Reporters and photographers find it easier to function independently.

Film cameras still have their advocates, who consider these cameras more portable and flexible than tape cameras, cheap enough to be taken home daily by photographers, the choice for features and feature documentaries, the choice for stories far from home base when time is no problem.

Another advantage of a video camera is weight. Although the early videotape cameras were heavier than the 16 mm sound cameras available at the time, the weight of the video cameras has been dropping sharply while a lower limit exists on the lightness and size of a sound film camera because of its need for a drive motor and for insulation to block motor noise from reaching the audio recording mechanism.

At present both film and tape present library storage problems. Storing large amounts of either requires space and both media can deteriorate. The costs of buying tape for library storage can mount, but the future may be on the side of tape if research in solid state digital duplication proves successful. An electronic image reduction system could concentrate electronic information--the image and sound of videotape--on a small recording medium. The information could be retrieved and "blown up" if needed for broadcast.

The ability to duplicate tape cheaply and quickly could give rise to independent news services which cover stories and beam them to client stations. A private videotape service located in the capital city of any state could feed small television stations around the state at a fraction of the cost to a station of keeping a reporter at the capital, providing each station with more stories than any single reporter could cover. A regional service could cover one or more states.

Pooling

Pooling of mag stripe film is a cumbersome, time-consuming process requiring intermediate steps and a laboratory that can duplicate optical prints. Time pressures in daily news coverage virtually rule out pooling of film. Pooling of tape is extremely simple, either through tape duplication or microwave transfer.

Pooling is an idea whose time may be coming. It can be considered at both the policy level and the technical level; that is, whether pooling should be done at all, in what ways it should be done, and how it can be done, for pooling conceivably could become one of the most important parts of the ENG "revolution."

For television news, pooling simply means a sharing among competitors. Just what is shared or made jointly available and what is to remain privately acquired and competitive must be worked out by the members of the pool. Pooling is not a new concept at the networks. Every four years the nation gets pooled coverage of the Democratic and Republican Party conventions. Based on the drawing of lots, CBS might handle the Democratic Convention, ABC the Republican Convention, and NBC the remotes for both conventions, which in the past has put five pool cameras inside each convention hall, with all three networks free to assign other cameras wherever they chose. Nothing but cameras are pooled.

The networks make similar camera pool arrangements for inaugurations, state funerals, space shots, presidential addresses and news conferences, certain committee hearings, and presidential debates. In Washington, D.C., each afternoon representatives of ABC, CBS, and NBC hold a conference phone call to consider the stories suitable for pooling the next day. If two networks agree, a pool camera crew is provided. Each network, of course, sends its own reporters. Sometimes the only pooling is the lighting of a committee hearing. Camera pooling for live coverage is provided when newsmakers, such as committee chairmen, want to limit the number of cameras. And sometimes a travel film pool is arranged, as it might be when the president flies to another city to give a speech.

The pooling agreement in no way limits any network. NBC covers any event it chooses to cover, no matter what CBS and ABC choose to do. To the network news bureaus in Washington, D.C., pooling is simply a way to cut expensive duplication.

The News Election Service is another example of pooling. Faced in 1964, as in previous election years, with the enormous task of tallying the votes from all the precincts in the nation, a task done in quintuplicate, the three networks plus AP and UPI decided to pool. N.E.S., the News Election Service, was born. The networks still compete vigorously in every other phase of information gathering and dissemination on election night: key precinct projections, analysis, remote units, and elaborate anchor sets. The N.E.S. pool feed is open to any other wire service, local station or group of stations willing to "buy in" to receive faster and more complete returns than they could acquire by any other means.

The European Broadcasting Union pools through the Eurovision News Exchange, a television cooperative involving about 25 news organizations, mostly in Western Europe. Iron Curtain countries maintain their own pool, Intervision, and since 1965 there have been exchanges between Eurovision and Intervision.

Newspapers have long had pooling arrangements of one kind or another. The Associated Press and, in practical terms, United Press International, are news pools fitting the definition that pooling is a sharing among competitors. Newspapermen do not talk about it much, but many a big city press room at police headquarters or city hall maintains an easy going spirit of cooperation among competitors, the Tribune reporter covering for the Express reporter.

In local television news, examples can be cited involving the cracks which have opened in recent years in Canon 35. News departments in Wisconsin, Washington, Colorado, Alabama, Georgia and Florida have all participated in pooled coverage in courtrooms where a judge is willing to permit a single camera to cover a trial. Except in such special instances, local station experience with pooling is not as common as it is on the network level. Competition between stations in the same city has meant duplicated facilities of all kinds, despite the obvious facts that many news budgets are slim, that some technological sharing would save money which could be more judiciously spent, and that a degree of pooling could be established with no loss of competitive edge. For instance, transmission of ENG signals from vans to television stations requires a line of sight that some stations achieve by putting relay equipment atop tall buildings or hills. With a cooperative network and an agreement not to steal another station's signal, pooling is possible. Those few real beats that a news crew does not want to tip off to the competition can be transmitted by driving the van to a direct line of sight with the station. The practice would be similar to the familiar use of regular telephones when a station assignment editor or a news crew doesn't want to put information over mobile radio.

Like the network bureau agreement in Washington, D.C., the television news departments in a city might agree to place, say, one video crew from each station into a pool. If a city has four television stations participating and if each crew can cover, say, four stories on an average day, the cost of maintaining one pool crew would bring each station 16 news stories a day instead of 4. What stories they use and how they edit the tapes are for the stations to decide. The stories that pool crews cover would be of the routine type: news conferences, speeches, openings, exhibits, and similar standard fare which all stations learn about in advance. Of course, there would be no pool reporters. Editorial competition should always be maintained, but "herd journalism," the massing of cameras and reporters at the scene of an event, would be reduced. Any station wishing to send a reporter to a pool assignment, such as a news conference, would do so. the pool crew at the service of each reporter who appeared. At the same time, each station would have its other video and film crews out to get exclusives.

As every experienced assignment editor is aware, most stories are pre-arranged. It may be argued that too many stories are planned in advance, announced on wire service budgets or drawn from future folders, but the fact that pre-arranged stories are the meat-and-potatoes menu of many newsrooms points to the use that can be made of a pool.

There is always the danger that a station manager would use a pool as an excuse to cut its own news staff, but stations where this would not happen would have greater independence of action, its non-pool camera crews largely liberated from routine coverage to pursue exclusive stories in greater depth. The responsibly managed station might, in fact, increase the number of reporters on staff.

None of this would have been possible a few years ago. ENG has made it feasible. Whether pooling becomes operational at the local station level must depend upon policy decisions.

Costs

With so many advantages, why haven't all television newsrooms converted from film to ENG? The biggest reason is the cost of the equipment. A live capability system might require an investment of $250,000. As a station already owns film cameras, capital costs may range from nothing at all to, say, $10,000 for another single system camera. It is, of course, possible to get into ENG for considerably less than $250,000, but the question of what to buy is a difficult one, especially for a small station. More must be considered than a choice of one brand over another. The question is really how far to dip the station's toe into ENG waters and when to dip it. Should the station acquire a relatively inexpensive Akai camera and recorder? Should it spend more for an Ikegami? One or two? What about computer editing? A microwave system? Or should the station wait?

"We've purposely dragged our feet," one news director explained. "We thought, and properly so, that the equipment would change quickly. Our feeling was, let's wait it out. Now we've got some equipment coming in June or July."

No station wants to spend a lot of money for, say, third generation equipment when next spring will bring improved, fourth generation equipment at lower prices. On the other hand, no station in a competitive market wants to see rating points slip away to another station which decided to buy now.

Once the initial purchase is made, using tape is cheaper than using film. Twenty minutes of 16 mm raw film stock costs approximately $80. It can be used once. Twenty minutes of videotape costs approximately $15. The tape may be reused 20 times or 200 times. KMOX-TV estimated that it had spent $83,000 annually for film stock plus $18,000 for processing chemicals, compared to $6,000 for tape.

Labor costs are not so easy to compare because camera crew size varies. A small station may send out a one-man band to be both photographer and reporter, then return to the station as editor. A New York station or a network may send a committee: reporter, producer, cameraman, soundman, electrician. KMOX-TV, which has had experience with both a complete film operation and a complete tape operation figures labor costs are cheaper using tape:

> A 2-man crew rather than a 3-man crew is required and no courier service is needed to transport the record of the news coverage back to the News Center. In addition, the film-processing technician has no counterpart in the electronic system. Electronic editing costs are however higher than for film, where a single technician was employed to physically cut and splice film at the indicated points. In the aggregate, however, labor costs are lower for ENG than for film.[4]

Electronic equipment, being more complex and sensitive than film equipment, requires special handling and maintenance. A video camera may be out of service more frequently than a film camera. A station may have to hire extra engineers or send engineers to special schools for maintenance training.

Unions have disputed jurisdiction over videotape cameras. Does a videotape engineer use this new piece of videotape equipment or does a photographer use this new camera? At several stations the dispute was extended, bitter and eventually settled by arbitration.

The survey by Stone and DiCioccio showed that most ENG photographers were formerly film photographers:

> When news directors were asked where they get ENG camerapersons, 95% checked "film photographers." Only 9 percent checked "studio camerapersons," and 6 percent said most were specially trained ENG camera operators. (Multiple responses were accepted.)[5]

Which Picture is Better?

Film, usually running at 24 frames per second, is fed through a telecine chain to match the video image of 30 frames per second. A video camera image, requiring no such conversion, seems to have more presence, to be more natural and smooth. Said KSTP-TV news director Ron Magers, "The plus we have with the video image is a very real, live picture that stands out, that is so crisp that it stands out to the audience, which says, 'Boy, there is something that's different, that's really different. I can almost feel I'm there.' "

On the other hand, the film image is stable, which is not always true for the video image, especially as equipment grows older and offers up a variety of roll bars, glitches and scanning twists, depending, of course, upon how well the engineering staff maintains the equipment. Newer video equipment has eliminated most of these problems.

In video's early years, at least, color was much better on film and much more stable. Faces on color did not shift from red to green with each camera cut. Now, ENG produces a far superior color image for television, being itself a television image. ENG is also preferred for low light situations. A Sony BVP 300, an Ikegami 79 A, or a Thompson Microcam, the latest cameras at the time of publication, shoot in much less light than film. Both film and video have improved markedly in recent years. Eastman Kodak's 7240 and 7242 are good, fast films, while each new portable video camera marketed seems to have improved low light level sensitivity. The strong fluorescent lights found in many schools and government buildings provide good illumination for video cameras, especially when augmented by portable lights now on the market. Partisans of film have argued that a sturdy CP-16 sound camera weighing 17 pounds gives the photographer more flexibility than 35 pounds of video equipment which must be handled gingerly and takes time to set up. And back at the station, it is argued, film editing is simpler, quicker, more personal and more versatile for documentaries, thanks to film optical effects not yet available on tape. For many documentaries, the chosen solution is a mix of film and tape, with the final product transferred to tape for replay.

The Television Camera

The word "television" derives from Greek and Latin roots meaning "to see at a distance." What the television camera sees, it makes an electronic image of. (It must be clearly understood that a *film* camera is not a *television* camera.) Cables and/or a broadcasting transmitted carry the VHF (Very High Frequency) or UHF (Ultra High Frequency) signals, a constantly changing television image, into monitors, which receive a closed circuit signal, or receivers, which receive their signal through the air. The home television set is a receiver.

Depending upon the tube or tubes inside, a television camera may be referred to as a vidicon camera, a Plumbicon camera or an image-orthicon camera. Among other types of tubes are the Saticon, the Isocon, the SEC vidicon, and the SIT vidicon, a low-light camera designed for military night operations. Researchers are now developing a "charge-coupled device" (CCD) camera that uses no tubes at all. Cameras may one day be smaller than their lenses.

All present-day television cameras have a lens section that focuses a picture on an image section, which produces an electrical charge whose strength is determined by the light and dark elements of the picture. An electronic beam from a gun structure converts the picture into its electronic image, which is then transmitted.

The Plumbicon tube resembles its older sister, the vidicon tube, in most respects. Like the vidicon, the Plumbicon transmits the lens image to a photo cathode target, which is then scanned to produce the video signal.

The Plumbicon differs from the vidicon principally in that it produces a better picture at low light levels. The difference may be compared to the advantage of a faster film over a slower film. The Plumbicon has less image retention, or "burn in," than a vidicon. The 2/3-inch diameter Plumbicon tube is preferred by several manufacturers of ENG cameras.

The image-orthicon, or I-O, camera remains the most widely used television studio camera. The I-O tube is much larger than a vidicon tube, so the I-O camera is seldom, if ever, used where a portable camera is required.

The image-orthicon tube has an additional electron multiplier section which produces larger video signals than do either the vidicon or Plumbicon tubes. With a larger lens, a larger target area, and greater signal output strength, the image-orthicon can give better detail and crispness than the other cameras and, consequently, a superior picture. On the other hand, the image-orthicon camera is considerably more expensive than the vidicon camera. New I-O tubes have longer life spans than vidicon or Plumbicon tubes.

Video Transmission

The picture received by the television camera is fed by cable to a camera control system, which contains additional circuitry to improve the picture, amplify the signal and add synchronous pulses to lock the picture to the television receivers.

Microwave, which must travel in a straight line, is more versatile and more flexible than cable transmission, and has a higher quality. However, it cannot be used in every situation because of terrain, and the initial cost of a microwave transmission system is higher (the cost difference between microwave and cable can be compared to the cost difference between using a walkie-talkie to send messages or using a coin telephone — buying the walkie-talkie equipment is initially more expensive than dropping coins into a telephone box, but subsequently walkie-talkie calls are cheaper).

Film-to-Videotape

Where a complex film story requires three or more film chains, the director may put the story on videotape before the newscast begins. A pre-newscast dubbing session in the studio is the time to make the mistakes. During the newscast, it is easier to roll one tape than to roll three films while cueing the anchorman and swinging Camera 2 over to Easel 1.

Videotape carries four separate tracks: From top to bottom they are:

1) The audio track, which carries the sound.

2) The video track, taking up most of the width, which carries the picture.

3) The cue track, on which videotape engineers can record information using a microphone or a beep signal. For example, a beep might mark the start of a newsclip, such as the point in a recorded baseball game where a home run was hit with bases loaded.

4) The control track, which consists of the electronic equivalent of sprocket holes. All tracks are monitored on oscilloscopes or VU meters.

The Videotape Machine

Videotape, or VTR (for Videotape Recording), machines have either a helical scan or a quadrature scan.

Helical scan machines have a video head which rotates horizontally, for recording or playback. They have two basic advantages: (1) they are relatively cheap, so they can be sold for home and hobbyist's use; (2) they can freeze frame; that is, they can be stopped at any point to show a still picture. The disadvantage of helical scan machines is the poor quality of their pictures compared with quad scanning.

Quadrature (or quad) scan machines use a video head which consists of four separate heads set in a wheel at 90 degree angles from each other.

Each of the four heads that comprise the video head is responsible for 4/16ths of the tape. Imagine the two-inch-wide tape divided into 16 bands. One of the four heads would serve bands 1,5,9,13. The next would serve bands 2,6,10, and 14. And so on. Much of the work of the VTR engineer is the adjustment of the four heads to synchronize with one another. The video head wheel makes 240 rotations a second. A capstan drives the tape at a constant speed of 15 inches per second. As each of the four heads passes the moving tape, it lays down an electronic track. If the tape were not moving, the track would be perpendicular to the tape. But because the tape moves, the track is laid at a slight angle.

Maintaining a constant head-to-capstan relationship is another important part of the VTR engineer's job. The adjustment of this relationship or distance, is called "tracking." A tracking control knob centers the rotating video head upon the center of its "information." A guide at the video head is an air pressure vacuum which keeps the tape at an exact distance from the video head. If the head-to-guide relationship is not correct, the resulting video picture will be skewed, giving it a venetian blind effect, or it will be "scalloped," which is a rounding effect.

Besides the video head, there is an audio head consisting of several separate heads:

1) An audio record-playback head.
2) An audio erase head.
3) A cue record-playback head.
4) A cue erase head.
5) An audio and cue control monitor head.

The videotape "feed" reel is loaded on the left side or the top of the machine, depending on the model.

The take-up reel is loaded on the right side, or on the bottom. From left to right (or top to bottom) the tape passes, in turn:

1) The master erase head.

2) The video head and control track head.
3) The audio head.
4) The capstan.
5) The timer, graduated in seconds.

Some other terms used by the VTR engineer should be added to the broadcast newsman's lexicon:

High band: a frequency range of the broadcast carrier frequency used mainly for color reception and transmission. It can also be used for monochromatic (black and white) reception and transmission, but seldom is. High band frequency VTR machines are newer than *low band* receivers. They produce a better quality picture, with sharper resolution and without the distorting "noise" of low band transmission. High band transmission also suffers less deterioration in dubbing.

Modulator: an electronic device which takes the incoming carrier signal and modulates — or alters — it. The signal goes from the modulator to the recording head, and then to the videotape.

Demodulator: the reverse of the modulator, used when the videotape machine feeds a picture. It takes the modulated carrier frequency and strips the carrier signal off to leave the video picture, which is then transmitted.

The signal is modulated (some kind of carrier frequency is present) when it is on videotape, when it is being transmitted by microwave, and when it is being broadcast through the air. The signal lacks a carrier frequency when it is moving along a cable, such as its transmission from a TV camera to a videotape machine or from master control, by cable, to the transmitter.

Reel-to-Reel Editing

Reel-to-reel editing machines, now limited mostly to schools, offer a choice of assemble edits or insert edits. The assemble edit lays down a sync track, the insert edit does not. For a simple edit, like connecting two shots, an assemble edit will do nicely. For more complex edits, it is advisable to lay down a sync track first in the assemble edit mode, perhaps with a camera pointing at a sweep second hand clock as an additional aid in locating particular shots. Once the track is laid down the edits should be done in the insert edit mode. The editing machine will offer "video only," "audio only" and "video and audio" options.

A back-timing scale will help to make sure that the start point you want is the start point you get. It cannot be done just by winding the feed (playback) and master (record) take-up reel back five turns each because the take-up reels of each will hold different amounts of tape; five turns of a nearly empty take-up spool wind far less tape than five turns of a nearly full spool. This scale should be cut out and attached to each take-up reel, with the target hole directly over the center.

When the incue edit point has been located on the feed reel and the outcue edit point has been located on the master reel, the levers of both machines should be put in the pause mode and the power should be turned off. Now each machine

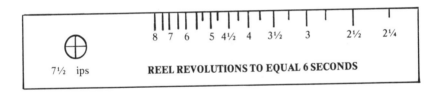

should be backtimed six seconds. The scale reading of the outer layer of tape on each take-up reel tells how many turns of that reel equals six seconds. Each reel should be turned by hand with the machine in the pause mode.

Before rewinding, make any needed skew and tracking adjustments on the feed, or playback, machine, set the video and audio levels on the master, or record, machine, and select the edit mode, assemble or insert. After rewinding with the power off, turn the power on again and roll both machines from the pause modes. Punch the edit button on the recording machine. Then, at the visual or verbal cue, punch the record button. After passing the next outcue, punch the cut-out button. Stop both machines, rewind the master reel to a point in front of the edit, pull the sync-defeat lever and check the edit. If it is good, go on to the next edit. If not, do it again.

Computer Editing

A story which has been transmitted by microwave or physically brought into a newsroom equipped with computer editing facilities is assigned by the executive news coordinator to a writer-editor. The incoming transmission is received on two separate tapes while tape physically brought in is copied onto an identical pair of tapes. One, a master tape, has an invisible time-code track electronically imprinted on it. The other, a "work-print," has a corresponding time display visibly supered at the bottom of the picture area with white lettering over a black strip. The writer monitors the work print tape, just as film footage would be monitored, logging interesting shots and potential incues and outcues. The writer decides how the story should be cut and draws up an edit decision list for a technician. To get a precise cutting point, the writer pushes a button on a time-code reader panel below the monitor. This freezes the time display, enabling the writer to jot down a frame number. The edit decision list consists of a series of frame numbers. Audio-only and video-only options permit assembly of B-rolls. The technician then enters the frame numbers on the keyboard of an editing machine, which pulls the scenes from the master tape. (Some editing systems use control tracks rather than time codes to achieve similar results.)

All of this — recording, editing, assembling — has been done on helican-scan machines, probably ¾-inch color cassette machines. The executive news coordinator now reviews the finished story package. If approved, the story is fed through a time base corrector onto a 2-inch quad tape cassette for playback in the newscast. The helical-scan master tape, like all videotape, is never cut or physically marked, which enables the writer to return to it for a new package to be used in a later newscast.

In a typical ENG newsroom, writer-editors work in what are sometimes called edit-decision booths: the technicians put together the story from master tapes in tape-assembly rooms. The executive news coordinator can summon up any story by pushing buttons on a console housing several monitors. In sum, little physical tape handling is involved. Outside the station, the video picture moves via microwave relays. Inside the station, it moves via closed circuit cables. And the entire newsroom may double as the newscast studio, as at KMOX-TV, St. Louis.

After the last newscast, or the first thing next morning, a technician transfers the entire day's recording, tape that was aired plus outtakes, onto a cassette for storage.

The Future

A dilemma of television news is the inability of the photographer to observe without being observed, unless he can shoot from afar through a zoom lens. To repeat what was said in earlier chapters, you can't wish yourself invisible and you can't put a camera close to a person's face without attracting his attention. None of this matters, of course, when news coverage has been set up in advance, but this is arranged news and usually it is "pseudo news," an event which would not have occurred were it not that reporters and cameras would witness it. Yet the most interesting and exciting news is of a breaking event, something unexpected covered while it is happening. And it is precisely here that bulky camera equipment by its mere visibility may alter what is happening. A photographer standing in the middle of a group of angry farmers protesting milk prices is almost certain to affect what those farmers will do. A photographer standing in the middle of a race riot may be lucky to escape with his life, let alone with his camera intact. One reason that photographers have been barred from courtroom trials has been the distraction they cause. Cameras have been too visible, too obvious. Now, year by year, cameras grow smaller. Lights become less necessary as light-gathering power increases. Microphones grow more sensitive. Auxiliary equipment like recorders, batttery packs and cables shrink.

Because tube cameras are approaching a minimal limit, researchers at several companies are working at developing solid state cameras, with silicon chips replacing pickup tubes and scanning beams. They call this type of image sensor a "charge-coupled device," or CCD. In theory, a CCD camera would be small, lightweight, require only an equally small and lightweight backpack, have high sensitivity, a high signal-to-noise ratio, and be able to take the rough handling which television news photographers give to cameras.

Edwin Diamond described one possibility for the near future:

> In a few years the telephone company will be able to install permanent sockets in the base of street telephone poles, permitting live television broadcasting simply by plugging in on the line; in a city the size of New York, 30 to 40 such street plugs might be installed. These street plugs could drastically alter the kind and amount of material that could get on the air, taking the news farther from the studio and "managing editor." The evening news, at a guess, could come to resemble the kind of television event the medium does best, the multiple switching and pickups of the political convention coverage. [6]

NBC News Services general manager James W. Kitchell described the television reporter/photographer of the future:

> He will wear a small hearing-aid type of device that is actually a micro-miniaturized satellite receiver to maintain constant communication with his office. He will carry a small videotape recorder about the size of today's (audio) cassette units. He will have a TV camera the size of present home movie cameras, and he will carry a brief case size satellite terminal that will allow him to transmit from anywhere at any time. [7]

If that day arrives, technology will have come close to solving the dilemma of how to observe without being observed. The reporter/photographer in action will look almost like any other observer, and perhaps with a little ingenuity even the tiny camera can be disguised and hidden so that the presence of the reporter will not affect the story at all.

Cable television, now in about 10 percent of the television homes in the United States, promises to bring us the "wired city" and even the "wired nation." CATV (community antenna television) potentially could send news and other kinds of information into homes in several new ways. An article in *Fortune* stated:

> The possibilities of cable are breathtaking. If all of the homes that now have television sets were wired for cable reception, it would provide a network that could be used in countless ways. If the era of the home computer is ever to arrive, for example, it will almost certainly be via CATV, with the home television set as the information terminal. Cable capacity is great enough to make practical the facsimile reproduction of newspapers or magazines in the home, and to make TV transmitters available to almost any group with something to say. And one of the most attractive features of cable is that it uses none of the increasingly crowded radio-frequency spectrum. [8]

Cable is much more extensive in Canada than in the United States. The average Canadian city in 1980 had cable service to 60 per cent of the homes. Some communities were 90 per cent wired. In Ottawa, the federal capital, for example, a home on cable could receive three local stations, three Montreal stations, a Hull station, the educational network, the three U.S. networks via stations in Rochester, N.Y., and PBS. Some of the Canadian stations broadcast in English, some in French. In Toronto, 25 channels were available via cable.

Two-way CATV offers much more than a chance to shop for groceries in a new way. Conceivably, wire copy, from one or more news services, fed into a computer could be called up from telephones or keyboards and displayed on individual television sets (or computer CRT's), bringing to schools, libraries and homes more news on a subject of interest (for instance, the economy) than any home daily newspaper would carry. This kind of "television news" would be totally unlike a present television newscast, of course. It is called "teletext."

Also in the future, maybe not too many years away, is the use of laser light to carry messages. Unlike radio frequencies, laser light spreads very little as it travels. Its power output remains concentrated in a narrow cone, and therefore less power is required to reach a distant relay point. By aiming a laser beam from a helicopter near a ground camera directly to a satellite in stationary orbit, live transmission may one day be beamed from the remotest locations.

Water, electricity, telephone service and gas are "piped" into our homes. Broadcast signals and CATV wiring provide a kind of pipe too, bringing information and entertainment. But a few words of caution are in order, lest we become blinded by technology. It has been said that a message may take an instant to go around the world, but months to penetrate a skull. Edward P. Morgan summed it up on the air one night:

> Journalism has come quite a way, I guess. Thucydides carved some of his accounts of the Peloponnesian war on wax-covered tablets with a stylus which incidentally had a blunt end to erase errors. Quite a stretch to live TV in color and the instant sound of battle news from Saigon — with speed often seeming more important than time to correct mistakes.
>
> Some authorities maintain that the world's first reporter was Herodotus — the Greek historian of the Peloponnesian wars in the 5th century B.C. That was Thucydides' time too, but Herodotus was 25 years older.
>
> It's said Herodotus used a quill pen scratching his notes on animal skin or papyrus with ink from the vital parts of an octopus. The octopus today is the many-tentacled electronic equipment necessary to get a news show on the air.
>
> A reporter used to begin as a cub, but in the magic media he can quickly become a lion of the headlines to unseen millions, especially if he is a ham.
>
> Today for video purposes, a broadcast reporter has to think about the condition of his necktie more often than the condition of his typewriter ribbon.
>
> The vital question is whether all this paraphernalia is helping to get

a more understandable account of current history on your TV screen than if we scratched it out and mailed it to you on an animal skin.

I hope the answer is yes, but it won't be if we keep our mouths to the mike more than we keep our ears to the ground.

For the Student

1. List five features that an ENG crew could cover live during a 6 p.m. newscast.

2. List five others that could be covered live during a 10 p.m. newscast.

3. Should a newscast present a story live that it would ignore if on film?

4. In class, debate the merits of local stations agreeing to contribute one ENG crew to a permanent pool.

5. Should local reporters ever be pooled? Can you think of any situation where a station would show a story done by a reporter from a competing station?

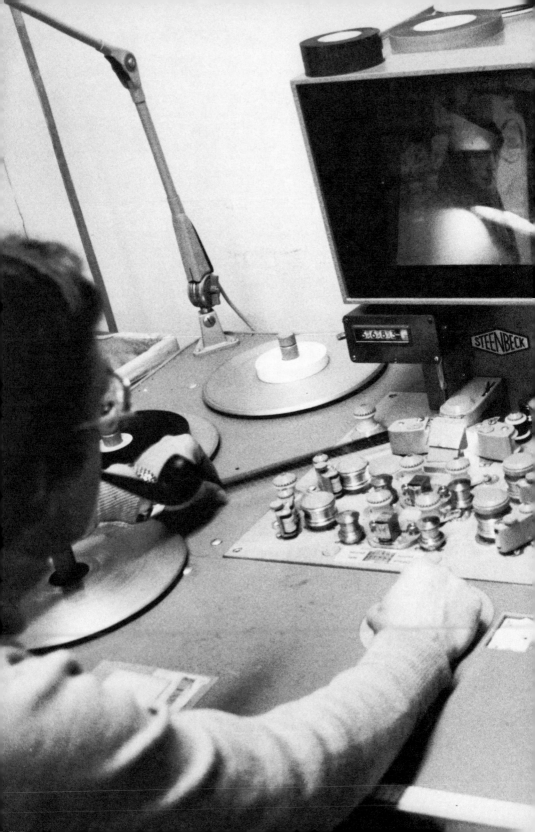

TV Photography 22

Reporting the news on television is like writing with a one-ton pencil.

— Fred Friendly

What makes television news special is the moving picture of events. Without the moving picture and the still picture television news is radio news with faces attached. Until electronic news gathering came along, almost the only moving picture the viewer saw came from film. Film and film cameras will continue to be a factor in the television news industry for years to come, although somewhat diminished by the spread of ENG.

Some Basic Concepts

Most television news film today is shot with single system sound cameras. Single system means that picture and sound are recorded in the camera. Some film is shot double system, which means the sound is recorded on a tape recorder locked in synchronization with a silent camera. And some film is shot with just a silent camera. Most television news film is shot with 16 mm cameras; that is, the film is 16 millimeters wide. Some film is shot with Super 8 cameras; the film is 8 millimeters wide, the film image one-third larger than standard 8 mm film.

The film photographer, like a still photographer, must be concerned with the relationship of the aperture, the lens opening, to the film speed, plus depth of field, the use of light meters, and other elements of basic photography. A beginner who plans to shoot film for broadcasting should take a course in photography or learn under a skilled television news photographer. Among books, *Television Newsfilm Techniques* by Vernon Stone and Bruce Hinson, can especially be recommended.[1]

The Sound Camera

A survey published in 1977 reports that television news stations, large and small, are phasing out film cameras in favor of ENG.[2] However, thousands of sound and silent cameras are in daily use at television stations and will continue in use for many years. Many news directors indicate a preference for film over video for certain types of stories.

The best liked sound camera, the survey noted, was the CP-16. Also liked were the Frezzolini LW-1 and the Canon Sound Scoopic. All are lightweight, "one-man-band" cameras. The old standard of the television news industry, the Auricon Cine-Voice, continued in wide use but news directors were more sparing in its praise, probably because of its weight.

The CP-16/A, fully loaded with a 400-ft. magazine, weighs 17 lbs. That includes an Angenieux zoom lens, a battery and an amplifier, all built into the camera, plus plugged in microphone and headphone. The only cords needed are for the mike and headphone. It can be carried directly on the shoulder or fitted with a shoulder brace. A light can be attached, running off the battery. Like the LW-1 and the Scoopic, the CP/16A was designed for the "one-man band," the small city television journalist who covers a story alone, serving as reporter and photographer and handling both sound and lights.

The Arriflex remains a well-liked camera, but it is often preferred for documentary work rather than daily newscast coverage because it is more expensive and not as rugged as some of the other cameras. Its technical advantages and fine quality make it the camera of choice for film makers who are less likely to give it rough handling.

The sound in a sound camera is created either optically or magnetically along one edge of the film. Nearly all television news sound cameras use the magnetic system. The opposite edge of the film, of course, has the sprocket holes.

Along the sound edge, there will either be a brown layer of magnetic striping or one of two kinds of optical striations. The optical image is created by a hairline light from a galvanometer responsive to audio modulation. While optical sound quality can be excellent under motion picture studio conditions, it has proved inferior to magnetic sound under the rough-and-ready conditions imposed by television news.

The sound camera has been the heart of television journalism, steadily pumping film for news stories, documentaries, specials, and editorials. It is now joined by, and may eventually be replaced by, the video camera.

The Zoom Lens

On sound cameras the most popular zoom, or variable focal length, lens is the Angenieux, with a range of 12 millimeters to 120 millimeters. This zoom lens enables the news photographer to expand the camera's field of vision by a 10 to 1 ratio from the extremely wide angle 12 mm frame to the extreme close-up of the telephoto 120 mm lens. For example, while filming a horse race, the photographer can "zoom in" from a wide angle of the entire track to a close-up of the lead jockey at the far turn spurring her horse on.

The zoom lens is controlled by a straight rod or a crank mounted in front of the camera, or is battery-powered. For a fast zoom, the photographer disengages the crank and turns the barrel of the lens by hand.

The work in flipping a three-lens turret is a continual nuisance, compared with the simplicity of cranking a small handle controlling a zoom lens. The photographer using a turret is tempted to take shortcuts, such as remaining on the middle, or 1-inch lens. Staying on one lens not only cheats the viewer of the best framing, but also limits the film editor who prefers a change of frame when splicing two similar scenes together.

When a plane or car goes past, there is a tendency on the photographer's part to follow it and zoom in on the departing plane. This is a poor decision, because the plane does not appear to recede. Rather it looks as if it is standing still or even backing into the camera! The photographer is better advised to pan and hold the shot, letting the plane grow smaller as it vanishes in the distance, or as an alternative, letting it fly out of frame.

The amateur photographer pans too much. Most shots don't require panning, which is usually used to establish a relationship between two separated points, to encompass a wide scene, or to follow motion. It is in the last category that the experienced photographer shows competence. He does not pan to follow motion without a reason. Instead, he holds the camera still to let the moving object enter the camera's field of vision, move across it, then leave it. The object moves. The camera does not. And the film editor is grateful, for he will be able to splice this segment of film to other segments showing the same object in a different locale. A shot of an airplane which takes off and flies out of frame can be spliced to a shot of sky in which the airplane flies into frame, or even a shot of the plane coming in for a landing.

Just as the photographer should not pan unless he has a specific reason for panning, he should not zoom without a reason.

Unless done for shock effect or done with the expectation that the zoom will be cut out on the editing bench, no zoom should be rapid. The "pop zoom" or "snap zoom" is disturbing to the viewer. Like the swish pan, which suddenly and blindingly moves from one scene to another, the pop zoom is a cinematic convention that says something to the viewer. The swish pan says, in effect, "Meanwhile, back at the ranch . . ." The pop zoom says, in effect, "My gosh, will you look at that!"

At 120 mm, a zoom lens is equivalent to a five-power pair of binoculars. At 250 mm, which can only be achieved with a special and rather expensive zoom lens, the field of vision and magnification is equivalent to 10x binoculars. Obviously, a shoulder pod is useless here. The camera must be fixed on a tripod, or else the viewer will think he is being pitched in a hurricane at sea. A rule of thumb for a competent photographer using a shoulder pod is to avoid zooming in past 50 mm unless he can brace himself against a solid object such as a wall, a tree, a car, a fence or a table. At any focal length, the photographer can keep his camera steadier if he pans than if he holds a fixed shot. He is steadier following an airplane across the sky than he is trying to hold on a balloon in the sky, because his arm tires under the camera's weight and his efforts to overcome the physical trembling accompanying fatigue are more noticeable if the camera is still.

The Silent Camera

Besides a sound camera, the television news photographer usually takes along a silent camera. Lightweight, battery-powered or spring-wound, rugged, it offers flexibility sometimes lacking with the sound camera.

The silent camera is available on an emergency basis, in the event the sound camera malfunctions or the photographer happens across an event occurring when he arrives, and he hasn't time to bring his sound camera into action (although a competent photographer will not let himself get into such a fix often).

Sometimes the silent camera is used when there is no room for a sound camera and no need for one; for example, in a small helicopter.

Sometimes a subject will permit pictures to be taken, but forbids sound; judges occasionally set this stipulation in courtrooms during recesses.

The one-person camera crew, "the one-man band," may be better off with a single, lightweight camera and a lightweight sync-sound recorder than loaded with sound gear. You can get arguments on both sides.

Combined with a tape recorder, the silent camera can shoot a sound story which does not require lip synchronization. The audio tape can perform double service in a radio newscast. The combination of a silent camera and a tape recorder is superior to a sound camera where lip sync is not needed, because it produces double system filming.

To make life simpler for the director when the newscast goes on, the photographer loads mag stripe film in the silent camera. He also carries a tape recorder. This gives him silent film and accompanying wild track sound. After the film is edited, the sound is transferred onto the mag track from the quarter-inch tape by plugging the tape recorder into an ordinary movie projector.

Also, using two projectors, background sound from mag stripe shot in a sound camera can be transferred to mag stripe shot in a silent camera, thus eliminating the audio drop in silent cutaways.

Even lip synchronization is possible in shooting with a silent camera if the camera is equipped with a sync motor and it is hooked up to a synchronized tape recorder, like the Nagra. But allow extra time for editing.

Accessories

1. *Portable light.* (See also section on lighting in this chapter.) One of the handiest pieces of equipment carried by a photographer is a small portable light.

Powered by its own small nickel-cadmium battery, the portable light is either attached to the camera or held by hand. For fast-breaking, dimly lit story situations, the portable light is an absolute necessity. Photographers often refer to their portable light as a "Frezzi" (for manufacturer Frezzolini) or Sun Gun (made by Sylvania).

2. *Tripod.* A lightweight, sturdy tripod with a fluid head to provide smooth pans is the standard sound camera base in such stationary situations as interviews and news conferences. When the tripod is placed on a marble floor, where it might slide, or on someone's rug, which it could tear, it should be supported either on grooved rubber cups or on a canvas or aluminum triangular spreader.

3. *Light meter.* This ubiquitous device is usually found dangling from a photographer's neck on a string. One of the newest types of light meter is as highly directional as a shotgun microphone. Without leaving the camera, a photographer can aim it and get a reading on a subject dozens of yards away, quite an advantage when arriving late at a large news conference or at a sporting event or rally where the center of action is a long way from the camera. At least the professional silent cameras, the Bolex H 16 Rex 3 and the CP 16 R have a built-in electric eye, eliminating the need for a light meter.

4. *Changing bag.* This is a light-proof black bag which permits a photographer to remove exposed film from magazines and load fresh film while he is in the field. Without a changing bag, the photographer would either be required to carry a great many loaded magazines wherever he went, or forever be seeking out darkrooms.

5. *Spare magazines.* At least one, and preferably two loaded magazines should be part of a photographer's gear.

6. *Special lenses.* Occasionally, a photographer will take along a lens for a particular job. Extra-long telephoto lenses, for example, are useful at boxing matches. Extra wide angle lenses are needed occasionally.

7. *A set of filters.*

8. *Spot sheets.* A pack or pad of spot sheets (also called scene sheets, breakdown sheets, white sheets, shot cards, etc.) is used to record what is on film, which reel it is on, and roughly how long it runs. When time is tight, the writer may put together a silent film story from the spot sheet and wire copy, without seeing the film, either editing the film after he hands the script in for the newscast or leaving instructions for the film editor, based on the spot sheet.

9. *Lead foil,* such as Film Wrap, to protect film from x-rays in post offices and airports.

Lighting

The art of lighting is a complex one, and goes far beyond the scope of this text. However, it might be instructive to describe briefly the basic lighting of a man at a desk. All other lighting may be considered a departure from this basic lighting situation, but even the lighting of so common a subject as a man at a desk varies from photographer to photographer.

The subject is lit by three lights: a key, a fill and a back light.

1. *The key* is the brightest light. The photographer might use a 1,000-watt quartz lamp 10 to 15 feet away, depending upon such factors as the shade of wall paint, the size of the room or the color of the subject's skin. The key light is often placed at a 45-degree angle from the camera. If the light is too close to the camera, the lighting will be too flat. If it is at too great an angle, the key light will provide only side lighting. The key light is not focused narrowly. It lights the subject and the area around him.

2. *The fill light* is used to fill shadows caused by the key light. The photographer lighting a subject at a desk might use a 1,000-watt quartz lamp widened to a flood beam with scrims to further diffuse and soften the light. This lamp might be placed close to the camera.

3. *The back light,* placed out of camera range, lights the subject's back and shoulders, gives depth to the picture, and helps separate the subject from the wall behind him. A 650-watt quartz lamp or a photoflood is common. A "barn door" on the lamp can block a portion of the light so that the camera doesn't pick up a flare from the lamp and so that the light shines only where the photographer wants it to shine.

The photographer may want to add other lights to remove shadows or lighten specific areas. For example, he may use a small eye light just to add sparkle to the subject's eyes.

In a memo to photographers and correspondents, Gary Franklin, formerly ABC News film review manager, made these points:

> The background to a standupper must be photographically compatible.
>
> That means doing your bit to avoid that most common photographic problem: shots of correspondents and interview subjects backgrounded by glaring sky, water, desert and beach — so that the color system finds itself unable to handle the great difference between that bright background and the lesser light, being reflected from the face (especially, a sun-tanned or black person's face). The too-often result: loss of tones and detail.
>
> Of course, the cameraman has his collection of fill-lights and reflectors — but under some conditions, even these are not enough. (That's why Hollywood location crews have trucks, to lug arc-lights and huge reflectors.)
>
> One solution which often works: making the standupper shot a slight "high angle" shot, the camera shooting downwards, to avoid sky and/or a too-bright background. Not too high, though, otherwise you'll look uncomfortable, trying to talk to that thing up there.
>
> Try to avoid being hit by near-vertical, midday sunlight. It sends dark shadows running down from eyebrows, noses and cheek-bones. (Again, even fill-lights and reflectors sometimes won't cure such visual ills.)

Furthermore, beware of in-and-out-from-behind-the-clouds sunlight. Although the cameraman can and does compensate for the varying light, through manipulation of his f/stop ring, it is usually obvious, visually distracting, and much easier to move on to a shaded location.

Indoors, try to avoid flat, old-fashioned newsreel lighting, when we have control over the light and/or camera position.

When limited to two lights, the backlight *or* the fill can be eliminated. (The fill is expendable especially when the subject is a man, whose face can stand harsher light.) The effect is then one of a strong sidelight, covering almost all of the visible face, with the backlight highlighting the right cheek and side and the hair.

Portable lights need not be kept immediately adjacent to the camera. When more than one light can be set up, don't forget the backlight for depth and separation.

Let your light do more than just move the exposure meter needle to the desired reading. Let light work for you creatively, even in straight news coverage.

Film and Processing

News events happen under a bewildering variety of lighting and temperature conditions. Eastman Kodak and other companies which manufacture news film engage in continuous research to improve their products. The present virtually universal use of color film by American and Canadian television stations has compounded the problems of manufacturing consistently high quality film. Nevertheless, new films and new chemistries appear from time to time. They may even offer some competition to the manufacturers of videotape.

In choosing a film type, the photographer must compromise between speed and graininess. Fine grain films are, unfortunately, slow, requiring plenty of light. High speed films (which record images under poor lighting condition) are, unfortunately, grainy. The photographer must decide how much speed he is willing to sacrifice for the quality of granularity he desires; or, vice-versa, how much graininess he will put up with in order to get the speed he wants.

At present the most commonly used television newsfilm is Eastman Kodak's EF 7240. Photographers also use EF 7239 for daylight shooting and EF 7250, a very high speed film, where available light is low such as at nighttime sports events. These are all reversal films; that is, the image is recorded negatively but is reversed during processing so that it comes out of the developing tank as a positive print. When "daylight" film is shot under tungsten lights, or "tungsten" film is shot outdoors, the photographer attaches filters to the lens. Daylight film shot without a filter will have a red tone. Unfiltered tungsten film looks blue if shot outdoors and green if shot under most fluorescent lights. Unfortunately, different kinds of fluorescent lights affect film differently. Some television photographers have asked government agencies to stock uniform lights in offices and auditoriums. A color temperature of 3200 degrees Kelvin allows for shooting without filters.

When a photographer brings in film shot at less than ASA (American Standard Association) specifications, because of poor lighting conditions, processing can be either slowed or altered by temperature change. The film is then "pushed" or "forced" through development. The photographer should also alert the lab technician from the field, if there is deadline pressure, so that the processor can be readied. If film is exposed at double the rated speed (tungsten, 125; daylight, 80, with a filter) the film can be forced with a small loss in quality. With a greater loss in quality, the film can be forced two f-stops, which is quadruple the rated speed.

Graininess increases if film is overexposed or overdeveloped, or if the chemicals in the development tank are heated to increase film speed ("to push it up one more stop") in order to salvage film which otherwise would be too dark. It is the photographer's responsibility to tell the lab technician when developing speed must be altered.

The relationship of poor exposure and poor development causes these results:

a) overexposure and overdevelopment: graininess.
b) overexposure and underdevelopment: washed out image.
c) underexposure and overdevelopment: contrastiness and fog.
d) underexposure and underdevelopment: fog.

Wherever possible, normal exposure coupled with normal development should be the rule.

Super 8

For television stations with limited budgets and for universities teaching broadcast news film courses, Super 8 offers an alternative to the more expensive 16 mm and ENG. Several stations, notably KDUB-TV, Dubuque, Iowa, have happily used Super 8 for years.

Its advantages

Equipment is cheaper. A variety of single system and double system cameras are available, with prices in the hundreds of dollars, up to about $2,000, instead of the high thousands or, in the case of good ENG equipment, the tens of thousands of dollars. Because the primary market for Super 8 cameras, processors, editors and projectors is the huge amateur photographers' market, manufacturers compete strenuously to improve quality, keep prices down, and add such useful features as sound, automatic exposure with manual override, reflex viewing through the lens, electric drive, power zoom, plus those two necessary features for in-camera dissolves, backwinding and a variable shutter to stop down a lens.

Film is cheaper, approximately one-third the cost of 16 mm. EF 7242, for years the standard magnetic-striped 16 mm tungsten film, is available now in snap-in cartridges. A shortcoming of the cartridges has been the plastic pressure plate used to seat the film, which affects the sharpness of the image. By the time of publication, however, finely tooled metal plates or some compensating device may be available on some models. A 50-foot cartridge runs about 2½ minutes. Cameras are available which will take a 200-foot load. It's also possible to shoot double Super 8 in a modified 16 mm camera, the aperture exposing only half the film at a time. The film is then reloaded and the other half exposed.

A good camera may be augmented at the station by such equipment as an 8 mm double system editing deck similar to the Steenbeck 16 mm editing table. Kodak sells a film video player which substitutes for the Super 8 film chain. The device, the VP-1, transfers Super 8 film to video tape and contains a built-in image enhancer, which is needed to bring Super 8 film up to broadcast quality. Editing can be done electronically, leaving the original film uncut.

A small camera is easier to tote around and is less noticeable, less forbidding to some people the photographer wants to film. Dave Hamer, of KMTV, Omaha, noted with a grin:

> ...what happened to the "cinematographer"? He discovered sound-on-film.
>
> Down with the Filmo (8 lbs.) and up with the Auricon (16 lbs.). Off with the fixed lens (4 oz), on with the zoom (3 lbs), and strap on an external magazine (7 lbs) and carry a crateful more.
>
> Tote that Pro-Junior (13 lbs)...lift that Frezzolini (13 lbs)...push that amplifier (5½ lbs)...tug that mike (2 lbs)...trip over those cables (7 lbs)... cart those Sun Guns (7 lbs each)...drag that Cinekad, the spare parts, tubes, bulbs, batteries, fuses, etc. Smile, be a good ambassador for the profession, and oh yes! take the Filmo (8 lbs) for a "cover shot"...I don't mind. Really.
>
> But it does sort of bug me when the neighbor down the street pops in with his Super-Eight, f 1.8, ten-to-one zoom, mag sound, nicads, and electric eye. He's toting it in his pocket between takes!
>
> There but for the grace of the manufacturers and suppliers go I![3]

A big advantage of a Super 8 system is the fact that so many people own cameras. Hundreds, even thousands of potential stringers, are out there. The station which advertises that it will pay for newsfilm used, plus giving credit on the air, will tap a big market. Amateurs who keep their cameras handy in the cars may profit from some advice:

1. Use Ektachrome film, which is easier for a television station to process than Kodachrome.

2. Shoot at 24 frames per second.

3. Leave a margin in the viewfinder. Television receivers cut off the edges of film frames.

4. Shoot low contrast.

5. Let your shots run long, 10 to 20 seconds.

6. Avoid special effects like in-camera dissolves. Shoot straight.

7. Do as little panning and zooming as possible. Hold a shot. If you must zoom, use a power zoom.

8. Get a variety of angles. Take plenty of close-ups.

9. Use a tripod or balance the camera so that shots are not shaky.[4]

Its disadvantages

Film editors find Super 8 harder to work with than 16 mm. Editing is often slower as a result. A film viewer is always necessary.

Super 8 does not have the sharpness and fine grain of 16 mm. If care is taken at every step, the differences are hardly noticeable, but *care must be taken.* Super 8, in other words, is a "less forgiving" medium. Cleanliness is particularly important because hair, dust, dirt and scratches are blown up twice their size in projection. An electronic image enhancer is a *must* in the film chain. Transferring the edited film to 2-inch quad tape before the newscast may help.

Sound quality may be poorer than 16 mm.

For the Student

1. Why does a photographer use a silent camera?

2. Compare the advantages of single system shooting with sync sound using a silent camera synched to a tape recorder.

3. Without looking back, can you recall the effects of combinations of over- and under-exposure and development?

4. Cite three news story situations which could use swish pans and three which could use pop zooms.

5. Suppose you were allotted 100 feet of 16 mm film for a parade. Plan your assignment.

Sound

23

Television is the ultimate triumph of equipment over talent.

— Fred Allen

Networks and stations in major cities hire a sound technician to accompany a photographer. He is the person in the background, quietly listening and monitoring his amplifier while the focus of attention is on the reporter and the photographer. This does not diminish the sound tech's importance in covering the news story, for the skills and experience he brings to the story can mean the difference between excellence and disaster.

Photographers for most of the television news departments in the nation handle the sound themselves along with the picture. Usually this means they set up the mike and the amplifier, check the level before they start filming, and then occasionally glance at the meter to make sure sound is being recorded on the mag track. On "one-man band" cameras, the photographer attaches a directional mike to the camera. An earpiece or earphones help. When a reporter is not busy and a photographer is, the reporter lends a hand with the audio.

Equipment

The basic sound equipment is:

An amplifier

A standard amplifier that is not part of a camera may weigh about three pounds. It is a "black box," maybe measuring 10″ X 8″ X 3″ with two or more microphone inputs, volume controls and a transmission cable leading to the sound camera. This "umbilical cord" ties the sound tech to the photographer whenever they "go portable," so that they work no more than six feet apart unless special cables separate them. Normally battery powered, the amplifier also uses A.C. power. Cordless amplifiers are built into cameras like the CP-16/A and into ENG equipment.

Microphones

Microphones vary according to how they vibrate, their pickup coverage pattern and their impedance, a measure similar to electrical resistance.

The old-fashioned ribbon, or velocity, mikes contain a metallic ribbon that vibrates when struck by sound waves. Once used in studios, they are being replaced by condenser microphones, in which a diaphragm attached to a backplate vibrates when sound strikes it. A condenser mike is extremely sensitive to sound, so it can be used as a shotgun mike, like Sony's C-77 FET. Condenser mikes require their own power supply, a battery inside the mike.

Most television news microphones are dynamic mikes. A diaphragm attached to a coil vibrates when sound waves strike. The dynamic mike is more rugged than the condenser, but less sensitive. It does not pick up wind noise easily, which is one of several reasons why dynamics are the all-purpose mikes. Hand-held mikes, lavaliers and wireless mikes are usually dynamic. So are several shotgun mikes like the Electro-Voice 642. The Electro-Voice 635-A is a standard among television news reporters. Its pickup pattern is omnidirectional. Dynamic mikes can also be made thumb size. A disadvantage with all dynamic mikes: unless you are careful, it will pop your *p*'s and hiss your *s*'s. Among the more popular models are Electro-Voice's RE-15, RE-55, and 666; RCA's BK-1A; Shure's SM-57, SM-58, and the newer SM-82, which has a built-in "pop" and wind filter.

Other types of microphones include crystal mikes, which depend upon a voltage change when pressure is applied to a certain kind of salt. Crystal mikes are not commonly used in television news. Neither are ceramic mikes, in which sound vibrates against a ceramic plate. Both are sold with inexpensive tape recorders.

Mikes are also classified by the way they pick up sound. Unidirectional: only sound in front of the mike is transmitted. Bidirectional: sound picked up in front and back, but not to the sides. Omnidirectional: sound in any direction. Cardioid: sound picked up to the front and sides. Multi-directional: pickup patterns may be altered by turning a screw. Most hand-held microphones, lavaliers, and wireless microphones are omnidirectional.

And they are classified by impedance. Dynamic mikes and some ribbon mikes have a low impedance, which permits the reporter to stay as far away from the amplifier as he likes, perhaps with as much as 100 yards of cable. But the sensitivity of a low impedance mike is lower and a transformer is needed if the mike is feeding high impedance equipment. A high impedance mike, such as a good ribbon mike, a condenser mike or a crystal mike, is quite sensitive but is limited to a cable length of, at most, 20 feet. Also, high impedance mike cables make noise if you move them.

Four kinds of microphones are used in the field:

1. *Hand-held mike.* With a stand, the hand-held mike becomes a desk mike. Frequently used: EV 635-A, EV 655-C, EV 665, RCA BK-1-A. Outdoors, especially with a noisy background, the hand-held mikes should be close to the speakers. With noise all around, the reporter should hold the mike a few inches from whomever is speaking, pointed straight up so the voice crosses the mike, avoiding the problem of plosives and sibilants. During an interview in noisy surroundings he will hold the mike now in front of the interviewee's chin, now in front of his own. If the setting is not noisy, the mike should not wiggle back and forth. The reporter can hold it midway between himself and the interviewee. Or, if the interviewee has a soft voice, closer to him.

2. *Lavalier* with a cord is hung from the subject's nect or is attached with a lapel clip or tie clasp. The microphone reaches to the breastbone, and can be placed either in front or behind a necktie. A small amount of audio quality is lost when the "lav" goes behind a necktie, but it may go there for appearance sake. A "lav" can also be fitted beneath a jacket lapel. Popular "lavs": RCA BK-6B, EV 659-A, Sony ECM-50.

3. *Shotgun mike.* This microphone picks up sound at a distance. Examples: EV DL-42 lightweight dynamic shotgun, EV 643 super shotgun, Sennheiser MKH-815. Being highly directional, the shotgun mike picks up sound emanating mostly from the direction in which it is pointed. Very little comes from sources outside the narrow cone which constitutes its receiving area. The cone is much like that of a flashlight beam.

When the distant sound comes from a wide area, such as a football cheering section or a marching band on a football field, an ordinary desk mike pointed at a small parabolic reflector gathers the sound very well. For truly sharp shotgun mike effect, use a large parabola. Example: Dan Gibson EPM parabolic mike.

4. *Wireless mike.* Also called a radio mike or an FM mike, it usually hangs like a lavalier microphone, connected by a short cable to a small transmitter worn inside a pocket or hooked to a belt, with an antenna pinned to the clothing. The sound is picked up over a range of up to 6000 feet by a receiver plugged into the amplifier. Budelman, Stevens and Sony build broadcast-quality wireless mikes, but they are expensive and reportedly lack the quality of hard-wire microphones. They also require separate FCC licenses because they are FM transmitting stations of a sort. Among others used: Vega 55/56B, Vega 55/57, Comrex, Swintek.

A tape recorder

A small, lightweight, battery-operated tape recorder of good quality is useful for catching wild track (independent) sound, which is recorded on quarter-inch tape, the same audio tape used in any tape recorder.

A charger

Amplifier batteries run down and must be recharged. The charger, another small "black box," performs this job, and this also serves as an A.C. adapter. The amplifier runs off the camera batteries on many models. These batteries, of course, also need recharging.

Cables, adapters, extension cords, etc.

Problems and Solutions

1. On long establishing shots where a cable cannot be visible and — because this is news coverage — a boom mike is unavailable, the sound technician may use a radio mike. The audio quality is not always satisfactory. For instance, a passing automobile in an outdoor shot will sometimes be heard on the audio track as a series of pops. The pops are caused by spark plugs. Nevertheless, the audio track produced by a wireless mike is better than no track at all. Later, if the editor finds it objectionable, some or all of the track can be blooped out.

2. At this point we may note a documentary technique using such sound in a unique way. Where a narrator on location is speaking in the midst of a noisy establishing shot, the sound track from the radio mike is used as a cue track in a studio to redo the sound. The narrator sits in the studio listening on earphones to the sound of his own voice, and speaks his lines again, matching his own lip movements. A track of background sound from the track of a tape recorder or camera is then added. The result is a reproduction of the scene with satisfactory audio quality. This process, also used in shooting feature motion pictures, is called "dialogue looping" and saves reshooting a scene which has poor audio quality.

3. Where it is necessary to join two pieces of film with sharply different audio quality in the narration, an audio bridge serves the same purpose that a cutaway serves to connect two mismatched pieces of film. A documentary often begins with a narrator on camera in an outdoor location. Such an opening keeps the narrator from being merely a disembodied voice. But this opening may be followed by a narration track done in a studio. The difference in quality is evident to all listeners, unless an audio bridge is used. For example, if the documentary is about automobiles, the narrator's on-camera introduction could be followed by an engine starting up, followed in turn by a matching engine noise in the first scene over which the studio narration track is laid. The advance planning necessary for this sound bridge produces a more professional product in the critical opening minutes of a documentary.

4. The quality difference between outdoor and indoor sound is mainly in the dispersion of sound waves outdoors because there are no walls to reflect them. To compensate for the drop in the narrator's volume a sound tech outdoors must raise his audio levels, which unfortunately increases the amount of "white noise" in the signal-to-noise ratio.

5. The effect of wind is a particular outdoor problem. It is compensated for by one of two devices. One is a windscreen. This is a microphone cover made

of a material like foam rubber. The other device is a wind bypass filter, which filters out frequencies below 100 cycles.

6. The lower frequencies add strength and resonance to voices. Almost all lavalier microphones cut off low frequencies unless the microphone is touching the speaker's chest. Lavalier microphones were designed to rest against the chest cavities. Reporters who hold lavalier mikes in their hands are often unaware that by doing so they are giving their voices a slightly higher ring. Lavalier mikes should rest on or beneath neckties, or against shirts or dresses, where they can pick up the resonance of the thoracic cavity.

7. When a reporter is tired, his voice level drops. The drop appears as a movement of the needle on the amplifier meter. The sound tech compensates by raising his gain, or volume level, especially on stories that take a full day to cover, in this way matching the reporter's fresh morning voice with his weary evening voice. A tired voice may also possess a harsh edge. Soundmen can do nothing about this. The reporter helps himself best by continuing to be relaxed, to speak slowly and to enunciate clearly.

8. A cheaply made microphone gives a voice a harsh quality. The frequency reception of a poor microphone is slightly distorted, so that listeners strain to hear. Listeners may become irritated after hearing the voices for a minute or so. A cheap mike also picks up crackles from movement of the mike cord.

The microphone is not an ear. In some ways it is superior to the ear purely as a receptor of sound, because the human brain filters out extraneous background noises. We are familiar with the story of the veteran newspaper copy editor who sits beside a bank of teletype machines, barely conscious of their clacking. A visitor comes in and asks, "How can you work in all this noise?" The editor responds innocently, "What noise?" On the other hand, an annoying sound will be heard far out of proportion to its intensity.

9. The experienced technician, aware of the difference between the microphone and the ear, tries to place his microphone where it will pick up not what the ear picks up, but what the brain filters through — in other words, what the listener thinks he would hear if he were at the scene.

Sometimes he cheats a little to establish this perspective. For example, the wife of former Governor Ronald Reagan of California was dismayed at the condition and location of the governor's mansion in Sacramento. Among the things which concerned Mrs. Reagan, mother of a young son, was the busy traffic outside. A television news camera crew filmed Mrs.Reagan inside the mansion describing its limitations. A lavalier microphone hanging from Mrs. Reagan's neck would not give listeners a true perspective of the amount of traffic outside her window. The sound technician solved this problem by placing a second microphone on the window ledge. He then balanced the sound levels coming into his amplifier. When Mrs. Reagan referred to the traffic outside, the soundman briefly raised the gain of the window ledge microphone for emphasis. He was also considering the possibility that a film editor might choose to double chain film of the traffic at this point. Had he wished to, he could have made the traffic on the street in Sacramento, California, sound like Times Square.

10. Riding the amplifier gain offers opportunity for editorial judgment or for blatant distortion. The unscrupulous technician present at a political speech to which he is hostile, can twiddle the knobs to make rousing applause seem lukewarm.

11. The greatest of all broadcast journalists was Ed Murrow. His daily broadcasts from London during the Blitz generated in Americans a rapport with the English people which is credited with helping to change American public opinion from isolationist to interventionist. Murrow knew how to use a microphone to heighten perception. For one broadcast after a particularly nasty fire-bombing of London, he wanted to show how resilient Londoners were. He placed a microphone on a sidewalk to catch the footsteps of people in the city hurrying to work the next morning.

12. Each story location requires its own audio reception arrangements, just as it requires individual arrangements for optimum filming. As an example, where the people are seated at a table, a single omnidirectional microphone on a stand often provides better sound than the overlapping reception of three lavalier mikes hung around the speakers' necks. However, if the room is "boomy" with a lot of hard wall space near the mikes, lavaliers may be better adapted to the conditions because they are closer to the speakers. It may even be necessary for good sound reception to move the speakers to another part of the room if they happen to be sitting at an equidistant from two hard wall corners, which sharply reflect sound waves.

13. During news conferences or speeches covered by several stations, to get rid of the clutter of microphones and their call letters, audio multiplexers are used. The President of the United States and other top officials use them. In at least one city, Hartford, Conn., one television station WTIC, provided a multiplexer as a pool service. It is simply a box into which tape recorders and sound camera amplifiers are plugged. The WTIC multiplexer, made from $250 worth of parts, connects up to 18 audio terminals with a single microphone. WTIC carries along adapters for just about every camera, tape recorder or microphone in use.

14. The microphone may pick up the noise of the camera motor. The best solution is to repair a noisy motor or to modify the camera so that its motor is "blimped." Newer cameras are already blimped.

15. Microphones placed too far from the sound source pick up a lot of "white noise" along with the wanted sound. Compensating by increasing the gain on the amplifier is a "quick and dirty" solution. Better: move the microphone closer or use a more suitable microphone. Automatic gain control, which is built into almost all portable cassette tape recorders including the popular Sony TC-110 also adds a lot of "white noise" when the microphone is any distance from a sound source. Sometimes reporters using portable recorders have them modified by adding a switch that can overcome automatic gain control.

Awareness of audio problems and solutions comes with attention and experience. Considerations of sound usually take second place to considerations of picture and story. Within limits, it must be this way. The problems of sound are a matter of perspective, but the problems exist, should be recognized, and should be dealt with. The best compliment that can come to the person handling sound in a news story is that the product draws no attention to itself.

For the Student

1. For what reasons, if any, should sound reception be altered?

2. What problems of sound may come with double chaining? How can they be solved?

3. If possible, spend a day or two with a photographer who handles his own sound. Ask him to teach you to use the amplifier and the mikes. If no union rules are violated, assist him on a few stories by monitoring the amplifier while he shoots film.

4. Audio tape a lecture or a public meeting. What technical difficulties did you encounter? How might they have been solved?

5. What could you record to heighten radio or television coverage of a political demonstration? A high school graduation exercise? High rise construction?

Film Editing 24

The film editor is both artist and technician. If he fails as an artist — if he lacks experience, imagination and, occasionally, flair — his work will be usable, although pedestrian. But if he fails as a technician — if he is sloppy or slow — he sows ruin for a news operation. Film stories do not get on the air. Film breaks in the projector. Frames which should be eliminated are seen in homes everywhere in the city.

The artistic elements in film editing will not be learned from a textbook. They are instilled by practice combined with alertness. A textbook can only offer a few descriptions, some techniques, a trick of the trade here and there, and some ideas which others tried and liked.

The Editing Process

The writer and the film editor begin by looking at the film. A short, silent film can go right on the bench, mounted on rewinds and cranked slowly through a film viewer. Sound film should go on a sound projector. Whoever makes the judgments — reporter, producer, writer or film editor — ought to keep a rundown sheet, noting what is seen and heard, including likely incues and outcues, and where these occur. The "where" (actually "when") is provided by a stopwatch or a built-in counter.

After viewing, it's decision time. How much is the story "worth" based upon the news itself and the visual value of the film? (*The tape editor goes through the identical decision process.*) A "talking head" of the mayor is obviously worth more if he is resigning than if he is campaigning for reelection, although the two stories are visually identical. A flower show is worth less if the film is limited to flowers than if a couple of children are seen taking obvious delight in the displays.

Once the approximate length is known, the individual shots must be picked and placed in order. The sloppiest statement that can be made at this time is by the writer or reporter to the film editor: "Give me 30 seconds." Much more professional: "Let's open on the long shot at 3 minutes 15 seconds in...for seven seconds, then the shot of the sign at 5:08 for three seconds, then the...." and so on.

The next step is the cutting of the film. The editor finds the long shot at 3:15 in from the start of the picture, and snaps the film with his fingers, both fore and aft the wanted segment. This he may stick to his bench with a bit of masking tape and, if the story is complex, may mark the masking tape: 1. He then uses another bit of tape to rejoin the two reels on the rewind, and goes 5:08 in, looking for the sign. When all the pieces are pulled, the film editor splices them together. Or, if he is very experienced, he will build his air reel on the same rewind as he searches for the right clips.

Whe he finishes, he lables the air reel with the story slug the writer gave him, rewinds his outtake reel to heads out and sets it aside, then cleans the bench of bits of film and tape. The air reel, or reels if there are both A and B rolls, is then sent to the videotape room to be transferred to a cartridge or it remains in the film editing room awaiting the building of master reels in the order the films will be aired. Sometimes the producer or someone else will want to screen the finished reel, perhaps to check it against the copy.

Equipment

Splicer.

The mechanical device which bonds two pieces of film together with film cement (Ethyloid) can be either a hot splicer or a cold splicer. The latter is cheaper by far, but a splice is more difficult to make on a cold splicer, and it is more likely to break. A hot splicer, which is plugged into a wall socket, should be a standard piece of equipment in every television newsroom.

Another type of splicer uses tape to bond the film. This splicer is slower than the more commonly used overlap splicer and may put dust on the splice unless the editing room is kept antiseptically clean. On the other hand, the tape splicer, by butt-ending the film, avoids the double thickness which can cause a jiggle in a projector gate.

Viewer

This usually sits on the editing bench near the splicer and the sound reader. Like the splicer, it is brought to a part of the bench between the rewinds when it is needed, so that the film passes through it smoothly. The viewer is simply a device to magnify the film which runs through it on a sprocket wheel track. Although film can be viewed instead through a projector or merely by holding it up to the light, a film viewer is a handy and valuable piece of equipment. A projector is bothersome to thread, and may scratch the film. Too much is missed by holding a strip of 16mm film up to the light.

Sound reader and Amplifier

Like the viewer, the sound reader, which picks up and plays film sound tracks, enables the film editor to work at his editing bench. It usually consists of one or two sound receiving sources, an amplifier, a counter and one or more film tracking wheels. One of the most popular sound readers consists of a "mag head" (to transmit the sound of magnetic striping), a separate amplifier, a counter that counts in minutes and seconds (a footage counter is a nuisance, requiring a conversion table to translate feet to seconds), and a four-gang synchronizer. The newsfilm editor will probably never need more than two tracking wheels unless he edits a documentary requiring dissolves and double system shooting (which will be explained later in this chapter).

The four-gang synchronous sound reader can be equipped with a motor drive which runs at 16 mm projection speed. This produces normal speech, instead of the meandering or rushing pattern resulting from manual operation of the rewinds. By using the motor drive, the editor is freed from the trouble of taking his film off the editing bench and mounting it on a projector just to hear the audio track. Another type of sound reader often found in editing rooms consists of nothing but a magnetic sound head and a sprocket track, without a counter.

Editing barrel

Also called a "trim bin," the barrel is actually a large white cloth bag, about two feet in diameter by three feet deep, held in a frame or set in a bin. As the editor removes scenes from an unedited reel preparatory to assembling a film story, he dangles the film in the bag, keeping it from dragging onto the dusty floor, perhaps to get stepped on. The film strips hang from a frame of some sort — such as a bar holding spring steel hooks — or are pasted with bits of masking tape to the edge of the bench. If a frame is used, it can consist of rows of pointed hooks over which film sprocket holes easily slip, or the frame can consist of a row of spring clothespins. The pointed hooks can be dangerous. Clothespins may be more trouble than they are worth. Using bits of masking tape is the simplest method, one which can be recommended.

Reels

The editor should keep a supply of reels of the following lengths: 100 feet (these are usually plastic); 400 feet (most useful); 1200 feet; 1,600 feet; and 2,000 feet. The 400-foot reels take 10 minutes of film, the 1,200-foot and 1,600-foot reels hold half-hour documentaries, and the 2,000-foot reels hold nearly an hour of film. For exact figures, divide the length of the film by the film speed, 36 feet a minute. The editor should also have a 400-foot split reel and a 1,200-foot split reel for coring film, plus a supply of 100-foot and 200-foot cores. The cores are used for storing and shipping.

Grease pencil

A grease pencil allows the film editor to mark the place he wants to cut, without the finality of actually cutting. For example, if the editor is considering an overlap jump cut (matched action) which would not be obvious on the air, he will want to roll the two pieces of film through his viewer several times before he actually cuts the film in order to assure himself that the splice will not be obvious. Also, when the film editor is working with a reporter or writer, he should mark the places to be cut. Not only does this permit the reporter or writer to go off sooner to write his copy but it also gives the film editor a second chance, by himself, to consider the editing decisions they have made. A bright yellow or white grease pencil mark is easier to locate than a black mark. A grease pencil can be used to mark numbers on the bits of masking tape attaching film segments to a bench, noting the order in which they will be spliced onto the reel. And it can be used to mark a piece of tape identifying each reel of arriving film.

Other supplies

Needed, too, are *editing gloves; film cement; magnetic film cleaner* (other cleaners may take off the magnetic track); *acetone* (a good cleaning fluid for the splicer); a *degausser*, or *bar magnet*, to wipe out the sound track where it is not wanted; *a velvet pad* (on which film cleaner is sprinkled; the editor pinches the film gently with the dampened pad and runs the film through the pad using the rewind); and a roll of *masking tape*. The film editor should also have reels of academy or SMPTE leader (which contain numbers spaced to show the seconds remaining before picture appears) and at least one other kind of leader (black or yellow opaque are common).

Splicing

Any piece of film — silent, mag track or optical track — may be spliced to any other, provided they both are of the same width (8mm, 16mm, 35mm) and the same polarity (positive or negative). Black-and-white film *could* be spliced to color film, but this would cause a sharp change in shading, for which a video shader could not compensate quickly enough to avoid a sloppy appearance on the home set. Such a splice is not recommended. If it is necessary to connect dissimilar pieces of film, it is better to write a "roll-thru" into the script: the director cuts back to the newscaster or to a still for enough seconds to enable the video switcher to change polarity or adjust his shading, and for the projectionist to replace a magnetic head with an optical head, in the rare event that these dissimilar types of sound film must be on the same reel.

Before splicing magnetic film, the mag track at the juncture must be wiped away. Place a drop of film cement on the mag track of the film in the right side of the splicer. Using a white glove or a clean rag, wipe away the mag track, which lies along the shiny, non-emulsion side of the film. Because the film lies in the splicer emulsion-side up, it is necessary to reach under the film to wipe away the track. The splice may now be made in the usual way, scraping the emulsion from the film lying in the left side of the splicer.

Sometimes it is necessary merely to wipe away the sound, not the entire mag track. To erase magnetic sound, use a magnet. Several styles of "degaussing" magnets are available. The only consideration in choosing and using a magnet is wiping away as much sound as you intend, and no more.

To "degauss" or "bloop" a segment of film, place the magnet on the mag track, making sure that the magnet does not dig into the film, for this might peel the track itself. Then, in one motion, move the magnet along the area of track to be erased. After erasing, run the film through the sound reader again to make sure that all the unwanted sound is gone. There may be times when a single pass of the magnet fails to get every vestige of noise on the track. If any sound still remains, a second pass of the magnet should take care of it.

When the magnet is not in use, store it in a place where it is not likely to fall or accidentally brush against film.

Where to Splice

Because sound preceds picture, edit on the *audio* cue at the *start* of a statement. That is, if you want film of a man saying, "Boy, it sure is a hot day," cut at the start of the sound of the "B" in "Boy."

Edit on *video* at the *end* of a statement. Cut when his mouth finishes forming the "ay" sound in "day." And if the statement is the last piece of film in the film clip, leave an extra two or three seconds of film beyond that, giving the director and the TD time to cut back to the newscaster. Be sure to bloop any sound beyond "day," using the magnet *after* splicing tail leader to eliminate the possibility of a popping sound at the splice.

The film editor will cut the *end* of the statement on *audio* if he wants the last word or two to be heard over film of something else; for example, a cutaway of a reporter listening, or the back of the head of the man speaking, or even an outdoor scene of a hot day. Cutting the end of a statement on *audio* is known as an overlap cut.

Overlap Cuts

In 16mm motion picture film, the sound track precedes the picture by 26 frames on optical film and 28 frames on magnetic film. That is, the sound that belongs to any given frame of film can be found by counting 26 or 28 frames forward — frames which have already gone past the projector lens. The picture and the sound are separated so that the lens and the sound head in a 16mm projector pick up picture and sound simultaneously.

This spread between picture and sound presents some problems. The biggest problem is known as "lip flap," which occurs when someone says something the editor wants immediately after he says something the editor does not want. The sound track which begins the wanted statement lies beside the picture of the person concluding the unwanted statement. Hence, lip flap, the lips moving to form words which have been blooped. In order to pick up the wanted sound, it is necessary to use the unwanted picture adjacent to it.

Sometimes — and only sometimes — two statements by the same speaker can be overlapped to avoid lip flap. Let us say that, at a news conference, Ms. Smith makes two important statements, one at the beginning, the other near the end of her news conference, and that her second statement was immediately preceded by a long, dull statement which will not be aired. Let us also say that Ms. Smith did not pause between the dull and the important. The way to avoid lip flap, without a cutaway or double chaining, is to overlap the two important statements. The editor cuts the first statement on sound — that is, he cuts the film a few frames past the frame of film which carries the final sound of the last word, not the picture of the lips forming that final sound. He then splices this to the start of sound on the next statement. Viewed through a projector, it appears that Ms. Smith's lip movements just before the start of the second statement form the word we hear at the end of the first statement.

Sometimes this works well. Sometimes it is botched. An experienced editor can judge, before he makes the splice, whether or not the overlap is likely to look natural.

An overlap involving the same speaker will probably not be successful if both pieces of film are close-ups or both are medium shots. Cutting from close-up to close-up of the same face would almost certainly result in an obvious jump cut. The jump cut is far less obvious if the cut is from a close-up to a medium shot or, better still, a long shot, or if it is from a long shot to a close-up. The change in framing distracts the viewers' attention from slight changes in facial expression or the angle of the head. Of course, no change in framing can hide such major differences as a head swiveled from left to right, or the sudden appearance or disappearance of a hat, a pair of glasses, or some other item on or near the head of the speaker.

Overlapped splices produce a more tightly edited piece of film. The pause at the end of a statement, during the single second of time when a speaker's voice is not heard but his lips move with the words of the next statement, can be eliminated. Viewed through a projector, the last word or two might be heard while we are looking at a one-second or one-and-a-half second silent cutaway of the reporter appearing to listen attentively. A one-second cutaway without lip flap following it provides a smooth and natural transition.

Double Chaining

When a film story consists of one film clip, it is known as a single chain story, because it uses only one projector. There are times when a film story should consist of two film clips fed at once from two projectors through two telecine chains. This is a double chain story.

Before attempting to double chain, the editor must be sure two projectors will be available when he needs them. Should he learn he cannot get facilities to project a double chain story, the editor, or the writer, must sharply revise his organization of the story.

The editor may decide to double chain for no reason other than to mask a bad cut or lip flap. If the lip flap at the juncture of two statements is obvious, a simple cutaway cannot hide it. Instead, the cutaway should go onto a second reel, and it should be long enough to enable a director to cut to it immediately prior to the splice on the first reel and cut back immediately after the splice, without the danger of showing leader on the air.

With the letters "A" and "B" representing reel 1 and reel 2, a double chain script might look like this:

VIDEO	AUDIO
DOUBLE CHAIN. CLIP RUNS 2:53.	
ROLL A AND B TOGETHER.	
A VIDEO AND AUDIO AT START	
AFTER 12 SECS, DISSOLVE TO B VIDEO	
	AT 37 SECS IN, AFTER END CUE: "....at last report." CROSSFADE TO B AUDIO
	AT 1:02 IN, TAKE A AUDIO
AT 1:47 (MAN WALKING UP STEPS), DISSOLVE TO A VIDEO	
AT 2:15, CUT TO B VIDEO FOR 5 SECS.	
AT 2:20, CUT BACK TO A VIDEO	
	ENDS: "....intended to go." PLUS 8 SECS, SHOWING DIVING BELL SPLASHING INTO WATER AND DISAPPEARING

Guided either by a clock or a scene description or an audio cue, the director orders the technical director to "Take 2" just before the splice on Reel 1, then immediately prepares to return to Reel 1 with the command "Ready 1," followed after the splice by "Take 1." All three commands could occur within four seconds. If the technical director is alerted beforehand, the "Ready 1" command can be eliminated, and the length of time the cutaway actually appears on air can be shaved to three seconds, or even two seconds. However, to avert the likelihood of leader showing, the editor should insert a cutaway of anywhere from five to ten seconds in length, expecting only the middle three seconds or so to appear.

Naturally, the technical director can dissolve into and out of the cutaway, instead of cutting. But a dissolve is not desirable here. For one thing, there is no aesthetic reason for a slow dissolve or even a fast dissolve. For another, a longer cutaway is aired than the story requires. Two quick and clean cuts, in and out, do the job best. And the job is to hide a bad splice.

Dissolves ought to be employed when the double chaining method is used for silent film which illustrates a sound track. For example, if Fire Chief Sam Wilson describes a blaze for two minutes, the viewer should not be made to endure the sight of the chief for the full two minutes. The viewer will be interested in what the chief says, not what he looks like. The film story should be cut to establish the chief and listen to him start his description for perhaps ten seconds. Then, while the chief talks away on reel 1, the technical director should dissolve to reel 2, showing the fire.

FIRE. DOUBLE CHAIN. 9/24. CLIP
RUNS 2:00

ROLL A AND B TOGETHER TAKE
A VIDEO AT START :12 SIL

Fire at the Suregrip tire factory north of Five Points sent a column of thick black smoke a mile into the air. It began around noon. The smoke and stinking fumes forced firemen to use gas masks.

1:40 SOF   TAKE A AUDIO

AT :15, SUPER: SAM WILSON

AT :25, DISSOLVE TO B VIDEO

HOLD B AUDIO UNDER, FOR BACK-GROUND

A AUDIO ENDS: "....will smell all week."

WHEN A AUDIO ENDS, AT 1:52, BRING B AUDIO UP FULL FOR RE-MAINING 8 SECONDS.

This script carries silent or sound film of the fire or the ruins it left behind. The writer and the editor who assemble the story retain the option of ordering a dissolve back to the chief at the conclusion of his tale, or simply staying with the silent film and going to black when the chief finishes. For an added effect, the silent film can be continued for four or five seconds beyond the conclusion of the audio, possibly followed by a fadeout. Sometimes, especially when the film is a light feature, a musical tag may be used, but this is a matter of news policy.

Double System

Almost all television newsfilm is single system, which means the picture and the sound are carried on the same film. The sound track, either magnetic or optical, runs along one edge of the film. Sprocket holes run along the opposite edge.

However, feature motion pictures are filmed double system, and so are most pre-planned network documentaries. Double system filming, as the name implies, consists of two systems running concurrently. The film camera carries only the picture. The sound is recorded either on a sprocketed 16mm film base covered with magnetic track or — more commonly — on quarter-inch audio tape controlled by a 60-cycle sync pulse track, which is transferred later to mag film for editing. This mag film is called "full coat."

Some photographers carry 16mm full coat for the reporter's voice-over narration, because the full coat mag film is reusable. Other photographers load ordinary mag strip film for the voice over. In this case, it is not necessary to develop the unprocessed film carrying the narration. It can be pulled from its can and exposed to the light. The mag track is unaffected. But the photographer had better be sure he labels his can correctly!

Single system filming can become double system editing by transferring the sound to full coat. The original reel is cut on picture. The full coat reel is cut on sound.

By transferring all their film and sound tracks to videotape before the newscast, many television news departments avert the danger that dealing with several tracks will result in on-air sloppiness. Using a different approach, Washington's WRC-TV put together a mixing system to combine up to five sound tracks into one. The reporter in a sound booth narrates the edited film while the editor at a console funnels the narration and other sound sources onto a 16mm full coat track.

Advantages of Double System Filming

1. Several film cameras may be used, offering the editor a variety of angles of the same scene.

2. Tighter editing is possible; for example, "lip flap" is no problem.

3. Audio quality is better.

4. Additional audio tracks may be added, such as: music, sound effects, narration and voice dubbing. All audio tracks are later combined in a "dubbing session."

5. Dissolves and fades can be built into the film.

6. Special visual effects may be added, such as sub-titles and cartoons.

7. Work prints, not originals, are used for the creative editing. The editor need not be afraid of scratching the film or making a splice which he might later regret.

9. A splice-free print emerges. No splice marks will be seen on the air.

10. The microphone can operate independently of the camera, recording "wild track."

When the film editor completes his work, a motion picture lab transfers the picture and sound elements to a composite print on a single reel. This is a positive print with an optical track.

Disadvantages of Double System Filming

1. More processing is needed than simply developing the film. Quarter-inch tape must be transferred to 16mm full-coat magnetic film if a tape recorder was used.

2. Editing is slower. The extra time required to process and edit double system film militates against its use in daily news coverage.

3. Although television film projection rooms can double chain the double system picture and sound reels, they are normally not prepared to do so and the result may be badly out of lip sync.

4. Film and lab costs are higher.

In summary, where time is not crucial and budgets permit, double system is superior to single system filming. For normal news coverage, single system filming, perhaps with some double system single or double chain modifications, works better.

For the Student

1. Attend a speech or a news conference being covered by a television news crew. Later, compare the way you would have cut the story with the air version. Was an important statement chosen over an interesting statement? Vice versa?

2. Watch several newscasts for film editing. List sloppy cuts.

3. Interview a film editor. What was his training? What are his chief problems? His biggest gripes?

4. When should a film editor cut on sound? On picture?

5. Practice erasing sound on sound film.

Stills 25

Visual aids are hardly ever used to the maximum on TV.
— Karl Deutsch
Political science professor
Harvard University

In television news, still pictures and other graphics are as vital as motion pictures. There are times when only still pictures are available, and there are times when a lack of motion is preferable. For example, film or tape can do little to increase the information of a simple map. A Chromakeyed quotation gives a verbal story added impact and snap. A graph made of two numbers and a line tells a tale. The supered name is indispensable.

A recently developed piece of electronic hardware, the frame storage unit, can pull stills from motion and motion from stills. It can pick up individual frames from videotape, store them, and feed them out at the director's command. It can also store a series of stills which it can feed out at a rapid speed, creating a video time lapse photography, or it can produce a somewhat jerky slow motion from tape shot by a minicam.

Outside Sources

Both the Associated Press and United Press International sell photo facsimile services. Because of the large number of wire service bureaus and stringers, and because of the speed of handling and transmission, still pictures of a breaking news event often reach television newsrooms around the nation much quicker than film or tape except where television cameras have been set up in advance for a scheduled event. The quality of these transmitted photos has steadily improved over the years, although they still leave something to be desired.

Because television news broadcasts are now in color, the Associated Press has investigated the technical feasibility of transmitting color stills by wire. According to the AP, the cost of transmission represents the major drawback.

Black and white wire photos can be transformed into colorful, eye-catching graphics. An artist can use several techniques:

1. A photograph of an individual has more impact if extraneous background is cut away. Mount the head on a sheet of colored construction paper. Trim the paper to a silhouette of the head. Then mount both on a different color poster board. Some colors that work well together are yellow on orange or red and light blue on medium blue.

2. Mount a trimmed head shot directly on a color poster board. Outline the head shape with ¼″ black plastic tape.

3. A variation is to use a box outline to frame a cut-out shape. This technique works well with lettering since it provides a line for the letters. When the story calls for head shots from two different wire photos, the silhouette, outline, or box frame make a cohesive background for the photo collage.

4. A wire photo can be combined with clip art (a colored picture clipped from a magazine). A story about the *Hustler* magazine publisher prompted one graphics artist to combine a wire photo of Larry Flynt with a clip art picture of a *Hustler* magazine cover. The overall effect was of an all-color graphic.

5. A wire photo can be used with a color map. To illustrate "Khomeini's Iran," a color map of Iran was mounted on a contrasting color poster board. In one corner of the map a wire photo of the Ayatollah was mounted.

6. On occasion, it is possible to color in a "fax." A yellow Magicmarker was used to color in a photo of gold bars for a story about rising gold prices. Press on letters and plastic tape should be black or white for high impact.

Library Stills

A television station can buy 35mm color slides of major news figures from a commercial service. For instance, United Press International sells news slides not only of national and world figures, but of important people in the station's region. These "Unislides" remain on file at each station for re-use, of course. The Associated Press offers a similar color slide service.

ABC News sells slides for rear projection and Chromakey of stylized drawings of news subject areas. For example, a drawing of a dollar bill would be used as a rear projection for an on-camera story about the economy, a half-black and half-white schoolhouse would serve for stories about integration, etc. ABC News has used these graphics for its own newscasts for several years.

Most of the slides provided by AP and UPI show head shots of famous people. The slides are meant to be stored in television newsroom libraries. Thus, if the name of a well-known national or international figure unexpectedly appears on the teletype — often, unfortunately, by dying — newsrooms can show his face either as a rear projection (designated in a script as RP; VIZ, for Vizmo; or CHROMA, for Chromakey) over the newscaster's shoulder or fully on screen by "punching up the slide chain."

Each newsroom should keep a library of stills, as complete as possible, slides and/or cards, both head shots and news photos which have previously moved on the wire. The still library must be winnowed regularly. Otherwise, it will be inundated with stills, which is nearly as bad as having no library at all. Finding the right still in a picture file without a filing system is a frustrating task which a busy journalist soon abandons.

A library file ought to contain head shots of local and state personalities. It is a good idea to introduce the matter of head shots at a newsroom staff meeting, in order to determine whose pictures should be on file. The person placed in charge of the library can phone or write for pictures needed to complete the file and bring it up to date (so that the grizzled U.S. senator does not appear as he did when he was a freshman state legislator). A few stills of familiar places should also be filed — for example, the state capitol, the White House, a courtroom or the outside of the courthouse, any of which might Chromakey a story where no other illustration is available.

Maps

The first rule for drawing a television news map is: *keep it simple*. The second rule is: *hold it on camera longer than a photo would be held*, giving viewers plenty of time to read place names, understand the relative distances and absorb all the information even a simply drawn map conveys. A map should contain not one place name, not one highway line, not one mark more than is absolutely necessary to locate the spot where whatever happened happened. For example, a map locating a brush fire might show nothing but the two nearest towns, or a town and a highway, plus an X to mark the fire or, better still, a drawing of flames or smoke to locate the fire.

To show movement in a map or on a graph, an electronic Telemation unit connected to a switcher can draw lines and produce flashing spots. For news operations without the electronics, consider the pull-tab. A pull-tab map is relatively simple to construct, and looks good on the air, telling a story clearly. The pull-tab works because of the optical illusion that makes black invisible in a television receiver when it is next to a light color. The pull-tab consists of three layers of cardboard: a top layer on which the map is drawn in white on a black card, with a strip cut out for the path of the pull-tab; a black, movable middle layer, the pull-tab itself; a white bottom layer glued to the top layer. Pulling the tab slowly exposes the white bottom layer. To the viewer at home, it seems as if an invisible hand is drawing a line. Pull-tabs can also be black-on-gray or colored. Once a television newsman gets accustomed to making such maps to show, for instance, the path of an airplane, there are few limits to what can be done with a little imagination and patience: multiple pull-tabs, perhaps showing solid, broken, or dotted lines uncovered separately or in unison; pull-tabs showing graphs or financial "pies"; even pull-tabs creating a kind of animation.

Cartoons

As everyone who reads newspaper editorial pages knows, cartoons are not always funny. Both funny and serious cartoons have a place in television news, but they should be displayed with caution. Surprisingly, a drawing is strong medicine in a television newscast. It may be remembered long after the day's film and videotape are forgotten.

A cartoon can be used by itself, with or without a caption, with the newscaster voice over. More commonly, the cartoon — or a line drawing — with or without a caption is used as introduction to a film story. Sometimes, a story is told using a series of drawings.

Besides cartoons and line drawings, newscasts make use of collages, often several newspaper articles or headlines artfully pasted on a card to show the interest a certain matter has stirred up.

Because cameras are still barred from most courtrooms, news departments send artists to sketch people at newsworthy trials. These quick drawings of the defendant(s), lawyers, the judge and witnesses are an inadequate substitute for film or videotape, but without them the public would have no visual record of a trial which may have public importance, unless cameras were allowed in the courtroom.

Supers

If a character generator is not available, the super (for superimposition) card also works, on the optical principle that black is invisible over a lighted image in a television receiver. White lettering on a black card shows only the white. The black shows as a neutral gray. If a television camera focusing on a super card is punched up at the same time as a television camera focusing on a person, or at the same time as a film is being shown, the result will appear as white lettering over the person or film. In practice, an identifying name of a person, place, or whatever, is "supered" over the person or place to be identified. The black card will cause the television picture to darken slightly, but the darkening is not objectionable and, except to the accustomed eye, hardly noticeable.

Character generators can electronically super over stills, film or live action, roll vertically for credits, and crawl horizontally for bulletins and announcements. Depending upon the particular model, electronic supering devices offer such features as: 1) flashing or blinking words to attract attention, with each word in a different color and black borders around each letter; 2) upper and lower case printing; 3) titles retrieved from a storage library.

Electronic supering may be used to super names on film, to identify studio guests, to show the score and standing of a ball game (*Top of the Seventh, Yankees 2, Red Sox 1*), to super titles or dates, to report election returns over movies, to announce that news follows the movie, and so on. A blinking feature can be preset in combination with a map to show where the battle is, where the cold front is centered, or where the airplane crashed.

Because it can be hooked to a memory storage unit, one device can present candidates' names in what amounts to a lot of "limbo boards" (i.e., boards viewed in limbo, not part of a set). As new returns come in during an election, each "limbo board" can be updated with the latest figures, eliminating the need for a background set with the latest returns behind the newscaster. A board is punched up on the air at the touch of a button.

Slides

A slide does not require a studio television camera, while a card does. Television projection rooms include slide projectors as basic equipment and 35mm projectors often share an electronic chain with a film projector, thanks to a mirror system which may be flipped around to take an image from either of them.

But a slide cannot be handled as flexibly as a card; for example, it is impossible to pan across a slide without projecting it on a screen and picking up the image with a studio camera.

Animation

By definition, animated is the opposite of still, yet in television terms they may be considered together because animation consists of a series of stills. Television news makes little use of animation techniques that are widely used in television commercials and television entertainment, especially for children. That's too bad, because animation is pleasant to watch and can be more informative and moving than straight film.

At KABC-TV, Los Angeles, the author helped put together what may be regarded as animation sequences to observe such major events as the funeral of a famous person. In this case the camera moved in relation to still pictures. A silent film camera that can single frame, like a Bolex, can be fitted with a cable release and attached to a movable platform or, better, to a frame which gives the camera freedom to pan in all directions; the frame can be cranked forward or backward. Stills are taped to a board in front of the camera. The camera can be backed up to create double exposures and to permit dissolves in the camera.

An event such as the funeral of a prominent national figure will trigger a series of pictures on the Photofax or Unifax, both historical photos and pictures of the funeral itself. That the pictures are black and white instead of color may add to the mood. In the television newsroom the producer selects the stills that best capture the famous person and the feelings and events of the day. The producer puts them into a sequence, then decides how the camera will treat each picture.

For this one, the camera will dolly in for ten seconds; for the next, it will hold for three seconds; for the next, a six-second pan from right to left; for the next, a tight shot of two faces in the upper left corner, two seconds; next, a montage of six shots for one second each; next, a slow pull back using the zoom lens, dissolving to the next still, which it holds for four seconds before dissolving to a card with the name of the personage and dates of birth and death. The script will carry instructions to the television studio director to fade to black after the card has been up for three seconds. The script will also carry copy or, if words are superfluous, just the reference to the music the producer chose.

What KABC-TV used was a knocked-together animation stand. For the station willing to go beyond home-made solutions, professional animation equipment is available such as the Oxberry animation stand, which a station can use for much more than news. With professional equipment and a skilled animator, work can be done with collages, producing the kind of animation viewers of the Monty Python series remember so well. And, of course, cell animation, made famous by the Walt Disney studios, is done with professional equipment, and so is figure animation, like the Pillsbury commercial of the gingerbread man. However, it is unlikely that these techniques will find their way into the newsroom for use in editorials. A more likely technique for an editorial cartoon or a weather report would be the sketch that draws itself; that is, the artist draws lines a fraction of an inch, then gets out of the way and pushes the cable release to snap a still frame and advance the film.

For the Student

1. Monitor a newscast, looking for stories that could have been improved by graphics.

2. From today's newspaper, clip six stories that could be illustrated on a television newscast with a chart, map or drawing.

3. Put together a two-minute news segment using stills. Be sure each still has the 3 x 4 aspect ratio. Use fairly large pictures.

4. Prepare a map for one news story and a graph for another. Add them to your news segment.

5. On your next visit to a television newsroom, introduce yourself to the person who makes slides. Learn how it's done.

Glossary

A ROLL: One of two film clips in a double chain. The A roll may carry narration while the B roll carries most of the picture, or vice versa.

A-WIRE: The AP and UPI teletype services which emphasize world and national news; the primary news wire.

ACADEMY LEADER: Film numbered in reverse from 10 to 1 or 5 to 1, used at the start of a film clip, or in a roll-thru of 10 seconds or longer. The numbers guide the projectionist and the director.

ACTUALITY: A radio report from the scene of an event, live or on tape.

ADD: An addition to a story.

AD LIB: Unscripted, spur-of-the-moment comment.

AFFILIATE: A station, not owned by a network, which contracts to take the network's programs.

AIR CHECK: The videotape recording of a television program or one performer's work, or the audio taping of a radio program.

AIR TIME: The time scheduled for a broadcast to start.

ANALYST: One who explains the meaning of a news event and considers its consequences.

ANGLE: In news writing, the approach to a story.

AUDIO: Sound; the sound portion of a broadcast.

BG: (abbr.) Background.

B ROLL: See A ROLL.

B-WIRE: The AP and UPI services emphasizing features and reports in depth; a supplementary service to the A-wire.

BACK-TIMING: Timing to a closing segment whose length is known. A script is back-timed to give it a strong, clean ending. Weaknesses of filling and stretching occur in the middle of the newscast, where they are less obvious.

BARN DOORS: Metal shades used to block light emission.

BEAT: (noun)

1. The reporting of a story ahead of the competition.

2. The list of places a reporter is assigned to cover, usually daily.

BEEPER: A telephone interview recorded on audio tape over a special telephone circuit which emits a regular beep sound to inform the parties to the conversation that they are being recorded.

BILLBOARD: In broadcast news, all the headlines at the start of a newscast.

BLACK: A blank screen (which actually appears mid-gray on a receiver).

BLOOP: Erase, or "wipe" sound from a magnetic track with a magnet.

BLURB: A publicity release (derogatory).

BOOTH ANNOUNCER: A television announcer who speaks from a small booth, heard but not seen.

BREAK: In reporting, a new development in a running (continuing) story.

BRIDGE: In a newscast, a few words tying one element of news to another. (In broadcasting generally, the musical bridge is better known.)

BRITE: See KICKER.

BROADCAST WIRE: See RADIO WIRE.

BUDGET: (noun)

1. The sum allocated for running a news department, for covering a special news event, or for producing a special program.

2. A listing of news stories a wire service plans to transmit.

BULLETIN: Important late news.

1. Teletype copy introduced by the word "bulletin."

2. News read on the air over a bulletin slide.

BUSY: Crammed with detail.

BUTT END: (verb) To splice one piece of film directly to another; the term often refers to the splicing of film of one speaker directly after another.

CAMERA CHAIN: A television camera, its camera control unit and its power supply.

CHARACTER GENERATOR: An electronic device for creating supers.

CHROMA: (abbr.) Chromakey, a process which places an electronic image on a screen behind the newscaster. The image may be a live remote, a still, film or videotape.

CHYRON: A brand name of a character generator. (Sometimes spelled CHIRON.)

CLIP (or FILM CLIP): An edited film story.

CLOSEUP: Framing which, roughly speaking, includes just the head, or head and shoulders, or an object seen at close range.

CLOSING (or CLOSE): The standard concluding segment of a newscast according to format.

COLLAGE: In a newscast, several photos, newspaper headlines or printed stories pasted onto a card.

COMMENTATOR: One who gives his own views of news events, especially political and international news events. See ANALYST, EDITORIALIST.

CONTINUITY: Non-news copy; e.g., commercial, promo, or station break copy.

COPY: News printed or typed. WIRE COPY is teletype news. HARD COPY refers to complete news items on paper, as distinct from LEAD-IN COPY or FILM COPY, both written for use with other elements.

COVER SHOT: See ESTABLISHING SHOT.

CRAWL: A display of words in a single line moving horizontally across a screen without interrupting regular programming. Also, the device which moves the display either horizontally (for a "crawl") or vertically (for a "roll").

CROPPING: Trimming a still to a ratio of 3 units of height by 4 units of width to match the aspect ratio of a television screen.

CROSSFADE: To change sources of sound by steadily lowering the volume of the outgoing sound while raising the volume of the incoming sound.

CROSSING THE LINE: Changing directional relationship on film.

CU (abbr.): Close-up.

CUE: In a newscast, a hand signal by the stage manager to the newscaster. Common cues are those to begin, slow down, speed up, or conclude in a certain number of seconds; e.g., one index finger upraised means one minute left, both index fingers crossed in a "t" means 30 seconds, a fist means 15 seconds, all 10 fingers held up means 10 seconds left.

CUE PUNCH: A spot mechanically scraped onto each corner of several frames of film as a warning that the film is about to end.

CUT: 1. (noun) A recorded segment of a record or an audio tape.
2. (verb) To end sharply, usually at a precise time or at the conclusion of a news item. In a studio the cut signal is a finger drawn across the throat, meaning "End it right now."

CUTAWAY: A short piece of film placed between two scenes of the same person or locale. The cutaway shows something other than the persons or places in either scene.

DEAD AIR: Silence, due to error, in a broadcast.

DEADLINE: That moment before each newscast when all copy and film should be prepared. The copy deadline and the film deadline may come at different times. Deadlines are ignored for bulletins.

DEGAUSS: Demagnetize. See BLOOP.

DISSOLVE: A smooth exchange of one image for another.

DOLLY: 1. A movable camera platform.
2. A shot taken from such a platform, or its equivalent, while moving to or from the subject.

DOPE SHEET: The paper on which a cameraman writes story and film information; e.g., names of crew members, story location, total film footage, developing instructions, etc. Also called POOP SHEET, SPOT SHEET, SHOT CARD, etc.

DOUBLE CHAIN: 1. (noun) A film story using two reels of film (designated

A Roll and B Roll) going through two projectors simultaneously. The studio's switching equipment, controlled by the technical director, determines which picture and which sound is fed at any moment.

2. (verb) Use two film chains.

DOUBLE SYSTEM: Separation of sound and picture in filming, using a camera synchronized to a recording device.

DUB: 1. (noun) A duplicate of film, videotape, or audio tape.

2. (verb) Make such a transfer; re-record.

EDITORIALIST: One who expresses opinions, usually those of station management, about news events, local conditions and pending legislation. See COMMENTATOR.

END CUE: See OUT CUE.

ESTABLISH SOUND: An instruction to play a sound track at full volume (usually for about 5 seconds) before lowering the volume, often to the level of background sound.

ESTABLISHING SHOT: A camera view of the entire scene.

ET: (abbr.) Electrical transcription, meaning a phonograph record.

ETA: (abbr.) Estimated time of arrival.

EVERGREEN: An anytime feature story.

FADE (or FADE TO BLACK): The electronic equivalent of a film fade out. A dissolve from a picture to darkness, which is a mid-gray rather than black.

FCC: (abbr.) The Federal Communications Commission. Among other responsibilities, it issues and renews television and radio station licenses.

FEATURE: A human interest story whose news value is not necessarily limited to the day of its occurrence, as distinct from HARD NEWS.

FEED: 1. (noun) A news story or an entire program electronically transmitted to other stations or broadcast to the public.

2. (verb) Broadcast or transmit.

FEEDBACK: The whine caused by loudspeaker output being picked up by a microphone feeding the loudspeaker. This sound circle is broken by separating mike and loudspeaker.

FILL: 1. (noun) A light used to fill shadows.

2. (verb) Read pad copy to fill a time gap.

FILM CLIP: See CLIP.

FLOP: A card, placed on a stand, to be viewed through a studio camera.

FLUFF: An on-air verbal error, such as a mispronunciation.

FORMAT: In television, the framework of a program (independent of content).

FREEZE FRAME: A frame of film or videotape, to or from which action flows; arrested motion.

FREZZI: A type of portable light.

FUTURE FILE: Also called FUTURE(S) BOOK, DATEBOOK, ADVANCE FOLDER, etc. A file of upcoming events, divided into 31 days.

GAFFER: A member of some film crews who is responsible for lighting.

GAIN: Audio volume. To RIDE GAIN is to adjust volume as needed during recording.

GOOF: An on-air technical error. Also referred to in less polite terms.

GRAPHICS: Any fixed, two-dimensional representations such as photos, maps, graphs, cartoons and super cards. A subset of the term "visuals" (film, videotape and props are considered visuals, but not graphics).

HAND-HELD: A portable color video camera.

HANDOUT: Free film or copy (a printed news release) mailed or hand delivered, issued by a private company, an organization, a government agency, a political candidate, etc., or a public relations agency or film company acting as agent.

HAPPY TALK: A newscast filled with humorous asides by on-camera personnel.

HARD NEWS: Reports of current events which are of interest because of their timeliness and general importance or violence (as in crimes and accidents). Feature stories are not hard news.

HEAD SHOT: A still photo of a person's head or head and shoulders.

HEADLINE: In broadcast news, a phrase or short sentence at the start of a newscast summarizing a story.

HIGH ANGLE SHOT: An above-eye-level view, often filmed by standing on a ladder or furniture.

HIGH BAND: A frequency range used mainly for color transmission.

IN CUE: The place where a newsfilm segment is to start, a start cue. Sometimes, the first words of a statement.

INTEGRATED FORMAT: The inter-relating of newscaster(s), weatherman, sports reporter, commentator, and field reporters doing studio reports. The studio set, the introductions, and occasional chatter give the newscast a mood of relaxed informality.

INTRO: 1. (noun) Introduction; introductory copy to film or tape.
2. (verb) Introduce.

JIGGLE: Derogatory term for activity shown on the screen instead of a newscaster reading the news.

JUMP CUT: A direct cut on film to the same person or scene.

KEY LIGHT: The main light.

KICKER: A short, humorous news item at the end of the newscast. Also called a TAG, a BRITE, or a ZIPPER.

LASERPHOTO: The Associated Press picture-by-wire service.

LEAD: A fresh introduction to a story, as in NEW LEAD. Also, the first sentence or two of a news story.

LEAD STORY: The first story in the newscast.

LEADER: Film placed at the head or tail of a film clip for threading through a projector, or in the middle of a film clip where a roll-thru is needed. Leader may be numbered, clear or blank, black or yellow.

LIMBO BOARD: A graphics display (e.g., showing election returns in a particular race) which is not part of the set. It exists "in limbo." To show it, the director usually "breaks" a camera from the set.

LINE-UP: Arrangement of items in a newscast.

LIP FLAP: The result of cutting a film of a speaker to begin in mid-speech, so that his lips are seen moving before he is heard.

LIP SYNC: Synchronized speech, with picture and sound matching frame for frame.

LIVE: 1. On-the-air. A live mike is broadcasting sound.

    2. In transmission, immediate, as contrasted with the delay of film and tape.

LOCAL NEWS: News of the city in which the television station lies, and its environs; sometimes, by definition, anything covered by the station's own news staff, or any news occurring within the station's reception range is considered "local."

LOGO: The identifying symbol of the newscast, usually on a slide.

LONG LENS: See TELEPHOTO LENS.

LONG SHOT: Framing which takes in the scene of an event.

LOOSE SHOT: A view which leaves lots of space, or "air," around the subject.

LOW ANGLE SHOT: A below-eye-level view, often filmed from a crouching position.

LS: (abbr.) Long shot.

MAG: (abbr.) Magnetic sound track film; a magnetic stripe on the base side of film, used to carry the sound. Also called MAG STRIPE or MAGNETIC STRIPE.

MAG HEAD: The device on a projector, a sound reader or an editing machine which plays back or "reads" the sound track of magnetic striped film.

MAGAZINE FORMAT: A news program with several long stories each day, instead of many short news items.

MEDIA: The plural form of medium, or means, of transmitting information. Media include television, radio, motion pictures, newspapers, magazines and books.

MEDIUM SHOT: Framing which roughly encompasses anything from head to waist of one or two persons to the framing of three or four people seated at a table, or the equivalent.

MONITOR: 1. (noun) A television or radio receiver.

    2. (verb) In radio, to listen, and in television, to watch and listen, taking notes, often of subject matter and running times.

MONTAGE: In television news, a rapid succession of moving or still pictures assembled to create an overall effect.

MOS: (abbr.) Man-on-street. The interviewing of average citizens for short responses to a question; the interviews can take place anywhere. By extension, "MOS" is sometimes also used to define the editing of a film to get several very brief comments on a subject, no matter what the sources of the film are.

MOVE: Transmit copy or pictures by wire.

MS: (abbr.) Medium shot.

NEG: (abbr.) Negative image film.

N.E.S.: (abbr.) News Election Service, the pool which gathers election returns.

NETWORK: Any interlinked group of stations; usually refers to CBS, NBC, ABC, or, in radio only, Mutual, which are corporations providing programming for O & O and affiliate stations.

NEWS WIRE: A news-by-teletype service.

NON-EXCLUSIVE: Refers to identical film clips, prints offered equally to competing newscasts.

NON-STANDARD FILM: Film having the emulsion on the reverse side of the base, compared with the most commonly used film.

O & O: (abbr.) Owned-and-operated; refers to stations owned and operated by networks.

O/C: (abbr.) On camera; a symbol typed in a script to indicate when the newscaster should be seen. The newscaster's name often replaces this symbol.

OPENING (or OPEN used as a noun): The elements which begin a newscast; by definition, the opening may refer to the standard daily announcement with music, film, sound effects, etc., but not headlines or tease, if any.

OPTICAL: Optical track sound film; sometimes abbreviated in a script as OPT or OP.

OSV: (abbr.) Off-stage voice, same as voice-over.

OUT CUE: The place where a newsfilm segment is to end; the last words to be included in a statement.

OVERLAP: A splice which causes the sound track at the end of one segment of film to appear with the start of the following segment's picture.

PAD COPY: News stories not expected to be aired, but available if needed. Pad is usually "pinned up" (i.e., stapled to 8½" x 11" sheets for ease of handling) wire copy. The stories are unrelated to other items in the newscast.

PAN: 1. (verb) Camera movement horizontally or vertically (tilting) from a fixed position.
2. (noun) Film resulting from such a movement.

PATCH: A connection between two pieces of electronic equipment, directly or by means of a patch board.

PIC: (abbr.) Still picture.

PLUG: Free advertisement; e.g., mentioning a product or a new motion picture in a news story.

POLARITY CHANGE: Electronic reversal of negative and positive images.

POOL: The combination of competing news media to achieve a particular result; e.g., several television stations in the same city agreeing to dub and share a single videotape, or the three major networks sharing cameras and personnel to cover the presidential inauguration.

POP ZOOM: A fast zoom in from a long shot to a close-up.

POT: (abbr.) Potentiometer; the volume control dial.

PROMO: A "house" commercial, advertising an upcoming program.

PROP: In news, a three-dimensional object which is part of a story or gives credence to a locale.

PROTECTION SHOT: A filmed scene of a changing news event. The photographer shoots this scene when he arrives to be sure he has someting "in the camera."

PUBLIC SERVICE ANNOUNCEMENT: PSA. An unpaid "commercial" for a non-profit cause; e.g., the anti-smoking spots.

PULL-TAB: A drawing, usually a map, with a movable portion which is physically pulled on camera to expose what lies beneath it.

PUNCH (or PUNCH UP): To cut to, electronically, in the studio.

QUARTER-INCH TAPE: Audio tape.

RADIO WIRE: A teletype service largely of news summaries written in broadcast style.

READY: A warning the director gives to the technical director and other studio personnel that a command is imminent; e.g., "Ready camera one" warns that the next command for a camera change will be a cut or dissolve to number one camera.

REAR PROJECTION: A process which places a visual on a screen behind the newscaster. The rear projection, or RP, may be a still photo, map, graph, cartoon, a film or videotape.

RECAP: 1. (noun) A news summary in headline form at the end of the newscast, or the summary of the main elements of a long story.
2. (verb) To summarize news.

REGIONAL SPLIT: A specified period (e.g., 10 minutes each hour on the half hour) set aside by wire services for regional news. Usually, the New York offices of the wire services relinquish control to their bureaus in the major cities. Only specified teletype lines are permitted splits from the trunk service.

REVERSAL FILM: Motion picture film which develops as a positive print. Most news color film is reversal.

REVERSE: A camera shot approximately 180 degrees from the preceding shot; an opposite angle shot; e.g., each of two people talking face to face.

RIP AND READ: A derogatory term describing the practice on some newscasts, especially radio newscasts, of simply reading the latest news summary torn from the radio wire, without rewriting or incorporating local stories.

ROLL: 1. (verb) To film, or tape; an order to start a camera or tape machine.
2. (noun) A spool of film; a reel.

ROLL-THRU: Film not meant to be aired, spliced into a film clip so that the clip may continue rolling through a projector at a known speed. Blank or black leader is often used. Just before the roll-thru goes past the projector film gate, the director "takes" another film chain, a camera on the newscaster, etc.

ROUGH CUT: A preliminary editing of film.

RTNDA: (abbr.) The Radio and Television News Directors Association.

RUNNING STORY: A story of continuing interest as new developments occur day after day.

RUNNING TIME: The time, in minutes and seconds, from the start of a program or segment. Monitoring normally includes a log of running time.

SCOOP: 1. A photoflood, used as a main light source.

2. (noun) A story reported before the competition reports it. Also called a "beat."

3. (verb) To report a story first.

SCREEN: To view film or videotape.

SCRIPT: In television news, the arranged collection of news stories, together with open, close and leads to commercials.

SECS: (abbr.) Seconds.

SEGUE: See CROSSFADE.

SHOOT: To film.

SHOT: A film scene.

SHOW: A newscast.

SIL: (abbr.) Silent.

SINGLE SYSTEM: Filming sound and picture on the same film using a sound camera. Most television news sound film is single system.

SLANT: The approach to a story, usually (but not always) from a political standpoint. See also ANGLE. A slanted news story is one written from a political bias.

SLIDE: A transparency shown with a slide projector, either through a film chain, a separate projector chain, or as a rear projection.

SLOT: 1. (verb) Place in a newscast; e.g., "slotting" a story to follow a commercial.

2. (noun) The position of a story or commercial.

3. (noun) The position of the chief desk editor (more common to newspapers than to broadcast newsrooms).

SLUG: 1. (noun) A length of leader film serving as a spacer in a double chain film clip.

2. (noun) An identifying name for a news story.

3. (verb) Label.

SOF: (abbr.) Sound-on-film.

SOT: (abbr.) Sound-on-tape.

SOUND BITE: A sound-on-film statement.

SOUND CREW: Basically, a photographer and a sound technician. In some union jurisdictions and electrician or a gaffer and/or an assistant photographer are part of the crew. A reporter and/or a producer may accompany them, but are not considered part of the crew. See also TEAM.

SOUND-ON-FILM: Film carrying its own sound track.

SOUND UNDER: An audio level which permits background sounds to be heard, but not so loudly that they interfere with the newscaster or reporter.

SOUP: 1. (verb) To develop film.

2. (noun) Developing chemicals in the tank.

SPLICE: 1. (verb) To connect two pieces of film or tape.

2. (noun) The connection.

SPLIT SCREEN: Two images, not superimposed, sharing the screen.

SPOT: A commercial. DOUBLE SPOTTING and TRIPLE SPOTTING are the assigning of two or three commercials back-to-back.

SPOT SHEET: Record of what was filmed.

SQUEEZE FRAMING: A technique of shrinking a full frame picture on camera until it occupies only a portion of the screen, which it then shares with the newscaster, alphanumeric information or other visuals.

STANDUPPER: A report at the scene of an event, with the camera focused on the reporter.

STILL: A photograph; may also refer to a map or drawing.

STRETCHING: Reading slowly to fill a time gap.

STRINGER: A free lance photographer.

STUDIO CARD: A still that is shot with a studio camera, not transmitted through a projector.

SUPER (or SUPER CARD): (abbr.) Superimposition. Lettering is combined electronically with another image on film or tape, or a live scene, identifying person, place or time.

SUSTAINING: Unsponsored.

SWISH PAN: A very rapid, blurred pan indicating a change of scene.

SYNC: (abbr.) Synchronous, synchronize or synchronization. The frame-for-frame matching of sound and picture. OUT OF SYNC: Inexact union of sound and picture, often due to the length of a film loop in a projector.

TABLOID NEWS: A newscast emphasizing violence and sex.

TAG: See KICKER.

TAKE: 1. (noun) A film or taped scene.

2. (verb) An order from the director to the technical director to cut to a certain camera or film chain. The take is an immediate cut, not a dissolve.

TEAM: Loosely, all personnel sent to cover a story.

TEASE: A headline or bit of news before the station break preceding the newscast. Also, an announcement of an upcoming news item.

TELEPHOTO LENS: A long lens, with a narrow angle of view and a long focal length.

THEME: Identifying music at the start and/or finish of a program.

THROWAWAY PHRASE: A few words delivered quickly and casually in an offhand manner.

TIGHT SHOT: Framing with little or no space around the central figure(s) or feature(s); usually a close-up.

TIMING: Noting the length of time of each story or segment and its running time (how far into the newscast each story begins and ends).

TITLE CARD: A card naming a story, sometimes used to begin a feature. Besides a title, the card may be illustrated with a design, a cartoon or a photograph.

TRACKING: Adjusting the head-to-capstan distance of a videotape machine.

TRUCK: In television news, to film while walking or riding. Also, camera movement parallel to the subject.

TWO SHOT: Camera framing of two persons.

UHF: Ultra High Frequency, the range in which a small but growing number of commercial and educational television stations transmit.

UNIFAX II: The United Press International picture-by-wire service.

UP-CUT: A loss of words at the start of film or tape. A newscaster's delivery is also up-cut if his microphone is cut in after he begins a sentence.

UPDATE: A new version of a story, requiring a change in script or, if a network newscast has been received on tape for later playback, a fresh story exactly timed to lay over the old story on the playback.

"UP ON ONE" (or TWO, etc.): An order by the director to the technical director to fade into the scene on number one camera.

VHF: Very High Frequency, the range in which most commercial television stations broadcast.

VIDEO: 1. Television.

2. The pictorial portion of a broadcast.

VIDEOGRAPH: The brand name of a type of character generator.

VISUAL: Anything seen on the television screen.

VIZ: (abbr.) Vizmo, a rear projection process.

VO: (abbr.) Voice over.

VOICE OVER: Speech by a newscaster or announcer over film or cards.

VOICER: A radio report, usually on tape, by a reporter on assignment. It may include other voices. STRAIGHT VOICER: Only the reporter's voice is heard.

VTR: (abbr.) Videotape recording.

WAYBILL: A freight ticket with an identifying number, address and statement of contents. When film is shipped (by plane) the sender must phone or wire the receiver to tell him the waybill number, the flight number and the estimated time of arrival (ETA).

WHITE NOISE: (sometimes called just NOISE) Undifferentiated background sound of all frequencies; static.

WIDE-ANGLE LENS: A lens with a wide angle of view and a short focal length.

WILD TRACK: Background sound recorded at the scene of an event by tape recorder or sound camera. The sound is not recorded to match any particular scene or to provide lip sync.

WIRE: See NEWS WIRE.

WRAP (or WRAP-UP): 1. (noun) Conclusion.

    2. (verb) Finish.

    3. Wraparound.

WRAPAROUND: Copy with a lead into SOF and a tag or further copy after the SOF.

WOODSHED: To practice reading copy before the newscast.

ZIPPER: See KICKER.

ZOOM: 1. (noun) A variable focal length.

    2. (verb) Alter framing while filming by means of a zoom lens.

Reference Notes

PREFACE

1. Lecture, Memphis State University, April 23, 1969.
2. Robert E. Kintner, **Broadcasting and the News**. New York: Harper & Row, 1965, pp. 46-47.

CHAPTER 1: WRITING FOR THE EAR

1. Larry Incollingo, "When Judge Becomes 'Defendant' Watch Out," **Daily Herald-Telegram**, Bloomington, Ind., May 29, 1974.
2. S.I. Hayakawa, **Language in Thought and Action**. New York: Harcourt, Brace and World, Inc., Second Edition, 1964, pp. 176-79.
3. Quoted in UPI's **Broadcast Stylebook**, 1969, p. 10.

CHAPTER 2: NEWS COPY

1. Edwin Newman, **A Civil Tongue**. Indianapolis: Bobbs-Merrill, 1976.

CHAPTER 3: THE LEAD-IN

CHAPTER 4: THE PICTURE STORY

1. March 11, 1967.
2. **Television Newsfilm Standards Manual**. New York: Time-Life Broadcast, Inc., 1964, p. 88.
3. **Television Newsfilm: Content**. New York: Time-Life Broadcast, Inc., 1965, pp. 57-58.

4. James Bormann, "Radio News Strives for New Format," **Quill**, January, 1959, p. 15.

CHAPTER 5: **THE RADIO REPORTER**

1. Mark W. Hall, **Broadcast Journalism**, 2nd ed. New York: Hastings House, 1978.

CHAPTER 6: **RADIO NEWS**

1. Robert Lewis Shayon, "Trobriandish," **Saturday Review**, April 25, 1970, p. 49.

CHAPTER 7: **THE TELEVISION REPORTER**

1. Ken Metzler, **Creative Interviewing**. Englewood Cliffs, N.J.: Prentice-Hall, Inc., 1977, p. 94.
2. **Television Newsfilm Standards Manual**, p. 75.
3. July 17, 1961.
4. **The Newsroom and the Newscast**. New York: Time-Life Broadcast, Inc., 1966, p. 78.
5. Dan Rather, **The Camera Never Blinks**. New York: William Morrow & Co., 1977, p. 136.
6. Reported by John Brady, **The Craft of Interviewing**. Cincinnati: Writer's Digest, 1976, p. 69.
7. Thomas D. Patterson and Robert D. McClure, **The Unseeing Eye**. New York: G.P. Putnam's Sons, 1976.
8. **Television Newsfilm Standards Manual**, op.cit., pp. 75-76.
9. Dan Drew, "The Roles and Decision Making of Three Television Beat Reporters," paper delivered at Association for Education in Journalism meeting, Columbia, S.C., 1971.
10. **Television Newsfilm: Content**, p. 30.

CHAPTER 8: **A TELEVISION NEWS DAY**

CHAPTER 9: **THE NEWSCASTER**

1. Walter Cronkite, "Mobility, Miniaturization: Broadcast Journalism's Future," **Quill**, November, 1962, pp. 16-17.
2. See Charles Kuralt,"All Those Pretty, TV News Anchormen," **Quill**, October, 1975, pp. 9-10.
3. Ron Powers, "Eyewitless News," **Columbia Journalism Review**, May/June, 1977, pp. 17-24.
4. **The Wall Street Journal**, October 15, 1976, p. 1 ff.
5. **CBS Evening News** commentary, April 22, 1974, reported in **Broadcasting**, April 29, 1974.
6. **The Camera Never Blinks**, p. 281.
7. Paper delivered at American Orthopsychiatric Association meeting, Washington, D.C., 1971.

8. **Television/Radio Age**, July 22, 1974.
9. **The Camera Never Blinks**, p. 66.

CHAPTER 10: **GETTING IT TOGETHER**

1. Reported in Robert MacNeil, **The People Machine**. New York: Harper & Row, 1968, p. 30.
2. Jeanie Kasindorf, "The Pay Is Rotten and the Hours Are Worse," **TV Guide**, April 26, 1975.

CHAPTER 11: **NEWS FOR EVERYONE**

1. Speech to RTNDA conference, Miami Beach, December 14, 1976.
2. Walter Lippmann, **Public Opinion**. New York: The Macmillan Co., 1922, pp. 38-39.
3. Ibid., p. 65.
4. See Wendell Johnson, **People in Quandries**. New York: Harper & Brothers, 1946.
5. **RTNDA Bulletin**, May, 1970.
6. "ABC News Affiliates Newsletter," February, 1978, p. 3.
7. John Doolittle, "The News Media's Captive Audience: Older Adults," paper presented at Association for Education in Journalism meeting, Madison, Wis., 1977.
8. Charles Atkin and Walter Gantz, "Children's Response to Broadcast News: Exposure, Evaluation and Learning," paper presented to the Association for Education in Journalism meeting, 1973.

CHAPTER 12: **WEATHER**

1. **RTNDA Communicator**, September, 1979, p. 19.
2. David Hyatt, Kathy Riley and Noel Sederstrom, "Recall of Television Weather Reports," **Journalism Quarterly**, Summer, 1978, pp. 306-310.
3. Arthur S. Harris, Jr., "Those Dull TV Weathercasts," **Quill**, December, 1970, p. 17.
4. See Stuart W. Hyde, **Television and Radio Announcing**, second edition. Boston: Houghton Mifflin Co., 1971.

CHAPTER 13: **SPORTS**

1. Bill Surface, "The Shame of the Sports Beat," **Columbia Journalism Review**, January/February, 1972, p. 51.
2. David Shaw, **Journalism Today**. New York: Harper's College Press, 1977, p. 149 ff.

CHAPTER 14: **SPEAKING OUT IN EDITORIALS AND DOCUMENTARIES**

1. Irving E. Fang and John W. Whelan, Jr., "A Survey of Television Editorials and Ombudsman Segments," **Journal of Broadcasting**, Summer, 1973, pp. 363-71.

2. Address to National Broadcast Editorial Association. **Broadcasting**, July 1, 1974, p. 41.

3. **Radio and Television Editorializing: Management Attitudes, Station Practices, and Public Reactions**. National Association of Broadcasters, undated, p. 7.

4. Herschel Shosteck, "The Structural Dimensions of Television Editorial Effectiveness," **Journalism Quarterly**, Spring, 1975, pp. 37-43.

5. Address to National Broadcast Editorial conference, Nassau, Bahamas, December 1, 1972.

6. **Television Newsfilm: Content**; plus a letter to the author.

7. September 13, 1976.

8. Ralph Renick, "News is Not a By-Product at WTVJ," Wometco Enterprises, Inc., pamphlet.

9. **Television Newsfilm: Content**.

10. Fred Friendly, **The Good Guys, the Bad Guys and the First Amendment**. New York: Random House, 1976.

11. Jerome A. Barron, **Freedom of the Press for Whom? The Right of Access to Mass Media**. Bloomington: Indiana University Press, 1973, pp. 150-151, 158.

12. Statement before the Senate Subcommittee on Constitutional Rights, February 16, 1972.

13. Minnesota Law Review, Vol. 52, 1967.

14. William A. Hachten, **The Supreme Court on Freedom of the Press**. Ames: Iowa State University Press, 1968.

15. **In the Matter of Editorializing by Broadcast Licensees**. 13 FCC 1246, June 1, 1949.

16. 48 Statute 1062, as amended (1959).

CHAPTER 15: **THE LAW**

1. Don R. Pember, "Privacy and the Press: The Defense of Newsworthiness," **Journalism Quarterly** 45:1 (Spring, 1968), pp. 14-24.

2. Letter, April 28, 1971.

3. **Broadcasting**, May 17, 1971, p. 10.

4. Sources of information include Freedom of Information Center reports on access laws, School of Journalism, University of Missouri.

5. Statement to Sen. Sam Ervin's Senate Subcommittee on Constitutional Rights. **Broadcasting**, February 7, 1972, p. 81.

6. **Documents of American Broadcasting**. New York: Appleton-Century-Crofts, 1968, pp. 111-12.

CHAPTER 16: **MIKE AND CAMERA IN THE COURTROOM**

1. See Donald Gillmor and Jerome Barron, **Mass Communication Law: Cases and Comment**. St. Paul: West Publishing Co., 3rd ed., 1979.

2. Guy O. Kornblum and Paul Rush, "Television in the Courtroom and Classroom" 59 **American Bar Association Journal** 273 (1973).

3. Ibid., p. 275.

4. **RTNDA Bulletin**, October, 1967.

5. **Cowley v. Pulsifer**, Supreme Judicial Court of Massachusetts, 1884.

CHAPTER 17: **THE PROFESSION**

1. David J. LeRoy, "Journalism as a Profession," **Mass News: Practices, Controversies and Alternatives**. Englewood Cliffs, N.J.: Prentice-Hall, 1973, p. 250.
2. Richard H. Hall, "Professionalization and Bureaucratization," **American Sociological Review**, February, 1968, pp. 92-104.
3. Speech at Washington Journalism Center, June 3, 1976.
4. **RTNDA Communicator**, March, 1977, p. 10.
5. Speech to National Press Club, February 4, 1970.
6. Speech to Georgia Radio and Television Institute, January 24, 1968.
7. David Dary, **Radio News Handbook**. Thurmont, Md.: Tab Books, 1967.
8. **Broadcasting and the News**, pp. 17-18.
9. November 14, 1969, p. 69.
10. Address to RTNDA, September 25, 1970.
11. Harry J. Skornia, **Television and the News**. Palo Alto: Pacific Books, 1968, pp. 210-11.

CHAPTER 18: **SHOW BIZ**

1. Alexander Kendrick, **Prime Time**. Boston: Little, Brown & Co., 1969, p. 411.
2. "News: Sine Qua Non in TV Programing," **Broadcasting**, February 25, 1974, p. 28.
3. Speech at Washington Journalism Center, June 3, 1976.
4. **RTNDA Communicator**, May, 1977, p. 7.
5. **The Camera Never Blinks**, p. 163.
6. Ibid., p. 270.
7. **60 Minutes**, March 10, 1974. Reported in **Broadcasting**, March 11, 1974, pp. 84-85.
8. **Broadcasting**, September 9, 1974, p. 22.
9. **Ibid**.
10. Ibid., p. 28.
11. Ibid.
12. Candice C. Harr, "A Study of Consulting Firms and Television Newsrooms," Unpublished M.S. thesis, Iowa State University, 1974.
13. Thomas Griffith, "Happy Is Bad, but Heavy Isn't Good," **Time**, May 17, 1976, p. 79.
14. Speech to CBS affiliates meeting, May, 1976. Repeated to RTNDA conference, Miami Beach, December 13, 1976.
15. April 10, 1977, p. 6.
16. **TV Guide**, March 9, 1974, p. 10.
17. Speech cited.
18. Interview with University of Minnesota student Jan Falstad, 1977.
19. **Television/Radio Age**, October 1, 1973, p. 65.
20. Ron Powers, "Eyewitless News," **Columbia Journalism Review**, May/June, 1977, p. 22.
21. Letter to author, October 30, 1974.
22. **TV Guide**, March 26, 1977, p. 10.
23. Prof. John Kurtz, Southern Illinois University, Carbondale, unpublished study.
24. "News Doctors: Taking Over TV Journalism?", **Broadcasting**, September 9, 1974, p. 28.
25. **Quill**, August, 1974, p. 13.

CHAPTER 19: THE ROUND EVENTS PEG AND THE SQUARE NEWS HOLE

1. **Saturday Review**, September 6, 1975, p. 2.
2. **Minneapolis Tribune**, December 1, 1979, p. 8A.
3. **TV Guide**, September 29, 1973.
4. Sander Vanocur, "How the Media Massaged Me," **Esquire**, Janury, 1972.
5. **Saturday Review**, June 7, 1969.
6. "Troubled Reflections of a TV Journalist," **Encounter**, May, 1970.
7. **Look**, November 17, 1970.
8. Robert Ardrey, "The Violent Way," **Life**, September 11, 1970, p. 65.
9. Edward Jay Epstein, "The War in Vietnam: What Happened vs. What We Saw," **TV Guide**, September 29, 1973.
10. **RTNDA Communicator**, April, 1977, p. 13.
11. **RTNDA Communicator**, December, 1975.
12. Don Farmer, "Heat and Light Through the TV Tube," in **Race and the News Media**, ed. by Paul L. Fisher and Ralph L. Lowenstein. New York: Frederick A. Praeger, 1967, pp. 73-74.
13. **RTNDA Bulletin**, February, 1970.
14. Speech at Washington Journalism Center, June 3, 1976.
15. D.R. Holdridge, "High versus Low Camera Angle in Film Production as a Factor Influencing Viewers' Prediction of Performance," Ph.D. thesis, **Dissertation Abstracts**, 36:1, 13-A, 1975.
16. **Newsweek**, January 9, 1970.
17. **RTNDA Bulletin**, February, 1970.
18. PBL interview, December 22, 1968.
19. Kenneth Stewart, **News Is What We Make It**. Boston: Houghton Mifflin, 1943.
20. **The Camera Never Blinks**, p. 71.
21. Speech, November 25, 1969.
22. **RTNDA Bulletin**, December, 1969.
23. Joe Saltzmann, "How to Manage TV News," **Human Behavior**, March, 1979, p. 65.
24. "Trap at Wounded Knee," **Time**, March 26, 1973, p. 67.
25. Stephen E. Rada, "Manipulating the Media: A Case Study of a Chicano Strike in Texas," **Journalism Quarterly**, Spring, 1977, pp. 109-113.

CHAPTER 20: SHOOTING THE STORY

1. Inquiry into WBBM-TV broadcast, November 1 and 2, 1967, of a report on a marijuana party.

CHAPTER 21: ELECTRONIC NEWS GATHERING

1. **TV Guide**, March 15, 1975, p. 6.
2. Vernon Stone and John DiCioccio, "A Survey of Electronic News Gathering and Television News Coverage," paper presented at Association for Education in Journalism meeting, Madison, Wis., 1977.
3. Ibid.
4. J.A. Flaherty, "All-Electronic News Gathering," **E.B.U. Review**, December, 1975, p. 298.
5. Stone and DiCioccio, **op.cit.**
6. Edwin Diamond, **The Tin Kazoo**. Cambridge, Mass.: The MIT Press, 1975, p. 76.

7. John P. Taylor, "The Future of Equipment: Tiny TV Cameras Spurred by Trend to 'Electronic News'," **Television/Radio Age**, September 2, 1974, p. 74.

8. Dan Cordtz, "The Coming Shake-Up in Telecommunications," **Fortune**, April, 1970.

CHAPTER 22: **TV PHOTOGRAPHY**

1. Vernon Stone and Bruce Hinson, **Television Newsfilm Techniques**. New York: Hastings House, 1974.

2. Vernon Stone, "ENG and Newsfilm Use Surveyed," **RTNDA Communicator**, April, 1977, pp. 7-10.

3. "Range Finder," National Press Photographers Association newsletter.

4. Don Sutherland, "Why TV Station KDUB Is Going Super 8 All the Way," **Popular Photography**, August, 1973, p. 115.

CHAPTER 23: **SOUND ON FILM**

CHAPTER 24: **FILM EDITING**

CHAPTER 25: **STILLS**

Index

abbreviations, 31

ABC News, 59, 62, 65-66, 104, 106, 201, 207, 227, 241, 292, 294, 303, 319, 325, 331, 350, 376

abstraction ladder, the, 25-26

access to public meetings, 242-243

accuracy, 22

"accused" and "alleged," use of, 35

acetone, 366

action verbs, 35

actualities, 49, 93-96

Agnew, Spiro, 12, 294

Air Canada, 291-292

Alabama Plan, 255

Allen, Fred, 355

American Bar Association:
Canons of Judicial Ethics, 250, 255, 265

American Indian Movement (AIM), 303

American Meteorological Society, 202

American Opinion, 236

American Society of Newspaper Editors, 265

American Stock Exchange, 191-192

American Telephone and Telegraph Company, 87, 239

American Telephone and Telegraph Bell Telephone Laboratories, 42

amplifier, 355-357, 365

anchor person, 61-62, 150, 158, 201, 280

Anderson, Jack, 238

animation, 205, 379-380

announcer, 135, 151, 158

Ardrey, Robert, 288

Arlen, Michael, 121

army — McCarthy hearings, 243

Arnow, Ed, 125

arranged news, *see* staging the news

assignment editor, 78, 122, 135-143, 145, 150, 176-178, 326, 333

Associated Press (AP), 103, 135, 166, 172-173, 176, 189-190, 192, 202, 332, 375-376

Associated Press Radio (APR), 106, 192

Atlanta Journal, The, 29

attribution, 36

audience opinion, 220-221

audio
  blooping of, 358
  problems and solutions, 359-361, 365
audio bridge, 358
audio cart, 93-95
audio control booth, 151
audio engineer, 95, 149, 151, 153, 186
audio news services, 104-105
audio tape, 179-180, 268, 348, 357, 371
  editing of, 93-94
"automatic gain control" (AGC), 89, 93

back light, 350-351
backtiming, 94, 153, 182, 338-339
Bagdikian, Ben, 300
Banzhaf, John, 227
bar magnet, 366
"barn door" in lighting, 350
Barron, Jerome A., 228, 235
Barron's, 240
BBC-TV, 288, 298
beepers, 88, 105
Benti, Joseph, 281
Beutel, Bill, 131
Bill of Rights, 263
Black Panthers, 240, 253
blacks, news for, 106
Blair, Sam C., 253
Bliss, Edward, 35-36
bloop, 53, 130, 367
boom mike, 151
Boorstin, Daniel, 300
Branzburg case, 239
Brennan, Robert, 76
Brennan, William, Jr., 253
Breslin, Jimmy, 211
Brewer, Norman,
Brinkley, David, 22, 32, 124-125, 160, 187, 274, 295
brite, 94, 138, 183
Broadcast Journalism, 91

Broadcast News (BN)
  wire service, 173
Broadcasting, 272
Brown, Bill, 303
Brown, Heywood, 211
Bryan, William Jennings, 251
Bubble Gum News, 195
Buddine, Richard, 299
Buehler, Don, 79
bulletin, 98, 109, 135-136, 146, 181
bulletin slide, 136, 176
bumper, 143
Burdick, Sen. Quentin, 87
Burke, Edmund, 78
"The Burned Child," 217, 222

cable transmission, 336, 338
Cable-TV (CATV), 173, 341-342
Caldwell case, 239
Callaway, John, 107
Canadian Press (CP), 173
Canon 3(A)(7), 249
  see Canon 35
Canon 35, 249-250, 252-253, 256-257, 332
Capital Film Laboratories, 76
Carlin, George, 244
Carson, Johnny, 274
cartoons, television news, 180, 219, 225, 378
  in weather news, 49, 203, 205
cassette recorder, 88-90, 93, 108-109
Cavett, Dick, 116
CBS Evening News, 176, 275
CBS News, 76, 104, 106, 118, 120, 125, 158, 194, 201, 239-241, 243, 274, 280, 286, 290, 298, 318-319, 324-325, 331
CBS Radio, 87, 107
CCD camera (charge-coupled device) 335, 340

censorship, 81, 91, 189, 227, 230-231
   243-244
Chancellor, John, 160
changing bag, 349
character generator, 143, 181, 378-379
Charnley, Mitchell, 328
Charny, Israel, 160
Chase, John, 219
checkbook journalism, 297
Chicago Seven, 300
Chicago *Tribune*, 240, 251
"Children's News," 195
children's newscasts, 194-195
Christian Science Monitor, 104
Chromakey (CHROMA), 49, 51,
   166, 181, 202, 205, 375-376
Churchill, Winston, 25
CITY, 325
City News Service (CNS), Los Angeles,
   67-70
CKOC, 108
Clark, Justice Tom, 252
clear writing, 24-25
   see also "Easy Listening Formula"
Cleaver, Eldridge, 240
Cleveland Plain Dealer, 251
Cleveland Press, 251
cliches, 37-38
close-up shot, 53, 55, 58, 70, 311,
   313-315, 354
close, 58-59, 61, 94
"Closer Look," 195
CMHL, 108
Cohn, Bruce, 319
collision, filming of, 311-312
Columbia Journalism Review, 159,
   209, 281
commercials, 61-62, 151, 182, 209,
   266, 286-287, 379
   Pillsbury, 380
Commodity News Service, 104
Communications Act, 225
Congressional Directory, 271

Considine, Bob, 251
consultants, 270, 273, 276-282
Consumer Inquiry, 222
consumer problems, 221-223
Consumer Reports, 222
contractions, 36
control room, 95, 150-151
Cook, Fred, 229
Cooney, C.E., 275
Coppersmith, James, 277, 279
copy:
   relationship to pictures,   50-52,
      55-58, 71-73, 94
   selecting and sorting, 181
Corrigan, Michael, 253
courtroom sketches, 176, 378
Cousins, Norman, 285
Creative Interviewing, 116
criticism of journalism schools by
   stations, 269-270
Cronkite, Walter, 135, 157, 160,
   239, 261, 265, 275, 280, 288
cropping, 180
crossing the line, 310-311, 314
Cummings, Gary, 246
cutaway, 53-54, 58, 76, 129-130,
   310-313, 316, 348, 367-368, 370

Danziger, Jerry, 278
Darrow, Clarence, 251
dates, 31
Davis, Elmer, 160
Day, Robin, 288, 298
debates, political, 231
Degausser, 366
"Deep Throat" sources, 239
Democratic National Convention 1968,
   294
demodulator, 338
Denenberg, Herbert S., 222
The Desperate Hours, 238
d'Estaing, Giscard, 324

Deutsch, Karl, 375
dialogue looping, 358
Diamond, Edwin, 341
DiCioccio, 327, 334
Dictionary of Pronunciation, 164
Dietz, Bill, 325
director, TV news, 51-52, 62, 149-153, 164, 166, 179, 180, 182, 207, 269-270, 367
Disney, Walt, 380
dispatcher, 138, 140, 142
dissolve, 52, 55, 143, 316, 352, 354, 365, 370, 371
documentaries, 139, 217, 219, 229, 230, 240, 246, 335
Dodd, Senator Thomas, 238
Doerfer, John C., 218
Dominic, Virgil, 290
double chaining, 58, 82, 179, 368, 369-371
double out, 95
double system filming, 345, 348, 352, 365, 371-372
downlink, 325
Drew, Dan, 125, 126, 127, 128
dubbing, 53, 90, 93, 95, 109, 145, 336, 338

easy listening formula, the, 25-26
editing a speech, 81, 82, 83
editorials, TV, 217, 218, 219, 223, 224, 225, 226
education for journalism career, 266, 267, 268
Eisenstein, Sergei, 76
Electronic News Gathering (ENG), 166, 179, 205, 310, 315, 324, 325, 326, 327, 328, 332, 333, 334, 345, 346, 352
Emory, Patrick, 281
emphasis, 42
ends up, 95

English Pronouncing Dictionary, 164
Ephron, Nora, 121
ERA Research, 281
Ervin, Senator Sam, 241
establishing shot, 53, 54, 58, 76, 77, 144, 310, 311, 312
Estes, Billie Sol, 252, 253
ethics in journalism, 264, 265, 266, 313, 317, 318, 319
  bias, 296, 297
  broadcast journalism, 132, 290, 295
  checkbook journalism, 297
  live coverage, 328-329
ethyloid (see film cement), 364
European Broadcasting Union, 332
Eurovision News Exchange, 332
executive news coordinator (newsroom), 326, 339, 340
Eyewitness News, 49, 165, 280

fades, 55, 62, 207, 368, 369
Fairness Doctrine, 218, 220, 221, 224-229, 231, 240
Falk, Peter, 246
Farber, Myron, 239
Farmer, Don, 292
Farmers' Union v. WDAY, 232, 237
Farr, William, 241
Federal Aviation Agency, 98
Federal Bureau of Investigation (FBI), 265
Federal Communications Commission (FCC), 99, 108, 142, 218, 220, 225-227, 229-232, 240, 243, 244, 245, 247, 263, 281, 301, 303, 318
Federal Rules of Criminal Procedure, Rule 53, 250
Federal Trade Commission (FTC), 227
fill light, 350-351

film,
  black and white, 366
  color, 351, 366
  development of, 352
  Eastman Kodak, 351
  Ektachrome, 353
  graininess of, 351, 352, 354
  magnetic track, 346, 366-367, 371
  optical track, 346, 366
  relationship of poor exposure
    and poor development, 352
  silent, 49, 53-54, 58, 72, 363, 370

film editing, 349, 354, 363-371
  equipment, 364-366
  problems of, 129-130, 375
  process of, 54-55, 66-81, 82, 129-
    131, 363-364
film editing barrel, 365
film editing bench, 347, 364, 365
film editing gloves, 366
film editing room, 148, 363
film editor, 53-54, 61, 77, 82, 83,
    129, 130, 131, 145, 148, 150,
    153, 178, 179, 310, 316, 330,
    347, 349, 354, 363, 372
film magazines, 349
film reels, 365, 366
film viewer, 354, 364, 365
filming techniques, 309-319, 345-354
filters, 349-351
fire, filming of, 310-311
First Amendment, 225, 227, 229,
    231, 232, 233, 235, 239, 241,
    242, 252, 262, 277, 290
First Amendment and the Fourth
    Estate, 235
Flesch, Rudolf, 24
floor director, 151, 153, 161
Flynt, Larry, 376
Ford, Gerald R., 289, 324
formats for news programs, 165
Fortune, 341
fractions, 31

frame storage unit, 375
Frank, Reuven, 115, 122, 294, 295
Franklin, Gary, 59, 118, 350
Franklin, Marc A., 235
freedom of the press, 217, 231-233
    235-237, 252-254, 257, 262,
    263, 265
freight train phrases, 35-36
Friendly, Fred, 220, 227, 228, 243,
    345
Frost, David, 297
Frost, Robert, 296

gag orders, 241-242
Gallico, Paul, 211
Gallup Poll, 294
Gannett v. Pasquale, 241
Gertz v. Welch, 236
Gillmor, Donald M., 235
Ginsburg, Douglas H., 235
global village, 13, 186
gobbledygook, 34
Goldwater — Extremist of the Right,
    229
Goodman, Julian, 227, 285
Gottschald, Dick, 280
Graham, Billy, 125
Graham, Jerry, 105
Graham trial, 250
graphics, 180, 181, 376
grease pencil, 366
Gresham's law, 275
Griffin, Merv, 274
Griffith, Thomas, 279
Grissom, Virgil, 118
Gunning, Robert, 24
Gurfein, Judge Murray L., 242

Hachten, William S., 232
Hackes, Peter, 263
Haldeman, H. R., 297

Hall, Mark W., 91
Hamer, Dave, 353
Hand, Judge Learned, 217
Handberg, Ron, 329
handouts, 137, 141, 176, 181
Hanna, Lee, 276
hard news, 138, 183-184, 199, 201, 316, 319
Hargis, Rev. Billy James, 229
Harlan, Justice John Marshall, 253
Harris, Arthur S., Jr., 204
Harris Poll, 262, 286
Harvey, Paul, 157, 277
Hatteberg, Larry, 193
Hauptmann, Bruno, 249
Hayakawa, S. I., 26, 299
Hearst, Patricia, 324
Heatter, Gabriel, 250
helicopters as mobile units, 108
Hemingway, Ernest, 211
Henson, Bruce, 245
Herbert v. Lando, 239
Hernandez, Lencho, 303
Hickey, Neil, 289
high band, 338
Hill, James, family, 238
Hill, Sandy, 281
Hodnette, Robert E., Jr., 255
Hoffman, Abbie, 300
Holmes, Oliver Wendell, 257
House Judiciary Committee debate on the impeachment of President Nixon, 243
Hughes, Charles Evans, 12
Huntley, Chet, 298
Hustler, 376

IFB (Interrupted FeedBack), 151
image-orthicon camera (I-O), 335, 336
In the News, 194
instant replay, 324
interview, 116-119
intervision, 332

intro, 49-51, 53-57, 58, 60, 94, 131, 179
inverted pyramid, 20
Issues and Answers, 117, 231

Jackson, Rev. Jesse, 298
jargon, 33
"jiggle," 184, 364
Johnson, Nicholas, 301
Joint Media Committee on News Coverage Problems, 265
Journal of Broadcasting, 272
journalists' privilege, 238, 239, 240, 241
jump cut, 58, 129, 368

KABC-TV, 118, 222, 379, 380
Kahn, Frank J., 244
KAKE-TV, 193, 253
Kampmann, Mel, 278
KBJR, 280
KBYU-TV, 195
KDUB-TV, 352
Kefauver crime investigation hearings, 243
Kendrick, Alex, 274
Kennedy, John F., 287
Kennedy, Robert F., 125, 254
Kesterton, Wilfred, 236
key light, 350
KFBB-TV, 221
KGO-TV, 275, 277
KGW-TV, 191
Khomeini, Ayatollah, 285, 376
Khrushchev, Nikita, 244
"kicker," 207
Kidswatch, 195
Kidsworld, 195
KING-TV, 217, 222
Kintner, Robert E., 13, 265
Kiritsis, Anthony, 289, 290
Kissinger, Henry, 324

Kitchell, James W., 341
KLPM, 253
KMBC-TV, 190
KMOX-TV, 323, 325, 333, 334, 340
KMTV, 353
KNXT-TV, 39, 72, 254, 256, 281, 324
KOB-TV, 278
KOLN-TV, 195
KOLT, 200
KOMO-TV, 192
KOMU-TV, 253
KOOL-TV, 326
KOTV, 205
KPFA, 245
KPIX, 275
KPRC-TV, 191, 193, 277, 327
KRON-TV, 195, 275
KSAT-TV, 275
KSFO, 99
KSTP Radio, 79
KSTP-TV, 282, 328, 334
KTTV, 191
Kunstler, William, 329
Kuralt, Charles, 157, 274
KVII-TV, 190
KWHY-TV, 192

Lando, Barry, 239
Lar Daly Amendment, 230
Lardner, John, 211
Lardner, Ring, 211
Laserfax, AP, 172, 176, 180, 379
law and the press in Canada, 236
law of mass communications, 235
lead foil, 249
lead-in, 49-57
    see also intro
leads, 43-47
lenses, 310, 346-348, 349, 352
Leonhardy, Terence, 87
LeRoy, David, 261, 262, 278
Levy, Dr. Mark R., 274

libel, 236, 237, 239
library, newsroom, 271, 272, 376-377
    film and tape storage, 204, 330
    slide, 176
library stills, see still pictures
licensing, broadcast, 99, 228, 229, 245
Life, 238
light meter, 349
lighting techniques, 349-351
limbo boards, 379
lip flap, 368, 369
lip synchronization, 348
Lippmann, Walter, 188-189, 274
live coverage, see Electronic News
    Gathering
Living Room War, The, 121
London Times, 319
long shot, 53-54, 58, 59, 70, 77,
    312-315
Los Angeles Times-Washington Post,
    173
lost child, filming of, 315-316
lotteries, 247
Lower, Elmer, 227

MacNeil, Robert, 177
Magers, Ron, 282, 328, 334
Magid, Frank, 276-279, 281-282
magnetic film cleaner, 366
Magnuson, Senator Warren G., 217
make-up for TV newscaster, 164-165
Man-on-the-Street interviews (MOS),
    92, 118, 119, 220, 221
map, television news, 176, 180,
    271, 375, 377
    weather map, 49, 52, 185, 195,
    203, 204, 205
Marshall, Jim, 282
Mass Communication Law: Cases
    and Comment, 235
master control, 109, 150
Mayflower Decision, 225

McAndrew, William, 265
McCarthy, Sen. Eugene, 89
McCarthy, Sen. Joseph, 243
McClure, Robert D., 124
McGaffin, Don, 217
McHugh, Philip L., 273, 280
McHugh and Hoffman, 273, 276, 277
McLuhan, Marshall, 13, 26, 186, 319
Means, Russell, 303
medium shot, 53, 55, 58, 70, 77, 310, 311, 313-315
Meet the Press, 116, 179, 231
Menninger, Dr. W. Walter, 262
metaphors and similes, 37-38
meteorologist, 202, 205
Metzler, Ken, 116
microcam, or Thompson-CSF microcam, 335
microphones, 88-90, 93, 94, 151, 252, 356-357
microwave link or transmission, 179, 323, 326, 327, 330, 336, 339, 340
Miller decisions, 245
Miller, Ray, 193, 277
minicam, 53, 323, 326, 375
Minnesota Press Council, 265
Minow, Newton, 218-219
Missouri Network, 104
mobile radio units, 96, 98, 107-109
modulator, 338
monitors, 125, 145, 150-151, 162
Monroe, Bill, 227-228
Monty Python, 380
Morgan, Edward P., 342-343
mult-box, 88-89
murder, filming of, 312-313
Murphy, Lee, 244
Murrow, Edward R., 21, 49, 65, 87, 125, 159-160, 219-220, 264, 273, 295, 296, 360
Mutual Network, 104-106
My Lai massacre, 298

Nader, Ralph, 262
narrative treatment, 32-33
NASA, 116
National Association of Broadcasters, 230
National Educational Television, 253
National Labor Relations Board, 261
National Law Center, George Washington University, 228
National News Council, 265, 297
National News Council, 265, 297
National Oceanic and Atmospheric Administration (NOAA), 201-202
National Press Photographers Association TV newsfilm workshop, 309
National Public Radio (NPR), 104
National Weather Service, 201
NBC Handbook of Pronunciation, 164
NBC-TV News, 70, 104, 106, 122, 195, 223, 256, 263-265, 274, 276, 289, 298, 331, 341
Nebraska Press Association v. Stuart, 242
Nelson, Harold L., 235
Nessen, Ron, 289
Neustadt, Rick, 301
New York Daily News, 275
New York Times, 29, 122, 172, 188, 237, 239, 252, 275, 301
Newman, Edwin, 160, 207
Newman, Paul, 274
News, radio,
  advantages over television, 89, 91
  audience of, 98-99
  audio feed services, 104-105
  economics of, 98-99, 103-104
  editorializing, 101, 103
  equipment, 88-89
  examples of operations, 99-102
  newscast schedule, 105-106
  remote tape reports, 92-93
  special networks, 105

techniques of reporting, 90-91
news, TV,
arts, 193
editorializing, 223
farm, 193
happy talk, 165, 275, 279, 280, 287
impression left by, 70-71
late, 146, 181
local station approach, 79
objectivity in, 82, 160, 161, 223, 264, 265, 294-296
pictures (visuals), 70-71
relation of words to pictures, 71-73
selection of material, 70, 78, 79, 80-81, 182-183, 187
show business in, 273-275, 277
sources of, 137-138, 171-177, 239
tabloid, 165, 275, 279, 280
truth in, 188-190
v. newspaper news, 182, 185-188
news beat, 139
news conferences, coverage of, 53, 76, 88, 90, 128-129, 141
news director, 50, 80, 132, 138, 143, 150, 158, 223, 224, 269, 270, 275-282, 290, 299, 309, 316, 326
"news doctors," 276, 277
news editor, 136, 274
News Election Service, 331
newscast, radio preparation of, 80, 94-95, 183
newscasts, TV, 50, 61, 79, 159, 269-270, 375
audiences for, 142, 146-148, 150, 151, 153, 187, 193-195
formats of, 165, 207
make-up of, 171, 178-179. 183-184
newscaster, TV, 49-52, 56-58, 132 140, 146, 148-151, 153, 157-162, 164, 166
image-maker, 158-160
presentation, 160

newsmen's privilege, *see* journalists' privilege
newspapers, as sources of TV news, 173
newsroom set, 62, 149, 165-166
Newsweek, 119
Newsweek Broadcasting, 175, 219
Nixon, Richard, 238, 243-244, 297, 324
Nixon tapes, 243
North, Don, 65
Not on the Menu, 218, 222
note-taking, radio reporting, 89-90
numbers, 31, 39

objectivity in journalism, 223, 264-266
obscenity, 236, 243-247
Oklahoma City Times, 208
one-man-band, 334, 346, 348, 355
Osgood, Charles, 33
Othman, Fred, 27
overlap cuts, 54, 367-368
overlap jump cuts, 366
Oxbury animation stand, 379

pad copy, 50, 94, 146, 153, 182
Paisner, Richard, 301
panning, or pan shot, 54, 310-312, 347, 348, 354
Pappas case, 239
parade, filming of, 313-315
Paskman, Ralph, 118, 125
Patterson, Dave, 159
Patterson, Thomas E., 124
Pearson, Senator James B., 241
Pegler, Westbrook, 211
Pensions: The Broken Promise, 230
personalization, 41
Pettit, Tom, 172
photofax, 172, 176, 379
see also Laserfax

photographer, 53, 71, 77, 81, 137, 139, 142, 144-145, 208, 309-317, 345-353
Pickard, Larry, 281
Plato's *Republic*, 188
Plumbicon camera, 335-336
Polillo, Pat, 282
political news, 115, 123-125
pooling of video tape, 331-333
portable light, 348-349
Powell, Justice Lewis Franklin, 237
Powers, Ron, 159
Pressler, Senator Larry, 285
producer, radio newscast, 94
producer, TV news, 81, 143, 146-150, 153, 265, 363
professionalism in journalism, 240, 261-264
projection room, 150, 179
projectionist, 151, 153, 179
promo, 147, 151, 159
Pronouncing Dictionary of American English, 164
protection copy, 182
Proxmire, Senator William, 228
pseudo-event, 300, 303, 317, 327, 340
Public Broadcasting System (PBS), 177
Public Opinion, 188
public opinion polls, 221
pull-tab map, 144-145, 377

quartz light, 350
question leads, 32
Quill, 272
quotes, 36-37

Rabe, Robert, 290
radar, 200, 205
radio Amex service, 192

radio news financial reports, 192
radio newscasts as source of TV news, 173
Radio-Television News Directors Association (RTNDA), 99, 158, 218, 262, 265, 282, 291
Ramsey, Doug, 275
Rather, Dan, 120, 160, 164, 274, 296, 323
ratings, 158, 220, 273-276, 327, 333
Rayburn, Sam, 243
readability, 24-25
Reagan, Ronald, 231, 244
Reagan, Mrs. Nancy, 359
rear projection (RP), 49-52, 165-166, 176, 205, 376
Reasoner, Harry, 160
Red Lion Broadcasting v. FCC, 224, 229, 232, 236
redundancy, 34
Reece, Mason, 195
regulation of broadcasting, 235
Renick, Ralph, 224, 277
repetition, 38
reporter, radio, 87-94, 96
reporter, TV, 49, 53, 57-61, 81, 115, 138-139, 144-145, 158, 160, 165, 177, 263, 266, 268, 270, 279, 285, 326, 341
Reporters Committee for Freedom of the Press, 242
research, in TV news, 270-271, 282
Reston, James, 211
resume, 268
Reuters, 173
reversal film, 351
reverse shot, 130, 203, 310-311
rhetoric of TV news, 124
right of privacy, 236-238, 328
riots, coverage of, 289, 292-294, 309, 313, 317-318
Robinson, Glenn O., 232
roll-thru, 57-58, 129, 153, 366

Rooney, Andy, 201
Rosenbloom decision, 236
Roth decision, 245
RTNDA Communicator, 272
Rule, Elton, 363
Runyon, Damon, 211

Salant, Richard, 241, 280. 290
Salisbury, John, 282
Sandburg, Carl, 201
Saturday Review, 285
Scared Straight, 246
Schmidt, Larry, 222
Schmidt, Richard, Jr., 257
Scopes trial, 251
Scranton Commission Report, 300
script, assembling of, 30-31, 95, 146-149, 162, 164
sealed records, 242
Searle, John, 300
Section 315 of Communications Act of 1934, 225, 229-231, 237
Section 326 of Communications Act of 1934, 244
Section 1464 of the Criminal Code, 244
See It Now, 220
Segell, Hyam, 249
Seib, Charles, 285
Sell, Suzanne, 279, 281
Selling of the Pentagon, The, 240-241
Senate debate on the Panama Canal Treaty, 243
Senate Watergate hearings, 243
Sevareid, Eric, 19, 159, 185, 262, 274, 294
sex bias, 41-42
Shannon, Dr. Claude E., 42
Shaw, David, 211
Shayon, Robert Lewis, 107, 286
Sheppard, Dr. Sam, 251-252
Shirer, William L., 87
Shostick, Herschel, 218

shoulder pad, 347
Sigma Delta Chi, 262, 265
silent camera, 53, 137, 310, 345-346, 348
Simmons, Bob, 325
Simon and Garfunkel, 22
simplicity, 38
single chain story, 369
single system filming, 330, 345, 352, 371
Sirhan, Sirhan, 254, 256
Sirica, Judge John, 242
Sixth Amendment, 254
Sixty Minutes, 220, 224, 239
Skornia, Harry J., 270
slander, 237
slang, 37
slides, 52, 72, 146, 176, 180, 181, 376, 377
Small, William, 29
Smith, H. Allen, 201
Smith, Howard K., 13, 274, 294-296
Smith, Marty, 76
sound, *see* audio
sound bite, 53, 55, 57
sound camera, 345-346
SOF (sound on film), 49-50, 52, 55
sound reader, 364-365
Spain, John, 193
speeches, coverage of (radio), 89-90
Spencer, Herbert, 188
Spink, C. C. Johnson, 209
splicer, 109, 364
splicing, 57, 130, 178, 347, 364, 366-370
of audio tape, 109
Sporting News, 209
sports news, 147, 183, 207-208
ethics in, 208-209
jargon, 209-210
sports reporter, 147, 207-211
spot sheets, 349

Stafford, Jean, 29

Staggers, Rep. Harley, 240, 318

staging the news, 317-319, 340

standupper, 49, 58-59, 120, 143, 326-327

Stanton, Frank, 218, 243, 298

standards, professional journalism, 262-264, 275, 278-279

station managers, 159, 275-276, 280, 333

Statistical Abstract of the United States, 271

Stewart, Kenneth, 296

Stewart, Justice Potter, 252

still pictures, 49-52, 138, 149, 172, 225, 271, 375-378

stock market reports, 191-192

Stone, Vernon, 327, 334, 344

Stoner, J. B., 230

stringers, 99-103, 174-175, 264, 313, 353, 375

studio cards, 52, 143, 180

studio, TV, 150-151

Sullivan v. The New York Times, 236

summary lead or item lead, 32

Superior Films v. Department of Education, 232

Super 8 film, 195, 345, 352-354

supers, 50, 143-144, 176, 181, 194, 221, 319, 375, 378-379

Supreme Court, U. S., decisions of, 229, 232, 236-244, 251-253

switcher, 150, 366, 377

Symbionese Liberation Army, 324, 328

tag line, 120, 136

talking head, 192, 363

tape editor, 363

tape recorder, 88-90, 93, 100, 102, 104, 108, 109, 357

Talese, Gay, 211

tease, 62, 151

technical director, TV news, 143, 153, 180, 207, 367, 370

Teeter, Dwight L., 235

Telemation unit, 377

teleprompter, 149, 151, 153, 162

television camera, 52, 151, 153, 335, 336, 378, 379

Terkel, Studs, 191

Thames, 204

Thompson, Rep. Fletcher, 240

Thoreau, Henry David, 277

Thornberg, Bob, 87

throwaway leads, 31

Time magazine, 222, 265, 279, 303

tipster, 103-104

tracking, 337, 339

transitions, 31-32

Trese, Patrick, 70

tripod, 53, 347, 349, 354

trucking, 311

Tuckner, Harold, 223

TV Guide, 280, 289

Twain, Mark, 38

Unifax, UPI, 172, 176, 379

Unislides, 376

United Press International (UPI), 135, 163, 166, 172, 173, 176, 202, 319, 375-376

UPI Audio, 104, 106

United Press International Television News (UPITN), 176

U.S.A. v. The New York Times, 242

U.S. Code, 271

U.S. v. Paramount Pictures, 232

The Unseeing Eye, 124

up-cut, 55, 77, 129, 149

updating network feeds, 175, 181

uplink, 325

Van Messell, Jim, 275
Vanderbilt University, Vanderbilt
  Library, 270
Vanocur, Sander, 286
velvet pad, 366
video,
  editing of computer, 179, 339-340
  editing of reel to reel, 338-339
  use of, by judges, 254
video camera, 330, 334
video computer terminal, 103
video transmission, 336, 338
Vidicon camera, 335-336
Videoprompter (Q-TV), 149
videotape, 175, 179, 208, 211, 268-
  270, 324-325, 329-330, 334,
  335, 337-340, 353, 375
  advantages v. film, 329-331, 335
videotape recorder (VTR), 179, 337-
  338
videotape recording engineer, 145,
  151, 153, 175, 179-180, 334, 337
videotape service, or feed, 145, 175
Vietnam War, television coverage of,
  65, 66, 71, 72, 223, 239, 286,
  289
violence, television news, 288-290,
  290, 309
Visnews, 293
visuals story, or picture story,
  absence of detail, 66-70
  chronology, 73-76
  tying copy to pictures, 55-56, 71-73
Vizmo, 376
voice-over, 58-61, 66, 95, 150, 280,
  326, 371
Von Hoffman, Nicholas, 223

WABC-TV, 131
WAGA-TV, 282
Wald, Richard, 241, 309
Walker, Judge Herbert, 254
Wall Street Journal, 26-27, 104

Wallace, Mike, 116, 160, 240, 275
Warren, Chief Justice Earl, 252
Washington Post, 223, 242, 285-286
Watergate, 242-243
Watson, Lauren R., 253
WBAY, 282
WBBM-TV, 107, 318, 327
WBRZ, 193
WCAU-TV, 222
WCBD, 327
WCCO Radio, 87
WCCO-TV, 328-329
WCVB-TV, 221, 281
WDAY-TV, 221
WDSU-TV, 219
weather news, 199-205
Weinshienk, Zita, 253
Weis, Joseph F., 256
Westin, Av, 171, 228
WEWS, 159, 191
WFAA-TV, 222
WGN, 251
WGR-TV, 239
What's It All About? 195
WHDH, 281
white noise, 358, 360
WHK, 251
Who's Who in America, 271
Wide World of Sports, 210
wild track sound, 60, 310, 315,
  348, 372
Williams, Howard S., 256
Winchell, Walter, 251, 277
WINS, 244
WIP, 236
WIRE-AM, 289
wire copy, 172
wire services, 172-173
WITI-TV, 225
WJBK-TV, 225
WJW-TV, 191
WKBN-TV, 190
WLAC, 330

WLWC, 202
WMAQ-TV, 191, 195, 246, 292
WMTV, 270
WNAC-TV, 277, 279
WNCC, 195
Wolfson, Mitchell, 218
Working, 191
Wounded Knee, 303
wraparounds (wraps), 58, 94, 120
writer, radio news, 94-96
WPIX-TV, 319
WPVI-TV, 277-278
WRC-TV, 195, 371
WRGB, 204
WSLS-TV, 299
WSVA-TV, 327
WTCN, 191
WTIC-TV, 360
WTLV-TV, 222
WTOP-TV, 222
WTTG-TV, 222
WTVJ-TV, 218-219, 224, 277
WWJ-TV, 190
WWL-TV, 326
Young, Andrew, 290
Yount, Steven, 289-290
youth news, 194-195
Zelman, Sam, 120
Zimmerman, Carl, 225
zoom lens, 61, 76, 340, 346-348, 352-354
Zurcher v. Stanford Daily, 239